A Marriage of Convenience

A MARRIAGE OF CONVENIENCE

Relations Between Mexico and the United States

SIDNEY WEINTRAUB

A TWENTIETH CENTURY FUND REPORT

New York   Oxford   OXFORD UNIVERSITY PRESS   1990

Oxford University Press

Oxford New York Toronto
Delhi Bombay Calcutta Madras Karachi
Petaling Jaya Singapore Hong Kong Tokyo
Nairobi Dar es Salaam Cape Town
Melbourne Auckland

and associated companies in
Berlin Ibadan

9|0253   B&T   29.95

Published by Oxford University Press, Inc.,
200 Madison Avenue, New York, New York 10016

Oxford is a registered trademark of Oxford University Press

Library of Congress Cataloging-in-Publication Data
Weintraub, Sidney, 1914–
A marriage of convenience: relations between Mexico and the
United States / Sidney Weintraub.
p. cm.
"A Twentieth Century Fund report."
Includes bibliographical references.
ISBN 0-19-506125-X
1. United States—Foreign economic relations—Mexico.
2. Mexico—Foreign economic relations—United States.
I. Twentieth Century Fund. II. Title.
HF1456.5.M6W45 1990 337.73072—dc20 89-39386

Printing 9 8 7 6 5 4 3 2 1

Printed in the United States of America
on acid-free paper

To Jeff and *Freedom and Community*.

May both make a difference.

The Twentieth Century Fund is a research foundation undertaking timely analyses of economic, political, and social issues. Not-for-profit and nonpartisan, the Fund was founded in 1919 and endowed by Edward A. Filene.

FOREWORD

During the 1970s, Mexico profited from the convergence of two forces: the quintupling of oil prices and the almost profligate eagerness of Western banks to recycle petrodollar surpluses to developing countries. Mexico's rapid economic growth in this period helped it to absorb a labor force growing by 1 million new workers per year. But as oil prices eroded in the late 1970s, the country's economic boom collapsed, and Mexico found itself entering the new decade saddled with a vast foreign debt, about one-quarter of which was owed to U.S. banks. The economic collapse also led to a record number of undocumented Mexican workers streaming north.

Since then, the economic structure of Mexico has undergone a profound change: its markets have been opened to imports, which has forced its domestic industries to compete. Further, Mexican producers have been encouraged to export to world markets. Changes also have occurred, albeit at a much slower pace, in the political structure of the country. The PRI retains control of the presidency and the two houses of the legislature, but it is a more tenuous, a more shared, control than at any time during the past sixty years.

Sidney Weintraub, Dean Rusk Professor at the Lyndon B. Johnson School of Public Affairs at the University of Texas, believes that these changes provide an opportunity for the United States to further the industrial integration of its economy with Mexico's, an integration that he believes is in both countries' best interests. Mexico's interest in economic cooperation is evident—in its increasing welcome to foreign investment, its seeking out of the U.S. market for nonoil exports, and the signing of two bilateral trade agreements—but the U.S. interest is less clear; indeed, growing domestic protectionism, coupled with a certain incivility, threatens to impede integration.

Weintraub urges policymakers on both sides of the Rio Grande to recognize that in good times, and perhaps even more so, in bad, the behavior of each of these nations deeply affects that of the other. In particular, he urges U.S. policymakers to encourage Mexico's economic opening in word and in deed. To do this is to ask U.S. industries to adjust as Mexican industry becomes more competitive; it is to accept that U.S. workers will need support and that the support cannot be through U.S. import restraints. Further, the United States must rethink its approach to Mexico's foreign debt, recognizing that if Mexico's new president, Carlos Salinas de Gortari, does not achieve significant results on debt relief, the entire policy of restructuring the economy will be endangered.

The Fund is grateful to Sidney Weintraub for his clear, yet impassioned, examination of the transformations in U.S.–Mexican economic relations. His study, which probes Mexican and American interests, is an important contribution to understanding the forces at work in both countries.

August 1989   Marcia Bystryn, Acting Director
                                                                              The Twentieth Century Fund

ACKNOWLEDGMENTS

I was a diplomat in Mexico City from 1951 to 1954. A daughter was born there, and that forged an unbreakable personal bond with Mexico. I fell in love with the country—with its natural beauty, diversity, and gentle people. It was evident then, and this too has endured, that half its population was shamefully exploited. Some of this was caused by foreign exploitation, but Mexico's political-social-economic system was created primarily at home. There was nothing foreordained about Mexico's authoritarian politics, its economic backwardness, or the shocking poverty alongside great wealth and the unequal access to education and health services. The underlying structures are now changing, rapidly and for the better I believe. The United States, for its part, is no longer the self-confident nation it was for most of its history. It is important to understand the changes taking place in each country because they will profoundly affect the relationship between them. That is why I wrote this book.

Murray J. Rossant, then the director of the Twentieth Century Fund, had independently come to a similar conclusion. I would not have written this book without his encouragement. Many persons at the Fund worked with me, including especially Beverly Goldberg, who was my main point of support after Rossant's death, and Marcia Bystryn, who served as acting director. I received comments on successive drafts of the manuscript from a changing group of program officers at the Fund, Ron Chernow, Steve Andors, Gary Nickerson, and Richard Sinopoli.

My main dedication, however, is to the Mexican people. Most of those who assisted me were not aware they were doing so, but I imbibed a sense of the diverse personal and national aspirations that exist from countless conversations, intense during the past few years, but building on a familiarity spanning close to forty years.

I owe debts to many Mexicans—officials, politicians, businesspersons, academics, artists, cultural leaders—who provided information and, more important, insights on how Mexicans think and how the system works. El Colegio de México offered a base where I could receive telephone messages. I wish particularly to thank Víctor Urquidi, who for many years was the president of the Colegio, for his willingness to spend many hours, in his office, at conferences, and socially, discussing the Mexican scene and United States–Mexico relations. Mario Ojeda, the current president of the Colegio, provided me with a welcome to the institution. Gerardo Bueno, who was then managing the program dealing with United States–Mexico studies, arranged a luncheon seminar at which I was able to test ideas that eventually emerged in the book on the linkage between economic and political change. I benefited from the opportunity to discuss issues on Mexico–United States relations with many scholars at the Colegio. Some provided comments on portions of the manuscript. I will mention only a few: Saúl Trejo Reyes, Francisco Alba, Lorenzo Meyer, Jaime Serra Puche, Adalberto García Rocha, Manuel García y Griego, Gustavo Vega Cánovas, and Celia Toro. Jesús Tamayo read and commented on the entire manuscript when he was at the University of Texas at Austin as a Fulbright scholar.

M. Delal Baer and Georges Fauriol were kind enough to invite me as a guest scholar one summer at the Center for Strategic and International Studies, enabling me to discuss Mexican issues with the policy community in Washington. I was able to travel to Mexico on a number of occasions as a consultant to the Commission for the Study of International Migration and Cooperative Economic Development, established by the U.S. Congress.

William P. Glade, then secretary of the Latin American Program at the Woodrow Wilson International Center for Scholars, gave me the opportunity to explore ideas in a series of five seminars at the center. Several reviewers who read the entire manuscript made valuable suggestions. Except for two, George Grayson and Robert Pastor, the others are unknown to me. John Bailey's comments were particularly useful and also kept me out of trouble. Carolyn A. Rutsch, then a graduate student at the Lyndon B. Johnson School of Public Affairs at the University of Texas at Austin, read an early draft of the initial chapters and made helpful comments.

Two editors were invaluable in making my prose more precise and more readable: Alex Holzman, during the phase of commentary by the Twentieth Century Fund, and Rosemary Wellner, after the manuscript reached Oxford University Press. I wish to thank Valerie Aubry, my editor at Oxford University Press, for her gracious help; the title of the book is better now because of her.

The University Research Institute of the University of Texas at Austin provided an award that released me during one academic year from carrying a full-time teaching schedule, permitting me to carry out research and begin the writing.

During my many trips to Mexico over the past several years, Maxine and Bob Cohoes and I fell into a pattern of testing Mexico City's better restaurants. It is an understatement to say they are very good. This made the research particularly enjoyable. Professionally, Bob, who was the acting and then the deputy public affairs officer at the U.S. embassy, provided me with much information and valuable contacts throughout Mexican society.

Geoffrey Bannister, a doctoral student at the University of Texas at Austin, helped me compile and then verify information. He read the manuscript and made valuable suggestions. A Mexican student at the LBJ School, Rafael Fernández de Castro, helped me understand many ongoing developments in Mexico. Successive drafts of the manuscript were entered into the word processor, first by Linda

Borchardt and then by Elsbeth Taylor. They were reentered by persons unknown to me at the Twentieth Century Fund.

I am particularly thankful to a number of persons who provided updated statistics during the last-minute rush to complete the manuscript. While there were many, I will mention only four: John J. St. John, director of the Office of Mexican Affairs, U.S. Department of State; Brian Brisson of the U.S. Department of Commerce; Samuel Hernández L., private secretary to the director for information and public relations of Pemex; and Stephen F. Lande.

I, alone, bear responsibility for what is in the book.

The most patient collaborator was my wife, Gladys. She tolerated many absences and the long hours I spent closeted in a room with my word processor.

Austin, Texas   S.W.
August 1989

CONTENTS

A Marriage of Convenience

INTRODUCTION

And yet I believe that Mexico and the United States are so far from resolving
their problems that, in truth, it can be said that the process of understanding has
not yet even begun.

DANIEL COSÍO VILLEGAS, 1947

Sociological analysis can tell us only that the development of democracy in
Mexico is within the realm of the probable, owing to the over-all level of
development in the country, and that effective democracy is the indispensable
prerequisite for continued peaceful development.

PABLO GONZÁLEZ CASANOVA, 1965

We will continue reordering our productive structures and processes in order to
be able to compete in the international economy instead of locking ourselves
inside structures that are, if not archaic, poorly adapted to the changes in international trade.

PRESIDENT MIGUEL DE LA MADRID, 1984

Whether either side likes it or not, geography has made the relationship between the
United States and Mexico the most important one for Mexico and one of the most
important, if not the most significant, for the United States. This has long been
evident to Mexicans. It is only now, because of oil discoveries and then the fallout
in the United States of the protracted economic depression in Mexico, becoming
apparent to Americans (or *norteamericanos,* as the Mexicans would call us).

This is a book on policy. The discussion looks to the future, but realism requires
that judgments be based on a sympathetic understanding of what has shaped the
present. For instance, every Mexican schoolchild learns that the United States
invaded Mexico more than a century ago and seized half the country's territory, and
Mexican history books are replete with references to U.S. economic exploitation.
Lázaro Cárdenas, who was president when Mexico nationalized foreign oil-com-
pany properties, and the young cadets who defended their land against the U.S.
invaders are Mexican heroes, but are largely footnotes in U.S. history texts.

While history is the foundation for fashioning the future relationship, the building
blocks are the current situations inside the two countries. It is necessary to examine
internal developments to understand foreign policy, particularly for two countries as
economically integrated as Mexico and the United States. The prosperity of either

leads to increased exports by the other, just as economic decline in one leads inexorably to lost jobs in the other's export industries. The need to pay interest on the debt to U.S. and other foreign banks requires that the Mexican population be deprived of these resources. American macroeconomic policy that raises interest rates increases the hardship in Mexico, just as a decline in interest rates permits Mexico to invest more at home for its own development. As economic opportunity for individual Mexicans diminishes, as during most of the 1980s, the pressure mounts to emigrate to the United States. This, in turn, affects the ethnic mix, cultural makeup, job opportunities, and politics of those regions of the United States that receive the immigrants.

The interaction between the two countries can be either a positive- or a negative-sum game. As one country grows economically, it pulls along the other. As either contracts, the other is also dragged down. The ideal relationship, therefore, is one of mutual prosperity, with each country's economic growth supporting that of the other. This is the objective that drives the policy recommendations contained in this book.

The quotations at the beginning of this introduction were chosen to signal the central themes of the relationship: the lack of mutual comprehension, to which the famous Mexican historian Daniel Cosío Villegas referred more than forty years ago, the interplay between politics—the subject of Pablo González Casanova's statement—and the need for economic restructuring in Mexico, to which President Miguel de la Madrid was referring.

Politics in Mexico is not a purely internal matter, since it forms the basis for the totality of the nation's foreign relations. The same can be said about internal U.S. politics, which shape macroeconomic policy and a host of other U.S. positions—on Central America, drug traffic, trade protectionism, and, more generally, the ramifications of a growing economic nationalism. Each of these positions has a major effect on the United States–Mexico relationship.

Even our language is an issue that can have foreign repercussions. Two of the U.S. states that have strong movements in favor of establishing English as the "official" language are California and Texas, in which the majority of the Mexican-origin population lives.[1] Politics, ethnicity, emotion, education, and nationalism all come together on this issue.

The reinforcing nature of the internal and the external, of politics and economics, are themes permeating the analysis in this book. An appreciation of the interplay among policy measures is also necessary for understanding the relationship between the two countries. Migration is influenced by job opportunities, income distribution, and the level of wages; the burden of debt servicing, an economic matter, is a paramount domestic political issue in Mexico; trade and industrial policies in the two countries affect incomes and the level and quality of their employment; the rapid growth of the population along the border is reshaping the economics, politics, culture—indeed, the very pattern of thinking—of the people who live there. This book's chapters are divided into such themes as trade, industry, oil, debt, the border, and migration, but this is for convenience of exposition, not because the issues are truly separable. It is not possible, for example, to think of drug use in U.S. cities without considering Mexico's drug-eradication program, the factors influencing demand in the United States, the profits generated by the traffic, and the corruption made possible in both countries by the vast sums of money involved.

Economics or issues that derive from economics, such as migration, are at the heart of the United States–Mexico relationship. Mexico is not powerful enough and the United States is too powerful for Mexico even to consider arming against U.S. predation.[2] Neither country poses a military threat to the other, and there is no nearby powerful enemy, such as the Soviet Union, whose proximity so thoroughly influences the U.S. posture in Western Europe and Asia. Yet the economic aspect of United States–Mexico relations is sometimes subordinated to what should be extraneous features of the relationship. These include the opposing outlooks on Central America, disputes on how to control drug production and traffic, and the instinctive reaction in the United States that pervasive corruption in Mexico makes cooperation difficult. These issues are dealt with in this book precisely because they embitter the relationship.

One other impediment to cooperation is that the relationship is not a warm one. The style of governmental exchanges is formal. This may be inevitable; the United States is a world power, and Mexico a struggling developing country. Annual per capita income in the United States is now about $18,000; in Mexico, less than $2,000. The Mexican culture is Hispanic, and that of the United States, while complex, derives much of its sustenance from a British, Western European, non-Latin tradition. Mexico was the territorial loser and the United States the gainer in their nineteenth-century war.

All these differences complicate but do not preclude cooperation.[3] Lack of affection has not prevented the French from working harmoniously with the West Germans since World War II, to cite one example where history would have predicted continued conflict but where conscious policy decisions brought cooperation instead.

The Mexican economy has been disastrous since 1982, the entire span of President Miguel de la Madrid's six-year administration, or *sexenio,* as it is called in Mexico. The gross domestic product (GDP), after discounting for inflation, remained about the same after fifty years of steady expansion of about 6 percent annually. Since population has been increasing in recent years at about 2 percent annually, the decline in per capita income over the six-year period of the de la Madrid administration totaled about 15 percent. Take-home pay of wage earners— that is, salaries after accounting for inflation—fell during the *sexenio* by 50 percent.[4] The wage earners were the lucky ones; they had jobs.

Unlike in many other Latin American countries, inflation was not a major problem during Mexico's halcyon half-century of economic growth, but rose to 160 percent in 1987. As recently as 1981, the exchange rate was 24.5 pesos to the dollar. It took more than 2,300 pesos to buy $1 during most of 1989.

Disaster, however, is not the complete economic story of the de la Madrid *sexenio.* President de la Madrid inherited rigidities that contributed to the economic decline during his watch that included a mostly inefficient industrial complex protected from competition, an elaborate system of government subsidies, and a public-sector deficit that was running out of control. Mexico is now going through a profound change in its economic structure involving rapid opening of the market, which is forcing domestic industrialists to compete. The depreciation of the exchange rate encouraged Mexican producers to export to world markets. From an economy that looked inward, the changes during the de la Madrid *sexenio* forced Mexicans to cast their gaze outward and join the rest of the economic world. This is a transformation of historic proportions, and now that the economy is being opened, it can be turned back to the earlier, closed model only at great economic cost. The longer the economic opening endures, the more irreversible it becomes.

The Mexican economy is changing at an unprecedented rate, but until the presidential and congressional elections of July 6, 1988, the political structure was unfolding at a snail's pace. The contrast between the two could not have been more stark. The official party, the Partido Revolucionario Institucional (Institutional Revolutionary Party, PRI) had never lost a presidential or gubernatorial election since its formation (under another name) in 1928 and 1929; sixty years of political control is a long time in the modern world. The PRI lost four senatorial seats in 1988 and one governorship in 1989. Even the word "official," which is habitually used to describe the PRI, is revealing. A democracy should not have an official party. The PRI has provided the symbols of democracy without the reality, and the July 1988 elections revealed that this was no longer acceptable to the electorate.

The disparity between economic opening and a closed political system had to give way because Mexico is too developed a country, too steeped in the rhetoric, if not the practice, of democracy, to maintain political closure. The political opening came more abruptly than had been expected, however. The growth of democracy elsewhere in Latin America added to the drive for a more competitive political structure in Mexico. The authorities lacked any moral international standing in the absence of a truly popular mandate at home, and, as a qualified democracy, Mexico could not play the role on the world stage to which it aspires. The PRI retains control of the presidency and the two houses of the legislature, but it is a more tenuous, a more shared control, than at any time during the past sixty years.

When the Mexican economy faltered in 1982, its authorities looked outward. As the U.S. economy over the same period has experienced setbacks in the form of large trade deficits, there has been the opposite tendency, to look inward. In the full flush of earlier confidence, U.S. authorities advised Mexico to play a more active role in the world economy. Now that Mexico is doing so, the United States is becoming more protectionist in its economic policies. Synchronization of the two countries' industrial and foreign-trade policies has been elusive.

A major theme of this book is that such policy synchronization of two countries whose economies are already highly integrated would serve both well. Such integration can be resisted, as it often is, through restrictions on the import of goods, services, capital, and people by one or the other. It can be allowed to proceed as the market dictates, which requires an essentially laissez-faire policy that neither country is prepared to accept. Or it can be encouraged by mutual policy frameworks that give the promise of consistency. The recommendation here is that encouragement will serve to raise incomes in both countries by exploiting the advantages that each possesses.

Relations between Mexico and the United States are carried out on two levels, the substantive and the stylistic. Official intercourse is more formal than friendly, and at times can be patronizing and rude. A Mexican speaker can win applause from a domestic audience by describing relations with the United Sates as unequal, exploitative, or even imperialist—in short, a relationship that benefits the United States more than Mexico. A U.S. speaker earns nods of concurrence by describing Mexico as corrupt, antidemocratic, and inefficient, and then using these characterizations as justification for noncooperation. Both sides play the scapegoating game, but this is zero-sum thinking. These denigrating approaches, found in speeches by politicians, official documents, and the media, contain elements of truth, half-truth, and outright distortion, and they surely frustrate cooperation. The United States does not respond graciously when accused of being economically imperialistic. Mexico cannot be expected to behave obsequiously when it is publicly charged with being corrupt.

The United States is often unbearably condescending. Its officials denigrate Mexican authorities in ways that are unthinkable when dealing with other allies. The U.S. ambassador to Great Britain would not last long if he regularly and publicly lectured the British government on its policy shortcomings, but John Gavin, who was U.S. ambassador to Mexico for five years until May 1986, did precisely that to the Mexican government. It would be remarkable for a subordinate U.S. official to openly charge senior French authorities of complicity in the drug trade, yet William von Raab, commissioner of customs, did just that against Mexican officials during a Senate hearing on May 13, 1986. One can hardly conceive of a Senate vote threatening reprisals against the Federal Republic of Germany based on an unconfirmed (and ultimately false) report that a Soviet warship was about to visit a German port, but one-third of U.S. senators did exactly that in September 1985 with respect to Mexico. There were no hearings, no attempts at verification, just a gut reaction that this action was routine in dealings with Mexico.

Much effort is invested by Mexico to separate the verbal from the substantive; most of the verbal excess is directed to domestic audiences and not intended for U.S. ears. The attempt to separate audiences also shows up in disparate approaches to foreign political and economic policies. The first is heavily ideological; the second, much more practical. Stephen Krasner has noted, "Foreign policy has long offered Mexican political leaders opportunities to resolve some of the tensions inherent in their political situation."[5] Jorge Castañeda has asserted that cooperation with the United States on drug control and treatment of foreign direct investment requires the demonstration of Mexican independence in other ways, particularly by opposing U.S. policy toward the Marxist regimes in Cuba and Nicaragua.[6]

The following discussion focuses on the substantive rather than the stylistic. Yet the latter poisons the former; internal and external audiences cannot be separated. Those who make U.S. policy hear and read what is said and printed in Mexico. Foreign political policy cannot be divorced from foreign economic policy. New presidents in each country began their terms more or less simultaneously at the end of 1988 and the beginning of 1989. They can set a courteous tone in the discourse between the two countries, both by example and by punishment of those officials who overstep the bounds of decency.

My approach is more practical than ideological. Stanley Hoffmann has written that "it should be easy to understand that pragmatism, which ought to be a universally valid approach, becomes highly parochial when it is so deeply rooted in a unique experience.''[7] I admit that the conclusions of a pragmatist from the United States may differ from those of a Mexican pragmatist.

Two other important values are brought to this study. The first is the conviction that democracy, unfettered by qualifying adjectives and stultifying limitations, is the only modern system for a country that has pretensions of playing a moral role on the world scene. The second is that a just society requires a more egalitarian distribution of income and of education, health, and other vital services than exists in Mexico. Mexico's income distribution is one of the most unequal in the world for countries at its stage of development.[8]

There are other pairs of countries whose destinies are intertwined. These include Canada and the United States, France and Germany, Australia and New Zealand. But in no other case has fate placed populous countries so disparate in levels of economic development and cultural tradition next to each other as Mexico and the United States. (China and the Soviet Union come closest to this.) These differences make the challenge of cooperation extremely delicate and difficult, but geography leaves no other choice.

I

THE CONTEXT

1

EXPLOITING INEVITABLE INTEGRATION

Underestimating the importance of Mexico's economic bonds with the exterior, especially in finance, has contributed to weakening, even to arresting, the development process, particularly in recent years.

PROGRAMA NACIONAL DE FINANCIAMIENTO DEL DESARROLLO 1984–1988

Despite the impossibility of understanding U.S. Mexican relations in a purely national framework, the fact remains that the grip of "we/they" thinking is still very strong.

RICHARD R. FAGEN, 1981

In dependent societies cultural institutions play a dual role: first, to justify the power wielded by a colonial class, by instilling at every social level its values and ideas, as if they reflect the natural order of things; second, to exert their authority in the interest of both the class they represent and the international imperialism to which they are subordinate.

CARLOS MONSIVÁIS, 1978

Interlocked Destinies

The central argument of this book is that Mexico and the United States are increasingly becoming captives of each other. The degree of captivity, however, is asymmetrical; only at great cost can Mexico separate its future from its relations with the United States. Put more forcefully, Mexico cannot even isolate itself from internal decisions made in the United States. Mexico is more caught up in the web of U.S. internal policy than any other country, except perhaps Canada, where a comparable situation exists. It is evident that U.S. foreign-trade policy, whether it accepts imports or is protective, must affect Mexico. It is somewhat less obvious but equally significant that U.S. fiscal and monetary policies have profound repercussions in Mexico. This was evident in 1981 and 1982 when restrictive U.S. monetary policy led to high interest rates that greatly complicated the servicing of Mexico's external debt. Other examples of internal U.S. imperatives limiting the independence of Mexico's economic policy abound. For example, the need for a production base for labor-intensive operations for many U.S. industries explains the growth of both assembly plants and the automotive-parts industry in Mexico.

This dependence, to use that loaded word, can be deplored by Mexicans con-

11

cerned over national sovereignty, but it cannot be ignored if Mexico wishes to maximize its long-term growth.[1] The *Economist* has noted that successive Mexican governments from the 1950s to the 1980s struggled to find a third way between protectionism and reliance on the U.S. market, but "there simply was not one there."[2]

United States dependence on Mexico, while unequal, is also significant. This was driven home when U.S. exports to Mexico declined by $8.7 billion between 1981 and 1983.[3] Using the relationship of 25,000 jobs per $1 billion of U.S. exports, this translated into almost 220,000 jobs lost, most of them in manufacturing, at a time of recession in the United States, when alternative jobs were not available at wages equivalent to those lost.[4] Another poignant example of integration is that Mexico's inability to create enough good jobs for its young population emerges as an immigration issue in the United States.

Since divorce is not practical, what other options exist for the relationship? Some introductory comments can provide the context for answering this question.

Integration in Fact

The most frequently used indicators of United States–Mexico integration are economic. In most years, between 60 and 70 percent of Mexico's merchandise exports are sold to the United States, and the same proportion of Mexico's imports comes from the United States. Mexico has no present substitute for the U.S. market for most exports, although, in theory, import sources are alterable. In practice, however, this would involve a costly wrench; a large part of Mexico's imports are transactions between related parties—that is, a parent trading with a subsidiary—and these parties are also crucial in fostering Mexico's nonpetroleum exports. The two aspects of trade, Mexican purchases and Mexican sales, are thus part of the same process.

The growth of U.S. direct investment in Mexico over the years has led to many transactions between related parties that are an integral part of the pattern of imports and exports. More than one-third of all nonpetroleum exports from Mexico to all destinations are accounted for by firms with foreign capital.[5] This is an indicator of either dependency or integration, depending on one's point of view. What it illustrates is that foreign direct investment in Mexico leads to trade between Mexico and the investing country and, further, that companies with foreign capital are more export-oriented than those with purely Mexican capital. If increased exports are a sine qua non of Mexican recovery, as Presidents Miguel de la Madrid and Carlos Salinas de Gortari have said, then the case for accepting foreign direct investment is strengthened.

Trade integration with the United States is even greater than indicated by the overall import and export percentages. The critical sector for Mexican exports is manufactures, since these products are less prone to the large price variations that beset trade in raw materials, including petroleum. Manufacturing is also more labor intensive than extracting petroleum and natural gas from the ground and under the sea, and creation of jobs is a critical requirement of Mexico's development process.

The United States is particularly crucial for Mexican exports of manufactures, which made up 48 percent of Mexico's exports to all destinations in 1987, but 55 percent of exports to the United States. The value added in *maquiladora* production, which is almost entirely composed of manufactures, is not shown under trade in Mexico's balance-of-payments presentation, but if these exports for 1987 ($1.6 billion) are added, the proportion of manufactures in Mexico's exports to the United States rises to more than 60 percent. (*Maquiladora* are plants, mostly near the U.S. border, in which imported products are further elaborated, using Mexican labor, for re-export, usually back to the United States.) The reliance on the United States can be stated even more starkly. In 1987, more than 80 percent of Mexico's exports of manufactures to its ten largest customers went to the United States.[6]

This is often decried by Mexican critics as double dependency: dependency of market and colonial subservience, since many of these exports are intermediate goods produced with low-cost labor that enter into subsequent production in the United States. The latter dependency argument is superficially attractive but essentially specious because many U.S. exports to Mexico are also of intermediate goods, as indeed is much of world trade.

Whatever the label, the U.S. and Mexican markets are closely intertwined, a connection that did not diminish even during Mexico's years of successful import substitution. What changed then was the composition of trade, from finished consumer goods to intermediate and capital goods going to Mexico and intermediate and final consumer goods going from Mexico to the United States.

The other economic aspect of integration that has taken on much importance in recent years is capital flow between Mexico and the United States. Capital moves in large amounts in both directions. There is more U.S. foreign direct investment in Mexico than from any other country, roughly two-thirds of the total.[7]

About 85 percent of Mexico's external debt is with private creditors. Of the commercial bank portion, which makes up about 80 percent of the total debt with private creditors, one-third comes from U.S. commercial banks. Of even greater moment is that the leadership role for new bank lending comes from U.S. banks. This is involuntary to a great extent because of pressure from the U.S. government and the banks' need to protect existing portfolios, but the key connection is still with the U.S. capital and money market. And when funds move out of Mexico, once again the key destination is the United States for debt-service payments and capital flight. For better or worse, there is no escape from the United States for trade and capital flows.

The integration of the two countries extends beyond the economic. It is no accident that the most turbulent Mexican elections took place in Chihuahua, a border state, in 1986, and in Coahuila, another border state, in 1987. The opposition was particularly strong in several border states in the 1988 presidential election, the left in Baja California Norte and the right in Chihuahua and Sinaloa. Proximity has tied the economy of the Mexican border closely to developments in the United States and has led also to an infection of democratic norms familiar north of the border. Mexican intellectuals often argue that Mexican democracy must fit the Mexican scene and not be built on the U.S. model, and U.S. apologists for Mexican authoritarianism often make the same point. This argument is valid enough as far as it goes, but loses force if what is advocated does not include effective suffrage— since it is hard to conceive of "democracy" without choice by the people.

The border is an avenue of integration through what Karl Deutsch, in another context, has called transaction flows.[8] There were 293 million legal crossings of the U.S. border via Mexico in U.S. fiscal year 1987, which was 64 percent of all legal border crossings.[9] Many persons who live in Mexico cross the border repeatedly to go to their daily jobs in the United States. No other two countries have this many legal border crossings. The number of foreign tourists entering Mexico in 1987 was 5.5 million, of which 1.8 million came overland, practically all from the United States.[10]

Another significant aspect of transaction flows is that represented by trade and capital movements. These occur by the thousands daily, in small and large transactions. As with human flows, some are legal, others are clandestine, and most occur without government intermediation. The only countries with which the United States may conduct more daily trade transactions are Canada and Japan.

The impact of these transaction flows is cumulative. The transmission of political ideas is reinforced by the flow of people, goods, and capital. Ideas and habits also flow from the media. Radio programs from the United States can be picked up all along the border, and U.S. television is available in most of Mexico, directly at the border and by cable or satellite dishes elsewhere. It is fashionable in Mexico to deplore consumer habits imported from the United States, but it is not possible to stop them—short of converting Mexico into a closed society.[11] The cultural infection is not merely from soap operas, rock music, and baseball, as prevalent as these are, but also from the education of a large number of Mexico's elite at U.S. universities. Both Miguel de la Madrid and his successor as president, Carlos Salinas de Gortari, received graduate degrees in the United States. Members of extended families live on both sides of the border. Indeed, it is hard to find a Mexican, from whatever social or economic class, who does not have a relative in the United States, a kinsman or *compadre,* or who has not personally visited the United States, legally or without papers.

These interactions have a cumulative effect that permeates Mexican society. A poll conducted by the *New York Times* in October and November 1986 found that 48 percent of Mexicans had a favorable opinion of the United States as opposed to 27 percent who had an unfavorable view.[12] When asked what was best about the United States, 16 percent, more than for any other specific attribute, cited its democratic system of government. This answer is both a commentary on the Mexican scene and an indicator of the transmission of ideas.

These cultural and kinship flows move in both directions. An estimated 10 to 20 million Spanish-speaking persons in the United States listen to the broadcasts of the Mexican-owned Univisión, the former Spanish International Network. Univisión news telecasts are beamed directly from Mexico City and have an *oficialista* (pro-government, pro-PRI) bias. Mariachi music moves north, just as rock music goes south. Cultural patterns in both countries are changing as a result of the reciprocal movements, and what is emerging will be a mixture of the two national influences.

The creeping integration has become so extensive that the power to control it has effectively passed out of the hands of governments. The authorities can no more control the cross-border connections than King Canute could hold back the sea. Each government has tried in the past to do this, as in the U.S. "operation wetback" in 1954, which resulted in cruel mass deportations of Mexicans, or Mexican efforts in 1982 to prevent capital flight by decree. These examples are now anomalies in the total relationship. Traders do business legally when governments cooperate, but they also do so clandestinely when governments are obstructive. The drug traffic is an integrated whole across both countries. California and other states may pass laws making English the official language, but Spanish will continue to flourish in the United States. Consumer tastes, music, and ideas will flow in both directions.

Mario Ojeda, a Mexican political scientist, unwittingly explained why. He saw the connection in terms of vulnerabilities with respect to the United States that must be reduced if Mexico is to have an independent future. The three dominating vulnerabilities he cited were geographical propinquity, power asymmetry, and economic and technological dependence.[13] Ojeda, of course, recognizes that propinquity cannot be altered and power asymmetry will persist for the indefinite future; the prescription therefore boils down to reducing Mexican reliance on the United States in the economic and technological fields. This is precisely what has proved to be impossible because of an even more imperative objective—maximizing economic growth.

Managed Integration

Since the two economies are becoming integrated despite repeated national efforts to arrest the process, one response would be for governments to step aside and let the process proceed. However, neither country is completely laissez faire in its policies. Each encourages certain industries, limits some imports, imposes minimum wages, has social welfare programs, and regulates activities in the name of health, safety, and competition. The two tax systems differ, and that imposes different constraints and incentives on economic activity. The Mexican state has been activist for as long as any current participant in the economy can remember, and this tradition is not easily discarded *in toto*.

The more feasible role for the two governments would be to establish the policy and regulatory framework that optimizes the integration taking place in any event. This would be a model of managed integration as opposed to the anarchic integration that is now occurring. Both governments already manage their economies at a macro level through fiscal, monetary, and exchange-rate policies, and at a micro level through a variety of regulations, antitrust actions, and direct and indirect subsidies. Except for libertarians, the debate is not over government management as such, but its extent and correctness. What I propose are two fundamental changes in this management: it should recognize the growing integration of the two economies and abandon the "we/they" mentality that Richard Fagen deplores in the epigraph to this chapter; and it should seek to extract maximum advantage from the integration rather than futilely fighting it.

Managed integration implies concrete measures:

- The exploitation of each country's comparative advantages.
- Seeking out rather than deploring economic complementarities.
- Recognizing that each country has a natural market in the other.
- Encouraging intra-industry production sharing where this is appropriate.

Detail on these recommendations is contained in later chapters dealing with trade, industry, and border relations. At the broad policy level, and using Ojeda's terminology of vulnerabilities, the proposal is to take advantage of propinquity and the complementary nature of economic and technological development. This is done now for the assembly plants, the *maquiladora,* whose expansion is based on the combination of low-cost labor in Mexico and market availability in the United States. *Maquiladora,* however, only touch the surface. At the end of 1988, there were about 1,450 of these assembly plants, about 90 percent at the border, employing upward of 400,000 workers and providing more than $2 billion of value added to the Mexican economy.[14] Mexico has tens of thousands of manufacturing plants, over 27 million workers in the labor force, and a GDP in the neighborhood of $150 billion. The *maquila* structure, as important as it is, represents a small part of the economy. Beyond that, the plants are mostly an enclave activity not integrated into the Mexican economy, and the exploitation of comparative advantage proposed here is intended to be part of the two economies.

The use of low-cost labor—the equivalent of 78 cents an hour, including wages and benefits, at the end of 1988—is quite naturally a sensitive issue in Mexico; it smacks of exploitation.[15] Olga Pellicer, for example, has argued that industrialization based on the exploitation of cheap labor would only confirm Mexico's dependence.[16] The issue is sensitive in the United States as well; it suggests runaway industry at the expense of U.S. workers, and precisely for this reason the *maquiladora* are disliked by organized labor in the United States.[17]

To the Mexican concerned about labor exploitation, the alternative in practice under the import-substitution model that prevailed for half a century was involuntary part-time employment for millions of Mexicans; this was even greater exploitation under a structure that led to great inequalities. It is possible to set minimum wages that lessen the exploitation, as long as they are not so high as to drive away potential investors, and to regulate working conditions. However, wages in Mexico will increase for the majority only as demand for labor increases; under the model that protected any domestic industry through subsidies and import restrictions, some Mexicans worked at relatively high wages, while others had no work or part-time work at low wages. This was a system of privilege that excluded the majority.

To the American worker concerned about runaway industry, the answer is that short of import protection against products that can be made competitively by low-wage workers abroad, U.S. employment is increased by producing part of these products at home and part abroad. This is what production sharing is all about. It seeks to ensure sources of supply of intermediate products, usually within an industry, by exploiting comparative advantages, whether they are relatively cheap labor, cheap capital, cheap land, the availability of a particular technology, or whatever. Mexico's advantage as a location for this type of added value is the combination of propinquity and low wages.[18]

Mexican objections to such a strategy include a historical antipathy to actually fostering integration with the United States; an ideology which argues that the state should directly foster development rather than give the primary role to private industry; and deep concern that Mexico, as the weaker partner, will become even more dependent and that its future would be determined by decisions taken elsewhere and designed to enrich actors in the United States at Mexican expense.

The historical antipathy exists, and not much more can be said about it. It resides more among politicians and intellectuals than among the general populace, as various public-opinion polls show. This can be phrased more precisely: while the historical distrust exists even among the general populace in Mexico, most individuals believe that this need not prevent United States–Mexico economic cooperation. If the economic integration is taking place in any event, antipathy, whatever its motivation, is largely extraneous.

The major alternative development model, what Rolando Cordera and Carlos Tello called the ''nationalist project,'' has a more solid intellectual base than anti-Americanism.[19] Cordera and Tello contrast their model with what they call the neoliberal approach.[20] The nationalist approach would make the state the guiding force in development, directly and through its management; foster the production of capital goods in Mexico; strive for food self-sufficiency; deal with inflation by means other than wage containment; and expand large, state-owned projects in energy, petrochemicals, steel, and fertilizers. This, in its essentials, was the approach from 1932 to 1982, almost down to the last detail. It worked for decades but has now spent itself.

It is not the Cordera–Tello proposal that is at issue, but the approach that argues that the way out of Mexico's economic crisis is by a large dose—that is, a new large dose, more far-reaching than those of the past—of state management and direct involvement. This policy did not prevent effective integration of the two economies in the past; it is not clear that it would in the future, unless the growth objective were sacrificed.

There is great fear among Mexicans that deliberate steps toward economic integration with the United States under the current conditions of economic and power asymmetries would perpetuate dependency. The asymmetrical interdependence that exists with the United States is already seen by some Mexicans as a form of ''transnationalization'' of the capitalist economy.[21] In discussing why a common market between the United States and Mexico would be unwise, Carlos Rico has argued that this ''would be equivalent to recognizing the failure of the aims of independence and sovereignty that are central to the ideology of the Mexican Revolution.''[22] But the managed integration I propose is a far cry from a common market, even though the heat of Rico's position makes clear that the same criticism would apply.

To many Mexicans, the degree of integration that has taken place is evidence of failed government policy. What emerges when one probes deeply into the thinking of the proponents of a state-dominated model is that there was just not enough state involvement and direction in the past. The basis for concern over economic and power asymmetry is that the balance of bargains struck between actors in the two countries will inevitably favor the United States. But the bargaining that takes place between the two governments or private parties in the two countries is more complex than a simple asymmetry model implies, a point I will amplify later in this chapter.

Managed integration with Mexico might be acceptable to the body politic in the United States precisely because it does not involve free trade—but acceptance is by no means ensured. An American must ask what is in it for the United States, just as Mexicans must ask how Mexico would benefit. The answer for the United States is roughly the same as for Mexico. Economic integration is taking place in any event, and managed integration would provide the basis for exploiting the complementarities of the two countries. The growth of intra-industry production at the United States–Mexico border shows how quickly private enterprise can react once the two countries establish the conditions that make this form of production possible.[23] And, perhaps most important, it is hardly in the U.S. political interest for Mexican underdevelopment to endure, since this would perpetuate emigration and stimulate social instability in Mexico.

Managed integration is straightforward in concept but would be complex in actual management. It is *not* a Mexico–United States common market, a Mexico–United States free-trade agreement, thoroughgoing laissez faire, or a nationalist project of the type advocated by Cordera and Tello. Managed integration need not prevent each government from pursuing industrial and social policies that it considers to be in the national interest, as long as they did not overwhelm the integrative tendencies. If Mexico did not wish to alter its legislation on foreign direct investment, that would complicate industrial integration, but not any more than it has in the past. The United States need not alter its efforts—whatever they turn out to be—to restrain illegal immigration. Greater anti-immigration efforts would lessen the extent of labor-market integration, but, again, probably no more than in the past.

What is necessary is to accept that the combined industrial structures of the two countries would be more efficient if their complementarities were fostered rather than resisted. Managed integration requires that trade in intermediate products, which for manufactures is becoming increasingly significant in the trade between the two countries, be promoted. This integration can be within a framework that encourages particular industries and sectors in each country—what in European Community countries are referred to as national champions—but the balance in industrial policy requires that a binational approach be specifically encouraged by both governments. Bela Balassa, in discussing the European Community, made a relevant point in this context: "It has further been shown that trade creation has resulted largely from intra-industry specialization in manufacturing which brings benefits through the exploitation of economies of scale."[24] The degree of public ownership of industry can still be determined by each country as it sees fit—the pattern in the European Community despite an economic integration far more thoroughgoing than that contemplated here.

The difficulty of management stems from internal political, economic, and social differences between the two countries. The use of the phrase "industrial integration" masks vast differences among industries, both between and within countries. Labor in each country is by no means homogeneous. Labor involved in U.S. industries already facing severe competition from producers in low-wage countries, such as Mexico, views foreign trade quite differently from labor in industries in which the United States is a strong competitor in export markets. And labor in the most highly organized sectors in Mexico, particularly in government-owned enterprises, has a different stake in industrial integration from that of nonorganized and underemployed Mexican labor. Mexican scholars often argue that the United States must accept either Mexican goods and services or, if there is a lack of job opportunities at home, Mexican labor. This may be valid in the abstract but has little resonance in a particular case of import competition.

These realities emerge in practice today in production-sharing arrangements within industries and will continue as industrial integration proceeds. Conflict is inevitable among particular labor and industrial interests, but governments must promote the national interest while protecting particular interests to the extent feasible without prejudice to the broader picture. This balancing act is difficult enough in any case, with or without managed integration. But management is most difficult at times of economic stagnation and high unemployment and least complex in a growing economy. The case for managed integration is that it will encourage economic growth in both countries.

Bargaining

Managed integration puts an emphasis on bargaining. The seeking out of complementarities, exploitation of comparative advantages, maximizing of intra-industry specializations, and entry into each other's home markets all require negotiation. Negotiation of this type is not new; however, its augmentation under managed integration would be significant.

Negotiation is often implicit: a producer of semiconductors in the United States can now set up an assembly plant in Mexico for the labor-intensive parts of the operation without detailed negotiation; the manufacturer of women's blouses can open a factory in Mexico for embroidery and finishing; *maquila* plants are established to complete the manufacture of automotive parts for reshipment to U.S. assembly plants. The main bargaining in each of these cases was finished earlier, when Mexico permitted in-bond production without payment of duty and the United States in turn permitted the reentry of goods subject to duty only on the value added outside the country. Even this intergovernmental bargain was indirect in that it stemmed from two separate decisions and not a specific negotiation.

The bargain is sometimes explicit, too, however. The 1985 agreement between the two governments on subsidies and countervailing duties was of this nature, as were the negotiations between the two governments leading in 1987 to a broad economic framework agreement to deal with bilateral trade problems, foreign investment, economic dispute-settlement procedures, and intellectual property rights.[25] When IBM agreed in 1986 to establish a plant to produce personal computers, a specific bargain was struck between a private company and the Mexican government. This agreement spawned a series of subagreements between IBM and technical institutions, some private and others public, and with many private Mexican companies for inputs into the production process and for the sale and servicing of the final product.[26] When the Ford Motor Company agreed to establish plants in Mexico both to assemble vehicles and to produce parts for later incorporation in cars assembled in the United States, this also involved multiple bargains, most of them explicit.

Table 1.1 shows a broad categorization of bargaining modes. The actors to bargaining are a mixture of private parties and governments, although it is not always clear where the private ceases and the public becomes dominant. When a U.S. investor agrees to take a minority equity position in a Mexican enterprise, a series of negotiations takes place with the government and potential Mexican associates, who may be either public or private. Bargaining between the two governments or their dependencies is omnipresent, a necessary concomitant of increasing

Table 1.1 Patterns of Bargaining

Players	Key Elements	Examples in United States–Mexico Relations
Government to government	Effective national power	Central America
	Domestic politics	Tariff preferences
	Quid pro quos	Import limitations
	Relative zeals	Balance-of-payments support
	Linkages—implicit and explicit	Trade negotiations
		U.S. strategic petroleum reserve
Private to private	Economic power	Technology sales
	Alliances	Production sharing
	Quid pro quos	Import and export transactions
		Private borrowing
Private with government	Shifting power	Oil and natural-gas sales
	Domestic politics	Foreign direct investment
	Alliances	*Maquiladora*
	Quid pro quos	Debt rescheduling
	Zeal	
Hybrids	Elements as under purer forms	Export-performance requirements
Private–private under government regulations		Domestic-content provisions
		Debt rescheduling (Paris Club)
Government–government under international constraints		Natural-gas controversy (1977–1978)
		Import restrictions
Private–government under constraints imposed by either government		Export financing
Combinations involving all the above		

economic interaction. Managed integration would intensify these negotiations, since it implies greater specialization within industries than now exists.

Ojeda puts Mexico's negotiating capacity at the center of its relations with the United States. The gist of his argument is that Mexico is vulnerable in government-to-government negotiation when its economy is weak, as during a balance-of-payments crisis.[27] This is not disputable, as is evident from Mexican negotiations with the International Monetary Fund (IMF). Ojeda and others, including President José López Portillo, saw the oil boom of the 1970s partially in this light—that Mexico need no longer be the *demandeur* in all respects.

Relative levels of absolute power obviously have relevance here, but the exercise of power is more complex than posited by Ojeda. The key to negotiating advantage is less the respective levels of *absolute* power (that is, the United States has the larger economy and the greater military force) than those of *effective* power. The Iran hostage case provides a good example of the difference: U.S. military power served not at all to free the hostages held in the embassy in Tehran, but U.S. control over Iranian assets eventually proved to be decisive. The effective power turned out to be economic, but only after Iran made this so through economic policies that created a need for foreign exchange. With respect to United States–Mexico trade, the U.S. market is larger and Mexican dependence on this market is substantial, and thus U.S. absolute power in trade matters is greater. However, most trade negotiations deal with specific products, and it is not possible to determine in advance which side will have greater effective power in a concrete negotiation. The complexity of automotive negotiations between the two countries or those leading to the establishment of IBM and other computer companies in Mexico illustrate that it is too glib to talk about absolute power being crucial in a specific case. As I. William Zartman and Maureen Berman have noted, the terms "weak" and "strong" are often used in a sloppy manner.[28]

When Mexico seeks unrequited benefits, such as trade preferences, it is clearly in a weak bargaining position. This has always been the weakness of the position of developing countries when they insist that they should not be expected to grant reciprocity in multilateral trade negotiations with developed countries. If there is no quid pro quo, it is not a serious negotiation; it is a grant. The grant may be given for a variety of reasons, as much political as economic, but it should not be confused with the kind of bargaining that would be involved under managed integration.

The relative degrees of effective power in many bargaining situations, including those between private parties, are influenced by government intervention. When multinational corporations (MNCs) negotiate with either the government or private groups in Mexico, they bring oligopoly power to the bargaining table. They also bring technology, financial power, and marketing ability that usually give them a bargaining advantage.[29] Mexican laws and regulations are largely designed to reduce this MNC bargaining advantage. These provisions, such as those dealing with proportions of domestic content that must be incorporated into final products, then become an essential aspect of MNC negotiations with the Mexican government and private suppliers. Mexican requirements on export levels were a major ingredient of the Ford decision to assemble cars and produce engines in Mexico. The U.S. government also occasionally uses its power to influence private negotiations, as when it coercively withheld agreement on the subsidies and countervailing-duties accord to secure a revision of the treatment of the U.S. pharmaceutical industry operating in Mexico.

These examples indicate how private negotiating power is effectively altered by governmental actions. There are also examples in which effective governmental power has been constrained or augmented by private decisions. Official U.S. dislike of export performance requirements imposed by Mexico in the automotive industry has not been effective in preventing these requirements because the U.S. auto firms were prepared to live with them. The private companies gave greater weight to the potential Mexican market than to U.S. commercial policy. Similarly, U.S. government opposition in 1977 to the price of natural gas to be sold by Pemex to U.S. pipeline companies led to the cancellation of the letter of intent, but the plan was revived in 1979 when an understanding between the two governments permitted the conclusion of a commercial arrangement between Pemex and a consortium of U.S. companies.[30] This was a more complex conclusion than that arrived at in the automotive industry in that the price of the natural gas in the 1979 agreement was lower than that agreed to in 1977; but it shows that U.S. government policy prevented a private bargain at one point, yet private preferences eventually forced the government to alter its policy to permit a bargain (which is not now operative in that no gas is being exported) to be concluded.

Governments can alter effective power in private bargaining. Private pressures can also influence the effective bargaining power of governments. The two positions may be reinforcing or in conflict. The essential point is that bargaining under managed integration would involve all these complexities.

The main misgiving on the U.S. side is a variant of the Mexican concern about the power disparity in a negotiation. Many groups in the United States fear that there would be deep disagreements among the U.S. parties to the negotiations. Thomas Colosi has pointed out that team members in a negotiation often have conflicting goals, strategies, tactics, perceptions, assumptions, and values.[31] In negotiations with Mexico on specific industrial issues, there are almost certain to be differences between that industry's labor and management. General Motors management was quite prepared, even anxious, at the end of 1986 to move Delco production to Mexico, while the U.S. workers involved had a different outlook and prevented the move. A similar difference of outlook between labor and management exists in other automotive companies and other industries. Each side in a negotiation under managed integration must go through its own negotiation as well as one with the other country.

The role of the U.S. government in the negotiations involving comparative labor costs is ambiguous. Government decisions support those industries moving labor-intensive *maquiladora* operations to Mexico in the form of privileged reentry of the goods by making them liable for duty only on the value added abroad; labor's opposition to this policy has regularly been overridden for decades. The U.S. government has complained but has taken no effective action to protect U.S. labor against Mexican domestic-content provisions or export requirements for U.S. companies producing goods in Mexico.

The position of U.S. labor may or may not be valid, but its protests have been consistently overruled. Labor's concern is that issues of complementarity and industrial integration will be decided not solely on economic grounds, but also on the basis of internal power relationships within the United States and official concern for foreign relations, specifically the economic development and social stability of Mexico. Mexicans often argue that they are sometimes treated with disdain by the U.S. government because of power and economic asymmetries; U.S. labor organizations often have precisely the opposite view, that they are treated with disdain in the interest of foreign policy. Complexity abounds, and will have to be reckoned with in creating a managed integration policy in both countries.

As Mexico opens its economy, as it seeks foreign direct investment, as it gives higher priority to efficiency in manufacturing operations, as it concludes that future economic growth will require more diversified exports—all current Mexican policy—trade and industrial bargaining will increase. Most will occur between private parties; there will be many cross-border alliances. Such alliances are already common—between Pemex and natural-gas producers in the United States, between computer producers and providers of inputs for the manufacturing process in Mexico, between auto assemblers in the United States and parts producers in Mexico, and between tomato and vegetable growers in Mexico and U.S. marketers.[32] Alliance bargaining is quite different from what Raymond Vernon has called the obsolescing bargain, which related primarily to foreign investment in natural-resource projects.[33] Vernon observed that since these investments involved large sums of capital at the outset of a project, the bargaining advantage was with the foreign investor; once the investment was sunk, the power shifted in favor of the country in which the investment was made. The alliance bargaining discussed here differs in that interests of different groups within both countries are at odds with one another, forcing intra-country negotiations of the type to which Colosi referred. In addition, bargains are constantly renewable as industrial processes change and specializations shift. Van Whiting has argued that this "renewable bargain" in the food-processing industry invariably favored the MNC, despite Mexican government intervention, but there are examples of other outcomes, such as for auto-parts production in Mexico.[34] Power relations can shift; this has been evident in the relative power changes back and forth in the oil industry between the major oil companies and the Organization of Petroleum Exporting Countries (OPEC) since 1973.

Policy by Inadvertence

The most significant aspect of the differences in mutual dependencies is not in transnational bargaining, but in the official attention devoted by each country to the other. The dependency difference also means that official actions taken by the United States have greater repercussions in Mexico than the reverse. Ironically, the most important decisions of the U.S. government vis-à-vis Mexico are not those taken deliberately, but those that come about through inattention or inadvertence. Mexico is damaged or benefited by U.S. actions taken without any thought about Mexico; U.S. policy toward Mexico is made in absentminded decisions.

Most U.S. government economic decisions regarding Mexico specifically are marginal in their effect. These relate to specific product preferences under the U.S. general system of preferences, decisions about whether to impose a countervailing duty on a particular product, or whether to admit Mexican tuna to the United States.[35] Other decisions more or less related to Mexico but affecting foreign nations generally, such as the import-duty features of item 807 of the U.S. tariff code (charging duty only on the value added abroad), can have a great impact on Mexico, but still less than U.S. actions designed to affect the domestic economy.

American macroeconomic policy—decisions affecting fiscal deficits, levels of interest rates, and the value of the dollar—turns out to be of infinitely more import to Mexico than the actions noted above. To cite one obvious example, with Mexico's external debt exceeding $100 billion, each percentage point of change in interest rates can shift the nation's annual obligations by as much as $1 billion.[36] Each $1 change in oil prices, which are partially dependent on the level of U.S.

economic activity, can have an annual $600 million impact on Mexico's exports. The level of U.S. imports from Mexico is influenced by the rate of growth of the U.S. economy. The transmission to Mexico of influences from the United States is particularly substantial because of Mexico's trade and financial dependence.[37]

The effect on Mexico is not considered when macroeconomic decisions are made in the United States. On the off chance that somebody raises the problem of aggravating the debt burden of developing countries generally and Mexico specifically when monetary policy is tightened, the conclusion would have to be that internal considerations must take precedence. Nobody in the U.S. government wants to hurt (or help) Mexico when making these internal decisions, but the effect is present nevertheless. Many U.S. commentators have been critical of Mexico's economic policies in recent years, but few of these critics are willing to admit that U.S. decisions during the early 1980s, at the very time the Mexican crisis was building and erupting, aggravated the situation.

Internal Mexican decisions influence the United States as well. Economic austerity has curtailed Mexican imports from the United States. On a deeper level, Mexico's economic and social structure gives an impetus to emigration to the United States. The difference in policies by inadvertence is that Mexico is more dependent on the United States than the reverse. Internal U.S. decisions can be devastatingly good or bad for Mexico. Most internal Mexican decisions have only a modest effect on the United States.

Can anything be done to make advertent what is now unintentional? The short answer is probably "no," and the more tortuous response is that this may, at least to some extent, come about in time.

The Carter administration, in 1979, appointed a coordinator for Mexican affairs, Robert Krueger, a former congressman from Texas, whose function was to raise the level of awareness when official decisions were taken specifically on Mexico. When making the appointment, President Carter asked the executive agencies "to consciously give good relations with Mexico a continuing high priority in your thinking and planning."[38] This was an effort to maintain attention by directive, supported by an advocate whose function was to force agencies to think about Mexico in their day-to-day activities. Richard Feinberg called this a "special attention strategy."[39] That was the intent. It is just as likely that by appointing a single person to give this special attention, the executive agencies felt released from doing it themselves.[40]

Krueger could point to some successes on issues of preferential treatment of Mexican imports. The conception of the office was somewhat broader—that agencies took inconsistent positions affecting Mexico, such as support for a trade restriction by one agency and advocacy of more ample preferential treatment by another. This was the basis for calling the position holder a coordinator. These inconsistencies arise because decisions made for internal U.S. reasons—to support U.S. labor, agriculture, or industry, or to curtail illegal entry into the United States—have external repercussions.

The coordinator never had entrée into the meetings at which the most important decisions affecting Mexico were made, those dealing with internal U.S. macroeconomic policy. Indeed, the secretary of state and the national security adviser in the

White House rarely have influence over these decisions because their duties look outside the country. Mexico temporarily achieved the kind of priority in the thinking and planning of executive agencies that President Carter had in mind only after the start of the continuing crisis since 1982. Attention is not easily obtained by orders or organizational constructs.

The experiment did not work, and the coordinator's position did not survive into the Reagan administration.[41] Many reasons have been given for the failure: the coordinator should have been located in the White House, drawing on the reflected power of the president, rather than in the State Department;[42] coordination is at least one step removed from operations; and there was uncertainty about whether the U.S. ambassador to Mexico was located in Washington, D.C., or Mexico City.

As a general proposition, attention is a consequence not only of crisis, but also of importance of the country in economic, political, and security matters. The United States is never out of Mexico's attention span for precisely these reasons, and officials from the U.S. Treasury and Federal Reserve meet regularly with their counterparts from Western Europe and Japan precisely to prevent policy surprises. The Organization for Economic Cooperation and Development (OECD) in Paris exists to facilitate economic consultation among its members, mostly developed countries. This is a far cry from policy coordination, but the regular meetings force some heed to be paid to the consequences of internal actions on other countries. Canada has long been given special attention when regulatory changes are made on access to U.S. financial markets because of both the importance of the U.S. market to Canada and Canada's economic importance to U.S. financial interests and traders.

Comparable treatment for Mexico does not exist and probably cannot effectively be ordered until Mexico gains the economic salience to make the regular consultation natural. Until then, it may take constant vigilance by Mexican officials to both legislative and executive plans in the United States. There is substantial, documented evidence that this type of lobbying by Mexico is less extensive than by Canada, the other U.S. land neighbor.[43]

Managed integration would not by itself alter official U.S. attention to Mexico. However, managed integration would intensify economic and industrial links between the two countries, and this would be more significant than a bureaucratic change or presidential directive to pay attention to Mexico. And if managed integration stimulated Mexican economic growth, this could result in more regular consultative arrangements between the two countries. Achievement of Mexican economic growth is really the only path to diminish the degree to which U.S. policy toward Mexico is made by inadvertence.

Managed Integration and Dependence

Managed integration is based on the observation that United States–Mexico integration is, in fact, occurring, but in a haphazard fashion. Each government takes actions that both impede and encourage the linkages between the two economies. United States trade restrictions retard the integrative process, and U.S. trade benefits stimulate it. Mexican limitations on foreign investment hold back the process, and Mexican flexibility in accepting foreign investment facilitates it. The schizophrenia on both sides is typical of government policies generally, since nations are collections of groups with diverse views and interests. Their pulling and tugging of interests within countries would not be altered under managed integration. The change would be at the margin in some areas dealing with industry and trade and by extension with economic and political relations generally. Official policy would encourage bargaining for integration that is occurring in any event.

Would this make Mexico even more dependent on the United States? Would it make U.S. labor and industry even more vulnerable than they now are to low-wage imports from Mexico? The superficial answer to both questions is "yes." As U.S. and Mexican industry become increasingly intertwined, the ups and downs of either will have sharp repercussions on the other. If Mexico were to become a more efficient producer of both manufactured inputs and finished goods, competition with U.S. producers would grow, as would the impact on U.S. labor engaged in these activities.

But the deeper answer is that industrial efficiency would simultaneously reduce dependence, if that word is defined to mean the ability of a country to cope with internal economic and social problems. Mexico is not a formidable competitor in most markets for manufactured goods; many sales of manufactured goods in its domestic market depend on protection against imports. The United States has become increasingly vulnerable to competition from foreign manufacturers, and the recent tendency has been to resort to increasing protection. The argument in favor of managed integration is that exploiting factor complementarities would increase total efficiency in both countries and make each more competitive in world markets.

2

OPPOSING POSITIONS WITHIN MEXICO

> There are always arguments to limit, postpone, or detract from democracy. It is always too late or too early.
>
> ENRIQUE KRAUZE, 1983

> Down in Chihuahua, there ain't nothin' much to do.
>
> RALPH YAW AND JOHNNY RICHARDS, "DOWN IN CHIHUAHUA," 1947

> The PRI believes that the only party qualified to govern is it.
>
> HEBERTO CASTILLO, 1986

The Players and the Stakes

As elsewhere, struggles for political power and income shares are at the heart of government decisions made in Mexico. In a society where incremental change has been the norm, at least since the 1910 Revolution, interests are durable once they are vested, and the ability of earlier winners to maintain their gains has been a major feature of the modern Mexican scene.

The big winners of the past fifty years have been the business community, professionals (such as lawyers and engineers), organized labor, large-scale farmers, and the bureaucracy, both in government and in the official party. These groups dominate the political structure and have the largest incomes. Those who have benefited less include unorganized labor, small farmers, especially those cultivating crops in rain-fed areas, and persons flooding into cities because of the lack of opportunity in rural areas. Intellectuals have mostly been in the more privileged group. The absolute incomes of most groups rose when the gross domestic product (GDP) was growing at more than 3 percent per capita annually, but even then the spread between the incomes of the poor and of the rich widened. The *absolute* incomes of practically all groups have been declining since 1982, but the *share* going to labor has declined and that to business has increased.

President Luis Echeverría attempted to alter the division of political power and national income through essentially superficial means that involved co-opting many radical young people into the PRI and the government and using government expenditures to make income distribution more equal. But the class divisions were not altered; Echeverría accomplished little more than to stimulate the earlier winners to organize themselves more effectively to stave off future attempts at political and economic redistribution.

27

Another attempt at economic change is now taking place, driven not by a social ideology of income redistribution but by imperatives of efficiency. The change involves opening the Mexican economy, and if carried to its logical conclusion, future economic development will be more export-led. A different array of interests, only partially overlapping with the past division, will be vested.

The political challenge also deals with opening the political system to truly democratic freedom of choice, or maintaining a system in which a dominant party will continue to make major decisions in internal cabals. These related issues involve the very nature of Mexico's future; their outcomes could change the status quo as thoroughly as all the institutionalized revolution of the past half-century.

Buildup to the Present

The continuity of a single party in power in Mexico for sixty years has been a remarkable feature of the world scene. The precursor of the current PRI was established in 1928 and 1929, and the same party, twice renamed, has dominated Mexican politics ever since.[1] The name, the Institutional Revolutionary Party, is an oxymoron designed to connote constant change, but that change has hardly been revolutionary. Continuity rather than revolution better describes developments since the 1930s.

There were nine presidents from Lázaro Cárdenas (1934–1940) to Miguel de la Madrid (1982–1988), each serving a single six-year term mandated by the constitution. Policy shifts over this period were not radical and reflected the relative emphasis different administrations gave to such issues as land reform, the content and philosophy of the economic development program, and the weight assigned to economic growth as compared with a more egalitarian income distribution. Lázaro Cárdenas is best remembered in Mexico for his social program, in particular land reform, as well as the oil nationalization; Miguel Alemán, for the development of Mexican industry behind protective walls; and Luis Echeverría, for seeking to change the development model from what had been called stabilizing growth to shared development. Miguel de la Madrid will be remembered for his policy of economic opening at a time of economic hardship.

In terms of absolute economic growth, the PRI achieved good results from the 1930s through the 1970s. This economic miracle, as it was called, of fifty years of consistent GDP increases, averaging around 6 percent annually, altered Mexico from an economic backwater to a potential middle-level power. It helps explain the durability of the PRI, and the absence of such growth since 1982 is a major reason for current disillusionment with the PRI. Qualified democracy was an acceptable form of governance as long as the system provided economic growth of 2.5 to 3 percent per capita, year in and year out.

Economics does not wholly explain the PRI's durability. Cárdenas established a corporatist support structure for the official party that, in the main, has persisted to this day—at least until the presidential and legislative elections of July 6, 1988, when it was cast into doubt. The original elements in this structure included labor, the peasants, and the military. The military was later dropped, and a diverse urban group was added; arrangements between the political elite and military commanders are now accomplished outside the formal organizational structure of the PRI.

The labor pillar, the Confederación de Trabajadores Mexicanos (Confederation of Mexican Workers, CTM), remains the most important labor confederation in Mexico. Fidel Velázquez, now an octogenarian, has been its leader since 1941, and remains a significant figure on the Mexican political scene. But his power is easily overstated: while he can obtain limited favors for organized labor because the CTM is part of the official party, he is also a captive of that party. Today, organized labor in Mexico is complex, and the CTM is far from holding a monopoly on the loyalty of working men and women.

The peasant support group, the Confederación Nacional Campesina (National Peasants' Confederation, CNC), is the party's main force for organizing the countryside, but like the CTM, is no longer as influential as it once was. Mexico's population, 80 percent rural in the Cárdenas period, and 70 percent urban in the mid-1980s, is a significant factor in this weakening, since a lower proportion of the population diminishes rural power. Another is rural dissatisfaction with the benefits provided by the official party to impoverished peasants as compared with wealthy landowners. Nevertheless, the CNC remains important in mobilizing the countryside and delivering the peasant vote in support of PRI candidates. The CNC delivered a larger vote to PRI candidates in the July 1988 elections than the CTM.

The "popular" segment of the party, added in 1942, is the Confederación Nacional de Organizaciones Populares (National Confederation of Popular Organizations, CNOP). While the CNOP provides some basis for urban political organization by pulling together diverse groups, it is more inchoate conceptually than the other two pillars of the PRI.

The one significant group omitted from the structure established by Cárdenas was private business and industry, and this omission persists. Nevertheless, business has been the main beneficiary of the political stability and economic growth that Mexico enjoyed for half a century. The PRI established a system of benefits for business without formal representation and representation for labor and *campesinos* with lesser benefits.

The Pressure Groups

Those who benefited from Mexico's development practices developed a vested interest against major change and sought to defend this interest each time it was challenged. Mancur Olson's book *The Rise and Decline of Nations* deals primarily with developed, industrial democracies, but its thesis that extended political stability leads to the entrenchment of powerful self-interested lobbies that eventually frustrate national economic efficiency is certainly applicable to Mexico.[2]

The self-interested basis of positions is obviously not stated as such in Mexico or elsewhere; the arguments are phrased in more lofty terms, to defend a system in the interest of national progress. As elsewhere, slogans embedded in national history are used extensively. The Revolution and the symbolism surrounding its evocation arouse powerful emotions in Mexico, and, hence, a party of the status quo, the Institutional Revolutionary Party, calls itself revolutionary. The justification for continuation of policy, with only modest changes, carried conviction as long as policy was succeeding, as it was for some fifty years until the 1980s. In addition to

Table 2.1 Mexican Quality-of-Life Indicators, Selected Years, 1940–1988

	1940	1950	1960	1970	1980	1988
GNP per capita (in dollars)	73	178	344	692	2,090	1,800
Population (in millions)	19	26	35	48	70	83
Life expectancy at birth[a]	40	56	58	62	65	66
Crude birth rate per 1,000 population	43	45	45	45	37	30
Crude death rate per 1,000 population	23	16	12	10	7	6
Infant mortality at age less than 1 year per 1,000 live births	123	96	78	80	56	50
Child death rate, age 1–4, per 1,000 children	112	28	14	10	4	3[c]
Urban population, percent	35	43	51	59	68	70
Population per physician	8,647	2,400	1,830	1,445	1,260	1,037[c]
Persons enrolled in primary school as percent of 6–11 age group[b]	n.a.	64	80	106	120	115[c]
Persons enrolled in secondary school as percent of 12–17 age group	n.a.	2	11	18	37	55[c]
Persons enrolled in higher education as percent of age group	n.a.	3	3	6	15	16[c]

n.a. = Not available.

[a]Number of years newborn children would live subject to mortality risks prevailing for the cross section of population at birth.

[b]The years since 1970 show more enrollment than there were persons aged six through eleven; that is, older persons enrolled in primary school.

[c]Data are for 1985.

Source: World Bank, *World Development Report,* various issues; United Nations, *Demographic Yearbook,* various issues; United Nations, *Statistical Yearbook,* various issues; Population Reference Bureau; Secretaría de la Economía Nacional, *Anuario estadístico,* 1940; Nacional Financiera, *La economía mexicana en cifras, 1978*; Banco de México, *Asamblea general ordinaria de accionistas,* 1939–1941.

the persistent economic growth during that period, the majority of Mexicans benefited in other ways—for example, increases in life expectancy and education. Table 2.1 shows that these benefits were substantial. However, the 1968 student demonstrations and the attempt during the Echeverría administration to redistribute benefits demonstrated that, below the surface, all was not well. Many Mexican intellectuals preceded Echeverría in their concern about the inequalities in Mexican society.[3] Concern about the autocratic nature of governance has now become substantial.

Business and Industry

The key elements of the post–World War II Mexican economic model, at least until the mid-1980s, were a large state sector, a protected industrial structure, requirements to purchase most intermediate goods used for industrial production within Mexico, limits on foreign direct investment, and an overvalued exchange rate that permitted imports of needed intermediate and capital goods at what amounted to subsidized prices. The development-from-within model placed little stress on exports, and the overvalued exchange rate caused many exports to be subsidized. These policies were not unique to Mexico in the postwar period, but their survival even after their inefficiency was demonstrated reflected the power of vested interests. The power of protectionist interests was exemplified by small-scale industrialists who succeeded in keeping Mexico out of the General Agreement on Tariffs and Trade (GATT) in the López Portillo administration because the implication of GATT membership was that the protective structure would gradually be reduced.[4]

Many Mexican business organizations exist by law. These include chambers of specific industries and several large confederations. The two large obligatory business chambers, one for industry and the other for commerce, are the Confederación de Cámaras Industriales (Confederation of National Chambers of Industry, Concamin) and the Confederación de Cámaras Nacionales de Comercio (Confederation of National Chambers of Commerce, Concanaco). Local, state, and national chambers, which include firms of all sizes, are affiliated with the large confederations. These confederations sometimes criticize government economic policies, but their diversified membership normally requires bland positions to achieve consensus.

Other business groupings were formed independently precisely to counter government positions with which powerful business leaders disagreed. Two of these deserve mention. The Confederación Patronal de la República Mexicana (Mexican Employers' Confederation, Coparmex) was founded in Monterrey during the Cárdenas administration to serve as an opposing voice to the president's leftist orientation. The Consejo Coordinador Empresarial (Businessmen's Coordinating Council, CCE), established during the Echeverría administration to provide a focus for business opposition to many of his policies, has become particularly important because its membership includes the major national organizations. It undertakes more substantial research, through its Centro de Estudios Económicos del Sector Privado (Private Sector Center for Economic Studies, CEESP), than other business organizations, and this adds to its influence.[5] Table 2.2 summarizes the sizes of the leading business organizations.

The government influences the appointment of mandatory national confederation leaders. Indeed, some, such as Canacintra, the National Chamber of Manufacturing Industries, have been described as captives of the government.[6] The government has less control over the voluntary organizations, which have become powerful voices of dissent; indeed, they are among the most powerful in the society. Mexico's political system, authoritarian though it is, has permitted this diversity.

Despite the adversarial relationship that exists between the government and many business organizations, cooperation of a basic nature has taken many forms: protection of and large subsidies to national industries; favoritism to national industry in government procurement; support to national industry in meeting external debts following the financial crisis in 1982; and the tacit division under which the government puts into place the necessary infrastructure to facilitate the well-being of the private sector. Except at moments of heightened conflict, the struggle for dominance between the public and the private sectors usually is dwarfed by the vast area of cooperation. This cooperation has helped make private business the main beneficiary of the institutional "revolution."

Table 2.2   Main Mexican Business and Industrial
Groupings

	Affiliated Enterprises
Concamin	71 industrial chambers (more than 100,000 firms)
Canacintra	86,000 enterprises
Concanaco	261 chambers plus 120 members (more than 400,000 firms)
Coparmex	297 enterprises plus 3,250 members
Anierm	850 enterprises plus 1,500 members
Cemai	212 members
CCE[a]	7 confederations

Note: Concamin   Confederación Nacional de Cámaras Industriales (Confederation of National Cham-
bers of Industry)

Canacintra   Cámara Nacional de la Industria de Transfor-
mación (National Chamber of Manufactur-
ing Industries)

Concanaco   Confederación de Cámaras Nacionales de
Comercio (Confederation of National
Chambers of Commerce)

Coparmex   Confederación Patronal de la República Mexicana (Mexican Employer's Confederation)

Anierm   Asociación Nacional de Importadores y Expor-
tadores de la República Mexicana (National
Association of Importers and Exporters of the
Republic of Mexico)

Cemai   Consejo Empresarial Mexicano para Asuntos In-
ternacionales (Mexican Entrepreneurial Council for International Affairs)

CCE   Consejo Coordinador Empresarial (Businessmen's
Coordinating Council)

[a]The CCE membership includes Concamin, Concanaco, Copar-
mex, Asociación Mexicana de Instituciones de Seguros (Mexican
Association of Insurance Institutions), Asociación Mexicana de
Casas de Bolsa (Mexican Association of Stockbrokers), Consejo
Mexicano de Hombres de Negocios (Mexican Council of Business-
men), and Consejo Nacional Agropecuario (National Agricultural
Council).

Source: Personal inquiry of each group, May 14–15, 1987.

Overt conflicts include such economic issues as the size of the public deficit, availability of credit to the private sector, the exchange rate, and especially the direct and regulatory involvement of the government in activities the private sector believes should be reserved for it. However, no unanimous business position exists on any of these specific economic issues. The head of the CCE may criticize the large public-sector deficit, as he has done, but most businesspersons silently acquiesce to the deficit as long as it leads to procurement of their output.[7] Those businesses engaged in export deplored the existence of an overvalued peso, but the greater number engaged primarily in producing for the domestic market preferred overvaluation as a way to acquire imported inputs more cheaply, as long as other devices kept out competitive imports.

These differences in self-interest are what make the economic opening so laden with conflict within the business community. The small industrialist fears that he may be converted from a protected winner to a less-protected victim. His very business survival may be at issue. Some larger-scale industrialists fear that a less sheltered economy will translate into advantages for multinational corporations (MNCs), which already dominate many export areas, in no small part because of their ability to trade in intermediate products with their parent and other affiliated companies.

The full array of new winners and losers from the economic changes now taking place will depend on the degree of opening, the period allowed for adjustment, and the precise positioning of particular companies. What is certain, however, is that the economic opening does force change in industrial and commercial practices. For example, there was a major business premium in the past in having influence in the government. This influence could determine the degree of import protection and exemptions from import duties for goods necessary for production. The importance of cozy favoritism will not now disappear, but it will become less pervasive if import protection is more modest. Any analysis of corruption in Mexico must deal not only with overt bribery, excessive enrichment of public officials, and the spoils for members of the PRI, but also with the discretionary use of import licenses and import exemptions. An open economy has less scope for these discrete, discretionary life-and-death sentences by officials for specific businesses.

The peak business organizations, such as CCE, Concamin, and Coparmex, are on record in favor of economic opening, believing their future is more promising under an industrial structure closely intertwined with the world economy. They also see enhanced power for themselves if the government's roles as regulator and competitor are diminished. However, these organizations do not speak for the entire private sector, except on the most general level. When the CCE brings along its member organizations in favor of opening, it does so by compromises that will have to be struck and restruck as the liberalization process deepens.

Economic opening coupled with privatization will shift the fulcrum of the mixed economy in favor of the private side, turning the Cárdenas vision topsy-turvy. For many Mexicans with a visceral antipathy toward closer economic relations with the United States and for those with a Marxist bent in their political-economic thinking, this corollary of structural adjustment is a cause for concern.

The forces driving the debate are therefore both ideological and practical. The philosophical aspect is the familiar conflict between a state-led versus a private-dominated process of development. The Mexican mixture has had a large dose of state involvement ever since Cárdenas, and it expanded under Echeverría. It is now diminishing, a change that stirs deep passions in Mexico on both sides. The practical issue has to do with how discrete groups fare in the shift from a mostly closed to a more open economy. This is a pocketbook issue and, as such, arouses fierce defenses. The political lobbying taking place in Mexico in support of positions on both elements of the debate is intense precisely because so much is involved in the outcome.

Labor

There is no agreement among experts on the size of Mexico's employment and labor force, partly because there is no satisfactory way to measure part-time employment. One respected Mexican analyst estimated the economically active population (persons seeking employment) at 22 million in 1980, a figure that had increased by about 7 million by 1989.[8] Men aged twelve and over had a 71 percent participation rate in the labor force in 1980 and women only 21.5 percent. The male participation rate has declined since 1950, when it was 88 percent, and female participation has increased from the 13 percent at that time.[9] Both males and females between twelve and twenty-four years of age are staying in school longer.[10]

Open unemployment in Mexico was traditionally low, ranging between 3 and 6 percent, but now exceeds 15 percent as a result of the economic decline since 1982. Underemployment affects between 30 and 40 percent of the economically active population, but underemployment is an elusive concept that is hard to measure. Measurement is usually based on hours of work or level of income, but this leaves out the intentions of part-time workers, a factor particularly difficult to gauge for women and school-age workers. If young people are staying in school longer, this should not be considered underemployment, although sometimes it is. Mexico's frequently cited need to create about 900,000 to 1 million new jobs yearly may be overstated if there is a persistent surge in young men and women staying in school.

One other problem with the underemployment measurement is that the underground economy is not captured in official statistics. CEESP, the research arm of the CCE, concluded that in 1985 this constituted between 25 and 38 percent of the measured GDP.[11]

Finally, measuring labor's welfare also depends on how it is defined: as organized labor affiliated with the PRI, organized labor outside the PRI, nonorganized workers, urban or rural workers, full-time or part-time workers, or simply people who hustle for a living and are not captured in most official figures.

Organized labor and groups advocating structural reform often conflict. Leopoldo Solís offers an economist's technical reasons for this: unions seek wage increases in excess of productivity gains; they impede labor mobility through efforts at job security; and their members share in the profits of oligopolistic, natural-resource, and publicly owned industries. Solís also notes that support of the PRI is the quid pro quo for labor's wage and fringe benefits from nationalized industries.[12]

How well has labor as a whole fared under the state-directed, import-substitution economic model? Even looking only at the good years, roughly from the 1940s until the end of the 1970s, the answer is ambiguous. The average minimum wage increased fourfold in real terms between 1950 and 1980, and many industrial wages rose by even more. However, not everyone was working full time, and a broader view of how the average Mexican fared can be obtained by examining income distribution figures. As can be seen in Table 2.3, a substantial segment of the Mexican population—what the person in the street would consider the working man and woman, certainly the potential working man and woman—was in a worse relative position at the end of the good years than before them. This becomes even more clear in Table 2.4 (which is extracted from Table 2.3), which shows that the

Table 2.3 Family Income Distribution in Mexico (percent of income by deciles)

Deciles (in ascending order)	1950	1956	1958	1963	1968	1970	1975[a]	1977[a]
I	2.3	1.8	2.3	1.6	1.5	1.4	0.5	1.2
II	2.9	2.4	3.2	2.0	2.1	2.3	1.7	2.4
III	3.0	3.8	4.0	3.4	3.7	3.5	2.8	3.5
IV	4.4	4.5	5.0	3.4	3.8	4.5	4.0	4.7
V	4.6	5.7	6.0	5.1	7.9	5.4	5.4	6.0
VI	6.5	7.5	7.5	6.1	8.2	8.2	6.9	7.4
VII	7.4	9.1	8.3	7.8	8.2	8.2	8.8	9.3
VIII	10.1	11.0	10.7	12.3	8.2	10.4	11.7	12.1
IX	14.4	17.5	17.2	16.4	17.7	16.6	16.9	17.0
X[b]	10.4	10.3	10.2	13.0	10.4	11.5	41.6	36.3
	33.7	26.2	25.4	28.5	27.8	27.7		

Note: Figures may not add due to rounding.

[a] Adjusted with income elasticity of underreporting = 0.95.

[b] This decile is divided into two groups: the first from 90 to 95 percent, and the second from 96 to 100 percent.

Sources: From 1950 to 1970, Salvador Kalifa-Assad, "Income Distribution in Mexico: A Reconsideration of the Distribution Problem," pp. 56 ff. From 1975 to 1977, Joel Bergsman, "Income Distribution and Poverty in Mexico," p. 13.

40 percent of households at the bottom of the income scale received 12.6 percent of total income in 1950 and only 11.8 percent in 1977 (the most recent year for which there are consistent income-distribution data).

The ambiguity of how labor fared in the good years becomes unambiguous when examining more recent periods. Figure 2.1 shows the sharp, indeed startling, decline in real wages starting in 1982.

Another indicator of how poorly labor has fared since the economy started to decline is that salaries as a proportion of gross national expenditures declined from 37.4 percent in 1981 to 28.8 percent in 1983 and have stayed at that level or

Table 2.4 Income Distribution in Mexico (percent of family income in selected years)

Income Grouping	1950	1977
Lowest 40 percent	12.6	11.8
Fifth to seventh deciles	18.5	22.7
Eighth and ninth deciles	24.5	29.1
Top 10 percent	44.1	36.3

Sources: From 1950 to 1970, Salvador Kalifa-Assad, "Income Distribution in Mexico: A Reconsideration of the Distribution Problem," pp. 56 ff. From 1975 to 1977, Joel Bergsman, "Income Distribution and Poverty in Mexico," p. 13.

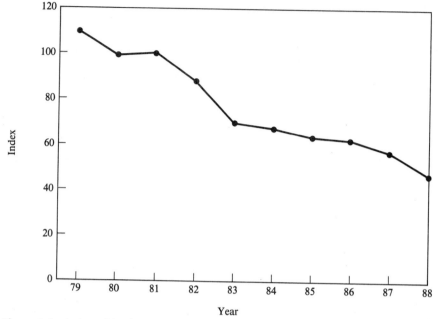

Figure 2.1 Index of Real Minimum Wages (1980 = 100)

Note: The results show comparable declines in real wages if 1978 is set at 100, or if manufacturing industry wages are used instead of minimum wages.

Sources: For the national consumer price index, Banco de México, *Indicadores económicos: Informe presidencial,* various years, statistical appendix for average daily minimum wage (except for 1979, for which the index was calculated using Bank of Mexico aggregate indicators of the economy).

declined further ever since. By contrast, the share going to capital, including depreciation, rose over that period from 54.6 percent to 60.9 percent. (In the United States at the start of 1989, compensation of employees was 73 percent of national income.)[13]

By whatever measure one uses, labor has not done well in the 1980s. This is true whether one looks at labor's absolute position or its treatment relative to business or professional groups. The situation has differentiated among labor groups, but the distinctions in recent years have been on the magnitudes of the income declines.

This raises the logical question of whether labor has benefited from its affiliation with the PRI. Because it is incorporated into the PRI, labor leaders help draft political platforms and are appointed to many executive and legislative positions in the central government and the states, but the economic system has not been particularly kind to most working men and women. For industrial workers during the good years, times were good; more than 90 percent of industrial workers were organized, and their real wages increased steadily over that period.[14] Workers affiliated with the large state-owned enterprises, such as Pemex, also fared well. But nonorganized labor has largely been left by the wayside, certainly in relative terms, in sharing the benefits of the Mexican economic system.

Even though labor has borne the brunt of the economic adjustment since 1982, there has been relative labor peace. The *New York Times* quoted an anonymous diplomat: ''In return for the political power that the CTM has and which Don Fidel (its leader) can wield, the payoff is that the CTM keeps the workers under control and in the workplace.''[15] The tradeoff seems of questionable value for the bulk of Mexican labor, and the durability of this bargain must therefore be questioned. The succession to Don Fidel will be a particularly vulnerable time.

Organized labor has consented to the ongoing economic modernization program, but the approval has been grudging, similar to that of the small industrialist. Each supports the political-economic structure developed since the 1930s, and although it is relevant that organized labor has benefited less economically than the small industrialist, this is not decisive. Organized labor has had compensating political benefits. The tradeoff between political power, which accrues mainly to labor leaders, and economic benefits, which can be more universally spread, is hard to calculate. The expectation that political influence will lead to higher wages has not prevailed in recent years. Nevertheless, the organized labor leadership affiliated with the PRI supports the government and has accepted steady declines in real wages, even while complaining. It has acquiesced to economic opening, without any enthusiasm. Organized labor will probably act like Canacintra—consent as economic opening proceeds, because it is a program the authorities on which each group depends have dictated, but both groups will want to keep the process as slow and as incomplete as possible. Organized labor leaders fear that a more open industrial structure would adversely affect wages to meet world competition, and that significant economic change would alter the comfortable labor–government political relationship.

Unorganized labor speaks with no clear voice, although in 1987 it constituted 65 percent of the economically active population of about 27 million. This labor majority has no settled position on economic opening. Views purporting to come from this group are given by leaders of organized labor. Unorganized labor undoubtedly has not really thought much about the issue of economic opening; it is too busy coping with survival.

Other Groups

As with unorganized labor, the question of economic modernization hardly creates a ripple among most Mexican farmers, particularly the *ejidatarios* (those living on *ejidos*, or communal landholdings) and others who eke out a living from nonirrigated land. These farmers produce mostly for their own consumption and for internal sale. They worry about other issues, such as product prices, credit, and the availability of water and other inputs at a reasonable cost. Large landowners, who do export and are closely allied with agricultural and agroindustrial interests in the United States, have already modernized.[16] They may want protection against imports of competitive products, but they also want access to the U.S. market.

The military must also be mentioned. Once the transition to civilian rule took place in 1946, the overt political role of the military mostly disappeared. It has not completely vanished because of concerns over instability near the Guatemalan border; and, as one U.S. analyst has noted, the military considers itself the guardian of the political system.[17] Military expenditures in Mexico constituted about 3 percent of GDP in 1980, and the military is therefore only a modest factor in the Mexican economy.[18] But it could become an important one in the event of instability.

Professional groups have fared well under the Mexican economic system until recently. So did many intellectuals, but the economic downturn has hurt both. Researchers lack funds to pursue their métiers; educators must augment incomes to live in a manner to which they have become accustomed; engineers and architects are hurt by the slowdown in construction; doctors and lawyers must operate in a less vigorous economy. These groups are still privileged compared with unorganized labor and most rural residents, but their absolute economic position has deteriorated and this has affected their behavior.

Since intellectual leadership in Mexico comes largely from these groups, their attitudes will greatly influence Mexico's future. Educators and writers are taking active positions on economic opening: some against, others in favor. Complaints about official corruption come mainly from these professional and intellectual groups; they are not generally the beneficiaries of the corruption that exists.[19] The economic decline has also focused their attention on the shortcomings of the political system, and they have become vocal advocates of change.

Intellectual currents in Mexico are difficult to sort out when it comes to economic policy. There is pride in past Mexican achievement as well as disaffection because of the large numbers of people excluded from the fruits of this accomplishment. The economic debate among academics is often vitriolic, and terms like ''Marxist'' and ''neoclassicist'' are thrown about loosely as pejoratives. Intellectuals are often sought out as allies by groups with self-interested objectives: the government seeks their support for its policy of economic opening, as does big business; small industry and organized labor seek intellectual backing for limited opening of the economy.

There is more disaffection among professionals and intellectuals today than at any time since the 1930s, with the possible exception of 1968, a time of student riots. This malaise is the result of the combination of a sick national economy and disillusion with a political system that is only qualifiedly democratic and ridden with corruption. There is even a modest brain drain from Mexico, not numerically significant, but noteworthy in that Mexico had been a haven for dissident professionals and intellectuals ever since the Spanish Civil War of the 1930s.[20]

Political Opening

Many U.S. observers new to the Mexican scene predict doom. A familiar picture is of another Iran on the U.S. doorstep. However, more serious students of Mexican affairs usually predict that Mexico will once again muddle through the hard times without violent political change.[21] This consensus is based on the past record and reinforced by the ideological differences of the opposition to the PRI on the left (despite the ability of many of the parties to the left of the PRI to jointly field a strong presidential candidate for the 1988 election) and the regionalism that has characterized the right. The PRI has adroitly dominated the center in Mexico; the party has forged an ample alliance covering the spectrum between the two extremes and has prevailed largely without violence or oppression.[22] William Glade attributes the PRI's durability to its extensive information network, its appropriation of cherished political symbols (the "revolution" in particular), and its ability to renew itself constantly.[23] The PRI controls the spoils. It can make or break political careers and distribute jobs to the faithful. The very existence of much of Mexican industry is due to the PRI, and so industrialists look to the government, and therefore to the PRI, for import privileges, tax concessions, and procurement. It takes a brave and economically independent industrialist to buck the party.[24]

This form of democracy was once familiar in many U.S. states, particularly in the South, where the Democratic party dominated state and local politics, chose its candidates in smoke-filled rooms or in rigged primaries from which inconvenient voters were excluded, and distributed largesse to keep itself in power. Remnants of such controlled democracy linger in many U.S. states, but they are an anachronism. The sentiment of many Mexicans is that this form of abridged democracy should become an anachronism in Mexico as well, as demonstrated in Enrique Krauze's 1986 book, *Por una democracia sin adjetivos,* which was widely read in Mexico.[25]

But the consensus opinion that Mexico will muddle its way through with an essentially unchanged political system began to come under increasing question in 1986. The PRI in 1986 drew the wagons in a circle to prevent political opening, implying a siege mentality new to the Mexican political scene. In addition, opposition arose inside the PRI to its closed method of making electoral decisions. Cuauhtémoc Cárdenas, the son of Lázaro Cárdenas and a former governor of Michoacán, declared for the presidency in 1988 under the banner of several small parties to protest the closed selection process of the PRI (and to promote his state-led model of economic development).

The political restlessness has both underlying and proximate causes. The immediate causes may be transitory, but the underlying or structural basis for the anxiety with the political system is less easily rectified. A structural change in the way Mexico is governed may be necessary to correct a systemic defect.

History, viewed incident by incident, argues that the PRI can make the marginal modifications necessary to continue. History viewed not by discrete incidents but by a tendency that has now covered at least three *sexenios* (Luis Echeverría, José López Portillo, and Miguel de la Madrid) argues that the past model of governance has about run its course. The basis for this statement is that the stability Mexico enjoyed during the good years is best explained by the ability of the growing middle class (loosely defined as the fifth through the ninth deciles shown in Table 2.4) to meet its aspirations within the Mexican political and economic system. It is precisely their inability to do this again during the past five to ten years, plus the lack of any convincing program that will reverse this trend, that is generating the current restlessness of these groups.[26] Their impatience is manifested in disgust with authoritarian practices previously tolerated.

The political unease Mexico is experiencing is based on systemic frustration that was bound to manifest itself under the proper circumstances, circumstances that presented themselves over three successive administrations, starting with that of Echeverría in 1970. In this atmosphere of general uneasiness, events once accepted with resignation became rallying cries for opposition. Two specific incidents were the mishandling by the authorities of the September 1985 earthquakes and the blatant fraud of the 1986 elections, especially in the state of Chihuahua. Each served to arouse the normally passive middle class. Complete mobilization of this anger into effective political organization has not occurred, but the discontent manifested itself in the July 1988 presidential and legislative elections. The PRI now has no choice but to change its mode of operation.

The September 1985 Earthquakes

Two large tremors, on September 19 and 20, 1985, caused extensive damage in Mexico City, including neighborhoods housing middle-class professionals. This turned out to be important because it led to independent mobilization of politically sophisticated persons.

Details were widely reported in the domestic and international press and will not be recounted here. The most comprehensive early analysis of economic damage was made by the Economic Commission for Latin American and the Caribbean (Eclac), by its office in Mexico City.[27] Its first estimate was of 6,000 deaths, 2,000 missing more than a month after the tremors, and 30,000 hurt. Houses, hospitals, schools, communication facilities, and other public buildings suffered major damage; services, such as water, energy, and transportation, were interrupted. Damage to industrial establishments was modest, save for the apparel industry, which was concentrated in the part of Mexico City hit by the earthquake. Eclac's preliminary estimate of the cost of the direct damage was $3.6 billion, a substantial figure, but not in itself critical. It represented about 2 percent of Mexico's GDP, and the outlays for restoration did not have to be made all at once. In addition, there was financial help from international sources, from governments, international organizations, and many communities and persons throughout the United States and elsewhere.

As bad as the physical and economic damage was, this paled when compared with the human trauma that beset Mexico City. The impression left with many observers (including the author, who visited Mexico City in the aftermath of the earthquake) was that the authorities failed to grasp the depth of this shock. The initial official actions did not pull the city together but gave rise to resentment and recriminations, thereby aggravating the already profound human distress. The sense of outrage at the mishandling of the aftermath of the earthquake had not fully disappeared on its first and second anniversaries (both of which times this author visited Mexico City); thousands of victims remained homeless.[28]

In the immediate aftermath of the earthquake, when private individuals organized themselves to clear the rubble and rescue people buried underneath, soldiers were dispatched mainly to stand guard (over what? rubble?) rather than to help. First offers of foreign aid were rejected on the grounds that Mexico had the wherewithal to deal with the problem by itself. The impression left with much of the public was one of brutal indifference, that pride and anti-Americanism took precedence over human lives. This criticism showed up in the Mexican press and led to calls for the dismissal of the foreign secretary, Bernardo Sepúlveda Amor, and the Mexican ambassador in Washington. Enrique Krauze was quoted in the *Wall Street Journal:* "They sacrificed concrete lives for abstract ideas."[29]

The U.S. ambassador, John Gavin, toured the damaged area and gave an estimate of the deaths of at least 10,000, around triple what the government estimate then was. (It is still not clear how many deaths there were; the Eclac estimate remains reasonable.) He acted in proconsular fashion (as was his tendency), but his intent was to help. A good deal of newspaper space and radio time was taken up with criticizing the ambassador, twisting decent U.S. emotions and giving higher priority to anti–U.S. sentiment than to human needs.[30] (The U.S. embassy mobilized a command center to coordinate its help in providing food and material, and individual experts were brought in.)[31]

Three conclusions gained currency in Mexico City in the days after the earthquake: that private citizens could organize effectively to deal with a crisis, indeed, more effectively than the authorities; that the government concerned itself more with form and politics than with substance; and that when the country needed a leader to pull it together, the president instead acted bureaucratically. All these conclusions were discussed openly in the Mexican media and even more extensively in private conversations.

Once the immediate, life-threatening emergency was past, the government compounded its mishandling by maladroitness in expropriating property in the damaged area, ostensibly to facilitate reconstruction. Many expropriated buildings had not been damaged, and the authorities of the Federal District backed off after much public and private protest. Underlying the concern with the handling of the earthquake was that the government could not be trusted to manage the reconstruction without corruption playing a role. This led to elaborate precautions by foreign governments and institutions when they gave assistance. There was a tendency to want to give help in the form of new buildings—say, a schoolhouse—and not with funds to build a schoolhouse.

Only belatedly did the government and the PRI realize how bad an impression had been created in the official handling of the disaster. The PRI actually then inserted full-page advertisements in newspapers to argue how much the government had done.[32] There was no recovery of full trust, however; the government had mismanaged a tragic incident, and the bungling had entered the public psyche.

There was speculation in the Mexican press about whether the independent citizens' groups formed to deal with the earthquake could consolidate themselves and expand as a counterweight to the *politiqueria* of the authorities. This did not manifest itself immediately in a concrete sense, although many middle-class persons date their activity in politics from that time. Still, the events following the earthquake provided a clear indication of the distrust that existed between the government and a large group of Mexico City's informed citizenry.

The earthquake was a tragic event whose human hardships will not soon be forgotten. It is not clear whether in the long term it will be seen to have been a major political event as well. Nevertheless, its handling added to the population's other political and economic frustrations with its government.

The 1986 Elections

The word "watershed" should not be used lightly, but the gubernatorial and municipal elections of 1986 merit that characterization because PRI cheating in the vote count was exposed in the press, leading to anti-PRI demonstrations and denunciations from both the political right and left. It is not clear whether part of the political fallout was the decline of the PRI in the 1988 national elections, but the preexisting structure was shaken at its very foundation.

The PRI, over the years, has been consistently losing its share of the total vote, dropping from 80 to 90 percent during the 1960s to 60 to 70 percent in the 1980s. A consistent vote of 80 to 90 percent ayes for a single party bespeaks an authoritarian society; it is too high to be believable. The acceptance of *only* a 60 percent majority implies greater obeisance to the voters' will. The PRI is finding that it must lower the size of its declared electoral majorities if the announced results are to have any credibility with the public. The abstention rate is showing a rising trend, indicating an attitude of why bother to vote when the outcome has already been decided.

One reason for lower announced majorities is to give the appearance of encouraging free choice and permitting dissenting viewpoints while still maintaining control. This was the purpose of the 1977 and 1986 political reforms. Each reform instituted a mixed system for selecting the legislature. Of the 400 deputies for the Chamber of Deputies chosen in the 1985 elections, 300 were selected on a plurality basis from single-member districts and the remaining 100 on a basis of proportional representation from five multistate electoral districts. Any party that won more than sixty plurality seats lost its eligibility to share in the proportional seats, thus effectively

Table 2.5 Percentages of Votes by Party in Single-Member Districts for Chamber of Deputies, 1985

Party	Percent
Partido Revolucionario Institucional	64.8
Partido Acción Nacional	15.6
Partido Socialista Unificado Mexicano	3.2
Partido Demócrata Mexicano	2.7
Partido Socialista de los Trabajadores	2.5
Partido Popular Socialista	2.0
Partido Auténtico de la Revolución Mexicana	1.7
Partido Mexicano de los Trabajadores	1.5
Partido Revolucionario de los Trabajadores	1.3
Annulled	4.7
Voting	100.0
Abstentions	49.3

Source: John J. Bailey, *Governing Mexico: The Statecraft of Crisis Management*, p. 174; based on data from the Comisión Federal Electoral.

Table 2.6 Congressional Representation, 1985

	Seats	
Party[a]	Single-member	Proportional
PRI	289	
PAN	9	32
PSUM		12
PDM		12
PST		12
PPS		11
PARM	2	9
PMT		6
PRT		6
Totals	300	100

[a]See Table 2.5 for full names of parties.

Source: John J. Bailey, Governing Mexico: The Statecraft of Crisis Management, pp. 172–173; based on data from the Comisión Federal Electoral.

eliminating the PRI from the proportional seats and reserving them for the minority parties.[33] In the voting in the single-member districts in 1985, the PRI received 65 percent of the votes cast. The abstentions came to 49 percent. The other votes were divided as shown in Table 2.5. The actual division of seats in the 1985 congressional elections is shown in Table 2.6.

One effect of the system introduced in 1977 was to split the opposition vote among many parties by allocating five seats to each party that won 1.5 percent of the vote. As Table 2.5 shows, this was accomplished by seven parties other than the PRI in 1985, thereby effectively allocating 35 of the 100 proportional seats. This rewarded the small minority parties at the expense of the main opposition party, the Partido Acción Nacional (PAN), whose number of seats would have been larger under a less complex system of proportional representation. Background on the PAN is given below.

The first elections under the 1986 reform were in 1988. There are now 500 seats in the Chamber of Deputies, 300 from single-member districts and 200 proportional. The essence of this reform is similar to that of 1977, but now the opposition is assured of 150 seats, or 30 percent of the total membership; the opposition share under the 1977 reform was 25 percent of the total. The new reform was intended to keep the opposition divided.[34] The 1988 elections, as noted below, did not follow the PRI script, however.

A multiparty system of the type entrenched by the 1977 and 1986 reforms can be stable when there is one dominant party, as has been the case throughout Mexico's modern history; or it can be stable when coalitions can form a majority, something that has not been tested in Mexico. In any case, by dividing the opposition, the PRI undoubtedly sought to make sure that it could stay in power longer while also giving the multifaceted opposition a cacophonous voice in a powerless legislature. But this may also make Mexico ungovernable if a true democracy, under which votes are counted honestly, ever emerges, because the large number of political parties with diverse philosophies may make the formation of effective coalitions impossible. There are two safeguards against this outcome: a strong-president system, and a provision in the 1986 law that the party with the most votes in the single-member elections will be given an absolute majority of the 500 deputies by allocation from the proportional seats. These safeguards will work as long as the PRI remains dominant; but even then, they may fail if this dominance is not overwhelming.[36]

No Senate elections were held in 1985. Each state and the Federal District in Mexico is entitled to two senators, sixty-four in total; before the 1986 reform, all senators were elected for six-year terms at the same time the president was chosen for a six-year term. Starting in 1988, half the senators stand for reelection every three years.[37]

Only a few comments will be made here on the nature of the opposition parties.[38] The most important single party, and the one whose strength has usually been most disturbing to the PRI until the 1988 presidential election, is the PAN. (The following discussion will use abbreviations to identify the parties. Their full names are given in Table 2.5.) The PAN was established originally by intellectuals and professionals with more of a religious outlook than found in the official party. Its purpose was to form a counter to the ideas and policies of the Cárdenas administration. Today the party's principles include greater separation of powers, more local control as opposed to the centralization of power that now exists, a smaller role for the government in the economy, and a larger role for the private sector.[39]

The party has had a stormy history ever since the 1970s, shifting between confrontational opposition to the PRI and competition as the loyal opposition. This division within the party was so great in 1976 that the PAN was unable to nominate a candidate to oppose López Portillo, but since 1978, and especially since 1982, the party's opposition to PRI has been confrontational. Its 1988 presidential candidate, a wealthy businessman named Manuel Clouthier, is known for his confrontational personality. The wing of the party that supports Clouthier's style is known as the *neopanistas*. The PAN gained strength during the difficult years, dating from the Echeverría administration. Echeverría's antibusiness tone and López Portillo's nationalization of the banks encouraged many in business to support the PAN.

The PAN's greatest electoral strength comes from urban manufacturing areas; regionally, it has been strongest in northern Mexico. Many critics of PAN argue that it is not a viable opposition party because its base is limited both geographically and popularly. This may be true, although overstated; in any event, regional successes could spawn offspring in other areas, which is precisely what the PRI feared in 1986.

The most important party on the left in 1985 was the PSUM, an alliance formed in 1981 among the Communist and other small parties. Other parties on the left in 1985 included the PPS, the PMT, and the PRT. As can be seen from Table 2.5, all four parties together won less than 9 percent of the vote in the 1985 elections for deputies from single-member districts.[40] The PAN alone got 15 percent of the total vote.

There was some promise early in the de la Madrid administration that the PRI would respect electoral outcomes in local elections. The opposition won seven major cities, including five state capitals, in these elections in 1982 and 1983. PAN victories came in northern and central states—Sonora, Durango, Chihuahua, Guanajuato, and San Luis Potosí. The string of victories was halted in September 1983 in Baja California Norte, when the PRI won the governorship amid claims of fraud. The electoral calendar was full in 1985, when seven state governors were chosen as well as the full 400 deputies. The PRI continued its clean sweep of gubernatorial elections, unbroken since the predecessor of the party was formed in 1929, but there were documented claims of fraud, especially in Sonora and Nuevo León. In her discussion of the 1985 elections, specifically those for the Chamber of Deputies, M. Delal Baer wrote:

> One might speculate that although the events of July did not produce an electoral watershed, they did precipitate a perceptual watershed in public awareness of the gap between political myth and reality. The inconsistencies generated by the political reform have accentuated public awareness of a gap between promise and reality.[41]

There were twelve gubernatorial elections in 1986, but none more visible and more sensitive than that on July 6 in Chihuahua, which also held municipal elections on the same day. Chihuahua, a border state, was known as a center of opposition. The border as a whole poses a difficult conundrum for the PRI. It is distant from the highly centralized government in Mexico City, increasingly linked with the United States for its well-being, and growing in population—all characteristics Chihuahua typifies. The PAN had won mayoral elections in the state's seven largest cities in 1983 and half of the state's congressional seats in the 1985 elections. Two leftist parties, the PSUM and the PST, had each won a mayoral election in 1983, and, as M. Delal Baer noted, the opposition at the local level governed an estimated 70 to 80 percent of the state's population.[42]

The PRI chose attractive candidates in Chihuahua, especially for governor. Fernando Baéza Melendez was a conservative with many ties in the state's business community, and, indeed, his family was close to the PAN. As the former mayor of the Chihuahua city of Delicias and a congressman from the state, he recognized the estrangement of the state from the capital and, indeed, ran against Mexico City. A good indication of Baéza's conservative philosophical outlook was captured in a remark made by the director of the PSUM in Chihuahua after Baéza's inauguration as governor and his selection of advisers: "If Francisco Barrio [the PAN candidate] were governor, there would certainly be more *priistas* [stalwarts of the PRI] in his cabinet."[43]

Francisco Barrio Terrazas was the flamboyant PAN candidate for governor. Barrio had been elected mayor of Ciudad Juárez in 1983, at a time when the PRI seemed to be respecting electoral outcomes in local elections. His affiliation is with the *neopanista* group of the PAN, and, like Baéza, Barrio conducted a vigorous campaign.

Two attractive candidates locked in a fiery campaign, the recent track record of PAN victories in the state, and an influx of journalists from Mexico, the United States, and elsewhere made this a particularly noteworthy electoral race. In the end, the PRI under Baéza was declared the lopsided winner, 401,167 to 231,109. PRI candidates were also declared winners in all but two municipalities, Nuevo Casas Grandes (to PAN) and Gómez Farías (PPS). Hardly anybody gave credence to the legitimacy of the results.

The PRI had been clumsy; because there were so many witnesses, the evidence of widespread fraud was obvious. The fraud took many forms: full voting boxes when the polls opened, denial of entry to opposition-party poll watchers, intimidation, carousel or repeat voting by individuals, the transport of ballot boxes by unauthorized persons, deliberate delays in voting places, and registrations in some municipalities exceeding the recorded populations. The actuality of fraud was documented in an article published in March 1987 in the Mexico City magazine *Nexos*.[44] In another article on the fraud in Chihuahua, Franciso Ortiz Pinchetti wrote, "The most complete, expensive, and sophisticated operation in the history of the official party was mounted in Chihuahua to carry out a decision of the federal government not to hand over this northern entity to the opposition, cost whatever it cost."[45]

The events following this fraud were unprecedented in modern Mexican history. Repeated mass protests took place. Bridges were blocked between Mexico and the United States, especially between Ciudad Juárez and El Paso. Catholic bishops strongly denounced the arrogance of the public forces and planned to not hold mass, an action prevented only by the intervention of the secretary of domestic affairs, Manuel Bartlett Díaz, with the papal nuncio in Mexico.[46] The press and journals were full of advertisements, including one from the Chihuahua bishops, denouncing the fraud and the lack of democracy demonstrated in Chihuahua. Local business leaders demanded that the elections be nullified. Three prominent *chihuahuenses* (Luis H. Alvarez, former mayor of Chihuahua city and later president of the PAN; Francisco Villarreal, a businessman; and Dr. Víctor M. Oropeza) went on an extended hunger strike.

More significantly, the opposition of both the left and the right joined in the name of democracy to denounce the PRI. Brought together by PMT president Heberto Castillo, the PAN, PSUM, PMT, and PRT formed the Movimiento Nacional Democrático to protest the fraud in the elections in Chihuahua and in August state elections in Oaxaca and Durango as well, and to call for electoral reform. This unified protest by such parties must be considered an event of some importance in Mexico.

Of equal importance, since political parties are often seen as taking actions as much out of convenience as conviction, was an open letter of protest, dated July 23, from twenty-one intellectuals to Baeza, demanding that the election be annulled. Few Mexican intellectuals are pro-PAN. While there was a large disaffection of intellectuals from the PRI following the handling of the 1968 student demonstrations, many intellectuals depend on the PRI for jobs.[47] It thus took some courage to protest to the PRI. This form of courage, of open disagreements of intellectuals with the PRI, has since become more frequent.

The PRI now controls the governorship and most municipalities in Chihuahua, but at the cost of increased public disillusion with Mexican "democracy." This has become evident in the growing open criticism of the electoral process in Mexico. The importance of the 1986 Chihuahua elections is that they marked a dramatic nadir in public support of the PRI, and this stimulated introspection in the party about how to adapt to the clear desire for effective suffrage while still maintaining political control.

Elections in other states did not attract similar attention. The combination of circumstances—two attractive candidates, the history of opposition success, the proximity to the United States—was not the same elsewhere. However, the outcomes were similar. The PRI continued to sweep gubernatorial elections. Indeed, the PRI has been putting up strong candidates; an active and potentially strong opposition has at least had this positive effect. Abstentions continue to grow. *Proceso* asserted that the abstention rate in the elections of Oaxaca on August 3, 1986, was 80 percent and that only 10 percent of the electorate supported the PRI.[48] No documentation was provided to substantiate this large abstention rate, but there is enough evidence that the electorate is losing interest in elections run and counted in the style that the PRI prefers.

The 1988 National Elections

The national elections on July 6, 1988, were to select Mexico's president for the six years beginning December 1, 1988, along with 64 senators (half for three years and the other half for six years), and 500 deputies (300 from single-member districts and 200 by proportional representation).

The official results for president were: Carlos Salinas de Gortari, the PRI candidate, 50.4 percent; Cuauhtémoc Cárdenas, running at the head of a leftist coalition, 31.1 percent; Manuel J. Clouthier, the PAN candidate, 17.1 percent; Gumersindo Magaña, 1.0 percent; and Rosario Ibarra de Piedra, 0.4 percent. More than 19 million valid votes were cast, yet over 18 million persons did not vote.[49]

The PRI won all but 4 Senate seats, 2 each in the Federal District and the state of Michoacán, all going to *cardenistas*. Sixty victories out of 64 contests has all the earmarks of a landslide, until one remembers that the PRI had never before conceded a senatorial election loss. In the Chamber of Deputies, the PRI won 249 of the 300 single-member seats, but the proportional distribution of the remaining 200 seats left the Chamber divided into 260 PRI and 240 opposition, reasonably evenly split between the PAN and the many parties supporting Cárdenas.

The results were unexpected. Presidential candidates from the PRI usually win with upward of 70 percent of the vote; Salinas had a bare majority, and the fact that the official count was slightly above rather than below 50 percent, thereby giving him an absolute majority, aroused suspicion of count rigging. The suspicion was heightened when the government delayed reporting the vote count, alleging computer problems. When one takes into account the nullified ballots and abstentions, only 22 percent of Mexico's 38 million registered voters voted for Salinas.

The big surprise was the strong showing of Cárdenas. He had been a member of the "democratic current" within the PRI, whose ostensible purpose was to make the party's decision making more transparent. After Salinas was chosen as the party's candidate in a procedure closed to all but a few insiders, Cárdenas decided to run for the presidency himself under the banner of the PARM, which was joined by two other parties, the PPS and the PST; all three were small and had had close ties with the PRI. The Cárdenas quest for the presidency had all the earmarks of a mutiny by insiders from the official party. For electoral purposes, the three parties called themselves the Frente Democrático Nacional (National Democratic Front, FDN).

The Cárdenas candidacy became formidable, however, after another candidate on the left, Heberto Castillo, withdrew about a month before the election. Castillo had been the candidate of five parties (the PSUM and the PMT, shown in Tables 2.5 and 2.6, plus three smaller parties) that joined together to form the Partido Mexicano Socialista (Mexican Socialist Party, PMS). Cárdenas, after Castillo's withdrawal, became the candidate of a left united for the presidential contest. The PRI had always taken comfort from the inability of the left to unite, thereby leaving the PAN, on its right, as the only serious organized opposition. The PAN did not do badly in the presidential election, but it was overshadowed by the Cárdenas coalition.

The monolithic domination of the PRI was seen earlier to be weakening, and the Chihuahua elections demonstrated this. They made it evident that the PRI would not shrink from fraud to win municipal and gubernatorial contests. The unmitigated economic hardship during the de la Madrid *sexenio* removed the solid foundation on which popular support for the PRI had been built. The handling of the earthquake contributed to middle-class disillusion with the administration. Yet the speed of the PRI's decline came as a surprise to most observers, both inside and outside Mexico. Two questions arise: Why? And with what consequences for Mexico and United States–Mexico relations?

As to why the massive defection from the PRI came in this election, one reason was certainly the symbolic significance of a man named Cuauhtémoc Cárdenas on the ballot. Both parts of the name have magic in Mexico—the first representing the pre-Columbian Aztec culture, and the second evoking the memory of Mexico's most popular president in the modern era, Lázaro Cárdenas, "a revolutionary soldier from the peasantry who is still venerated as a symbol of Mexican nationalism, social justice and mestizo pride."[50]

Cuauhtémoc Cárdenas, a former governor of Michoacán, is a man of sufficient personal stature to have appealed to many who were disaffected with the PRI but did not want to vote for the right. He brought together those who wished to register protests against economic conditions, corruption, and PRI arrogance. University students and many intellectuals supported Cárdenas. So did many small industrialists who resented the loss of import protection under the economic opening of the de la Madrid administration. Union members deserted the PRI; the decline in real wages over the previous six years undoubtedly took their toll.[51] *Ejidatorios* and their children, the beneficiaries of the land reform instituted by his father, were attracted to Cárdenas.

The answer to the question of why voters deserted the PRI in the 1988 elections is thus made up of a complex of frustrations built up over the years that found their release in Cuauhtémoc Cárdenas. Where this protest may lead is a more interesting and more speculative question. It depends on whether the unity of the left is sustained. And if it is, which is doubtful, it depends also on whether the left, especially in the legislature, acts as an obstructive force or a loyal opposition.

Had Cárdenas been declared the victor in the presidential election, his effective governance would have required coalition politics by a disparate group ranging from the Communists (part of the ex-PSUM, now part of the PMS) to former PRI insiders. Salinas may himself have to practice coalition politics to carry out his program. This is particularly relevant in the Chamber of Deputies, where it will not require very many defections for the PRI's 260 to 240 majority to evaporate.[52]

The abandonment of the PRI by a majority of voters from labor unions is evidence that the corporatist structure of the party is a nullity.[53] A political restructuring is thus required. The PRI continues to govern, but the game has changed.

Because the decline of the PRI was precipitated by the economic hardship of the de la Madrid *sexenio,* one imperative of the Salinas administration is to restore a respectable level of economic growth. This may require some compromise of the previous economic program, such as increasing government expenditures, restoring some subsidies on basic goods, and permitting salary increases large enough to reverse the decline in real wages. All these positions were part of the Cárdenas platform. One of Cárdenas's main planks was for substantial relief from interest payments on external debt, even by imposing a unilateral moratorium for as long as necessary as pressure to obtain agreement from creditor banks and countries. Salinas made it clear when he was elected that he also seeks debt relief.[54]

The political opening should lead over time to a warming of Mexico's relations with the United States in that the interchange will be between two democracies. This statement needs some qualifications. The shift from authoritarianism to "democracy without adjectives" is far from complete, and the speed of further change is uncertain. In addition, the relationship between the two countries will depend on the philosophical approaches and practical programs of the two administrations. A right-wing U.S. administration is not apt to seek a cordial relationship with a left-wing Mexican government. This combination may well arise from time to time.

Finally, Salinas's weak mandate may force a slowdown in the economic restructuring begun by the de la Madrid government. In this event, proposals for managed industrial integration between Mexico and the United States will be difficult to carry out. In his campaign, Salinas promised that as president he would continue the essentials of the economic program that he had a large part in devising as a member of President de la Madrid's cabinet, and his early actions confirmed this.

The degree of cooperation between Mexico and the United States in the years ahead will thus depend, on the Mexican side, primarily on outcomes in two areas: the nature and pace of the political restructuring that takes place and the economic program.

Economic Opening and Political Restructuring

The double development in Mexico—opening the economy as the political structure is shifting—is certain to have lasting effects, and the two developments are best viewed simultaneously because they interact.

The economic opening was forced on Mexico by a combination of internal and external circumstances that made evident the obsolescence of the model in use since the end of World War II. If carried to its logical conclusion, the market rather than the state will become the prime determinant of decisions, and the resulting decline in the party's ability to offer special, official favors will alter its role. The Mexican nationalistic tradition of looking inward will become more nuanced if Mexico's well-being becomes increasingly dependent on external markets, and an opening will deepen economic interaction with the United States beyond what already exists.

Because the consequences of this policy are far-reaching, it is appropriate to ask whether economic opening is durable. A corollary question is: What are the options? The answer that jumps immediately to mind is a return to a state-led model, intensifying state regulation and favoritism to domestic firms. This would require not only negating the internal decisions made by the de la Madrid administration, but also shifting position on a series of international undertakings in the GATT, the IMF, and the World Bank. An increase in oil prices might provide the financial means to make such a policy direction at least temporarily viable, and there are strong forces in Mexico who prefer exactly such a policy reversal. The Cárdenas campaign was based on precisely this position.

Much behind-the-scenes quarreling goes on between PRI operatives and technicians. The latter have been in the ascendancy for at least twenty years and dominated the de la Madrid cabinet—de la Madrid himself comes from a technical and not a party background, as does Carlos Salinas de Gortari. The economic positions in Salinas's cabinet are held by technicians cast in his mold. Salinas had no political experience other than appointment as a cabinet secretary before he was elected president. There is no ideological uniformity among either politicians or technicians—and both skills may be combined in the same person—but their natural tendencies are dissimilar. Politicians are less likely than technicians to be supporters of austerity.

Two diametrically opposed political arguments are being made in Mexico. The first is that basic economic change should not be continued while the political situation is in turmoil. This argument is that the populism required for political popularity precludes the success of carrying out basic economic change. The politician's argument for delaying economic opening is more straightforward: it would be political suicide for the PRI to perpetuate economic hardship.

It is obviously possible to combine economic opening and political restructuring. This is precisely what is being attempted in the Soviet Union. But is it possible in Mexico, which has a different tradition? The conclusion here is that the two openings must proceed simultaneously, so that they can reinforce each other.

Scholarly analysis of Mexico tends to concentrate on either the economic or the political structure. There is a large literature dealing with the dispute between those who favor an open Mexican economy and those who support a closed one, and between the relative economic weights to be given to the public sector as opposed to private enterprise in Mexico's version of a mixed economy.[55] A mostly separate literature exists on the qualified nature of Mexico's democracy, well exemplified by Enrique Krauze's *Por una democracia sin adjetivos*. The two strands have come together, as indeed they must, in the uncertain atmosphere of economic stagnation and political upheaval. It is doubtful that they can be ripped asunder any more.

Mexico's transition from a peripheral developing country to an intermediate economic power—which is the stated goal of the country's leaders—requires the nation's incorporation into the international economy. This is now taking place. Greater political opening is also coming, regardless of the outcome of the economic restructuring, but it will become irresistible as Mexico's integration into the world economy deepens. Political opening can be disruptive, but the suppression of opening is apt to be even more disorderly. The previous failure to open the political system also destroyed Mexico's ability to play a major moral role internationally— to which Mexico has long aspired.

Economic success in Mexico would benefit the United States—by increasing exports and investment opportunities, and by reducing emigration pressures. A prosperous Mexico would become increasingly integrated economically with the United States. But the U.S. objective is twofold—economic prosperity coupled with political stability—and the combination is crucial. In my view, anything less than a double opening, political and economic, will fail, and in the process frustrate an optimally beneficial bilateral relationship.

3

IMPEDIMENTS TO INTEGRATION

> In coming years, those aspects of relations with the United States which will demand most attention are economic interchange, migrant workers, and border relations, as well as the general Latin American policy of both nations.
>
> MEXICAN NATIONAL DEVELOPMENT PLAN 1983–1988

> Aspirants to political office now peacefully await their turn at corruption as well as power.
>
> DANIEL LEVY AND GABRIEL SZÉKELY, 1983

> And if the United States is to preserve its economic power and social progress in an increasingly dependent world, it must be prepared to exchange goods and services, labor, capital, and technology with Mexico on a scale unprecedented outside its own borders.
>
> CLARK REYNOLDS, 1983

The Uneasy Relationship

The relationship between the United States and Mexico is not warm. The two presidents meet frequently, but their encounters are not relaxed.[1] Bilateral commissions exist for a variety of themes, such as trade and the environment, but the give-and-take is not spontaneous. Counterparts in the two governments do not communicate with the casualness that typifies U.S. officials' exchanges with colleagues in Canada, the other land neighbor, or in many other countries.[2] It is not unusual for U.S. officials to act with imperiousness toward Mexico, and Mexicans, in turn, to respond in ways that are less than civil.[3] A stormy history is part of the complexity of the relationship. Evident inequalities in political power and economic development add to this complication. Different emphases, an East–West dominance in U.S. foreign policy and a North–South preponderance in Mexican foreign policy, augment other difficulties of intercourse. Mexico is usually the *demandeur* in economic relations and the United States the respondent, and this combination does not make for informality. In short, the dialogue is not between equals.[4]

The official coldness is reinforced by a critical press in both countries. The United States mostly relates Mexico's troubles, rarely its strengths. If all a U.S. reader or viewer knew about Mexico was what he or she obtained from the media, the impression would be of a corrupt, inept, and trouble-laden society, important only because it could cause a mass invasion of illegal immigrants. If all that a Mexican knew about the United States was what is contained in the daily press, especially in Mexico City, the impression would be of a callous, exploitative, war-mongering country.

The coldness of interchange, the posturing in intercourse, the superficiality of mutual reporting, and the propagation of stereotypes about each other impede the deepening of the integration between the two countries.

How Each Sees the Other

The cold war has been the dominant preoccupation of U.S. foreign policy since World War II, and Europe takes precedence in U.S. policy concerns. If foreign-policy emphases were based instead on economic self-interest, Asia would be given priority; the United States trades more with countries in that region than with Europe. If trade were the touchstone of foreign-policy emphasis, the most important countries in the world for the United States would be Canada, Japan, and Mexico, plus the collectivity of the European Economic Community. If future economic potential were the gauge of policy priority, Mexico would again rank high. Yet, it is evident that neither Canada nor Mexico is given the attention on a day-to-day basis that is lavished on, say, the United Kingdom or France.

The United States looks on its relationship with Mexico as one between superior and inferior. Mexico gets attention when its internal problems threaten to contaminate the United States or when its positions on foreign affairs might frustrate U.S. initiatives. And what attention it does get tends to be in terms of rewards and punishments. For example, what trade concessions can be granted or what benefits can be withheld to build pressure on Mexico to take positions that conform to U.S. desires? The sanctions, to use the terminology of one student of these issues, are either positive (granting a benefit) or negative (withholding a concession).[5] Positive concessions include balance-of-payments financing, other trade benefits, purchase of oil for the strategic petroleum reserve, manipulation of credit from the Export-Import Bank, and the encouragement of credit from the World Bank and other multilateral institutions.[6] Negative sanctions have included withholding trade concessions and refusing to sign a subsidy/countervailing duty agreement until Mexico altered its treatment of U.S. pharmaceutical companies operating in Mexico.

Rewards and punishments are part of bilateral relationships generally, but their dominance in the case of Mexico bespeaks the political and economic power asymmetry that exists between the two countries. As one scholar put it, "If the past is at all prologue, the United States and Mexico will continue to relate as a world power and a dependent state, rather than as neighbors bound in global relations of complex interdependence."[7]

The tone of this relationship inevitably results in friction and recriminations. American officials lecture Mexico. Senior executives of large multinational corporations repeat endlessly that Mexico will receive significant amounts of foreign investment only if the 1973 law limiting foreign equity to a minority role is changed; but the argument to countries that have been even more restrictive, such as Japan, is phrased in less peremptory terms.[8]

Viewing Mexico as a problem manifests itself in ways more significant than condescension. United States government officials openly speculate about the durability of the Mexican political structure, a type of conjecture common internally in governments, particularly at moments of travail, but seldom made public, as it was in 1984 when disagreements within the CIA and between it and the State Department broke into the open. In 1986, CIA analyst Brian Latell, on leave at the Hoover Institution at Stanford University, wrote a paper on the legitimacy of the PRI and the devaluation of the presidency under Miguel de la Madrid that attracted much attention in Mexico. Latell entered a disclaimer to the effect that his public comments were made in a personal capacity while at a research institution, but his personal position was undoubtedly reflected in official assessments before he took leave from and after his return to the CIA.[9] Latell argued that "corruption only became rampant in the years since technocrats and labor leaders have dominated the political system, and that when professional politicians were more prominent before 1970, there were few excesses."[10] The argument is ad hominem (and, in my view, nonsense); but the more important implication is the public denigration by a government official of the operation of the Mexican political system.[11]

Two former officials of the Secretariat of Foreign Relations (the foreign ministry, or SRE in its Spanish abbreviation) analyzed 1984 coverage of Mexico by the *New York Times,* the *Washington Post,* the *Wall Street Journal, Time, Newsweek,* and *U.S. News & World Report,* and found a number of recurrent themes: praise for economic austerity, reflecting a financial rather than a comprehensive view of the Mexican scene; corruption; alarm over social and political conditions; and Mexican foreign policy, especially in Central America.[12] The widely viewed CBS television program "60 Minutes" focused on corruption in Pemex, the national oil company.[13] As an article written by researchers at one of Mexico City's leading think tanks points out, the common denominator of U.S. coverage of Mexico has been U.S. national security—East–West issues, drugs, illegal immigration, and social instability.[14]

These are legitimate themes for the U.S. press. Nor can it be said that coverage of Mexico is intended by the leading U.S. newspapers, magazines, and television networks to be uniformly negative. The *New York Times,* the *Wall Street Journal,* and the *Washington Post* increased their coverage of Mexico after 1985 when conditions deteriorated. The *New York Times* ran a series of seven articles in October 1986 that, while drawing criticism in Mexico, were intended to be fair, despite being somewhat sensational.[15] CBS carried a Bill Moyers program on the Texas–Mexico border ("One River, One Country: The U.S.–Mexico Border") on September 3, 1986, which received praise in both countries for its evenhandedness and sophistication. However, the overall tone of the media coverage on Mexico in recent years can best be described as Mexico bashing, so much so that several leading U.S. newspapers carried either editorials or editorial articles deploring what one commentator called "the latest simple-minded sport."[16]

The Mexican domestic situation is indeed precarious. Economic hardship has been substantial in recent years; the political process is not democratic; corruption is endemic; and drug traffic has corrupted many official institutions, including the police.[17] All these developments affect Mexico's relations with the United States.

There was a jump in illegal immigration into the United States when the Mexican economy declined; the drug trade corrupts both countries. However, Mexico is more complex than these negative phenomena, and this diversity is not being captured in the surge of press coverage.

The combination of official condescension and media disparagement has done much to delegitimize the Mexican government in the United States. Mexican authorities have contributed to this, but foreigners would seem to have an obligation to couch their criticism in civil terms. That this is rarely done is one more manifestation of U.S. pretensions of superiority.[18]

Asymmetry in economic and political power does not by itself dictate a specific mode of behavior by either country. Mexico's behavior stems from a composite of asymmetry, history, and intellectual formation. Each country's response is conditioned by the other. When U.S. comportment is imperious, the Mexican reaction is arrogant. When Mexico seeks unrequited economic favors, it is treated as an inferior. Attitudinal changes do occur, but they require time.

Daniel Cosío Villegas, a well-known historian and the father of El Colegio de México, one of Mexico's leading research and teaching institutions, has, on various occasions, analyzed the effect of the U.S. agenda on Mexico. The national U.S. agenda, Cosío noted, was to spread the nation from the Atlantic to the Pacific, and, in its period of manifest destiny, some of Mexico's territory was in the way. Mexico's neighborhood has influenced its policy ever since. By way of introduction to current concerns and resentments of Mexicans, observers in the United States are reminded constantly that Mexico lost half its territory to the United States more than 100 years ago. The border industrialization program of the 1960s, which gave birth to the *maquiladora,* or assembly plants, had as one of its motivations to populate the northern region against further U.S. encroachment. To this day, Mexicans express concern about further U.S. territorial ambitions, as Guillermina Valdés-Villalba's quotation at the beginning of Chapter 8 demonstrates.

Cosío observes that after it became a continental nation, the United States required better transportation and communication between the Atlantic and Pacific coasts; this led to the cutting of the Panama Canal and fostered the spread of U.S. hegemony throughout the continent. The United States, when it emerged from World War I, decided "by universal consent" that its "immediate zone of influence would be Latin America, and Mexico first of all."[19] Mario Ojeda has asserted that "every time" the United States acted in foreign affairs on the basis of a "moral imperative" derived from U.S. ideals, the consequences for weaker countries have been "unfortunate."[20]

Mexican analysts tend to implicate the United States whenever something unfortunate happens in Mexico. Octavio Paz has stated, for example, that the students who rioted in 1968 were reacting, in part, against U.S. imperialism, and in commenting on Mexico's mixed public–private economic system, he said that the country's economic dependence was accentuated by making the private sector an essential part of the development program and by permitting the U.S. private sector to participate.[21]

Paz has contrasted American and Mexican attitudes in many ways. In discussing colonial and postcolonial development and the influence of Protestantism and Catholicism: "Continuity and change were not complementary terms as in the United States, but antagonistic and irreconcilable."[22] Or, in another analysis, "In the United States, the Indian element does not appear. This, in my opinion, is the major difference between our two countries."[23] On this basis, Paz argues that the United States was founded in a land without a past, whereas precisely the opposite was true for Mexico, which is a land of superimposed pasts. Mexico, he said in 1979, is still asking itself about modernization but must find its own way to modernity, making the "past . . . not an obstacle but a starting point."[24]

The Mexican emphasis on self-determination, on independence from the United States, shows up in many ways. Mexico refused to accept bilateral U.S. aid under the Alliance for Progress, but accepted U.S. assistance given indirectly through multilateral institutions such as the World Bank and the Inter-American Development Bank. Because all aid has its conditions, a distinction was thus made between aid conditions imposed bilaterally and those exercised multilaterally. At the same time, Mexico has no compunction about actively seeking trade preferences for as long, as one analyst put it, as "the time required for Mexico to reach maturity."[25]

A recurring criticism Mexican writers offer is the lack of U.S. sensitivity in the formulation of foreign policy to the Mexican historical and cultural context in which the policy is to be carried out. This theme, which can be found in the writings of Carlos Fuentes, Cosío, and Paz, undoubtedly has validity. However, the absence of Mexican sensitivity to the context elsewhere can also be irritating. For example, Mario Ojeda asserted that the reaction of Jews to Mexico's vote in 1975 in favor of the resolution in the United Nations General Assembly equating Zionism and racism was "exaggerated." Ojeda went on to argue that the government's effort to seek a reconciliation with Israel and Jews generally was "contrary to the national dignity."[26] A resolution of the Mexican Senate critical of pending U.S. immigration legislation, later enacted in 1986, was approved with little understanding of the U.S. context.

Mexicans expect the U.S. government to exercise restraint in the face of criticism, particularly of foreign policy. According to the U.S. Department of State, Mexico's position coincided with that of the United States in plenary votes in the United Nations General Assembly in the fall of 1985 only 14.5 percent of the time. The only countries with lower coincidence rates were Guyana, Nicaragua, and Cuba.[27] Yet the United States has been asked to tolerate Mexico's position in Central America on the ground that it helps to paralyze groups in Mexico that oppose the government from the left.[28]

What Mexicans are saying is that positions are taken in foreign policy not only because they are believed to be correct, but also because they are necessary for obtaining internal consent for cooperation with the United States in other fields, such as dealing with drug trafficking. Responsible Mexican officials also seek to prevent foreign-policy disagreements from contaminating economic cooperation. This separation does not always work.

Salience of Issues

There is a hierarchy of issues between the two countries, some clearly more important than others over the long term. The quotation at the beginning of this chapter

Table 3.1 Hierarchy of Issues Between Mexico and the United States

Type of Issue	Internal Aspect	Spinoff Effects on Other Country
Internal, with external repercussions	Maintenance of social order in Mexico	Transmission of turbulence
		Migration
	Economic growth in the two countries	Trade
		Capital flows
		Debt
		Migration
First-order foreign-policy issues	Economic relations	Trade
		Capital flows
	Political relations	Degree of cooperation
Second-order foreign-policy issues	Central America	Political cooperation
	Votes in United Nations	Effect on political cooperation
	Critical media coverage	Effect on political cooperation
Durable, basic issues	Water quality and quantity	Effect on economic growth
	Environment	Effects on Quality of life Economic growth Political cooperation
	Drugs	Political cooperation
		Social and economic effects
	Migration	Social and economic effects

from Mexico's national development plan for 1983 to 1988 lists what the Mexican authorities then deemed to be the most important issues in relations with the United States: economic exchange, migrant workers, border relations, and policy toward Latin America (this is a more inclusive way of referring to Cuba and Central America). Table 3.1 categorizes issues between the two countries in a different format. The bases for the classifications in the table are the importance and durability of issues and the ability of policy to affect them. The most important foreign-policy issues in this framework are spinoffs from domestic policies. It is evident that foreign policy is an extension of domestic policy, but the point merits particular emphasis in the U.S.–Mexico context because of proximity and integration. Indeed, it is hard to think of a significant "internal" economic issue in the United States that does not have repercussions in Mexico. It is equally difficult to imagine a social issue in Mexico that does not affect the United States. The integration of the two countries has become so extensive that it cannot be avoided even when internal decisions are made in each country.

The category labeled first-order foreign-policy issues in Table 3.1 refers to significant themes that are affected by policy. The second-order foreign policy issues receive much attention by governments, but are of lesser intrinsic importance.

Finally, those issues called durable or basic can affect the short-term relationship (such as drug traffic), but their importance is in their constancy. This is particularly true of water, which is probably the most important single issue for the American Southwest and the Mexican North.

The Problem of Corruption

Mexico has the reputation—at home, in the United States, elsewhere—of being a corrupt society. In reviewing Alan Riding's book *Distant Neighbors,* in which the corruption theme recurs throughout, Enrique Krauze commented that Riding, unfortunately, did not exaggerate: "Connections, patronage, embezzlement, nepotism, large bribes, the purchase of union favors, blackmail of the press, etc., have thrived in Mexico."[29] Lorenzo Meyer has noted that since 1940 corruption has taken the form of useless projects, inflated project costs, illicit enrichment, and an electoral process that is no more than a ritualistic formality.[30]

Nevertheless, it remains most indelicate for a non-Mexican to pronounce on Mexican corruption. Apart from nationalistic resentment, which would arise in any country, the context in which a foreigner views the Mexican scene must by definition be incomplete. But the Mexican public also believes that corruption of officials is a major problem. Miguel de la Madrid recognized this by stressing the theme of "moral renovation" in his presidential campaign in 1982. Since that time, moral renovation has become something of a cynical joke among Mexicans; some corrupt officials were punished, but they did not reach the very top of the Mexican political structure. Carlos Salinas, early in his administration, jailed two important persons on grounds of corruption: the head of Mexico's stock exchange and the leader of the petroleum workers' union.

The main reason for discussing Mexican corruption is not to titillate the non-Mexican reader with voluminous specific instances of wrongdoing (which would not be hard to do, in Mexico or elsewhere), but to ask how corruption, which undermines trust, hampers Mexican political and economic progress and, especially, the country's relations with the United States. The argument is that the forms corruption takes in Mexico are inherent in the political and economic structure that has developed, but *not* in the character of the people. As the structure changes (as is now occurring), so will the nature and perhaps even the extent of corruption.

Systemic Temptations. Most Mexicans are not corrupt, and corruption is viewed with increasing resentment. The very fact that each new president promises to reform the system is a backhanded form of evidence that popular Mexican preferences do not really differ from those that exist elsewhere—say, in the United States. But the very definition of corruption is not a settled matter. The dictionary offers such words and phrases as "evil or wicked behavior," "bribery," "rottenness," "acts that are morally unsound," and "deterioration from some norm or standard."[31] What is usually meant is self-enrichment, either outside the law or based on a person's position. The acceptance of bag money by Vice President Spiro Agnew (for which he was not jailed) was clearly corruption; the enrichment of Representative Fernand St. Germain of Rhode Island while he was chairman of the

Banking Committee of the U.S. House of Representatives was not considered corruption by his peers. Rigging the victory of the PRI in the elections in Chihuahua state in 1986 was an act of corruption; the practices that perpetuate incumbency in the U.S. House of Representatives are not considered corrupt. Acceptance of a bribe to influence the granting of a government contract is evidence of corruption; accepting campaign contributions and then voting in favor of the interests that made the contributions is considered normal politics.

The line between corruption and acceptability is fuzzy. The United States has its definitions of when the line is crossed, but these are not universal and not necessarily optimal. A majority of U.S. senators are millionaires; most Mexican senators are not. It is not clear why position dependent in large measure on wealth necessarily responds to a higher ethic than position flowing from party loyalty.

None of these observations is intended to excuse Mexican corruption or depict the United States as a corrupt nation. Rather, their purpose is to indicate that the patterns of corruption practiced in Mexico are a reflection of historical development and the organization of government and society. The deepest form of corruption of Mexican society is the unjust distribution of income and the unequal educational opportunities available to nationals based on their income and place of residence. The self-enrichment of a president is obscene precisely because so many Mexicans live below any reasonable definition of poverty.

Most Mexicans experience corruption in its most familiar definition, the paying of a petty bribe to avoid arrest or obtain some favor. Police expect *mordidas* (bribes) to forgive real or contrived traffic violations.[32] Minor officials expect a reward for providing a form or expediting some licensing procedure. This type of corruption is ubiquitous in Mexico and even affects tourists and foreigners seeking to do business there. But it is hardly unique to Mexico; such bribery is familiar in most societies in which public officials, especially police, are not paid an adequate wage. The practice was common in most U.S. cities less than half a century ago for precisely the same reason.

This corruption is destructive within Mexico—it is one reason why the general population has little confidence in the integrity of government or law enforcement. It would be naive, however, to expect this type of corruption to disappear as long as government budgets are inadequate and the opportunity exists to augment incomes.

The main source of substantial corruption in Mexico is the functioning of government, and the main encouragements are the size of the government, the degree of discretion allowed in thousands of economic decisions, and the monolithic dominance of a single political party.

Mexico's trade was typified for about forty years by the use of import licensing as the main protective device.[33] The grant of a license could make a firm viable; its withholding could affect cash flow and, at the extreme, determine a firm's very existence. Some general rules defined products for which licenses would be granted or rejected, but also allowed considerable leeway for administrative flexibility. Such a system grants great power to the bureaucracy, and because so much is involved in discrete decisions, it is a structure tailor-made for complicity between importers-producers and government officials.

Foreign investment is similarly typified by case-by-case consideration of investment proposals. As with import licensing, general rules exist regarding the types of investment that will be approved, but there is also scope for discretion by those granting the authority. This structure also maximizes the temptation for money and other favors to change hands during the negotiation of investment proposals.

What is being stated should not be misconstrued. Not all trade licenses involved collusion or corruption, and not all foreign-investment negotiations included improper payments or favoritism to particular Mexicans to share in the fruits of the enterprise by merely lending a name. However, the system made these outcomes more probable than one based on general rules.

Nothing inherent in the Mexican culture led to venality. It was a system that encouraged corruption, that is, bribery, collusion, and earning of rents (non-earned profits) by well-placed insiders. The old-boy network thrived under this discretionary system, and one of the reasons it has been so durable is that entrenched privilege is hard to dislodge.

The state role has been more direct in the operation of state-owned corporations, the so-called parastatals. There are hundreds of these, with the exact number depending on the date chosen and the policy of the particular incumbent. The numbers grew under President Echeverría; they diminished under President de la Madrid, when many were divested. However, key state-owned enterprises are durable, and many are extremely important, such as Pemex for oil, natural-gas, and basic petrochemical production and distribution, electricity generation and distribution, telephone service, steel production, and many other fields. Mexico has a unique entity to provide food throughout the country at subsidized prices to low-income groups: Compañia Nacional de Subsistencias Populares (National Staple Products Company, Conasupo), which, because of its great buying power, can establish domestic producer prices for many staples. All nonforeign commercial banks are now majority government owned.

There is nothing inherently corrupt in government ownership of operating enterprises. Conasupo fills an important need in Mexico, and there is nothing in the form this takes—operating retail stores throughout the country—that is necessarily better or worse than a food-stamp or other welfare technique. Pemex (the acronym for Petróleos Mexicanos, the national oil company) may or may not be less efficient than other large oil companies—although there is evidence that it is not a model of efficiency—but government-owned oil companies are prevalent throughout the world.[34]

But state-owned enterprises open vast opportunities for personal profit and political manipulation. The government and the PRI are not one and the same, but the intermingling is extensive. As with trade and foreign investment, Mexico developed a structure of government-owned enterprises that makes corruption inevitable. This takes many forms—job placement, nepotism, self-aggrandizement from purchases and sales, awarding of contracts, and the ability to be made part of related enterprises so that monetary benefits can continue long after service in the government-owned enterprise terminates. The analogy is inexact, but it is not inaccurate to depict the PRI as a sophisticated version of the political machines that used to thrive in U.S. municipalities and states by providing jobs and welfare to adherents and often riches to leaders.

One of the favorite whipping boys of observers of the Mexican scene is the union within Pemex, the Sindicato de Trabajadores Petroleros de la República Mexicana (Union of Petroleum Workers of the Republic of Mexico, STPRM). This is an important labor union, perhaps the single most powerful in Mexico. The criticisms leveled against it include enrichment of some leaders, control over hiring and firing of all Pemex employees save those denominated employees of confidence (*empleados de confianza*), participation in Pemex contracts, and control over gasoline stations.[35] Of these, the most significant is the control over Pemex's work force, including the practice of selling jobs in Pemex (*vendeplazas*). A union this powerful was made possible by the monopoly enjoyed by Pemex and the critical role of oil in the economy. Once again, however, powerful unions with unsavory leadership are not unique to Mexico, as witness the Teamsters in the United States.

Each structural program was established for a particular reason. Trade policy grew out of import-substituting industrialization; the case-by-case negotiating process for making foreign-investment decisions was designed to avoid foreign domination of key sectors of the economy; and the basis for the creation of so many government-owned enterprises was the conviction that state-led development was necessary in an underdeveloped country like Mexico. Whatever the merits of these underlying justifications, structures were established that systematized corruption. These structures were mutually reinforcing. The PRI has remained in power for as long as it has because it was able to deliver benefits both to the country and to its adherents. The trade, investment, and parastatal regimes provided the means to reward *priistas*.

Structural Changes Affecting Corruption. Mexico's economic decline since 1982 has undoubtedly abetted certain forms of corruption. As the purchasing power of wages declined, incentives for side income have increased. Most of this has come from perfectly legal means, such as holding more than one job and wives and children going to work. Others have coped by seeking income on the margin of legality in the informal economy. Petty theft has increased; in a country where walking the streets at any time, day or night, used to be relatively safe, this has brought about an unfortunate but, to Americans, familiar change in social habits.

Those in a position to extract bribes, like police and other officials whose services are needed by the general public, are doing so, probably more consistently than when economic times were better. There are complaints about *mordidas*, but just about everybody pays.

Many structural bases of corruption are changing, however. The growing clamor for democracy means that the political structure will change; as evident from the July 1988 presidential and legislative elections, the status quo is becoming increasingly untenable. The desire for change came from within the PRI itself, particularly under the label of the democratic current (*corriente democrática*), and from without, from other political parties and intellectuals and professionals. Political opening will not eliminate corruption, but it will inevitably change many of its forms. If there is a viable political opposition, the actions of the ruling party will be scrutinized more closely. The words "morality" and "democracy" are being increasingly linked in Mexico, and this can have its effect over time.[36]

There was a tendency in the past to justify corruption on the ground that it was a stabilizing factor. Daniel Levy and Gabriel Székely put this position as follows:

"Leaders who have taken care of themselves are more likely to leave office satisfied than to plot comebacks. And corruption decreases the chances of serious attempts at radical policy change insofar as political leaders have to work their way up by playing skillfully within the system as it is."[37] This patronizing argument suggests that Mexico is too immature to retain stability without corruption or, the reverse, that corrupt stability is preferable to the instability of honest political contest.

Other structures allied to the political monopoly are also changing. The import system is evolving from one of discretionary import licensing to protection by tariffs. When tariffs are used, the permission of a government official is not needed to import. Foreign investment is still negotiable, but some generality (not much) has been introduced for small investment in particular fields. The significance in the corruption context is the elimination of an opportunity for illicit gain in the negotiation process. And finally, the sale of many government-owned enterprises will reduce patronage opportunities, although the government will retain vast powers, both directly and through state-owned enterprises, to award contracts to favored bidders. All these changes will not eliminate corruption in Mexico, but they will reduce many of the temptations and opportunities.

The structure of political, economic, and social life of a country obviously influences the way people behave, whether they willingly pay taxes, the respect they have for authority, and the acceptance of corruption. Sissela Bok has noted that there can be a self-justification for lying when an individual confronts a network of corruption and oppression.[38] An atmosphere of corruption leads to further corruption, and such an atmosphere does exist in Mexico. However, and this is the main point of this discussion, societal structures as they affect corruption are not immutable. This has become evident in the use of special prosecutors in the United States to examine indications of official corruption to free the process from political influence. That toleration of corruption has its limits is obvious from the pariah status of former president López Portillo; this was not the case for previous presidents who had used the office to enrich themselves. The backlash from the fraudulent elections in Chihuahua and elsewhere has not dissipated. Major changes are taking place in Mexico's political and economic structures and in the interplay between the two, and they are affecting what until now has been the resigned acceptance of official corruption. Corruption will not end in Mexico, but perhaps its institutionalization will be weakened.

Mexico pays a high foreign-relations price for its reputation as a corrupt society. The government is not taken seriously when it makes statements about the morality of foreign regimes because the source itself is tainted. Part of the condescension that the United States exhibits toward Mexico reflects the instinct of dealing with corrupt officialdom. This reaction has been explicit in statements on the antinarcotics effort, but it also permeates other political and economic relations. This may be unfair, since the United States does not enter into relations with Mexico with clean hands, but the belief remains that Mexican corruption not only is more pervasive, but also is woven into the country's political and economic structure. Many Mexicans are convinced that accusations coming from the United States are designed to bring the Mexican leadership into disrepute because of its policy in Central America. Although this motive may exist, it is insufficient to explain the ubiquitous impression in countries other than the United States that Mexico is highly corrupt. And whether or not Americans' beliefs about the extent of Mexican corruption are accurate, they influence attitudes and policy.

What Does Mexico Want from the United States?

Mexican leaders have two objectives at the top of their agenda: maintenance of political control by the PRI, and steady economic growth. These linked domestic political-economic goals affect foreign policy, which is also driven by Mexico's repeated position in the path of drives by a greater power, the United States. The essentials of Mexican foreign policy are repeated on all possible occasions: nonintervention in the internal affairs of other countries; self-determination of peoples; and peaceful solutions to international conflicts. Mexico mostly follows these principles, but there have been exceptions, particularly in Central America.

What Mexico seeks most from the United States is cooperation in achieving economic growth and sympathetic understanding of the internal political-social situation. The historic foreign-policy principles are now mostly rhetorical, since the United States is no longer territorially expansionist or apt to intervene with troops in Mexico in the absence of some extreme crisis, such as a third-country invasion. The principles are important symbols, however, just as the Revolution is; they give intellectual coherence to Mexico's policy in Central America.

The practical aspect of Mexico's policy in Central America is more than symbolic, however. It is designed to neutralize the internal left, thereby buying exemption from opposition intrigue within Mexico. It is worth keeping in mind that Mexico is closer to Central America than the United States is, and that Mexico has a legitimate stake in events in that region.

The bilateral foreign-policy agenda is dominated by economic issues, although they naturally have political consequences. Mexico wants access to the U.S. market for its goods and services, with minimum restrictions. Mexico would like this access to be preferential, as is evident from the Mexican literature on the content of a "special" relationship with the United States. In trade, Mexico wishes to be treated as a developing country, which in concrete terms means that it wants U.S. acceptance of Mexican import protection, domestic-content requirements imposed on internal production, and legislation and regulations requiring foreign investors to export given proportions of their production. Mexico has opted not to default on its debt obligations, but it does seek the easing of servicing and the provision of new lending.

The official record is replete with disagreements between Mexico and the United States on economic policy, mainly because discord rises to the surface and harmony is taken for granted. Most economic interchange between the two countries proceeds smoothly. Governments get involved when there is conflict, but most of the exchange is extragovernmental, between private parties (or between a parastatal entity like Pemex and private parties in the United States, which is more akin to private than to intergovernmental exchanges). Mexico is not necessarily meeting all its foreign economic objectives; it has not diversified its markets, for example.

However, the shortcomings are primarily the result of policies made in Mexico rather than lack of U.S. cooperation. Mexico does not obtain all that it seeks from the U.S. government in the economic field: products are removed from preferential treatment even when not legally required; the U.S. government sometimes seeks to frustrate Mexican industrial-policy measures; and practices that Mexico pursues using the justification that it is a developing country are sometimes successfully resisted.[39] On the whole, however, economic cooperation is substantial.

Mexicans are wary of the U.S. response to Mexico's internal political agenda, however. The conservative Reagan administration was more in tune ideologically with the PAN, the conservative opposition in Mexico, even as its policy supported the continuance in power of the PRI for reasons of internal stability. This duality of sentiment emanating from Washington is evident in Mexico, and has raised PRI concern that the ambiguity may undermine its legitimacy and that of the Mexican government itself. It is in this light that many Mexicans see the critical press treatment of Mexico as a conspiracy to denigrate Mexican political practices.[41]

Mexicans also speculate whether the country's votes in the United Nations and its policy toward Central America are reasons for U.S. disparagement of Mexico in other respects.[42] The Mexican concern is that what is labeled second-order foreign-policy issues in Table 3.1 are overwhelming themes that are more important in the overall relationship.

Mexico's policy toward Central America reflects general sentiment in Latin America, as can be seen from the formation of the Contadora group (Colombia, Mexico, Panama, Venezuela), which sought to resolve the dispute in Nicaragua through negotiation, and the agreement of the presidents of the five Central American countries to seek peace in the region (the Arias plan). The policy toward Nicaragua is in accord with previous actions by Mexico, such as the maintenance of relations with Cuba under Fidel Castro despite the censure of Cuba by the Organization of American States. After all, the Revolution is Mexico's most potent symbol, and it is hard for Mexican leaders to be counter-revolutionaries. Finally, Mexico's Central American policy is undoubtedly based on the conviction that Mexico's own security is best achieved by nonmilitary pacification of the region. Mexico doubts that it is a potential domino to a Marxist regime in Nicaragua; and, indeed, it is convinced that potential aggression is best tempered by good relations with the Sandinista government rather than by opposition. (This, however, has not prevented the military from insisting on budget increases for modernization in order to defend the national territory from political turbulence in Central America.)[43]

Mexico's attitude is also based on opposition to U.S. hegemony. As René Herrera and Mario Ojeda put it, "Obviously, the Reagan government seeks stability in the area, but with the presumption [*pretensión*] of maintaining U.S. hegemony."[44] Is Mexico also a pretender to hegemonic status in the area? It undoubtedly was during the López Portillo period, when it joined with Venezuela to provide aid through concessional pricing of oil. It may still be, but Mexico's power to dominate is less convincing today.

Each country, Mexico and the United States, professes that it seeks stability in Central America. The means to and the nature of stability are not the same in the two conceptions. Yet it is folly to allow this disagreement to interfere with other issues of greater significance in the bilateral relationship. United States interests in Mexico are substantially more important than they are in Nicaragua or elsewhere in Central America, and the Mexican need for good relations with the United States is of greater salience than it is with countries in Central America. Mexico could afford to ignore Central America until the mid-1970s; it cannot afford to ignore the United States.

What Does the United States Want from Mexico?

The key U.S. desire is that Mexico remain a socially stable country. Despite all the petty irritations, such as foreign-policy disagreements and a press that is largely anti-American, the United States has been fortunate for the past half-century in having a stable neighbor to the south (as it has to the north). This stability permitted the United States to devote its attention elsewhere while mostly ignoring Mexico, but the reverse was never true. The asymmetry of focus has been attenuated, since there is nothing like prolonged economic crisis and political stirrings in a populous neighbor country to alter the national attention span.

Stability is not a simple concept. Mexico is not unstable today if instability is defined as widespread social disorder. And while Mexican democracy is certainly qualified, the country is not an absolutist state. The stability the United States would prefer is that of democracy unqualified by descriptive adjectives, but it is unclear that unqualified democracy would take precedence over stability in U.S. thinking if the two came into conflict. The United States would not want Mexican Marxists to win a free election, as it made clear in Chile, a distant country, when Salvador Allende was elected president. The stability sought by the United States is therefore a tempered objective—stability with a regime compatible with U.S. political mores.

Social stability in Mexico implies economic development. Economic growth has been the glue of past stability, and its absence is what now raises questions that U.S. policy could ignore for so long. If the first policy priority of the United States toward Mexico is stability and achieving it requires economic growth, the clear conclusion to the syllogism is that the United States should do what it can to abet Mexico's economic prosperity. At this point, the agendas of the two countries coincide, even if particular actions conflict. If Mexico's future calls for an outward-looking economy, as the United States has recommended and Mexico is pursuing, U.S. policy must accommodate this. The U.S. market must remain open to Mexican goods and services, and capital should flow from the United States to Mexico; in recent years, the net resource flow has been in the other direction because of Mexico's debt payments. Any inclination to punish Mexico economically for its policy in Central America or its votes in the United Nations would be self-defeating; the gratification would be momentary and the damage basic.

Behavior of the United States toward Mexico is mostly defensive—to prevent instability and avoid economic actions that might bring this about. Mexican behavior is more aggressive. It involves taking an independent position on Central America. Economically, Mexico seeks to increase its role in the U.S. market. Octavio Paz has stated that "North Americans consider the world to be something that can be perfected and . . . we consider it something that can be redeemed."[45] In comparing each country's foreign relations, it is more accurate to state that Mexico thinks the world is something that can be changed—or perfected, to use Paz's word—and the United States treats it as something that can be maintained. In external affairs, the United States is more the status quo nation than Mexico.

II

POLICY ISSUES

4

TRADE

[E]ven if officially Mexico is considered just another country in not being granted special treatment in matters of trade, the truth is that North American leaders will be obligated to take into consideration other elements of their relationship with Mexico.

OLGA PELLICER DE BRODY, 1981

As the world's thirteenth largest economy and the largest market economy trading country still outside the GATT, Mexico's decision was of great significance to the international trading system.

REPORT OF THE WORKING PARTY ON THE ACCESSION OF MEXICO TO THE GATT, 1986

[M]any of Mexico's exports to the United States, particularly agricultural and mineral products, have to surmount high trade barriers and arbitrary policies that protect special U.S. interests. In contrast, Mexico has erected no such barriers against imports from the United States, which tend increasingly to be capital equipment and food, nor are there measures that discriminate against the United States in relation to other suppliers.

VÍCTOR L. URQUIDI, 1979

Mexico has utilized . . . combinations of tariffs and surcharges, quotas and restrictive licensing practices, artificial valuation schemes, and a variety of export performance requirements and incentives . . . these policies have discriminated against the U.S. and Canada.

NORTH AMERICAN TRADE AGREEMENTS STUDY, 1981

New Policy Directions

American policy for most of the period since World War II has been to reduce trade barriers, while Mexico's commercial policy has been replete with import restrictions. The direction of each is now changing, that of the United States toward greater protectionism and that of Mexico toward more openness. United States protectionism is largely of a contingent nature, reacting to what are considered unfair practices by others. Mexican policy is shifting away from quantitative restrictions in favor of tariffs for most items. While the tariff levels are still relatively high, they are negotiable. The Mexican intention to follow through on the policy of greater openness is exemplified by its accession to the General Agreement on Tariffs and Trade (GATT).

The United States was the driving force behind the trade liberalization that took place after World War II under the aegis of the GATT. In successive rounds of multilateral trade negotiations, tariffs of industrial countries were drastically lowered and became a subordinate feature of trade in manufactures among these countries. Quantitative import restrictions were removed on most nonagricultural commodities, and a stab was made at dealing with other types of nontariff barriers in the Tokyo round of trade negotiations during the 1970s. The United States sparked the effort begun at Punta del Este in 1986 to deal with trade in agricultural products and services in the so-called Uruguay round of GATT negotiations.

American trade policy has not been pure. Its objective has not been absolutely free trade, but freer trade. Free trade was a limit that might someday be within grasp, but there was never a timetable.[1] Raymond Vernon caught the essence of U.S. practice when he observed that the general policy favored trade liberalization, even though specific cases of protectionism were common.[2] Many protective measures were the price that different U.S. administrations paid to particular interests to obtain a political consensus in favor of the liberal general policy. There are numerous examples of this: both Presidents Kennedy and Nixon restricted textile imports at the same time they undertook new multilateral rounds of trade negotiations; and the free entry of commodities into the United States under President Reagan's Caribbean Basin Initiative was circumscribed by many exceptions.

During the 1980s, the weight of specific restrictions has increased so much that the general policy of liberalization has been brought into question. The slogan has become fair trade as opposed to free or freer trade.[3] Another catchphrase is the need for a level playing field, which argues that since other countries intervene in a variety of ways to rig trade, the United States must respond.

Various other reasons have been given for this change in policy emphasis. They include the large U.S. trade deficits, the decline in many basic industries, unemployment and reduced wages among workers in declining industries, the emergence of many new competitors among the newly industrializing countries (NICs), the slowdown beginning in the 1960s of U.S. productivity growth, and, for many years, the overvaluation of the dollar.

Whatever the reasons, the United States is no longer the bulwark of freer trade, except as this suits the nation, as in services and parts of agriculture. The change has made a major difference on the world scene—no other country has replaced the United States as a leader for international trade liberalization.

Mexico, by contrast, embarked on a policy of substantial import protection in the post–World War II period, inspired by the country's underdevelopment and the conviction among officials that opening domestic markets in these circumstances was tantamount to accepting perpetual exploitation by wealthier, predatory countries. The theoretical development literature of the times, especially during the 1950s, stressed industrialization as the path to development and protection and import substitution as the means to industrialize.[4] Most of Mexico's restrictive import measures, those that lasted until the past couple of years, were introduced during this period. So were many stimulatory actions favoring industrialization. Restrictions included import licensing, domestic-content provisions, and export demands on foreign investors; and there was a rash of fiscal subsidies—the measures the U.S. government was referring to in the final quotation at the beginning of this chapter. They will be discussed in greater detail in Chapter 5.

This structure of protection and subsidy is now being dismantled under the pressure of events. The manifestations of this dismantling are the removal of the requirement for prior import licenses for most commodities, accession to the GATT, commitments to the World Bank to liberalize the trade regime, and reduction of fiscal subsidies.

The role reversal could not be more stark. In its search for modernity, Mexico is becoming a freer trading nation.[5] One must repeat that the operative word is "freer," not "free"; and in becoming more free, Mexico starts from a relatively high protective position. Unlike what was once the case in the United States, no responsible figures in Mexico talk of free trade as a limit. But the direction of Mexican trade policy since 1982 has been clear—it is toward greater freedom.

The direction of U.S. trade policy in the 1980s is also clear—it is toward greater protection. Although the United States is still vastly more open to imports than Mexico, the possibility now exists that the two policy lines will cross. This is the backdrop to the trade discussion in this chapter, which will examine both the historic and the currently evolving interaction between the two markets. The interesting operational question relates to the growth in trade integration that will occur between Mexico and the United States.

Increasing its exports has now become a crucial element of Mexico's economic development strategy. The critical export market, more now than ever before, is the United States. The success of Mexico's new development policy, even if not explicitly stated, is based on the country's interdependence with the United States.

The Interaction of Two Policies

The United States opted after World War II to make its trade policy truly multilateral. At the instigation of the United States and other industrial countries, GATT was organized. It, rather than bilateral discussions, became the forum for U.S. trade negotiations with other countries. The devotion of the United States to multilateralism was more complete than that of most developed countries, and bilateral agreements that existed with Cuba, the Philippines, and Venezuela were allowed to lapse. But multilateralism was never absolute; bilateralism, for example, was used to obtain reciprocal results in trade with the state-trading countries of Eastern Europe.

Alongside the multilateral structure, special arrangements grew among the countries in the European Economic Community and the European Free Trade Association, and then in the free-trade arrangement between the EEC and the EFTA. The EEC set up a vast network of special arrangements with former colonies of the member countries. European countries concluded an array of bilateral agreements, although many were nothing more than political expressions of intent with little bite regarding imports and exports.

It can be argued that the U.S. position of sticking to multilateralism while special arrangements flourished around the world was naive. United States dedication to multilateralism, at least in trade relations with market economies, also had implications for a special relationship with Mexico. Such a relationship implies departures from general rules in favor of particular countries, whereas pure multilateralism implies no such departures. This tension between principle and potential special practice in U.S. trade relations has always concerned Mexican officials, and, if truth be known, they never understood it.[6] The writings of many Mexicans make it clear that Mexico would have entertained a bilateral arrangement with the United States as long as it involved mostly one-way benefits in favor of Mexico. There was no bilateral agreement until 1985, by which time a host of other international developments led to changes in U.S. trade practices.

A related U.S. trade principle that affected relations with Mexico was the most-favored-nation (MFN) clause. This is another way of saying nondiscrimination, that all countries are treated as well as the country that is most favored. Unconditional MFN is the first principle of the GATT, set forth in Article I. Unconditional MFN and multilateralism logically go together; if there is no discrimination in treatment of countries, there is no trade reason for special bilateral agreements.

This absolute consistency has not prevailed on the world scene. Unconditional MFN and bilateralism have gone hand in hand. And so has special treatment as an exception to the unconditional MFN clause. Special treatment is what general systems of preference give to the generality of developing countries; it is what is done for limited groups of developing countries in the agreements between the EEC and the Africa-Caribbean-Pacific (ACP) countries and between the United States and countries in the Caribbean basin. Mexico, despite its location in the Caribbean basin, is not a beneficiary of the special preferences of this last initiative.

One argument made by Víctor Urquidi in the quotation at the beginning of this chapter is that Mexico did not discriminate against the United States in relation to other foreign countries in its trade restrictions. This is overtly true, but Mexico did try to use its oil exports to give and obtain concessions in special bilateral agreements during the López Portillo administration.[7] These marked a departure from multilateralism, but not a significant one. But even though Mexico was not a member of the GATT until 1986, the two countries did grant each other MFN treatment.

The difference between the two trade policies was based on their disparate degrees of development. The United States found itself a world power in the post–World War II period. It sought to lead in both economic and security matters, and dedicated itself to avoiding the mistakes of the interwar period while seeking to maintain the international economic status quo. Mexico, by contrast, saw little merit in the status quo. It viewed development of its own industry as the key to modernization, using its domestic market as the base to accomplish this goal.[8]

Trade conflict between the United States and Mexico was inevitable as a result of these two world views. As long as both countries prospered, as they did until the 1970s, the conflict was muted. What has brought trade disputes into sharp focus in recent years has been the deterioration in the U.S. trade account and the conviction of many domestic critics of U.S. trade policy that this was due partially to fatuousness in rigid adherence to principle, and, on Mexico's side, the protracted economic crisis of the 1980s. Each country has a tendency to blame the other. The United States sees Mexico as a country that uses a variety of techniques to deny U.S. producers a "level playing field." Mexico, in turn, regards the United States as imposing protective measures that complicate Mexico's emergence from its economic difficulties.

Table 4.1 Mexican Exports by Main Destinations, 1970, 1975, 1980–1987

Year	Total	U.S.	EEC[a]	Other Europe[b]	LAC[c]	Japan	Other[d]
Millions of Dollars							
1970	1,290	880	101	33	172	79	35
1975	3,062	1,772	264	68	453	131	374
1980	15,132	9,892	1,047	1,420	1,077	681	1,015
1981	19,420	10,543	1,629	2,192	1,944	1,203	1,909
1982	21,230	11,129	2,590	2,096	1,855	1,450	2,110
1983	22,312	12,988	2,273	2,014	1,745	1,535	1,757
1984	24,054	13,692	2,607	2,057	1,734	1,905	2,059
1985	21,866	13,388	2,245	1,849	1,269	1,719	1,398
1986	15,775	10,674	1,331	1,024	1,178	1,058	510
1987	20,656	13,358	3,008	133	1,559	1,349	1,249
Percent							
1970	100	68.2	7.8	2.6	13.3	6.1	2.7
1975	100	57.9	8.6	2.2	14.8	4.3	12.2
1980	100	65.4	6.9	9.4	7.1	4.5	6.7
1981	100	54.2	8.4	11.3	10.0	6.2	9.8
1982	100	52.4	12.2	9.9	8.7	6.8	9.9
1983	100	58.2	10.2	9.0	7.8	6.9	7.9
1984	100	56.9	10.8	8.6	7.2	7.9	8.6
1985	100	61.2	10.3	8.5	5.8	7.9	6.4
1986	100	67.7	8.4	6.5	7.5	6.7	3.2
1987	100	64.7	14.6	0.6	7.5	6.5	6.0

[a]Data exclude Spain, Portugal, and Greece, except for 1987, which includes them.

[b]Includes Eastern Europe, to which exports are modest; these exports were 0.2 percent of all exports in 1985. The largest single market in this group is Spain; in 1985, exports to Spain were $1.7 billion, or more than 90 percent of the category "other Europe."

[c]Latin American and Caribbean countries.

[d]Biggest "other" market is normally Canada.

Sources: SPP, *Sistema de cuentas nacionales, oferta y utilización de bienes y servicios* (1981) vol. 5, p. 599; and Presidencia de la República, *V informe de gobierno* (1987), and *VI informe de gobierno* (1988).

The Bilateral Trade Picture

Table 4.1 gives Mexican exports by main destinations and shows the dominance of the United States. The recent pattern is for 50 to 70 percent of Mexican exports, by value, to go to the United States. The decline toward the low end of this percentage range in the early 1980s reflects growing oil exports and the 50 percent limitation placed by Mexico on these exports to any one country. As oil revenue declined both absolutely and as a proportion of total exports after 1982, the relative importance of the U.S. market increased.

This is a significant point. The market for crude oil is worldwide, and the proportions traded between countries reflect location and business arrangements rather than a complete range of competitive conditions. Between 1980 and 1987, the United States absorbed about 70 percent of Mexico's nonoil exports, a truer

Table 4.2 Mexican Imports by Main Sources, 1970, 1975, 1980–1987

Year	Total	U.S.	EEC[a]	Other Europe[b]	LAC[c]	Japan	Other[d]
Millions of Dollars							
1970	2,463	1,567	633	a	142	105[e]	16
1975	6,575	4,128	1,354	a	667	347[e]	79
1980	18,832	12,604	2,583	874	1,072	1,018	681
1981	23,930	15,904	3,227	1,234	1,313	1,259	993
1982	14,437	9,006	2,222	866	757	855	731
1983	8,551	5,454	1,190	363	313	373	858
1984	11,254	7,365	1,350	510	506	519	1,004
1985	13,212	8,970	1,744	605	634	735	524
1986	11,432	7,427	1,644	622	392	684	663
1987	12,223	7,903	1,986	350	357	795	832
Percent							
1970	100	63.6	25.7	a	5.8	4.3	0.6
1975	100	62.8	20.6	a	10.1	5.3	1.2
1980	100	66.9	13.7	4.6	5.7	5.4	3.6
1981	100	66.5	13.5	5.2	5.5	5.3	4.1
1982	100	62.4	15.4	6.0	5.2	5.9	5.1
1983	100	63.8	13.9	4.2	3.7	4.4	10.0
1984	100	65.4	12.0	4.5	4.5	4.6	8.9
1985	100	67.9	13.2	4.6	4.8	5.6	4.0
1986	100	65.0	14.4	5.4	3.4	6.0	5.8
1987	100	64.6	16.2	2.9	2.9	6.5	6.8

[a]Data exclude Spain, Portugal, and Greece, except for 1987, which includes them. For 1970 and 1975, EEC and other Europe are lumped together.

[b]Includes Eastern Europe, from which imports are modest; those imports were 0.3 percent of all imports in 1985. The largest single source in this group is Spain; in 1985, imports from Spain were $218 million, or 36 percent of the category "other Europe."

[c]Latin American and Caribbean countries. For 1970 and 1975, data may include imports from Canada as well.
[d]Biggest "other source" is normally Canada.
[e]Figures for 1970 and 1975 are imports from all of Asia.
Sources: Presidencia de la República, *V informe de gobierno* (1987), and *VI informe de gobierno* (1988); for 1970 and 1975, Inegi, *Estadísticas históricas de México* (1985), vol. 2, p. 669.

measure of Mexican dependence on the U.S. market and of the integration of the two economies. Since Mexico sees its future as a middle-level industrial power and a country with a diversified export base, the 70 percent figure is more significant than the 60 percent of all exports, including oil, to the United States over this period.

Table 4.2 shows Mexican imports from all sources. The United States once again dominates the picture. But since a large proportion (about 50 percent) of nonoil United States–Mexico trade takes place between affiliates of U.S. multinational corporations (MNCs), it is hard to disentangle the import and export sides of the trade relationship. The same company buys and sells to itself through its affiliates in the two countries. Many Mexican exports to the United States under these circumstances are made possible by U.S. exports to Mexico. The inseparability of imports and exports is apt to become even more significant in the future as trade in components rather than finished products grows; much of this intra-industry trade implies two-way movement of the same products, with value added at each move. This is a significant indicator of how thoroughly the two economies are becoming integrated in that an ever-growing proportion of trade in manufactures is based on component production by affiliated companies located in the two countries.

By 1980, Mexico had become the third most important market for U.S. exports, after Canada and Japan. This position slipped in 1983 and 1984 as Mexico drastically curtailed its imports, but has since been regained. The asymmetry in trade importance is evident in that, even in third place, the Mexican market normally accounts for between 5.5 and 6.5 percent of the value of all U.S. exports, compared with ten times this reliance by Mexico on the U.S. market. Mexico in recent years has been the fourth source for U.S. imports, accounting for more than 6 percent when oil prices were high and about 5.5 percent when they were lower.

Manufactured goods made up 79.5 percent of U.S. exports to Mexico in 1985.[9] The proportion has remained similar ever since. About 50 percent of total U.S. exports by value that year and since have been machinery and transport equipment. About 37 percent of U.S. imports from Mexico in 1985 were crude petroleum and more than 41 percent when other fuels and lubricants are added. Manufactures were 47 percent of U.S. imports from Mexico in 1985, and agricultural products 9 percent.[10] These proportions change yearly depending on oil prices and Mexico's drive to export manufactured goods. The leading manufactured U.S. imports from Mexico in 1987 were automotive parts, especially piston engines; ignition wiring sets; and chassis and bodies. Automotive parts, including engines, were also among the leading U.S. exports to Mexico. This two-way trade illustrates the extent of market integration that exists in this industry.[11]

Table 4.3 summarizes the overall merchandise trade balance between the two countries as it has evolved since 1970. The trade balance showed a U.S. surplus until 1981; since then the surplus has shifted to the Mexican side, propelled less by increased U.S. imports than by drastic declines for several years in U.S. exports to Mexico caused by the latter's stabilization program designed to deal with the balance-of-payments crisis.

Particular Programs. Table 4.4 lists imports from Mexico under the U.S. generalized system of preferences (GSP). The data show that as Mexico's oil exports diminished after 1984, utilization of GSP increased. In 1980, during the heyday of Mexican oil exports, GSP imports from Mexico were 4 percent of total U.S. imports from Mexico. Since 1986, GSP imports have made up more than 7 percent of the total. This trend is supported by other U.S. data showing Mexico's utilization rate increasing from 50.7 to 85.4 percent from 1984 to 1988.[12] The utilization rate measures those imports that enter duty free as a percentage of all products from a country eligible for duty-free treatment under GSP. For many years, the Mexican utilization rate was low; the average for all countries in 1985 was 77 percent, compared with 52 percent for Mexico.[13] For some reason—perhaps the antiexport mentality that existed for so long—Mexico failed to take full advantage of the

Table 4.3 United States–Mexico Trade Balance, 1970, 1975, and 1980–1988 (millions of dollars)

	U.S. Exports (FAS)	U.S. Imports (customs basis)	Balance
1970	1,704	1,219	485
1975	5,141	3,067	2,074
1980	15,145	12,580	2,565
1981	17,789	13,765	4,024
1982	11,817	15,566	−3,749
1983	9,079	16,776	−7,697
1984	11,978	18,020	−6,042
1985	13,635	19,329	−5,497
1986	12,392	17,302	−4,910
1987	14,569	20,270	−5,701
1988	20,633	23,276	−2,643

Source: U.S. Bureau of the Census, *Highlights of the U.S. Export and Import Trade*, Report FT 990, various issues. The 1988 figures were obtained directly from the U.S. Department of Commerce.

Table 4.4 U.S. Imports from Mexico Under Generalized System of Preferences, 1980–1988 (millions of dollars)

Year	GSP	Total Imports from Mexico	GSP as Percent Total
1980	510	12,774	4.0
1981	634	14,013	4.5
1982	602	15,770	3.8
1983	728	17,019	4.3
1984	1,096	17,267	6.0
1985	1,240	19,392	6.4
1986	1,301	17,558	7.4
1987	2,188	20,519	10.7
1988	1,677	23,544	7.1

Note: Total import data may differ from those given in Table 4.3, which is based on customs value. Both GSP and total import data in this table are given in source on CIF basis.

Source: USITC, *The Impact of Increased United States–Mexico Trade on Southwest Border Development*, p. 59; U.S. Department of Commerce, *1986 U.S. Foreign Trade Highlights*, p. A-204; and data from the Office of the U.S. Trade Representative for 1986–1988.

opportunities offered by the U.S. GSP program. This has changed since the trade restructuring started in 1986. Mexico ranked third in 1987 among foreign providers to the United States under GSP.[14]

Imports from Mexico under GSP cover a range of products. The most important categories are chemicals and related products, followed by machinery and equipment, agriculture and fisheries, and some textiles and apparel. Between 1976, when GSP was instituted in the United States, and 1985, duties forgone on GSP imports from Mexico were estimated at $300 million.[15] By now, this figure exceeds $200 million annually.

GSP, while welcomed by Mexican authorities, has not been accepted without criticism. Gustavo del Castillo has asserted that hundreds of millions of dollars of Mexican GSP-eligible exports are eliminated by U.S. customs authorities because of improper documentation.[16] Isabel Molina has argued that in the 1984 renewal, GSP was made more protectionist.[17] The evidence supports this observation, certainly for an NIC like Mexico. In January 1987, GSP benefits to the NICs, including Mexico, were further limited. Because of the nature of its exports, Mexico is one of the lesser beneficiaries of GSP in terms of the proportion of trade that is theoretically eligible. The most significant export for which GSP is not relevant is petroleum. Finally, more Mexican products, involving more trade, have been graduated out of GSP eligibility than for Brazil, the other large GSP beneficiary in Latin America.[18] The main reason for this is that Mexican products were becoming increasingly competitive with U.S. production. Among the items excluded by graduation, which is an administrative rather than a statutory exclusion, are beer and other beverages, various vegetables, ceramic tiles, polyvinyl chloride resins, ferrites, parts of piston engines, silver articles, elevator winches, lead-acid storage batteries, transceivers, toys, and springs and leaves for motor-vehicle suspension.[19]

As noted above, GSP is a departure from the unconditional MFN provision of the GATT, although specifically sanctioned by the contracting parties. It is a one-way grant of free entry for products chosen by the importing country in favor of exporting developing countries designated as beneficiaries. The original U.S. statute provided that a country lost GSP eligibility for a specific product under two so-called competitive-need provisions: if U.S. imports from that country in the previous year exceeded 50 percent of all imports of that product; and if the value of imports exceeded a specific dollar value.[20] The 1984 revision altered the competitive-need provisions by removing them for the least-developed beneficiary countries, maintaining them for a middle tier of countries, and permitting the imposition of harsher terms (to 25 percent instead of 50 percent of U.S. imports of a specific tariff item) for the most developed of the beneficiary countries. Mexico fits into the last category, and this was the reason given for the exclusions announced on January 2, 1987. Countries can also be graduated completely out of U.S. GSP when per capita income exceeds $5,000, a figure high enough so that Mexico is in no immediate danger of losing eligibility on this ground.

Graduation has been the most controversial aspect of GSP in Mexico. Discretionary U.S. decisions on graduation are based on a combination of political pressures from Mexico and from competing U.S. producers. The fact that GSP imports amount to only about 7 percent of all U.S. imports from Mexico, or about 15 percent of nonoil imports, is not a convincing argument to a U.S. producer facing product-specific competition from Mexico. Enough discretionary cases have gone against Mexico for it to doubt its political weight in these internal U.S. deliberations. The restrictive actions of January 1987 made it evident that the United States is serious about graduation. The main impact so far has been on six countries: Taiwan, South Korea, Hong Kong, Singapore, Mexico, and Brazil.

Mexico nonetheless benefits from GSP's existence, although it is hard to measure by how much. An even less measurable aspect of GSP is the weight its existence has when nonrelated import restrictions are imposed on Mexican products. As one hand of the United States gives a GSP benefit, the other feels justified in imposing a restriction.

Table 4.5 shows U.S. imports from Mexico under U.S. tariff items 806.30 and 807.00.[21] These two tariff items represent another special form of U.S. imports. These imports come from *maquiladora,* assembly plants in Mexico, most of which are near the U.S. border. The *maquiladora* will be discussed in greater detail in Chapter 8, but their trade implications will be taken up now. The *maquiladora* represent a heightened form of production sharing under which components of manufactured goods are produced in the United States and then shipped to Mexico for further elaboration, especially to take advantage of cheap labor.

Note that TSUS (tariff schedules of the United States) items 806.30 and 807.00 exclude from liability for duty the U.S. portion of the value of certain imported articles. Item 806.30 deals with metal products, and 807.00, which is by far the more important, with other commodities. Put differently, the tariff on entry into the United States under 806.30/807.00 is imposed only on the value added abroad. This is the significance of the columns of Table 4.5. Column 1 includes the value of the U.S. goods originally sent to Mexico; column 2, on which the duty is levied, shows the value added in Mexico. From the Mexican viewpoint, therefore, column 2 is the relevant indicator of trade benefit. About 50 percent of U.S. 806.30/807.00 imports from Mexico constitute value added in Mexico; most of it is labor.

As Table 4.5 shows, 806.30/807.00 imports from Mexico have increased steadily since 1980. The most important 806.30/807.00 imports from Mexico are machinery and equipment. They made up 82 percent of all 806.30/807.00 imports from Mexico in 1987 on a gross basis and 87 percent of the dutiable value. The products involved were mostly parts for televisions, electronic and electrical equipment, office machines, and especially transportation equipment, although some final products were also imported. The second most important product category was textiles, apparel, and footwear. The textile and apparel items imported under 807.00 are included in the quota limitations imposed against Mexico under the multifiber arrangement (MFA).

Imports benefiting from the terms of 806.30/807.00 apply to all countries, developed and developing alike, and the system was not devised solely to benefit Mexico. The dutiable proportion from other countries in 1985 was 75 percent of gross 806.30/807.00 imports, a percentage considerably higher than the roughly 50 percent from Mexico. This means that a greater relative value of U.S. components was incorporated in 806.30/807.00 imports from Mexico than from the rest of the world. This can be seen also in the fact that Mexico in 1987 provided 13 percent of gross U.S. imports under 806.30/807.00, but only 7.5 percent of dutiable imports.

Table 4.5 U.S. Imports from Mexico Under TSUS Items 806.30 and 807.00, 1980–1987 (millions of dollars)

Year	Total 806.30/807.00 (1)	Dutiable Amount (2)	All Imports from Mexico (3)	Percentages 2/1	2/3
1980	2,341	1,155	12,580	49.3	9.2
1981	2,710	1,272	13,765	46.9	9.2
1982	2,839	1,389	15,566	48.9	8.9
1983	3,714	1,807	16,766	48.6	10.8
1984	4,808	2,253	18,020	46.9	12.5
1985	5,567	2,611	19,329	46.9	13.5
1986	6,457	3,036	17,302	47.0	17.5
1987	8,689	4,195	17,625	48.3	23.8

Source: USITC, *The Impact of Increased United States–Mexico Trade on Southwest Border Development*, p. 84, for 806.30/807.00 data for 1980 and 1981; USITC, *Imports Under Items 806.30 and 807.00 of the Tariff Schedules of the United States*, various issues.

This point has relevance for the future of 806.30/807.00 as it applies to Mexico. Labor unions in the Unites States dislike these provisions of the U.S. tariff schedule out of conviction that they encourage industries to run away, as they put it, to take advantage of cheap labor.[22] When the U.S. Tariff Commission, the predecessor of the U.S. International Trade Commission (USITC), studied this question in 1970, it concluded that 806.30/807.00, on balance, helped create U.S. jobs to provide the components for further processing abroad and servicing the imports and exports. The implied alternative to 806.30/807.00 was the loss to other countries of the entire operation. Because the use of 806.30/807.00 increased dramatically after 1970, the USITC was asked once again to study the issue of job loss, and its conclusion in 1988 was similar to that in 1970.[23] It is also clear that more U.S. components, and hence U.S. jobs, are used in the Mexican *maquiladora* than in comparable assembly operations in the rest of the world.

For Mexico, the *maquiladora* are a source of benefit and problems. Their existence in Mexico, coupled with the operation of 806.30/807.00 on the U.S. side, means that foreign-exchange earnings from domestic value added in Mexico are 8 to 10 percent above what is shown in the merchandise trade account. (The value added from *maquiladora* is not included in the trade account in Mexico's balance-of-payments presentation, but elsewhere in the current account.) The problems relate to the enclave nature of the *maquiladora*, social issues connected with female employment in these factories, environmental degradation from some plants, and the uncertain nature of an operation that is as mobile as most assembly plants. These issues are dealt with in Chapter 8.

Mutual Trade Restrictions

For many years, Mexican import restrictions against U.S. products were far greater than U.S. limits on imports from Mexico. The changing trade policy in Mexico leading to reduced import barriers is based on the expectation that less protection—

and hence lower production costs—will lead to expanded exports. Mexico is now joining the rest of the trading world more fully than at any time since the Revolution. And for Mexico, the trading world is represented overwhelmingly by the United States. Any significant growth in U.S. restrictions on imports from Mexico would thus frustrate the accomplishment of Mexico's economic development objectives. The United States cannot divorce its trade policy toward Mexico from the overall interdependence of the two countries.

There are many U.S. restrictions against imports from Mexico, but the damage is still more potential than actual. For a long time, a key Mexican complaint concerned the escalation of the U.S. tariff structure. Tariff rates increase as products are further elaborated to protect domestic value added, particularly labor. Tariffs are low or nil for raw materials, in a middle range for intermediate goods, and highest for final products. The Mexican argument was that protecting value added (labor) in the United States limited Mexico's own ability to add value (to use labor) in its exports to the United States. But the escalation issue is no longer significant because U.S. tariffs, as well as those of other developed countries, have been reduced significantly in successive rounds of GATT negotiations. Nominal (stated) U.S. tariffs, weighted by imports, are in the 3 to 6 percent range.

Overt nontariff barriers on U.S. imports from Mexico now exist for textiles and apparel and steel. Sanitary regulations limit imports of fresh vegetables and meat. Border-crossing and customs regulations may act as a deterrent to Mexican exports. And there are not enough bridges between the two countries in the lower Rio Grande Valley.

Both Mexico and the United States are parties to the multifiber arrangement (MFA), under which international trade in textiles and apparel is regulated. Pursuant to the umbrella of the MFA, the United States and Mexico have concluded a series of bilateral agreements calling for explicit quotas on some items, which now account for 80 percent of the value of Mexico's textile and apparel exports to the United States.[24] There are also provisions that permit the imposition of quotas on additional items if imports are seen as disrupting or threatening the U.S. market; consultations are triggered when imports reach designated levels.[25] But this U.S. import restriction, because it is global in scope, is actually probably a boon to Mexico. To cite the USITC, "Mexico receives benefits from the extremely tight quota restraints that are applied to the large Asian suppliers. As U.S. importers find it increasingly difficult to fill their needs from countries such a Hong Kong, Korea, and Taiwan, export opportunities increase for a large number of secondary suppliers, including Mexico."[26]

Following the submission of a number of unfair trade petitions against Mexican steel exporters, Mexico in late 1984 agreed to limit steel exports to the United States, and the U.S. government, in turn, agreed to seek the withdrawal of the unfair trade petitions. The 1986 limits for steel produced outside the *maquiladora* framework were 0.36 percent of apparent U.S. consumption (compared with 0.83 percent in 1984) and 100,000 tons of semifinished steel.[27] This limit was increased by 12.4 percent for 1988.[28] Nevertheless, Mexico was adversely affected by the forced export limitation, but the limits placed on Mexican steel exports should be seen in the context of U.S. restrictions on steel imports from a number of providers.[29]

The principal U.S. nontariff barrier is what has come to be known as contingent protection.[30] This refers to actual or threatened actions, mostly at the initiative of U.S. producers facing foreign competition, to either limit imports or impose supplemental duties on the grounds of what have come to be known as unfair trade practices. Such practices include foreign subsidies (that is, government support to facilitate low export prices) or dumping (sales at less than fair value, usually cost plus profit) by foreign producers. Since U.S. tariffs are low and legislatively applied import quotas take much time to get approved even when they are imposed, charges of unfairness—contingent protection—have become a popular protective device in the United States. As seen by the steel example, an unfair trade petition can either result in the negotiation of a ''voluntary'' limitation by the exporting country or lead to a countervailing or antidumping duty.

Table 4.6 lists all the subsidy and countervailing-duty cases in the United States against Mexico between 1980 and 1986.

Table 4.6 U.S. Countervailing-Duty Cases Against Mexico, December 1980 Through December 1986

Product	Initiated[a] (month/year)	Determination[b] (month/year)	Action at Determination[c]	Action at Most Recent Review[d]
Leather wearing apparel	12/80	10/81	5% CVD	0–11.75% CVD[e]
Ceramic tile	10/81	5/82	15.84% CVD	0–3.13% CVD
Toy balloons and playballs	1/82	12/82	5.97–6.23% CVD	1.98–2.92% CVD
Polypropylene film	7/82	4/83	Suspended (5.68)[f]	Suspended
Pectin	7/82	4/83	Suspended (11.19)	Suspended
Litharge	7/82	6/82	3.73% CVD	0% CVD
Yarns of polypropylene fiber	9/82	4/83	Suspended (4.28)	Suspended
Iron-metal construction castings	10/82	3/83	2.85% CVD	0% CVD
Anhydrous and aqua-ammonia	11/82	6/83	Dismissed	n.a.
Fresh asparagus	11/82	5/83	Dismissed	n.a.
Carbon black	12/82	6/83	2.55% CVD	3.08% CVD
Portland hydraulic cement and cement clinker	4/83	9/83	0–17.12% CVD	0–3.26% CVD
Pork-rind pellets	4/83	8/83	Dismissed	n.a.
Unprocessed float glass	10/83	6/84	Suspended (2.54)	Suspended
Fresh-cut flowers	10/83	4/84	Dismissed	n.a.
Carbon-steel products	12/83	n.a.	Terminated[g]	n.a.

(continued)

Table 4.6   (*Continued*)

Product	Initiated[a] (month/year)	Determination[b] (month/year)	Action at Determination[c]	Action at Most Recent Review[d]
Bricks	11/83	5/84	3.51% CVD	0–11.75% CVD
Bars, rebars, and shapes	4/84	8/84	2.03–104.58% CVD	Revoked[h]
Lime	4/84	9/84	0–55.89% CVD	n.a.
Oil-country tubular goods	7/84	11/84	5.84% CVD	Revoked[h]
Textiles and textile-mill goods	8/84	3/85	3.7% CVD	n.a.
Fabricated auto glass	8/84	1/85	4.63% CVD	0% CVD
Welded carbon-steel pipes and tubes	11/84	n.a.	Terminated	n.a.
Portable aluminum ladders and components	4/85	n.a.	Terminated	n.a.
Welded steel wire fabric for concrete reinforcement	12/85	n.a.	Terminated	n.a.
Porcelain-on-steel cookware	12/85	10/86	1.97% CVD	Lapsed[i]

n.a. = Not applicable.

[a]Date of petition.

[b]Date of final determination.

[c]When a subsidy is found, the determination establishes a past rate and estimates the deposit needed to compensate for future subsidies. The two rates are often the same. The percentage shown is for the past subsidy. CVD refers to the indicated countervailing duty to nullify the effect of the subsidy.

[d]Most subsidy cases are reviewed some time after the final determination, and this may change the earlier determination.

[e]When a range for the CVD is shown, this is to capture the subsidy determination for different exporters.

[f]Suspended refers to agreement by producer/exporter to cease the subsidization. The figure in parentheses is the rate of subsidy found that is being suspended.

[g]Termination refers to action taken before final determination.

[h]Various subsidy cases involving steel products were revoked after Mexico agreed to voluntarily restrain steel exports.

[i]This case lapsed after the United States–Mexico bilateral agreement was signed providing an injury test before the application of U.S. countervailing duties against Mexican subsidies.

Source: Based on table prepared by Richard C. Henderson, U.S. Department of Commerce.

Section 301 of the U.S. Trade Act of 1974, amended in 1984, permits the president to impose restrictions on imports if he concludes that foreign actions deny benefits to the United States under any trade agreement or if foreign practices are judged to be unjustifiable, unreasonable, or discriminatory.[31] This is broad power indeed. The authority of the 1974 law was expanded in 1984 by extending the president's scope to deal with foreign barriers to trade in services and denial of national treatment to U.S. investors. The so-called super 301 added in the 1988 Trade Act expands the retaliatory authority of the executive branch. The law contains procedures for dispute settlement with the foreign government, including recourse to the GATT if the issue is covered by the articles, but in the end permits the United States to take unilateral action if a mutually acceptable solution is not found. In other words, it is contingent protection writ large, and therefore limits the ability of producers that depend on exports to the United States to plan their production with certainty.

The most publicized unfair trade case in recent years was that involving Mexican fresh fruit and vegetable exports to the United States. In 1985, fruit, nut, and vegetable imports from Mexico amounted to $676 million.[32] In the 1984/85 U.S. crop year (November 1, 1984, to October 31, 1985), about 70 percent of Mexican fresh fruits and vegetables entered during the winter, November through April. The main product is tomatoes, but others include cucumbers, eggplant, onions, green peppers, squash, asparagus, broccoli, cauliflower, okra, strawberries, cantaloupes, and grapes. The Mexicans compete during the winter with produce from Florida, California, and Texas, as well as with cold-storage products. In 1978, producers of Florida winter vegetables submitted an antidumping case against the Mexican suppliers alleging that they were selling produce at less than fair value. This charge was preliminarily rejected by the U.S. Treasury Department in 1979 and then rejected in a final determination by the U.S. Commerce Department in 1980.[33] During this two-year period, the export trade was made uncertain in that a decision against Mexico would have resulted in increased duties, both prospectively and retroactively. The threat of renewed harassment is never absent.

The United States justifies contingent protection by charging that many foreign trade practices are unfair. Foreign suppliers in turn claim that unfairness is charged quite promiscuously whenever they increase their position in the U.S. market. The very label can disrupt trade by triggering a formal investigation whose outcome is unknown; consequently, the level of duties that will ultimately be levied is unknown.

The issue is difficult: unfairness in the form of subsidies or dumping often exists. How one defines dumping can be a complex issue; in the winter vegetable case, it hinged on whether sales of fresh vegetables at different prices at varying periods after harvest were a prudent business measure to avoid spoilage or predatory marketing. It was clear until Mexico and the United States signed a bilateral agreement in 1985 covering subsidy and countervailing-duty practices that it was open season on filing subsidy charges against imports from Mexico because the mere existence of a subsidy, regardless of the degree of injury it caused a U.S. producer, was enough to trigger a countervailing duty.[34] This is evident from the large number of cases filed against Mexico between 1980 and 1986 (Table 4.6).

The U.S. Congress is probably the main generator of contingency protection that Mexico must confront. The Canadian ambassador to the United States has pointed out that various types of U.S. legislative impulses can affect Canada: legislation directed specifically at Canada; generalized legislation to protect Americans against foreign trade practices; legislation directed inwardly, such as to protect the environment, that affects foreign countries; and legislation put forth by a single legislator that has an intended or unintended effect on Canada.[35] The point of the observation is that Canada must be constantly alert to protect itself. So must Mexico and for the same reasons.

This attention to legislative processes is necessary for all countries, but the separation of powers makes U.S. protective practice especially unpredictable. The unintended effects, moreover, are particularly strong for countries like Canada and Mexico, because of their great dependence on the U.S. market. What the U.S. Congress deems mostly internal, such as marketing regulations for fresh vegetables or a tax on petroleum to help finance the environmental superfund, can have significant economic repercussions on Mexico.[36]

Increasing U.S. protectionism is at the heart of the Mexican concern about future trade between the two countries. There is irony in this. Officials in the United States have urged Mexico to open its market, arguing that this would make Mexican products more competitive in export markets.[37] Mexico, for reasons of its own, is now following this advice, really for the first time in any serious way since the end of World War II. However, as the new policy succeeds, individual instances of U.S. protection are emerging in ever-increasing fashion, including attacks against preferences for specific Mexican products, questioning the validity of 806.30 and 807.00, forcing cutbacks in Mexican steel exports, and who knows what else next. Protectionist proposals made in the U.S. Congress are limited only by the imaginations of members of Congress and their interested constituents.

For many years, Mexican authorities cried wolf about U.S. trade restrictions. The fear of contingent U.S. protection, however, now has roots in reality. Actual U.S. restrictions against imports from Mexico—other than those on health grounds—are still relatively modest (certainly when compared with Mexican restrictions), but recent tendencies give little ground for optimism.

The U.S. complaint has not been that Mexican import policy has been discriminatory, despite the quotation cited at the beginning of this chapter, but that it has been excessively restrictive even for a developing country. Specific U.S. accusations generally are in response to importunings from U.S. producers and therefore usually reflect the reality of being locked out of or limited in entry to the specific Mexican markets. Yet in a broader economic sense, the narrow charges are simplistic. There is no evidence that U.S. exports, measured in their totality, were excluded from the Mexican market for reasons other than the availability of foreign exchange in Mexico. This was evident from the consistent U.S. surpluses in trade with Mexico before 1982. What the Mexican import-substitution process accomplished was to shift the composition of its imports, and hence of U.S. exports, from consumer to intermediate and capital goods. There was not enough foreign exchange available for Mexico to have imported increased consumer goods along with other goods. In the four to five years prior to the crisis in Mexico's balance of payments in 1982, increased total imports were based largely on an excessive debt buildup, a policy that collapsed.

Despite all the U.S. complaints, the restrictive Mexican import system really favored the United States. The imports curtailed by denial of licenses were mostly consumer goods in which the United States was losing competitiveness. The imports encouraged, of intermediate goods and capital goods, were those in which

U.S. competitiveness endured longer. The trade pattern fostered by Mexico resulted in advantages for intra-industry trade, which benefited U.S. producers because of their predominance among foreign investors in Mexico. The wisdom of Mexico's import-substitution policy can be questioned, but it is hard to make a case on other than a product-by-product basis that U.S. exports to Mexico were curtailed by the policy.

Lowering of Mexican Import Protection

Before examining the steps taken by Mexico that are opening the economy to foreign trade, recent developments in Mexico's trade should be set forth because they explain the motivations of the new policy. Table 4.7 lists Mexican imports by type of product. The decline during the past twenty-five years in the proportion of

Table 4.7 Mexican Imports, FOB, by Type of Product, 1960–1987

Year	Total	Consumption	Intermediate	Capital
Millions of Dollars				
1960–1969[a]	1,366	285	509	721
1970–1979[a]	5,599	616	3,091	1,798
1980	18,832	2,450	11,209	5,174
1981	23,930	2,813	13,541	7,575
1982	14,437	1,517	8,418	4,503
1983	8,551	614	5,741	2,197
1984	11,254	848	7,833	2,573
1985	13,212	1,082	8,966	3,165
1986	11,432	846	7,632	2,954
1987	12,223	768	8,825	2,631
Percent				
1960–1969	100	20.1	37.3	52.8[b]
1970–1979	100	11.0	55.2	32.1
1980	100	13.0	59.5	27.5
1981	100	11.8	56.2	31.7
1982	100	10.5	58.3	31.2
1983	100	7.2	67.1	25.7
1984	100	7.5	69.6	22.9
1985	100	8.2	67.9	24.0
1986	100	7.4	66.8	25.8
1987	100	6.3	72.2	21.5

Note: Totals may not add due to rounding and inconsistency of data from different sources, especially for earlier years. Showing only annual averages for 1960 to 1969 and 1970 to 1979 conceals steady import growth over each decade.

[a]Annual averages

[b]This figure is probably high, based on inconsistency of data.

Sources: Banco de México, *Indicadores económicos*; Nafinsa, *La economía mexicana en cifras*.

A MARRIAGE OF CONVENIENCE

Table 4.8 Mexican Exports by Economic Activity, 1960–1987

Year	Total	Agriculture[a]	Manufactures	Mining[b]	Other[c]
Millions of Dollars					
1960–1969[d]	1,035	522	244	189	80
1970–1979[d]	3,482	809	1,372	947	354
1980	15,308	1,544	3,379	10,381	4
1981	19,420	1,481	3,428	14,507	4
1982	21,230	1,233	3,386	16,602	9
1983	21,399	1,285	4,519	15,590	5
1984	24,054	1,460	5,452	17,140	2
1985	21,664	1,409	4,978	15,277	202
1986	16,031	2,098	7,116	6,817	0
1987	20,656	1,543	9,907	9,206	0
Percent					
1960–1969	100	50.4	23.5	18.3	7.8
1970–1979	100	23.2	39.4	27.2	10.2
1980	100	10.1	22.1	67.8	—
1981	100	7.6	17.6	74.7	—
1982	100	5.8	15.9	78.2	—
1983	100	6.0	21.1	72.9	—
1984	100	6.1	22.7	71.3	—
1985	100	6.5	23.0	70.5	—
1986	100	13.1	44.4	42.5	—
1987	100	7.5	48.0	44.5	—

Note: Totals may not add due to rounding and inconsistency of data from different sources, especially for earlier years. Showing only annual averages for 1960 to 1969 and 1970 to 1979 conceals steady export growth over each decade.

[a]Includes forestry and fishing.
[b]Includes petroleum
[c]Includes some services related to trade.
[d]Annual averages
— = Less than one-tenth of 1 percent.
Sources: Banco de México, *Indicadores económicos* and *Informes anuales*; Inegi, *Anuario estadístico*, various issues.

consumer goods in the total and the increase in intermediate products is evident. Yet the data actually understate the decline in manufactured consumer-goods imports, since a large proportion of what does enter Mexico under the consumer-goods category consists of basic foodstuffs, primarily grains and oilseeds.

Table 4.8 shows Mexican exports by economic activity, and demonstrates first the growth in importance of petroleum in total Mexican exports as prices increased, and then its decline when oil prices fell, especially in 1986. The table also shows the increase in manufactured exports, both absolutely and as a proportion of total exports, since 1983. Product diversification of exports came less by choice than from necessity, and the current import opening is designed to make this export diversification permanent.

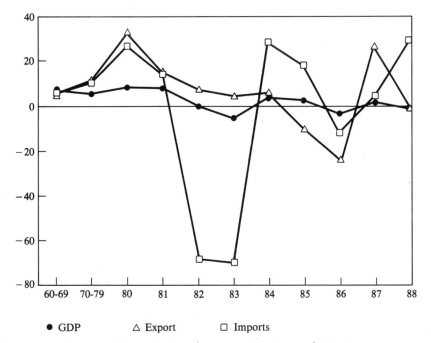

● GDP   △ Export   □ Imports

Figure 4.1   Mexican GDP, Exports and Imports (percentage change)

Note: Foreign-trade dollar data were deflated by the U.S. producer price index for intermediate goods on the assumption that these goods constituted the majority of trade with Mexico's main market and source. The percentage changes are quite close if the deflator used is U.S. producer prices for finished goods. While the precise percentages differ, the direction of changes and the nature of the relationships are not altered if foreign-trade data are not deflated.

Source: GDP percentage changes calculated from data in constant prices in Banco de México, Informes anuales, various years, and La economía mexicana en cifras 1981. Import and export changes from data in Banco de México, Indicadores económicos.

During the 1960s, the ratio between the growth of Mexican imports and the growth in Mexican GDP was 0.85; that is, GDP growth was sustained without swamping the country with imports (Figure 4.1). The ratio increased to 1.80 during the 1970s and then became explosively unpredictable in the 1980s. The increase in the ratio during the 1970s was caused by the rush to industrial development during the López Portillo administration. Once oil prices declined, the only resources that could sustain the import binge were from external debt, and this was not durable. In 1982, imports declined by about seventy times the fall in GDP and then by thirteen times in 1983.[38] The Mexican economy was starved of imports during these two years, but this situation could not be sustained indefinitely. Over time, the growing import demand must be met by growing exports. This explains the current export mentality.

One final table dealing with the development of Mexico's balance of payments is useful for understanding the Mexican foreign-exchange problem (Table 4.9). The turnaround in the current account starting in 1982 reflects primarily the change in the trade account. But, just as the trade surplus could not be sustained only on the basis of curtailed imports, the maintenance of a current-account surplus is tenuous

Table 4.9 Mexico's Balance of Payments (millions of dollars)

	1970	1975	1980	1981	1982	1983	1984	1985	1986	1987
Current account	-1,188	-4,443	-7,233	-12,544	-6,221	5,418	4,239	1,237	-1,673	3,881
Trade	-1,039	-3,637	-3,700	-4,510	6,783	13,761	12,942	8,452	4,599	8,432
Non-factor services[a]	-205	-939	-3,798	-8,323	-851	621	950	682	965	1,975
Factor services	*	*	*	*	-12,663	-9,265	-10,064	-8,899	-7,701	-7,195
Transfers	56	133	275	289	296	301	411	1,002	466	668
Capital account	849	5,459	11,948	21,860	6,754	-1,278	39	-1,527	1,837	1,199
Long term	561	4,373	6,835	11,696	15,203	7,108	3,617	261	1,146	4,356
Short term	288	1,086	5,113	10,163	-8,449	-8,387	-3,578	-1,788	691	-3,157
Special drawing rights	45	0	74	70	0	0	0	0	0	0
Errors and omissions	396	-851	-3,648	-8,373	-5,271	-1,022	-924	-2,134	439	855
Change in gross reserves	102	165	1,151	1,012	-4,738	3,101	3,201	-2,328	985	6,924

*Factor and non-factor services not broken down separately.

Note: Discrepancies in totals are in original source.

[a]This includes various transactions at the frontier for which the method of calculation was changed in 1982. Therefore, data for years before 1982 are not comparable with those of 1982 and later.

Source: Banco de México, *Indicadores económicos.*

because of large payments for interest on foreign debt. When the current account dips back into deficit, this implies an increase in foreign borrowing. The essential corrective to this situation is a growing export surplus. Table 4.9 brings out Mexico's large foreign borrowings in 1980 and 1981, shown in the capital account, and the substantial capital flight beginning in 1980, partly reflected in errors and omissions. Debt issues will be covered more completely in Chapter 7.

The trade account has thus become an essential element of the Mexican economic recovery. It will allow the generation of a current-account surplus necessary to meet debt-service payments without further debt buildup. Continued curtailment of imports would prejudice Mexico's industrial growth, since most imports are industrial inputs, and this places the main burden on the export side of the trade account. These imperatives explain the shift in trade policy more than all the importunings of the World Bank, the IMF, or the U.S. government. Although not all Mexicans accept this logic, preferring to believe there may be renewed life in a reprise of development from within, the official policy is based on a need to promote exports.

The Trade Policy Changes

Mexico formalized its accession to the GATT on July 24, 1986, and it became effective one month later, making Mexico the ninety-second contracting party.[39] The decision was a significant one, because of both the commitments made in the accession negotiations and the indications it gives of future trade policy.[40] The promise of GATT membership is that Mexico will be more open to imports in the future than in the past and that protection will take the form primarily of tariffs rather than quantitative restrictions.[41] This is not necessarily assured, since the GATT contracting parties, in practice, give much leeway to developing countries for departures from openness; but it makes little sense for Mexico to have joined GATT with the intention of violating its very premises.[42]

Following detailed negotiations, Mexico decided at the eleventh hour to reject accession in 1980. The question therefore arises as to why the Mexican authorities changed their collective mind in 1986. The major reasons are embodied in the trade and balance-of-payments data discussed earlier; they demonstrate that the closed economic model was no longer viable. Mexico did not have the cushion of oil revenue in 1986 that in 1980 had provided a false sense of security to policymakers. One Mexican analyst argued that the options open to Mexico in 1986 were the status quo, bilateralism, or multilateralism, and he rejected the first two as economically and politically infeasible.[43] The other argument put forward by proponents of accession, such as Ricardo Peña Alfaro, was that trade negotiations in a multilateral context improved Mexico's relative power.[44]

When accession had been rejected six years earlier, one argument was that membership would increase Mexico's dependence on the United States because of the great U.S. influence in the GATT.[45] But Mexico's decision to distance itself from the GATT and its instruments actually led to increased bilateralism with the United States.[46] Mexico's lack of adherence to the code on subsidies and countervailing duties resulted in the protective open season on Mexico noted earlier, and forced the government to conclude a bilateral agreement under which Mexico promised to alter its export subsidy practices in return for a U.S. promise not to impose countervailing duties unless it could be demonstrated that a U.S. industry was injured, or threatened with injury, from Mexican subsidies. What Mexico obtained bilaterally could have been acquired in a multilateral framework under the GATT code on this subject.[47]

The Peña Alfaro logic, that there is strength in developing-country unity inside the GATT, merits elaboration. Trade bargaining takes place between nations, regardless of their degree of economic integration, unless a country completely isolates itself from the world, as Albania did for many years. Because of the extent of their de facto integration, bargaining between the United States and Mexico, at governmental and extra-governmental levels, is pervasive.[48] It is difficult to understand why the weaker country, Mexico, would eschew membership in an organization with rules for certain types of trade bargaining in favor of ad hoc negotiations without these explicit rules. That, in essence, was the consequence of the 1980 decision to stay out of the GATT.

One final argument used by proponents of accession to the GATT was that this was a way, perhaps the only way, to introduce coherence in Mexico's trade policy. Despite the evident weakness with the development-from-within model, Mexico toyed in 1980 to 1982 with even greater import restrictions. The model was developed by a group of advisers from Cambridge University, the Cambridge Policy Group, and called for direct and selective import controls run by import boards, a reduction of interest rates, and suspension of gradual depreciations of the peso.[49] The policy entailed even more closing of the economy. The Cambridge proposals coincided with the position of some advisers to President López Portillo, and many of the recommendations were, in fact, tried at the close of his administration in 1982. Many of these advisers remain active in Mexico and could once again become influential if the current opening of the economy does not lead to favorable results.

The structure of protection in Mexico was clearly not conducive to export expansion. In a study in 1984, the Instituto Mexicano de Comercio Exterior (Mexican Institute of Foreign Trade, IMCE) demonstrated the dramatic growth in the bias against exports between 1979 and 1981 and then the gradual reduction in this bias because of the currency depreciations starting in 1982.[50] It makes the point that the discretionary, case-by-case choice of protective levels for products discriminates among activities, whereas protection deriving from the exchange rate is uniform across activities.[51] The main conclusion that can be drawn from the IMCE study is that the discretionary determination of levels of protection, by product and sector, coupled with the Mexican habit of maintaining an overvalued exchange rate, not only led to disparities in levels of effective protection and effective subsidies, but also contributed to the noncompetitiveness of Mexican products. This conclusion was generally confirmed by separate analysis of domestic resource cost ratios.[52]

We are now witnessing Mexico's first serious experiment with openness in foreign trade in the post–World War II period. In addition to the GATT commitment, Mexico received a $500 million loan from the World Bank in 1986 whose objective was to liberalize the trade regime by phasing down nontariff barriers and otherwise changing trade policy. These changes are to take place over a number of years, and the bank stated explicitly that it contemplated a series of loans over the 1986 to 1989 period *pari passu* with Mexican liberalization performance.[53] The loans from the World Bank reinforce the decision to enter GATT and thus strengthen the promise of trade reform.

Political Implications of Trade Opening

Several reasons explain the uncertainty about the durability of Mexico's trade opening. The first is that it is a significant change from past policy, and wrenches of this magnitude in the way business is done are unsettling. There have been past liberalization efforts, none as ambitious as those currently under way, and each foundered because of internal political opposition.

The more important reason to expect dissent about economic opening, really an explanation of why trade liberalization is so controversial, is that the stakes within the society are high. A system of controlled imports, reinforced by an overvalued exchange rate that makes it cheap to acquire foreign inputs, creates a particular set of winners. They include the protected industrialists, organized labor in these industries, and the bureaucracy, of both the government and the official party. Protected Mexican industrialists and their workers had no reason to fear external competition. They were generally not productive enough to export competitively, but the noncompetitive domestic market belonged to them at their prices. The official bureaucracy literally held life-and-death control over industrial activities through its ability to make general rules about imports, while also having discretion over individual decisions on import licenses and duty exoneration. The PRI can be seen as an extension of the official bureaucracy. Since organized labor has been strongest in unions of state-owned enterprises, the PRI had another element of control, while benefiting the workers involved.

There has been much debate in Mexico about the tendency to fill senior positions in the government, including the presidency itself, with technicians as opposed to politicians. One aspect of this debate that is rarely articulated clearly is that politicians would not be likely to open the Mexican economy, since this involves loss of a major aspect of patronage and control, and that it required the *técnicos* first to liberalize the economy and now to keep it open. This may be the most significant aspect of the choice of Carlos Salinas de Gortari, a *técnico*, to succeed Miguel de la Madrid as president.

Winners from an opening are hard to define precisely, and what winners there are will depend on the success of the experiment. If manufactured exports grow, as they have since 1986, the constraint placed on the Mexican economy from the balance of payments will be eased. This is the main objective of the liberalization. Those producers able to compete internationally will be winners. And if the opening succeeds, the big winner will be Mexican labor as a whole—those persons not affiliated with the protected or the government sector and whose rewards lagged in the protected model. The Mexican consumer should end up paying less for imported commodities, whether used directly or as inputs into other goods. The experiment, in short, deals with potential income shares, a profound political issue over which revolutions and civil wars have been fought.

There is an equally far-reaching political-economic consequence of opening an economy. In an open economy in which the decision to import grows out of price considerations rather than official discretion, the role of the bureaucracy changes. The bureaucracy will still control key aspects of the import environment through the level of the tariff and the manipulation of the exchange rate, but this control will decline as the tariff is lowered—provided the exchange rate is not allowed to become overvalued, thereby losing its function of protecting domestic producers against cheap imports. The elimination of case-by-case discretion over permission to import and the terms of this import can be telling in reducing the scope for official corruption. Flexible rules breed corruption; general procedures under which price, not fiat, determines outcomes remove this potential source of dishonesty. Corruption will not disappear in Mexico as trade is liberalized, but one important temptation will be diminished.

Finally, if trade liberalization is combined with diminution of the number of enterprises operated by the state, key tools of political control and patronage will be altered. Under these circumstances, the very political process in Mexico could be changed. This is one aspect of the technician–politician debate. There would be reason to be skeptical about Mexico's continued dedication to trade liberalization, subsidy reduction, and privatization—all of which were stated policy of the de la Madrid administration and of his chosen successor, Carlos Salinas de Gortari— should the politicians regain control of the state machinery.

Is trade liberalization reversible? The answer is obviously yes, but the longer the liberalization process endures, the harder it will be to change course once again. A new set of vested interests will have been established. Just as it is a trauma to shift from discretionary decisions to generalized price protection for imports, so would it be traumatic to shift back again if the new rules become entrenched.

The PRI is thus caught in an impossible position. If the trade opening fails to achieve its main objective of reducing the balance-of-payments constraint, the PRI will take much of the blame as the party in power. If the opening succeeds, much of the bureaucratic machinery on which the PRI relies for its strength will become obsolete. This process will take at least a few years to work itself out. What is involved is not just trade policy, but the economic-political ramifications of complex changes that have been set in motion.

Looking Ahead

One should not overstate. Mexico is opening its market, but the changes now taking place will not create a completely open market. Tariff levels will still be relatively high, and residual quantitative import restrictions still significant. The durability of the process is uncertain.

However, the direction in which Mexico is moving will tie its economy to what is taking place in the world economy more than at any time in the past fifty years. In view of the natural trade and industrial links with the United States, the current policy will reinforce the economic integration that already exists between the two countries. This is understood by those Mexicans who oppose the trade opening. Mexico's failure to enter the GATT in 1980 required the country to reach bilateral understandings with the United States, but Mexico's trade opening, symbolized by entry into the GATT in 1986, is almost certain to intensify economic relations with the United States even further. This, too, is clear to the Mexican authorities.

Despite the GATT multilateralism, Mexico did conclude a so-called framework trade agreement with the United States in November 1987 calling for negotiations and consultations on a variety of trade issues, investment policy, and treatment of intellectual property.[54] Both Mexico and the United States have decided that their mutual interests are best served by a combination of multilateralism and explicit bilateralism. Both elements of the combination are new for Mexico, and the duality provides Mexico with multiple future options in its trade policy.

There has been a secular tendency of the two economies to integrate, and any effort to alter this tendency would undoubtedly be costly in terms of reduced Mexican economic growth. The integration exists in factor markets—for labor and capital—and is growing in product markets as well, as exemplified by industrial complementarity and trade. It occurred even during Mexico's period of extreme import substitution and is likely to proceed even faster as this policy is jettisoned.

5

INDUSTRY

> The fundamental purpose of this program is for Mexico to succeed in becoming an intermediate industrial power toward the end of the present century.
>
> PROGRAMA NACIONAL DE FOMENTO INDUSTRIAL Y COMERCIO EXTERIOR 1984-1988

> The public sector is the principal buyer of capital goods in Mexico and its actions in this respect are decisive to stimulate import substitution and development of the capital goods industry.
>
> MÉXICO: LOS BIENES DE CAPITAL EN LA SITUACIÓN ECONÓMICA PRESENTE, 1985

> Except for the maquiladora at the northern frontier, the remaining industrial enterprises, including those most recently created, generally have negative external balances.
>
> SAÚL TREJO REYES, 1982

Changing Industrial Policy

Constants in post–World War II Mexican industrial policy have involved the protection of domestic industry, the imposition of domestic-content provisions to encourage production of intermediate goods, pressure to encourage exports by using the leverage of import permits needed by foreign-controlled industries, and the effort to Mexicanize industry. The policy can be said to have worked—a national industry was established. But it was costly and contained its own difficulties; the most important was that the combination of import protection and mandatory domestic-content proportions led to a lack of competitiveness in Mexican industry generally. Under the pressure of declining oil-export receipts and the need to replace this revenue with other exports, the rigidity of earlier import restrictions is being softened. It is not yet clear to what extent this emphasis on nonpetroleum (industrial) exports will endure if petroleum prices rise again, since there are strong interests in industrial protection, but Mexican industrial policy cannot return to the previous status quo.

Mexican acceptance of foreign direct investment has taken place on a negotiated, case-by-case basis that generally has continued through the economic crisis that has beset Mexico since 1982. What is different, however, is that Mexico is now beseeching foreign investors to come but the investors are not clamoring at the gates. Flexibility on Mexicanization (majority Mexican ownership) was passive earlier; it is now active and even being publicized abroad.

Mexico has a modest domestic market today, but a potentially large one in the future, and one objective of Mexican industrial policy is to use the attraction of the actual and projected domestic market as a lure to promote exports. This has been at the heart of policy in at least two industries, automotive and computers, and seems to be succeeding, as we shall see later in the chapter. Two essential reasons for success are the achievement of sufficient scale of production in Mexico to keep product prices competitive and the proximity and scope of the U.S. market. The success relies less on the exchange of finished goods than on that of intermediate products, goods that themselves are used in the production of final goods.

As trade increases, industry in Mexico and the United States will become more integrated. Earlier output was primarily for sale in Mexico, but intermediate goods will increasingly be shipped in both directions as Mexican production becomes more competitive. The stages of development can make industrial exchange complementary in that U.S. technology will be exported to Mexico and lower Mexican wage rates will be incorporated into products, particularly intermediate products, produced in plants of sufficient size and productivity for use in final U.S. products.

These developments often generate substantial controversy, as we shall see in the case of the pharmaceutical industry, but they inevitably also require cooperation. Industrial relations between two countries whose economies are becoming increasingly intertwined will thus involve constant negotiation, not just between governments, but at the industry level itself. These negotiations will concern such basic issues as what to produce, where to produce, and how to interchange this production.

Past Mexican Industrial Policy

After World War II, Mexico behaved like many other catch-up countries seeking to develop their industrial bases, assuming that underdevelopment was a consequence of underindustrialization. This logic came naturally, as it had to other relatively less-developed countries during previous centuries. From Alexander Hamilton's 1791 *Report on the Subject of Manufactures*, which argued the case for infant-industry protection in the young United States, to the United Nations Economic Commission for Latin America (ECLA) under its then director, Raúl Prebisch, the thesis was that unequal exchange was inevitable between countries exporting primary products and those exporting manufactured goods.[1] This inequality, ECLA argued, manifested itself in the movement of the terms of trade; the ratio between export and import prices allegedly deteriorated consistently for exporters of primary commodities but improved for exporters of manufactured goods. In practical terms, this implied that it took more and more exports of primary products to import the same volume of manufactured goods.

The cure was to industrialize, a powerful thesis that swept the field in Latin America during the 1960s and lingers in modified form to this day. This analysis was used to justify programs of import-substituting industrialization (ISI) in all Latin American countries capable of doing so, and even in many smaller countries that lacked the population and income base to rely predominantly on the internal market necessary for the policy to succeed. It was the basis for Mexico's development-from-within policy.

The progression Mexico followed began with the establishment of relatively simple industries for which there was an evident domestic market as measured by the level of imports. These were mostly consumer goods. Many of these industries already existed—for shoes, clothing, household pots and pans, and the like—and new ones were established, some similar to those previously existing and others more complex, such as for household durables like refrigerators, washing machines, and stoves.

It was relatively simple to protect this production for final domestic demand against imports. The principal device used by Mexico was import licensing; the denial of a license provided absolute protection, except for contraband goods. The result was that there was only modest competition within Mexico, and consumer goods were more costly than they would have been had imports been permitted. This is an inevitable price that consumers must pay for infant-industry protection. The objective is to compensate in the long term by establishing an industrial structure.

What was not made evident in the original conceptualization of import-substituting industrialization was that while a country could keep out competing final goods, its infant industries needed intermediate and capital goods in the production process. What became apparent in practice was that import substitution did not necessarily mean curtailment of imports, but a change in their composition. Mexico's merchandise trade deficit increased consistently until the scarcity of foreign exchange acted as a brake on imports in 1982, and most imports took the form of intermediate and capital goods. In 1985, for example, the proportion of imports was 8 percent consumer goods, 68 percent intermediate goods, and 24 percent capital goods. The breakdown was almost identical in 1987.[2]

This first stage, what is often called "easy" import substitution, thus required amplification. In theory, this could have taken the form of gradually reducing the protection offered for production of consumer goods—infants are expected to grow up. Several attempts were made to do this, all abortive until 1986, but the latest effort is apt to be more durable because it is embedded in a total development policy and in international agreements with the International Monetary Fund (IMF), the World Bank, and the General Agreement on Tariffs and Trade (GATT).[3]

What Mexico did instead was to seek import substitution in intermediate-goods industries by regulation and in capital-goods production by subsidization. The main technique used for intermediate goods, which make up the bulk of Mexico's imports, was to impose domestic-content requirements on producers of final goods. This was most notable in the automotive industry, but applicable also for computers, pharmaceuticals, and other industries. The philosophy behind domestic-content requirements was to force producers to buy goods in gradually increasing proportions of the value of final goods, a practice not unique to Mexico.[4] This inevitably raised the cost of inputs, since the ability to buy from the cheapest source was removed. Until domestic-content requirements reach the limiting proportion of 100 percent, this is less restrictive than denial of an import license, but it is of the same genre.

For capital goods, the main techniques for import substitution have been subsidies and government purchases. The quotation at the beginning of this chapter from the capital-goods study undertaken jointly by the Nacional Financiera of

Mexico and the United Nations Industrial Development Organization illustrates the latter point.[5] The *Programa nacional de fomento industrial y comercio exterior, 1984–1988 (National Program of Industrial Development and Foreign Trade 1984–1988*, Pronafice) is replete with the same recommendation of using preferential government procurement to stimulate domestic production of capital goods.[6]

Benefits and Costs of Industrialization

There is no simple way to measure the degree of success of past industrialization policy. Most Mexicans, and indeed non-Mexicans, who have examined Mexico's industrial development since World War II are convinced that the import-substitution or infant-industry-protection route was essential and that Mexico would not have the industrial base that now exists without it.[7] The proportion of manufacturing in gross domestic product (GDP) increased steadily under ISI, at least until the 1970s (Table 5.1). So did employment in manufacturing; some 12 percent of Mexico's economically active population was engaged in manufacturing in 1984, or 19 percent if a broader definition of industry is used to include related activities such as construction.

But the import-substitution policy also had costs. The policy required budgetary support, and government subsidies and transfers in Mexico grew from 3.6 percent of GDP in 1970 to 13.4 percent in 1981.[8] About 17.5 percent of these went to manufacturing in 1980; if petroleum and basic petrochemicals and construction are added, the proportion of subsidies and transfers came to 36 percent in 1981. And as manufacturing and related industrial subsidies and transfers increased, less was

Table 5.1 Sectoral Participation in Mexico's Gross Domestic Product, 1950s to 1980s (average percentages for decade)

Sector	1950s[a]	1960s[b]	1970s	1980s	1982–1987[c]
Agriculture	18	15	11	9	9
Mining[d]	5	3	3	4	4
Manufacturing	18	22	24	24	24
Construction	4	5	5	5	5
Electricity	1	1	1	2	2
Commerce	30	25	26	25	24
Transportation	3	5	6	8	8
Financial services	22	12	11	10	10
Government services[e]	n.a.	14	14	15	15
Total	100	100	100	100	100

Note: Totals do not add to 100 due to rounding.

n.a. = Not available.

[a]Data for 1950s computed from 1960 input–output matrix, with 1960 = 100.

[b]Data for 1960s and subsequently use a different methodology and are not strictly comparable to figures for 1950s. Base of 100 for data after 1950s is 1970.

[c]Shown separately, since these are the years of economic crisis.

[d]Includes petroleum but not petrochemicals, which are included under manufacturing.

[e]Includes only services, not government or parastatal production, which is shown in appropriate sector.

Source: Calculated from Inegi data on national accounts and information provided by the Bank of Mexico.

Table 5.2 Sectoral Growth in Mexico's Gross Domestic Product, 1950s to 1980s (average annual percentages growth for decade)

Sector	1950s[a]	1960s[b]	1970s	1980s	1982–1987[c]
Agriculture	4.2	2.8	3.2	2.8	1.2
Mining[d]	6.0	4.7	7.8	5.6	0.5
Manufacturing	7.3	8.2	7.2	1.3	−0.5
Construction	6.8	8.9	6.5	−0.2	−3.4
Electricity	9.2	13.9	9.9	6.1	4.2
Commerce	6.4	7.2	6.5	0.5	−2.1
Transportation/Communication	6.5	6.3	10.8	3.3	0.3
Financial services	5.7	5.4	5.0	3.0	1.7
Government services[e]	n.a.	7.0	6.5	3.0	0.9
GDP	5.9	6.5	6.4	1.9	−0.24

Note: Totals do not add to 100 due to rounding.

n.a. = Not available.

[a]Data for 1950s computed from 1960 input–output matrix, with 1960 = 100.

[b]Data for 1960s and subsequently use a different methodology and are not strictly comparable to figures for 1950s. Base of 100 for data after 1950s is 1970.

[c]Shown separately, since these are the years of economic crisis.

[d]Includes petroleum but not petrochemicals, which are included under manufacturing.

[e]Includes only services, not government or parastatal production, which is shown in appropriate sector.

Source: Calculated from Inegi data on national accounts and information provided by the Bank of Mexico.

available in a finite budget for other sectors.[9] For example, the proportion of government subsidies going to agriculture declined sharply between 1975 and 1980, from 36.7 to 11.2 percent.[10]

The evidence is straightforward: the agricultural sector was forced to finance the industrialization of Mexico and suffered in the process. Overall agricultural growth averaged less than 3 percent a year after the 1960s (less than population growth for many years) compared with growth rates between 7 and 8 percent a year for manufacturing during the 1960s and 1970s (Table 5.2).[11] One analyst argued that making agriculture part of the industrialization process, thereby also internationalizing it, accelerated the depopulation of the countryside into urban slums.[12]

The most serious consequences of the development-from-within model became apparent when the oil market weakened. In 1981, the year before the economic crisis became manifest, petroleum and petroleum products constituted 75 percent of all Mexican exports, and manufactured goods only 12.5 percent. It became evident then, as it was to Mexican economists even during the height of the oil bonanza, that this degree of reliance on a single export product is foolhardy. Oil's role in the development plans of the López Portillo administration was to act as the lever for other development, to provide the foreign exchange and tax revenue on which other activities could build. Oil was milked, as agriculture had been earlier.

Petroleum products were priced domestically not at their world scarcity value, but at subsidized levels. They were treated as partially free goods, as agricultural goods had been earlier. As transfers away from the oil sector became increasingly difficult to sustain, attention became riveted on the noncompetitiveness of the nonoil industrial structure. In 1985, the share of oil exports dropped to 68 percent of the total, and manufactures increased to 24 percent. In 1986, as oil prices declined further and the export of manufactures increased, the shares were petroleum 39 percent and manufactures 44 percent.[13] The Mexican economy is still lopsided, but the crisis focused official minds on the reality that a noncompetitive industrial structure can create jobs during the easy import-substitution period, but not growing incomes after that.

Those manufacturers who had a vested interest in maintaining Mexico's protective structure had a corollary interest in maintaining an overvalued peso. Most could not compete in export markets in any event because their production was inefficient by world standards, but it was convenient to import intermediate and capital goods cheaply. This elaborate structure, built over forty years, became anachronistic when the oil price collapse made it imperative to develop nonoil exports.

It is possible that a resurgence in oil prices will lead to restoration of the old system, but there is overwhelming evidence that the easier times of industrial development from within cannot be resurrected. This is mostly, although not completely, recognized in Mexico's 1984 to 1988 industrial development program (Pronafice). The plan explicitly rejects a sharp dichotomy between import substitution and export promotion, and, indeed, most countries' industrial policies have a mixture of the two. However, the stated intention is to shift the bias toward exports for most consumer-goods and some intermediate-goods industries and to retain the import-substitution option for industries producing significant inputs, such as chemicals and fertilizers, and capital goods. The way it is phrased in the plan is that import substitution in the future will have a decidedly selective character in favor of strategic inputs and capital goods.[14] The plan should not be regarded as a blueprint, especially since its release coincided with an austerity program limiting the government's operating options, but it did represent something of a consensus.[15]

Industrial Relations with the United States

Mexico's industrial policy has often brought it into conflict with the United States. One reason is that setting minimum proportions of domestic content in the production of final goods is a powerful nontariff barrier. However, since Mexico was not a contracting party to the GATT until 1986, the United States had no legal handle for its complaints. The argument had to be based on efficiency considerations, and if Mexico chose to be inefficient, that was its business. The complaint may have more legal validity now that Mexico is a member of the GATT, but not much more because many other contracting parties impose domestic-content requirements on their producers.

Complaints by the United States were more vociferous regarding Mexican performance requirements. They were used most comprehensively in the automotive industry and specified that vehicle assemblers cover the foreign-exchange costs of their imports through their own or related Mexican vehicle or parts exports. The purpose of these provisions was similar to the domestic-content requirement—to develop intermediate-goods production in Mexico by forcing some exports—but they went one step further by seeking to balance imports with exports in specific sectors. Again, while the U.S. legal case was not strong as long as Mexico was outside the GATT, there was a powerful practical argument against the practice because it mandated Mexican automotive exports to the United States as the price of automotive imports from the United States, a situation U.S. automotive companies investing in Mexico were more willing to sanction than the U.S. government.[16] Official U.S. protests accomplished little, though, perhaps because until 1983 Mexico had a large and growing deficit in this sectoral trade.

The totality of the Mexican industrial activities described above, coupled with the trade incentives noted in Chapter 4, have come to be called "targeting" in the United States. "Industrial targeting is defined as coordinated government actions that direct productive resources to give domestic producers in selected nonagricultural industries a competitive advantage."[17] The U.S. International Trade Commission (USITC) cited automobiles, petroleum, petrochemicals, mining, chemicals, electronics, cement, steel, pharmaceuticals, and various types of machinery and consumer goods as industries targeted by Mexico. The USITC is equivocal about the effects of Mexican targeting, conceding that growth in manufacturing coincided with the extensive import-substitution period, while noting some of the competitive disincentives that accompanied past Mexican policy.

More germane issues are whether past Mexican industrial policy compromised U.S. industrial interests, and whether future policy need conflict with those interests. A related issue concerns the scope of potential industrial cooperation between the two countries. The remainder of this chapter will first examine these issues broadly, and then focus on three specific industries that Mexican authorities consider strategic.

Trade and Investment Effects of Mexican Industrial Policy

Except for temporary discontinuities during Mexican stabilization programs, U.S. merchandise exports to Mexico increased steadily during the import-substitution period. The U.S. export decline was a blip in 1977 (less than $200 million from 1976, about 3.5 percent) because the austerity program was short-lived, but was substantial in 1982 and subsequently because the austerity and economic decline lasted longer. The year-on-year decline in U.S. exports to Mexico between 1981 and 1982 was $6.8 billion, or 38 percent; there was a further decline between 1982 and 1983 of $2.2 billion, or 20 percent. The data lead to two conclusions: the major determinant of total U.S. exports to Mexico is growth of the Mexican economy and not Mexican industrial policy; and while industrial policy determines the composition of U.S. exports, it is not conclusive in determining their volume or value. United States exports to Mexico shifted in line with the incentives established by Mexico's industrial policy, from consumer to intermediate and capital goods. Another way to state this is that Mexico's policy created some winners and losers among U.S. producers; but as long as Mexico's economy was growing satisfactorily, the winners gained more than the losers lost.

This can be stated more strongly. Since the United States generally has been losing consumer exports to all destinations during recent decades, Mexico's import-substitution policy can be said to have favored U.S. producers. The policy encouraged precisely those imports for which U.S. comparative advantage endured longest (intermediate and capital goods) and curtailed those the United States would have lost in any event. While U.S. trade principles were offended by Mexico's import-substitution policy, U.S. trade as such undoubtedly benefited from it. This reality may explain the subdued nature of U.S. protests.

Mexico's foreign-investment laws and procedures are an admixture of nationalism and deliberate industrial policy. The nationalistic aspect is to limit foreign equity in Mexican corporations to a minority (at least in principle). The policy element is to direct investment into activities that the Mexican authorities consider to be of high priority.[18] Three key laws affect foreign investment: the foreign-investment law of 1973; the technology-transfer law of 1973, modified in 1982; and the law on inventions and trademarks of 1976, amended in 1987.

Each investment proposal involves a separate negotiation between the investor and the national commission on foreign investment established under the 1973 foreign-investment law. These negotiations deal with the foreign equity percentage (including exceptions to the minority presumption), displacement of national companies, balance-of-payments effects over time, employment consequences, use of domestic content, and the technology that comes with the investment. Since foreign direct investment constitutes 3 to 4 percent of gross domestic investment, the immediate capital inflow into Mexico is not normally a major consideration; the technology that comes with the investment and the subsequent exports and imports it will generate are of greater moment.

A national registry for the transfer of technology was established pursuant to the 1973 technology-transfer law, which monitors the cost and value to Mexico of imported technology, facilitates transfer of technology to Mexican nationals, and assists nationals in technology negotiations with foreign companies. The law on inventions and trademarks controls the duration of patents in Mexico, and is generally more restrictive than comparable U.S. legislation.[19]

Additional laws and decrees apply to specific industries, each having its own regulations, and sometimes there are additional regulations without decrees. The result is a complicated network, with varying requirements depending on the size of investment, the sector, location, and the nature of production and technology accompanying the investment.

Tables 5.3 and 5.4 tell a story roughly analogous to that of trade, that the level of new U.S. foreign direct investment (FDI) in Mexico depends less on Mexican regulations than on the growth prospects of the Mexican economy, since the main objective of most foreign companies is to expand their internal market in Mexico.[20] The salience of Mexican economic growth as the stimulator of FDI can be seen clearly in Table 5.3. The capital inflows were large in 1980 and 1981 when GDP growth rates were high, declined in 1982 when the economy faltered, and then dropped sharply after when the economy was in crisis. (The large inflows in 1986 and 1987, shown in Table 5.3, result from debt-equity swaps, and their significance is ambiguous.)

About two-thirds of FDI in Mexico comes from the United States, and U.S. investors behaved as did other investors—they came to Mexico in the good eco-

A MARRIAGE OF CONVENIENCE

Table 5.3 Direct Foreign Investment in Mexico, 1950–1987[a] (millions of dollars)

Years	Total	New Investment	Intracompany Accounts	Reinvestment
1950–1959[b]	103.8	61.2	9.4	33.1
1960–1969[b]	171.2	96.1	10.5	64.6
1970–1979[b]	569.8	239.3	54.4	276.2
1980	2,164.6	860.4	369.3	935.0
1981	2,835.7	1,336.5	234.1	1,265.1
1982	1,657.3	956.7	−69.8	770.4
1983	460.5	70.2	193.0	197.3
1984	391.1	543.4	−367.6	215.3
1985	490.5	269.6	−10.9	231.8
1986	1,522.0	944.0	−9.1	587.1
1987	3,248.0	2,386.0	200.0	661.7

Notes: Totals may not add due to rounding.

[a]The figures are actual capital flows, not commitments to invest.

[b]Annual averages. The use of an annual average for a decade makes the jump in flows from 1979 to 1980 appear larger than it was. The foreign direct investment flow increased from $316.2 million in 1970 to $1,371.4 million in 1979. There were also annual increases during most of the 1950s and 1960s.

Source: Banco de México, *Indicadores económicos*, and data provided by the Bank of Mexico.

nomic years and stayed away in the bad ones (Table 5.4).[21] One reason is that MNCs came to Mexico primarily to exploit the domestic market, which is not really what the Mexican government had in mind.

The operations of MNCs in Mexico have been analyzed in many studies over an extended period.[22] The results tend to be ambivalent, reflecting concern over the loss of Mexican control of the leading sectors of the economy while recognizing the need for investment that reflects the priorities of the authorities. This double sentiment is inherent in the 1973 foreign-investment law, which was itself intended to be a compilation of previous regulations, although it turned out to be marginally more restrictive. The provision calling for minority foreign ownership continues to be sensitive despite the fact that it is now often breached, and Mexican authorities worry that it would be politically explosive to actually change the law. President de la Madrid reflected this Mexican sensitivity when, following a United States–Mexico interparliamentary meeting in May and June 1986, he responded to suggestions from U.S. delegates that the law should be changed to permit foreign majority equity:

> We are not about to receive lectures on what is appropriate structural change for Mexicans in a way that would cause Mexico to lose its national essence. . . . Regarding foreign investment, we will continue to do what we want. [Foreign investment] should submit to our laws, our sovereignty, and support the priorities of the economic course of action that we define.[23]

Some highlights of a study by Kurt Unger, a Mexican economist who examined the trade consequences of foreign investment, merit examination.[24] Unger divided

Table 5.4 U.S. Direct Investment in Mexico, Year End 1980–1987[a] (millions of dollars)

	1980	1981	1982	1983	1984	1985	1986	1987
Total, worldwide	215,578	226,359	207,752	207,203	212,994	230,250	259,562	308,793
In developed countries	158,350	165,396	154,381	155,736	157,461	172,058	194,691	233,315
In developing countries	53,277	56,182	48,058	45,746	50,131	52,764	60,270	71,174
Mexico: value	5,989	6,977	5,019	4,381	4,568	5,088	4,750	4,997
As percent world	2.8	3.1	2.4	2.1	2.1	2.2	1.8	1.6
As percent developing countries	11.2	12.4	10.4	9.6	9.1	9.6	7.9	7.0
Percent U.S. investment in Mexico in								
Manufacturing	75.0	74.1	78.1	78.7	79.5	79.6	79.4	79.2
Wholesale trade	12.1[b]	12.6[b]	6.8	8.0	9.0	10.6	7.3	5.5
Finance and insurance[c]	3.3	2.6	3.6	3.3	4.2	3.6	3.3	3.9
Other	9.6	10.7	11.5	10.0	7.3	6.2	10.0	11.4
	100.0	100.0	100.0	100.0	100.0	100.0	100.0	100.0

[a]The figures are based on book value of direct investors' equity in and outstanding loans to foreign affiliates, that is, firms in which a foreign investor owns at least 10 percent of voting securities or the equivalent.

[b]Investment in retail trade is included in these years.

[c]Excludes banking.

Source: Survey of Current Business, various issues.

exports into priority and nonpriority categories, basing these on the classifications used in the 1979 to 1982 industrial development plan. (About 60 percent of all production fell into the priority category in that plan.) He found that 25 percent of exports in 1980 were from nonpriority activities. The remaining exports were from priority activities: 47 percent either nondurable or durable consumer goods; 21 percent intermediate goods; and only 7 percent capital goods. Thirty percent of the exports of national companies were from nonpriority activities (1975), and only 16 percent of foreign firm exports were in this nonpriority category. Fully 45 percent of exports of national firms were of nondurable consumer goods (only 5 percent of foreign firms' exports were in this category). By contrast, 73 percent of the exports of foreign firms were either consumer durables or intermediate goods (compared with only 18 percent in these categories for national firms).

Unger defined dynamic exports (he used the words *en surgimiento*) as those priority goods whose exports were large and made up a significant proportion of production. For these products, he found that 74 foreign firms (of the 708 foreign firms that produced priority manufactures in 1975) handled 91 percent of the exports. He then constructed a ratio of the value added in Mexico to imports (VA/M) for all manufactured exports and this came to 2.73 (1975); for priority activities, the ratio was 2.36. The ratio for nonpriority goods was higher (4.41) and was highest of all for nonpriority, nondurable consumer goods (24.05). The significance of these ratios is that the import content of most exports is quite high (about 37 cents of imports for each $1 of manufactured exports), except in those nonpriority activities in which Mexican resources form the basis for exports (which require only 4 cents of imports for each $1 of exports). The import content of exports was high in the automotive, electrical equipment, basic chemicals, pharmaceutical, and capital-goods industries; most sales of foreign firms in these and other priority industries are in the domestic Mexican market. Unger raises the question of whether the high import content of Mexico's priority exports does not contradict conventional arguments about Mexico's comparative advantage. Only nondurable consumer exports use a high proportion of Mexican inputs.

These findings support one of the key criticisms made by opponents of industrial policy, that governments can propose but companies acting in their own interest do most of the disposing. Mexico's regulations may have raised domestic content in many productive activities but still left the country with a high import content in the exports most avidly promoted. Domestic content dominated precisely where the government did not explicitly seek it.

Mexican opponents of MNCs have sometimes used data on these firms' imports and exports, making estimates of the true value of intrafirm transactions, to show that MNCs as a group import more than they export. This evidence is then used to imply that MNCs are harmful to the Mexican economy.[25] There is a kernel of truth to the criticism, but it is overall a simple-minded analysis, valuable only as polemic. It omits many economic effects that MNCs have on employment and in stimulating the growth of supplier and buyer industries within Mexico. Although MNCs may have had a negative trade balance in most years, it is usually far less negative than the trade balance of domestic manufacturing firms. While MNCs are vastly more export oriented than domestic firms, their main market remains within Mexico.

The Mexican authorities established criteria in permitting foreign investment, and, for the most part, they have been met. Multinational corporations were sought in priority activities, and Unger's data and the other studies cited earlier show that this, too, was accomplished. Finally, MNCs were encouraged successfully by the import-substitution policy to produce final goods for sale in Mexico more than intermediate or capital goods. Yet the achievement of these objectives is the very source of most complaints against MNCs—that they dominate priority activities in Mexico and do not produce or export enough Mexican goods with high VA/M ratios. Mexico mostly got the foreign investment it wanted, but afterward did not want what it got.

Specific Industries

One of this study's central themes is that centripetal forces of geography and the desire to raise incomes and employment have resulted in an ever-increasing degree of economic integration between Mexico and the United States. But various aspects of Mexico's industrial policy are designed to separate rather than integrate, including limits on foreign equity holdings and domestic-content and performance requirements. The evidence indicates, however, that even where these national measures succeeded—indeed, precisely because they succeeded—economic integration intensified.

American MNCs hold large market shares in Mexico for food processing, chemicals, machinery, and electrical, electronic, and transportation equipment, and are a major factor in the trade between the two countries. More than half of U.S. manufactured imports from Mexico in 1979 were from intracompany, or related-party, sales.[26] Often much competition exists for market shares between producers in the two countries—evident in the steel and cement industries—but also substantial cooperation. The cooperation is facilitated by the large trade in components rather than finished products. The *maquiladora* exemplify intra-industry trade and production exploiting the factor and market advantages of each country—the cheap labor in Mexico and the market in the United States—but the cooperation extends beyond what are essentially assembly plants. What follows is an examination of cooperation and conflict, and the potential for more cooperation, in three specific industries: automotive, computers, and pharmaceuticals. All are of high priority in Mexico, and each reflects both the workings of Mexican industrial policy and the growing industrial integration between the United States and Mexico. Other industries, such as machinery and chemicals, demonstrate the same points.

Cooperation between unequals has the potential for duress and exploitation, a truth all too evident from the history of United States–Mexico economic relations. Coercion by the United States was most blatant in the oil industry and partly explains the popularity of the nationalization of the industry in 1938. However, as Robert Keohane has noted in an analysis of political-economic relations among developed countries: "Hegemonic cooperation is not a contradiction in terms."[27] Industrial cooperation operates primarily through bargaining, sometimes at an intergovernmental level but also at the industry level or between a private U.S. company and the government–industry combination in Mexico. The interference

that marked official U.S. support of the oil industry in the years before nationalization is no longer the norm in U.S.–Mexican relations.[28] Though the U.S. government still occasionally exerts pressure on behalf of U.S. MNCs operating in Mexico, this is no longer the rule, but the exception. On the Mexican side, outright
nationalization of foreign-owned enterprises has not been the practice since the oil
expropriation. When López Portillo nationalized the banks in 1982, he deliberately
refrained from taking over the U.S. Citibank operation in Mexico.

Both governments enter into the bilateral industrial bargaining process. Mexico
does so largely through its majority ownership, domestic-content, and export requirements, and also through controls on technology and prices; the United States
does so frequently by the threat to withhold trade concessions (discussed below). It
is unclear which government will act more hegemonically in any given industrial
negotiation. The U.S. government pressure is exerted on the Mexican government,
while that of the Mexican government focuses on the foreign MNC. Under these
circumstances, the very concept of hegemony loses clarity.

Automotive

The automotive industry is probably the best example for illustrating Mexico's
industrial policy. Mexican authorities have devoted much attention and substantial
resources to it. Because it was seen as the industrial activity *par excellence* for
stimulating a host of related activities to supply parts and services, automotive
development was guided by a series of decrees focusing on industry ownership,
domestic content, and export stimulation, supplemented by import restrictions and
vast direct and indirect subsidies.[29] In short, the government picked what it decided
was a winner, and then tried to validate that choice by its subsequent actions.
Whether the benefits in production, employment, and income exceeded the costs of
the policy over the past twenty-five years is hard to say—no easy measure of the
opportunity cost of devoting resources to one industry rather than another exists.

Automotive development has been described in many studies and will only be
sketched in here to provide perspective for the policy discussion.[30] Policy for the
industry was set in a series of decrees, the main ones being in 1962, 1972, 1977,
and 1983. These decrees were accompanied by detailed implementing regulations
that established the ground rules for foreign investors. The most important provisions involved domestic-content requirements, limits on vertical integration by
assemblers to encourage parts production by Mexican-owned companies, export
requirements as the quid pro quo for allowing assemblers to import parts, and
limitations on the number of models that could be assembled to achieve scale
economies in production.

The general intent of the government remained reasonably consistent for a quarter
century. One objective was to reduce the number of lines and models produced in
Mexico to obtain economies in the terminal industry; this was achieved only in the
years after the most recent decree, that of 1983. In 1984, seven terminal companies
produced 244,704 automobiles; these seven plus two others together produced
113,294 trucks in 1984.[31] The government also wished to Mexicanize the terminal
industry, but this has not happened; foreign companies still dominate this sector of
the industry.

Another goal was to balance imports and exports in the automotive industry, but this was slow in coming. The automotive trade deficit peaked in 1981 at $2.1 billion, 58 percent of the total merchandise deficit. The deficit declined sharply in 1982 and was more or less in balance in subsequent years. The bilateral trade balance with the United States in vehicles and parts was $1.4 billion in favor of the United States in 1981, but only $180 million in favor in 1985.[32] Automotive parts are now among Mexico's most dynamic exports. It is difficult to know whether the current pattern in automotive trade is durable, since in addition to growing exports of parts, it reflects the decline in Mexico's economy and the lack of availability of foreign exchange for imports.

The development of a parts industry dominated by Mexican-owned firms was mostly, but not completely, accomplished. The techniques employed were local-content regulations, the inclusion of parts exports as an element of the export-performance requirements of the terminal industry, the provision of the 1972 decree calling for 60 percent Mexican equity for new parts firms compared with the norm of 51 percent for industry generally, and the limitation on vertical integration by the terminal industry, which is mostly foreign dominated.

There are 750 firms in the parts industry, and, with some exceptions, especially the *maquiladora* near the U.S. border, most are completely or majority Mexican-owned. Employment in the automotive industry is about 115,000 (1984 estimate), with about 60 percent in the parts as opposed to the terminal industry. About 90 percent of automotive exports in recent years have been parts instead of finished automobiles or trucks.

These indicators of a successful policy are counterbalanced by some unanticipated outcomes. Most parts exports are from firms that, while Mexicanized, have substantial foreign equity.[33] This may be what should have been expected, that foreign (especially U.S.) parts suppliers prefer to rely on affiliated firms to which they are also more prone to supply new technology. Mark Bennett has also shown that when the parts industry is broken down by principal components, it is highly concentrated. He attributes this to barriers to entry, some inherent in the production process (particularly scale and technology), but others the result of policy. He highlights the need for prior approval by the interministerial commission before output of a new firm can qualify as local content and before new technology can be imported, and institutional difficulties of obtaining credit.[34]

The Mexican automotive industry has had its ups and downs, reflecting two related cyclical considerations—the state of the U.S. economy and particularly that of the Mexican economy. The year 1982 was essentially a neutral one for the industry, 1983 atrocious, 1984 bad but not seriously so, 1985 very good, 1986 a bad year once again, 1987 modestly improved, and 1988 slightly better once again. These characterizations correlate closely with growth of the Mexican economy in each year and, since 1986, with the growth in exports of auto parts to the United States. Looking ahead for the rest of this century, growth of the U.S. economy is apt in the long run to be almost as important for the industry as growth in Mexico. For better or worse, the export market is gaining in relative importance, and the critical export market is the United States, another example of the integration of the two economies.[35]

Despite official U.S. criticism of Mexican targeting in the automotive industry, U.S. and other foreign companies have responded to the rules laid down by Mexico.[36] Each of the big three U.S. companies has expanded Mexican operations in recent years. Ford, in 1983, invested in a stamping and assembly plant in Hermosillo, Sonora, and opened a new engine plant in Chihuahua City. Both these operations envisage exports to the United States. About 25 percent of Chrysler's engines worldwide are produced in Mexico, and General Motors plans a $500 million investment over five years starting in 1987. Roughly 250,000 automobiles and trucks were sold in Mexico in 1987, of which the American big three had half.[37] The other major foreign car and truck producers, especially Nissan and Volkswagen (which rank one and two in sales), have also expanded investment in Mexico.[38]

There is, of course, another major consideration prompting foreign investment in the Mexican automotive industry—the prospective market within Mexico itself. The largest potential growth for automotive sales is not in industrial countries, in which most sales are to replace existing cars, but in the more advanced developing countries in which income increases will lead to new sales. In a discussion of periodic transformations in the automotive industry, the automobile study program of the Massachusetts Institute of Technology projects that the next major change is apt to take place in the late 1980s and the 1990s when production will be concentrated in locations with low factor costs and growing markets.[39] Mexico fits this description.

The MIT study makes another point that ties Mexico's automotive destiny with the United States. The final assembler is the coordinator of increasingly intricate production and marketing systems, and the final assemblers in Mexico are mostly U.S. companies, the same companies to which parts are being exported by Mexico.[40]

The development of its automotive industry has been costly to Mexico. The program was conceived to achieve a large degree of independence for Mexico in automotive production, but at the very moment that many other objectives of the program are being achieved, particularly the growth in exports to compensate for imports and perhaps even to consistently exceed imports, independence is more elusive than ever. The Mexican automotive industry is closely tied to the United States because that is where the export market is. Except to an ultra-nationalist, however, this need not be cause for alarm. The dependence is complex, since the production and export platforms are in Mexico and the market is U.S. companies in Mexico and the United States. All parts of this exchange are necessary for the chain to hold together.[41]

Computers

The general philosophy underpinning development of the computer industry is similar to that of the automotive industry but with substantial differences stemming from the value of output, employment, and the timing of start-up. The computer-industry program contains such familiar features as majority Mexican ownership as the preferred norm, domestic content in production, and export expansion. Compromise on these features, especially on 100 percent foreign ownership of new investment, came quickly in the development of the computer industry. This was caused partly by the circumstance that the most important computer negotiation took place with IBM in 1984 and 1985, when economic uncertainty made Mexico more a seeker of foreign investment than the recipient of requests by investors. Mexico's power to dictate the terms of foreign investment was never complete, but was clearly greater during the halcyon years of the 1960s and much of the 1970s than it has been since 1982.[42]

A study prepared for the U.S. Department of Commerce estimated that Mexico's production of mini- and microcomputers and peripherals was $283 million in 1984 and was expected to increase at an annual rate of 21 percent to $609 million in 1988. The percentage increases are large because of the low base, but the absolute numbers are still modest for an economy as large as Mexico's. There were few computer or peripheral exports until the 1980s, but the situation has been changing since 1985 and should alter further under the agreement with IBM. The import level was estimated at more than $100 million in 1984, but the figure is not meaningful because of the large gray or clandestine market in imported computers and peripherals.[43] This, too, may change under the agreement with IBM, since the price difference between Mexican and imported personal computers will be modest.

The interest of foreign firms in the market for hardware and software in Mexico is based on expectations similar to those of the automotive industry, that what today is a modest market is likely to grow into a substantial future one. The study for the Department of Commerce estimated that the market for hardware and peripherals would grow to $666 million in 1988 plus about half of that for software. Apparent consumption in 1988 turned out to be $388 million for hardware, $410 million for peripherals, and $140 million for software. All markets—for hardware, peripherals, and software—are dominated by firms affiliated with U.S. companies, in each case with IBM in the lead (about 45 percent for hardware and 37 percent for software), but with other companies actively participating. In 1985, there were 18 minicomputer and 14 microcomputer suppliers, and about 200 software operations, both joint ventures and local operations.[44] These numbers change a good deal over time, reflecting the dynamics of this industry.

The Mexican authorities developed a plan for the computer industry in 1981, but it was not formalized into a decree. The plan had the usual features (Mexicanization, domestic content, export pressure) and did serve as the basis for approval of investment in the hardware and peripheral industry despite its lack of legal status as a decree. Its framework guided the Mexican authorities in their negotiation with IBM. However, the flexibility allowed Mexican negotiators under the foreign-investment law did permit IBM to achieve its standard policy of obtaining 100 percent equity.[45]

Various features of the IBM agreement are worth describing because they illustrate important aspects of Mexican treatment of foreign investment.[46] These include both the case-by-case negotiating procedure and the flexibility the Mexican authorities regularly publicize to downplay the Mexicanization features of the foreign-investment law, the tradeoffs the authorities are willing to make on ownership and even domestic content for export expansion and technological development, and the political booby traps that negotiators must confront in making these trade-offs. The negotiations with IBM took place over approximately two years, from February 1984 to late 1985, and since IBM is a large company it can spare personnel for this lengthy process. Smaller companies may not be able to do this, and it has only been since the IBM experience, and the lengthy negotiation with Ford, coupled with the Mexican quest for new foreign investment, that some relaxation of the case-by-case approach has been made for smaller companies, particularly those bringing high technology to Mexico.

Mexico was attractive to IBM for several reasons. A plant producing electronic typewriters and System-36 computers, employing 400 people, already existed in El Salto, Jalisco, near Guadalajara. IBM officials also cited other attractions of investing in Mexico: its political stability; the long period without exchange controls (other than at the close of the López Portillo administration in late 1982), which allowed conversion of pesos into dollars and profit remittances; the general lack of confiscations of foreign investment in Mexico since the petroleum experience in 1938; the proximity of the plant to the *maquiladora* production of semiconductors; and Mexico's membership in the Asociación Latinoamericana de Integración (Latin American Integration Association, ALADI), which potentially provided some trade concessions for exports to other Latin American countries.

The first proposal from IBM, omitting detail, was to make personal computers (PCs) in its plant, export about 90 percent of the output, or approximately $500 million a year in gross terms once in full operation, and set up a distribution network in Mexico. There was a complex formula on local content. The company's insistence on 100 percent ownership sparked opposition from other foreign computer firms (Apple and Hewlett-Packard, for example) that had already invested in Mexico, since they had accepted 49 percent equity for microcomputer production. Mexican-owned firms with a vested interest in minimizing competition also objected to the IBM equity proposal. The first decision of the foreign investment commission, in December 1984, rejected the IBM proposal, but the Mexican authorities let it be known that they wanted IBM to resubmit a proposal. The ownership issue, despite publicity in both the Mexican and the U.S. press, would not be a major negotiating item because the Mexican authorities had the power to agree to 100 percent IBM ownership, and it was clear that IBM considered it a sine qua non for an overall agreement.

The next round of negotiations was more focused and was preceded by a private discussion between IBM officials and President de la Madrid. The key issue was the amount of exports and the trade balance within the industry—the Mexicans wished to achieve positive net exports once the plant was functioning.[47] It is worth recalling that it took Mexico more than twenty years to accomplish this in the automotive industry. Domestic content, which is related to the trade-balance question, was both a technical and a practical negotiating issue to determine what should be counted in the percentage (labor, overhead, markup, indirect parts, and assembly, as well as the local value added in the direct parts used in assembling the final product) and the time to achieve a given percentage. The last point involved an assessment of a learning curve for production of domestic content. The agreement called for reaching 65 percent domestic content in 1987 and 82 percent by 1989 and thereafter.

Job creation was an issue, both in numbers of jobs at IBM and in the nature and extent of the technical development of Mexicans. A press release from the Mexican embassy in the United States refers to the creation of 1,700 new jobs over a five-year period. Some training elements of the agreement involve scholarships for Mexicans at IBM facilities throughout the world, planned at four to five persons a year; partnerships with Mexican universities (for example, for teaching CAD/CAM [computer-aided design/computer-aided manufacturing] at the Monterrey Institute of Technology); and the establishment of a semiconductor technology center at the National Polytechnical Institute in Mexico City.

The heart of the agreement, most of which has been made public, calls for an initial IBM investment of $90 million for the production, initially, of the PC XT, with the intent to export at least 90 percent of production, generating more than $600 million of gross exports and $100 million in net foreign-exchange earnings over five years. The understanding is that a particular effort is to be made to export to other Latin American and Caribbean countries and to buy imported parts from these countries. Software centers are to be established in Spanish-speaking countries. The difference in price for PCs sold in Mexico and those sold in the United States will be kept within 10 to 15 percent. Participation by IBM in the Mexican microcomputer market is not to exceed 33 percent unless the export ratio increases. The key elements of the agreement are summarized in Table 5.5.

The IBM agreement is a specific demonstration of the point stressed throughout this chapter, that there is apt to be increasing integration between the two countries in significant industrial activities. The important elements of the negotiation cen-

Table 5.5 Key Elements of the Agreement Between IBM and the Mexican Government, January 1986

IBM investment in Mexico over five years	$91 million
IBM equity	100 percent
Production of microcomputers over five years	603,000 units
New computer export proportion	92 percent
Local content—rising from 51 percent at end of first year to fourth year	82 percent
Price differential on microcomputers sold in Mexico and U.S. Limited to	10–15 percent
Exports, over five years	
Gross	$600 million
Net foreign-exchange earnings	$100 million
Time delay on introduction into Mexico of new PC line in U.S.	Six months
Expected employment	
Direct	240 jobs
Indirect	1,460 jobs
Establishment of semiconductor technology center	
Development of distribution center for exports	
Partnership programs with Mexican universities	
Scholarships for Mexican technicians	

Sources: Interviews with officers of IBM and Mexican government; Julia Christine Vindasius, "Mexico and IBM: A Look at State-TNC Negotiation and Bargaining Power," p. 61.

tered on three issues: the technology transfer, cooperation between IBM and Mexican parts producers and authorities; and increasing Mexican exports. The fact that the United States and Mexico are at different stages in the development of their computer industries facilitated this cooperation. The agreement should permit IBM in the United States to move on to other activities while upgrading Mexico's technical position and encouraging its exports.

Pharmaceuticals

The pharmaceutical industry in Mexico is an example of industrial integration marked by foreign domination. As such, it is at the stage of the automotive industry prior to the first decree in 1962. The Mexican authorities believe that the structure that exists in this industry is lopsided in favor of Americans and other foreigners, and the decrees and regulations being promulgated are designed to make the benefits more symmetrical.

The policy thrust of the Mexican authorities has the elements discussed for other industries: Mexicanization, domestic content, export insistence, and government favoritism to Mexican-owned firms. However, the industry has its own peculiarities because of the social and health implications of its products. Some background can put the policy issues into context.

Total industry sales in 1986 were more than $380 million.[48] Domination is by MNCs: of the forty most important companies by value of sales, thirty-eight are foreign dominated and thirty-five are completely foreign owned. The two Mexican-owned companies in the top forty are at the bottom of the list.[49]

Foreign domination has repercussions on research because MNCs prefer to do research at home, where there is a critical mass of technicians; with rare exceptions, Mexico is not innovative in the pharmaceutical industry.[50] The foreign companies cite this as evidence of Mexico's need for their presence, but the lack of research is also a consequence of the industry's structure.[51] This combination rankles: foreign domination, research done abroad, and then lecturing Mexico about its need for the MNCs because of the lack of domestic research. It is particularly annoying because the syllogism is accurate.

The pharmaceutical industry's ability to draw on the support of the U.S. government in its conflicts with the Mexican government also gets under the Mexican skin. It is a situation roughly analogous to the one faced by the petroleum industry before nationalization. In the first case, U.S. coercion dealt with basic issues, such as diplomatic recognition of the Mexican government and ownership of subsoil resources. In the pharmaceutical industry, the stakes have not been as high, but do deal with Mexico's ability to export nonpharmaceutical goods to the United States. The trouble started when the U.S. government delayed approval of an agreement concerning countervailing duties imposed against subsidized Mexican exports until Mexico made concessions in regulations implementing a February 1984 pharmaceutical decree, particularly the features relating to patent protection.[52] The issue of intellectual property rights has subsequently recurred and is still a subject of contention between the two governments. This is a major shortcoming of excessive and evident U.S. government pressure on behalf of specific private interests operating abroad; the skirmishes may be won, but the war continues.

The purpose of the February 1984 decree and subsequent implementing regulations was to make Mexico more self-sufficient in pharmaceutical production, particularly of the active ingredients. A second objective was to increase the supply of low-cost drugs, using a combination of generic labeling of basic retail drugs and stringent price controls. The decree singles out more than sixty active ingredients for which the objective is to replace imports by domestic production. The domestic-content provisions—the purchase of raw materials—were to rise gradually over three to five years to 50 percent. The industry trade deficit with the United States in 1984, the year the decree was promulgated, was $152 million (imports $190 million and exports $38 million), and the decree, in imprecise fashion, encouraged exports.[53] Companies were mandated to set aside 4 percent of feedstock sales for research and development in Mexico.

While dependent on foreign companies, the Mexican government has weapons of its own. Mexico has an extensive social security and public health system, and more than half of all pharmaceutical sales are to the government through a bidding process. At the time of the decree, seventy-five foreign companies supplied 72 percent of the domestic market but only about 50 percent of the government-controlled market, which implies national favoritism in government procurement.[54] As noted in one of the opening quotations to this chapter, the government makes no secret of its intention to increase industrialization and Mexicanization through its procurement power.

Government price controls are another element of potential government leverage. The controls have a social motive—to permit the poor to purchase medicines—but they can obviously affect company profits. The laws and regulations protecting intellectual property can be a further powerful tool of government pressure. The 1976 law on inventions and trademarks limits patent protection to ten years; if a patent is not exploited within four years of issue, it falls into the public domain. When the law was passed, MNCs held 85 to 90 percent of pharmaceutical patents, many of which then fell into the public domain. Many pharmaceutical products can now not be patented at all under the law. Foreign companies are concerned that these laws, already restrictive by standards of industrial countries, may be made more restrictive.

The purpose here is not to take sides between the industry, particularly the MNCs that dominate it, and the Mexican government, whose motives are a mixture of social concern, the desire to enhance domestic research, and the wish to have Mexico play a larger role in the production of pharmaceuticals for use in its own market. The pharmaceutical industry is one in which there is still much conflict. This may change with time, as it has changed in the two other industries discussed in this chapter.

6

ENERGY

> Considering that . . . the petroleum companies were ordered to impose new working conditions . . . and made known their rejection of the award, despite its having been recognized as constitutional by a judgment of the Supreme Court of the Nation . . . this carries as a necessary consequence the application of fraction XXI of article 123 of the General Constitution of the Republic . . . it is declared expropriated for reason of public interest and in favor of the nation the machinery, installations, buildings, pipelines, refineries, storage tanks, roadways, tank cars, distribution stations, ships, and all other goods and real property of [names of companies].
>
> PRESIDENT LÁZARO CÁRDENAS, PETROLEUM EXPROPRIATION DECREE, MARCH 19, 1938

> The 1938 takeover was the culmination not only of the reform process set in motion at Querétaro [relating to the 1917 constitution] twenty-one years earlier, but also to a certain extent of the Mexican Revolution itself.
>
> LORENZO MEYER, 1972

> The development policy adopted by our country reaffirms that we must avoid the petrolization of the economy and this signifies that structural change in energy must march to the rhythm of the structural change of the entire society and that, in the long term, the sector should lose relative weight in an economy that is more diversified, more modern, and more efficiently linked to the exterior.
>
> PROGRAMA NACIONAL DE ENERGÉTICOS, 1984–1988

Oil: The Changing Constant

National values, conditioned by a particular history, play a large role in policy determination of all countries. The checks and balances built into the U.S. political structure can be inefficient when the need for a decision is urgent, yet no branch of the government would explicitly advocate their elimination. They are too deeply embedded in the American belief of how a government should be run.

Mexican history has features just as deeply entrenched in the national psyche as the U.S. checks and balances. The most important is noninterference in the internal affairs of other countries. This aspect of Mexican nationalism is an outgrowth of its experience with the United States. Like U.S. checks and balances, there have been violations of the noninterference concept, such as withdrawal of recognition from the Somoza regime in Nicaragua while it was still in power, but these departures do not destroy the principle as it affects relations with the United States.

National control over Mexico's petroleum resources is comparable in its psychological and practical significance with U.S. separation of powers—it is taken as a given that brooks no argument. National control over oil resources could not be set aside even if it seemed temporarily advantageous; the thought itself would not occur. "Since 1938, petroleum and Pemex have symbolized the essences of nationalism: national dignity, economic independence, and state sovereignty."[1] The import of the Mexican attitude toward oil is not always grasped in the United States, and this has led to policy errors.

Oil has been both a blessing and a curse to Mexico. Oil provided resources for the nation's development, but it also was the lightning rod for foreign interference and the basis for some of the most egregious indignities inflicted on Mexico by the United States. The best known public example was the Bucareli agreements of 1923, under which Mexico was forced to make concessions to U.S. oil interests in return for U.S. recognition of the government of President Alvaro Obregón. The day-to-day control of a nonrenewable resource by foreign interests was inherently unpopular in Mexico, as it has been in country after country. (This is the essence of the quotation from Lorenzo Meyer at the beginning of this chapter.) It was the history of being treated as an inferior even more than the economics of who benefited most from Mexican oil resources that made the 1938 expropriation so popular.[2]

Mexican oil production prior to the expropriation had peaked in the 1920s. By 1938, the "foreign oil properties were in a state of abandon, their reserves depleted, equipment run down, and Mexican management and technical personnel nonexistent."[3] Daily crude production increased steadily but modestly in the decades following the expropriation, but the combination of increasing consumption and lack of discovery of important new fields led to a decline in the ratio of reserves to production from twenty-eight years in 1938 to eighteen years in 1970.[4] Mexico was a net oil importer in the late 1960s and early 1970s.

This all changed in the mid-1970s after Mexico found vast oil resources, particularly in the Tabasco-Campeche basin in the southern part of the country. Mexico was transformed from an oil-dependent economy to a leading producer and exporter. The foreign-exchange earnings and tax revenue from oil became an important component of Mexico's development plans—indeed, too important in that other aspects of Mexico's economic structure were ignored. When oil prices fell in 1981, this high dependence turned the oil bonanza of the late 1970s into the debt horror that Mexico has had to face ever since. Mexico has learned from this experience; planning for the future contemplates a decline in the importance of oil in the context of the total economy. However, continued tax revenue and foreign-exchange receipts from oil production and exports must be part of the solution to the nation's unhappy 1980s.

This chapter will discuss, first, the ups and downs of oil in the Mexican economy since the mid-1970s, or, more precisely, past and present production levels, pricing, and trade policy. The political basis of oil decisions will then be analyzed, with special emphasis on the relations with the United States, including the U.S. interest in Mexican energy policy. The final section will speculate about the future Mexico–United States oil relationship.

Table 6.1   Mexico's Estimated Oil
Resources as of January 1, 1982 (billions of
barrels)

Known Resources	
Original oil in place	193.0
Proven ultimate recovery	36.0
Cumulative production	8.8
Proven oil reserves	27.2
Indicated additional reserves	2.8
Total known ultimate recovery	38.8
Remaining recoverable oil	30.0
Undiscovered resources[a]	
Original oil in place	305.0
Recoverable oil	76.2[b]
Total recoverable oil	115.0

[a]The statistical mean value occurs at the 38 percent probability level.
[b]Assuming an average recovery efficiency of 25 percent.
Source: William D. Dietzman et al., *The Petroleum Resources of Mexico*, p. x.

The Ups and Downs of Oil

The U.S. Department of Energy (the Energy Information Administration, or EIA)
made the estimates shown in Table 6.1 of Mexico's oil resources as of January 1,
1982. Proven reserves were defined in the study as remaining producible oil as of
that date under operating practices then in effect; they include estimated recoverable
oil in undrilled portions of known structures.[5] Additional reserves refer to crude oil
that might be extracted by secondary recovery or pressure maintenance operations
in reservoirs not then using those techniques. Estimates of additional recoverable oil
are based on continuous probability distribution curves for undiscovered oil.

The key figures in the EIA estimate are the 30 billion barrels of remaining
recoverable oil from known deposits, the 38.8 billion barrels of ultimate recoverable oil from known deposits, and the total undiscovered recoverable oil with an
estimated statistical mean value of 76.2 billion barrels. Together, the last two
figures constitute the estimated 115 billion barrels of total recoverable oil.

The figures with the highest probability of accuracy are those from known deposits, the 30- and roughly 39-billion-barrel estimates of currently and ultimately
recoverable oil, both on the conservative side. The Mexicans estimated their proven
reserves as of the end of 1987 at 54.1 billion barrels, and noted there was little
change a year later.[6] The same estimate of Mexican oil reserves as of January 1,
1988 was given by the U.S. Department of Energy in its *International Energy
Annual 1987.*[7]

Based on the data published in the U.S. Department of Energy annual report for
1987, Mexico then ranked seventh in the world in crude-oil reserves, after Saudi

Arabia, Iraq, Kuwait, Venezuela, the Soviet Union, and the United Arab Emirates. Mexico's crude-oil reserves at the beginning of 1988 were 6.7 percent of the estimated world total. Those of the United States, by contrast, were 3.3 percent (27.3 billion barrels). Mexico still ranks among the world's leading countries for oil reserves, although not as high if the more conservative EIA estimates are used.

Table 6.2 shows Mexico's oil-producing regions by proven reserves. The first discovery in what is now Mexico's most important oil-producing area, the Tabasco-Campeche basin, was made only in 1960, and the biggest years for subsequent discoveries were 1976 and 1977. As a result, while this area contains the bulk of Mexico's proven and recoverable reserves, it has not provided the largest proportion of oil produced in Mexico.[8] That honor goes to the Tampico-Tuxpan embayment, which has provided about half the total amount of oil produced in Mexico since 1901. The EIA estimates that these two areas together account for about 95 percent of Mexico's proven oil reserves. Pemex, while it gives a larger absolute figure, also estimates that 95 percent of Mexico's proven oil reserves are situated in these two areas.[9]

The large crude-oil discoveries in the Tabasco-Campeche basin stimulated a debate rooted in the Mexican national historical experience. The issues were not merely how much to produce for national use and how much for export, which is the kind of debate one would expect after a large oil discovery in any country, but also how these decisions would affect Mexican dependence on the United States. The issues, therefore, were partly technical—the durability of oil reserves at different levels of production and the impact of production and exports on the national economy and the balance of payments—and they were partly rooted in past national experience—whether excessive exports to the United States would lead to even more economic integration than already existed.

Table 6.2   Proven Reserves of Mexico's Main Oil Regions (as of January 1, 1982)

	Millions of Barrels	Percent of Total
Tabasco-Campeche basin Includes Reforma area and Gulf of Campeche	19,329	72

Tampico-Tuxpan embayment
  Includes Ebano-Pánuco area, Golden Lane
  reef, Tamabra belt or trend, Chicontepec pal-
  eocanal, and San Andrés area
	5,916	22

Isthmus of Tehuantepec Includes Saline and Macuspana subbasins	1,124	4
Veracruz (or Papaloápan) basin	183	1
Burgos basin	129	—
Sabinas basin	20	—
Totals	26,711[a]	100

— = Less than 1 percent.

[a]The difference between this figure and 27.2 billion barrels of proved reserves shown in Table 6.1 is presumably the omission of certain fields in the material presented in the source.

Source: William D. Dietzman et al., *The Petroleum Resources of Mexico*, pp. 16–26.

The ''nationalist-conservationist'' position dominated the debate until the close of the Echeverría administration at the end of 1976, despite the growing evidence that the new finds were significant.[10] The extreme form of this position eased during the López Portillo administration, stimulated largely by the need to correct the large deficit in the current account of the balance of payments. The position eventually adopted in 1980 was for Mexico to have a flexible production platform of 2.5 to 2.7 million barrels of crude oil per day, of which 1.5 million barrels, plus or minus 10 percent, were for export.[11] To deal with the dependency issue, no more

Table 6.3   Mexican Crude-Oil Production, 1901–1988 (thousands of barrels)

	Yearly Total	Daily Average
1901–1910[a]	1,229	3
1911–1920[a]	51,776	142
1921–1930[a]	101,166	277
1931–1940[a]	39,163	107
1941–1950[a]	49,130	135
1951–1960[a]	86,799	238
1961–1970[a]	131,017	359
1971	155,911	427
1972	161,367	441
1973	164,909	452
1974	209,855	576
1975	261,589	717
1976	293,117	801
1977	358,090	981
1978	442,607	1,213
1979	536,566	1,470
1980	708,593	1,936
1981	844,241	2,313
1982	1,003,084	2,748
1983	981,222	2,688
1984	1,024,341	2,799
1985	960,114	2,630
1986	886,092	2,428
1987	927,333	2,541
1988	917,431	2,507

Note: The production figures in Dietzman et al. and in Pemex's *Anuario estadístisco 1985* are close to each other for most years, but not always identical.

[a]Figures are annual averages and daily averages based on annual means.

Sources: 1901–1970: William D. Dietzman et al., *The Petroleum Resources of Mexico*, pp. 14–15; 1971–1984: Pemex, *Anuario estadístico 1985*, p. 37; Pemex, *Memoria de labores*, annual reports for 1984–1988.

Table 6.4 Mexican Crude-Oil Exports, 1977–1988 (thousands of barrels)

	Yearly Total	Daily Average	Percent to United States
1977	73,736	202	88
1978	133,247	365	89
1979	194,485	533	84
1980	302,956	828	68
1981	400,778	1,098	50
1982	544,614	1,492	49
1983	561,005	1,537	54
1984	558,004	1,525	49
1985	524,943	1,434	52
1986	470,704	1,290	51
1987	490,925	1,345	47
1988	476,945	1,307	52

Sources: 1977–1982: Michele Snoeck, *El comercio exterior de hidrocarburos y derivados en México, 1970–1985*, p. 72; Pemex, *Memoria de labores*, annual reports for 1983–1988.

than 50 percent of crude-oil exports were to be shipped to any single country (that is, the United States), and Mexico would not provide more than 20 percent of the external crude-oil needs of any country. To avoid the petrolization of the country (or to use the word then in vogue in Mexico, the "Venezuelization"), no more than 50 percent of foreign-exchange earnings were to come from petroleum exports.

Table 6.3 gives data on Mexican crude-oil production since 1901. The table shows that the overall production target of between 2.5 and 2.7 million barrels a day has been adhered to after production reached that level in 1982, although there was some decline in 1988. Mexico has also largely fulfilled its aim of limiting exports of crude oil to the United States to 50 percent of the total, give or take 10 percent. Table 6.4 also shows that the proportion of crude-oil exports to the United States before 1981, when the 50 percent export decision went into effect, was substantially higher.

Mexico failed, however, to avoid the petrolization of the economy, a failure most evident in its merchandise exports. Crude-oil and petroleum products began a steady climb as a proportion of Mexico's total exports as crude production attained its targeted level in the Tabasco-Campeche basin, reaching a peak of 78 percent in 1982. As can be seen in Table 6.5, a decline occurred in subsequent years in the petroleum portion of total merchandise exports. The sharp drop to 39 percent of the total in 1986 came from a combination of a decline in volume exported, lower prices, and a diversification into other exports; the value of manufactured exports increased by a substantial 43 percent over 1985.[12]

Another aspect of petrolization is the role that revenues from Pemex operations, taxes paid directly, and those levied on gasoline and other product sales played in

Table 6.5 Mexican Petroleum Exports in Relation to
Total Exports, 1977–1987 (billions of dollars)

	Petroleum Exports (1)	Total Exports (2)	Percent 1/2 (3)
1977	1.0	4.6	22
1978	1.9	6.1	31
1979	4.0	8.8	45
1980	10.4	15.1	69
1981	14.6	19.4	75
1982	16.5	21.2	78
1983	16.0	22.3	72
1984	16.6	24.2	69
1985	13.3	21.7	68
1986	6.3	16.0	39
1987	8.6	20.7	42

Note: The petroleum export value includes both crude oil and products.
The crude-oil proportion has been 90 percent or more of the total every year
since 1975, with the exception of 1986, when it was 88 percent.
Source: Banco de México, *Indicadores económicos.*

financing the budget. These taxes rose from about 10 percent of federal government revenue in the mid-1970s to close to 40 percent in 1982.[13] On a cash-flow basis, petroleum receipts from export and domestic sales and taxes rose from about 33 percent of the receipts under budgetary control in the early 1980s to 45 percent in 1984. When petroleum prices declined, the financing of the public sector became more difficult.

The petrolization of Mexico was a symptom of policy measures taken or neglected. The intoxication of the oil-driven export boom permitted the authorities to ignore the need to stimulate exports of other products, particularly manufactured goods. The large oil receipts had the natural effect of strengthening the peso, and, on top of this, the political leadership equated a stable nominal parity of the peso with the dollar with defense of nationalism, despite Mexico's growing inflation. It would not have been possible to keep the official rate of the peso unchanged from late 1976 to early 1982 without the combination of oil revenues and foreign credit that was so readily made available on the premise that oil in the ground was ample security for the creditors. A thoroughgoing tax reform was delayed until the second half of the de la Madrid administration partly because oil revenue permitted such procrastination. Domestic prices for oil and petroleum products were subsidized despite the obvious outcome of frustrating conservation; oil reserves and the revenue that oil production was providing were seen as infinite, at least from the vantage of a single presidential *sexenio.*

Once the economic crisis erupted in 1982, these policies became untenable. Their correction, however, took place under the most adverse of circumstances, whereas more forethought might have avoided some of the most severe hardships that have since been inflicted on the Mexican population.

It is hard to avoid the conclusion that the Mexican authorities had their priorities wrong when they set the 1980 oil policy. Two objectives were met—limiting total crude production and exports and placing a ceiling on the proportion of exports going to the United States—but one was not—avoiding the petrolization of Mexico. The ceiling on exports to the United States is largely cosmetic as long as the oil production enters the world market. The U.S. Department of Energy was indifferent to this limitation precisely because there is a world market for oil and the economic interest of the United States was well served if the Mexican revenue from oil exports, to whatever destination, was largely used to buy U.S. goods and services.[14]

One assumption of the Mexican decision to limit crude-oil exports to the United States to 50 percent of the total is that a larger proportion would increase Mexican dependence on the U.S. market. It is not self-evident that the seller of a critical commodity is more dependent than the buyer, and the decision was based as much on Mexican history as anything else. The 50 percent export limitation, plus the accompanying limit that no country would be supplied with more than 20 percent of its crude-oil import needs, also reflected Mexican concern that if the United States relied too much on Mexican oil, the temptation for intervention in a crisis would be great.[15]

The second objective, that of limiting total production and exports, had a sounder basis in the desire to avoid both rapid exhaustion of a depletable resource and the petrolization of the Mexican economy.[16] But even though Mexico maintained its 2.5 MMB/d ceiling, it was not clear why it was wise to borrow heavily to limit current oil production, but this was what Mexico did.[17] Presumably, Mexican oil planners expected oil prices to rise forever.

Mexico failed to avoid the petrolization of the economy and in the process hypothecated the economy to foreign creditors. Such avoidance was a thoughtfully considered objective that should have taken precedence over a limit on exports to the United States, but did not in practice. The economic reasons for the failure included the desire for rapid economic growth and job creation at a pace that turned out to be unsustainable; the undertaking of projects (including hectic expansion of investment in petroleum facilities) not carefully thought through, coupled with excessive government expenditures on what was essentially consumption; and an unforgivable failure to build in contingencies against adverse shocks to the economy.[18] The superficial was accomplished—the limitation of crude-oil exports to the United States. The profound—the thoughtful use of the new oil resources to develop the economy—was not.

The overall economic planning at the time the energy-production limitations were adopted in 1980 placed great stress—it is now clear that this emphasis was inordinately great—on the use of oil resources as the springboard for overall economic growth. This was explicit in the two major economic-planning documents of the time, the global plan for 1980 to 1982 and the industrial-development plan for 1979 to 1982.[19] One element of these plans was to keep internal oil-product prices lower than prices for comparable products on the world market and, even to go beyond this, to provide additional subsidies for energy products when industries were located in specific areas of the country considered desirable for development.[20]

Mexico's internal oil-pricing policy prior to the 1982 financial crisis was thus in direct contradiction with the production limitation, encouraging profligacy in oil use, while the main purpose of the production limitation was to conserve this Mexican resource through efficient use.

Beyond this economic-development motive for preferential pricing, there was the internal political objective of keeping consumer prices low for gasoline, diesel, and home-cooking and heating fuels. Even as late as July 1983, prices for the most widely used type of gasoline were the equivalent of 16 cents a liter in Mexico compared with 32 cents in the United States and 58 cents in the United Kingdom. Liquid gas cost 6 cents a kilogram in Mexico compared with 29 cents in the United States; for diesel, the comparison was 9 cents a liter in Mexico and 32 cents in the United States.[21]

The results were predictable. As economic activity grew and the real prices of petroleum and energy products declined, consumption increased; the rate of increase was more than 8 percent a year between 1970 and 1982.[22] Between 1977 and 1982, when the energy subsidies were at their peak, the annual rate of increase was 10.5 percent.[23] The relationship during these latter years between the growth in energy consumption and the growth in GDP was 1.7 compared with 1.2 during the first half of the 1970s.[24] Energy use was becoming less efficient; simultaneously, the precisely opposite trend occurred in the United States and other energy importers. The major explanation for the difference was the maintenance of subsidized prices in Mexico and their abandonment in other countries.

Subsidizing energy prices is not unique to Mexico. The United States did this for many years, as have many other countries. When consumers are used to low prices for gasoline and cooking fuel, raising them becomes a major political issue. Subsidies were maintained in the name of industrial development and concern about the well-being of the poor, but the outcome was wasteful and the major benefit went to high-income groups. The internal prices of petroleum products began to rise after 1982, when it became clear that the government could no longer support the subsidies; these sharp price increases came on top of other austerity measures facing Mexican workers, particularly a decline in real income. Internal energy price policy turned out to be an issue delayed until the worst possible time.

Pricing of crude oil on the world market did not escape domestic politics either. Mexico did not join the Organization of Petroleum Exporting Countries (OPEC), but it was clearly sympathetic to the cartel and took advantage of OPEC's price maneuvers when they benefited Mexico. Several reasons have been adduced for Mexico's decision to remain out of OPEC, including the tradition of not compromising national sovereignty and the fear that the country would lose the tariff benefits under the U.S. generalized system of preferences.[25] Nonmembership did not mean noncooperation; contacts between Mexico and OPEC members still happen regularly. An example of cooperation is the action taken by Mexico in August 1986 to cut its crude-oil export ceiling from 1.5 to 1.35 million barrels a day and then again in January 1987 to 1.32 million barrels a day. As Pemex stated in its bulletin, these cuts were linked to the strategy and quotas adopted by OPEC.[26]

Mexico has sought to price its crude based on a formula that calculates the prices of competing crudes in each destination.[27] Because of lower transportation costs,

Mexican crude fetches a higher price in the United States than in most other markets. In other words, the ceiling on exports to the United States may involve an economic sacrifice in the interest of a political motive of avoiding excessive dependency.

Mexico's oil policy prior to the 1982 economic crisis was influential in devising later policies after de la Madrid became president. Many features of the old policy were retained, especially the production and export limitations, but others were altered, particularly those affecting conservation of energy resources. But before turning to those later policies, we need to consider Mexican policy on petrochemicals and natural gas, other important components of the oil industry, particularly as they affect relations with the United States.

Other Energy Products

Petrochemicals

The development of Mexico's petrochemical industry over roughly the past twenty-five years has entailed the dedication of a substantial amount of resources. The industry hardly existed until the 1960s, but once established, the growth in production of basic petrochemicals was significant, about 27 percent a year between 1960 and 1980. This declined to less than 10 percent a year between 1980 and 1987.[28] Data on production of the main basic petrochemicals for the years 1965, 1975, and 1985 are shown in Table 6.6.

The word "basic" as used in Mexico requires clarification. In the United States and generally elsewhere, basic or primary petrochemical refers only to olefins (the major olefins are ethylene, propylene, and butadiene) and aromatics (the major aromatics are benzene, toluene, and xylenes).[29] The definition of basic is broader in Mexico; it is also somewhat arbitrary and is altered from time to time. The significance of the distinction between basic and secondary petrochemicals as used in Mexico is that manufacture of the former is reserved to Pemex. Private companies manufacturing secondary petrochemicals (which elsewhere would generally be referred to as intermediate petrochemicals and petrochemical products) must be majority Mexican-owned and licensed by the government. There were 175 basic petrochemical plants in operation during 1988.[30]

The public–private division conformed to the general model of state hegemony over what were seen as the strategic levers of the economy. The state in Mexico, in addition to petroleum, reserves to itself the generation of nuclear energy and electricity, certain mining activities, the railroads, radio and telegraphic communication, and, since 1982, commercial banking. It is not clear that the state actually chose the most profitable part of the petrochemical industry for itself, since the value added is greater in producing secondary and derivative products, but it did select that portion that provides it with a means for controlling the entire industry.

There was also concern that the financial entry barrier to private ownership in the production of basic petrochemicals, an industry normally requiring a substantial initial investment, would lead to monopoly or oligopoly. The limitation of foreign ownership in the secondary industry, actually to only 40 percent as contrasted with a

Table 6.6   Production of Leading Basic Petrochemicals—
Mexico, 1965, 1975, 1985, 1988 (thousands of metric tons)

	1965	1975	1985	1988
Acetaldehyde	—	32	145	156
Acrilonitrile	—	20	49	61
Ammonia	121	801	2,261	2,515
Vinyl chloride	—	45	108	175
Dodecylbenzene	26	72	61	111
Styrene	—	27	33	132
Methanol	—	32	192	201
Orthoxylene	5	15	44	68
Ethylene oxide	—	27	71	102
Paraxylene	—	32	110	183
High-density polyethylene	—	—	68	82
Low-density polyethylene	—	99	160	317
Propylene	—	93	207	281
Butadiene	—	22	18	12
Others	310	2,318	7,896	11,066
Gross production	462	3,635	11,323	15,462

— = No production.
Source: Pemex, *Anuario estadístico*, 1985 and 1987; Pemex, *Memoria de labores*,
1988.

more general norm of 49 percent, was in conformity with similar limitations in all
industries.

The tensions that existed between the public and the private sector were resolved
by the compromise of imposing state control over an expansive definition of basic
petrochemicals, but with ample scope for the production of intermediates and products by the private sector. In keeping with the overall tendency in recent years for
more privatization of the economy, thirty-six petrochemical products earlier classified as basic were reclassified in 1987 as secondary, thereby permitting private
production.[31] This shift in definition did, in fact, lead to a number of applications
for private-sector production of the newly reclassified products.

The petrochemical industry was started at a time when import substitution dominated the thinking of Mexican industrialization. Mexico thought in terms of domestic value added and self-sufficiency, to be reached gradually, for basic petrochemicals. While there was a trade surplus in 1988, self-sufficiency has not occurred. In
1988, Pemex exported 517,458 metric tons of basic petrochemicals and imported
80,826 metric tons. In value terms, Pemex imports in 1988 were $17 million and
exports $73 million, for a surplus of $56 million.[32] As recently as 1985, the basic
petrochemical trade deficit had been $497 million; the export surge in 1988 was
largely in ammonia and ethylene. The import figures given above are only for
Pemex, not including those for the private sector. The United States is normally

Mexico's main foreign source for basic petrochemicals, overwhelmingly so in most years, and generally the most important market for exports.

The importance of the basic petrochemical industry in Mexico should not be exaggerated; its production generally contributes less than one-half of 1 percent of GDP.

Natural Gas

Mexico produced 3,478 million cubic feet a day of natural gas in 1988 (1,264 billion cubic feet for the year). Peak production was reached in 1982 (1,550 billion cubic feet for the year) and has declined consistently ever since.[33] Most of Mexico's production of natural gas is associated with crude-oil production in the southeastern part of the country and offshore; together 85 percent of natural-gas production in 1988 came from these two areas. Mexico seems to be keeping nonassociated gas (that is, gas exploited from fields unrelated to crude-oil production) mostly shut in, which can provide discretionary margins for both current and future production. Flaring of associated gas is not a serious problem; since 1986, about 5.5 percent of natural-gas production has been released in some form into the atmosphere.

The biggest purchaser of natural gas is Pemex itself, for fuel, for power generation, and as a raw material in the petrochemical industry, especially in the production of ammonia and methanol. Other large-scale consumers are the electricity, steel, cement, paper and pulp, and mining sectors.[34] Mexico does not now export natural gas—indeed, it imported minor amounts, $6.2 million worth, or 1.8 billion cubic feet, from the United States in 1986—and therein lies a story of the sensitivity of Mexico–United States relations when it comes to the petroleum industry.

The facts are the following: when the growth in oil and associated-gas production in the Reforma and Campeche fields occurred, the Mexican authorities assumed that natural gas over and above that allocated for domestic needs would be available and that one practical use was for overland export to the United States. A memorandum of intent was signed in August 1977 between Pemex and six U.S. gas-transmission companies for deliveries of up to 2 billion cubic feet per day by 1979, about 3 percent of annual U.S. consumption. The first shipments were to be priced at $2.60 per 1,000 cubic feet, and subsequent prices were to be adjusted quarterly based on the heat equivalent of No. 2 distillate fuel delivered in New York harbor. This was eight times the domestic Mexican price.[35]

A pipeline, 48 inches in diameter, was planned to transport the gas from Cactus, in Chiapas state, to the area around Monterrey, from which another line would go to Reynosa, on the border across from McAllen, Texas. The total pipeline would run about 760 miles and be financed in part by a U.S. Export-Import Bank loan of close to $600 million. The main purpose of the pipeline was to make the gas available for industrial and other uses in Mexico itself, but the U.S. part of the arrangement was extremely controversial in Mexico. The left castigated the government for selling part of the Mexican birthright to the United States and in the process increasing Mexico's dependence. Suggestions were made for liquefying the gas, if exports were necessary, so that other markets could be tapped, despite the obvious shortcomings of this proposal.[36]

While this controversy was going on in Mexico, a debate over prices was taking place in the United States. Natural gas was still regulated in the United States, and one proposal was to raise the price of newly discovered U.S. gas to $1.75 per 1,000 cubic feet. Canadian gas in the Pacific Northwest was selling at the time for $2.16 per 1,000 cubic feet. Opponents of the Mexican scheme felt that $2.60 for Mexican natural gas was excessive. Senator Adlai Stevenson III placed pressure on the Export-Import Bank to delay the credits for the Mexican pipeline until the price of gas came down.[37] Secretary of Energy James Schlesinger opposed the agreement because of both the high initial price and the tie to middle distillate No. 2, since the price of this product was manipulable by OPEC. The gas deal collapsed in December 1977.

Several years later, in 1979, a modest gas deal was concluded for sales of up to 300 million cubic feet of gas per day at an initial price of $3.625 per 1,000 cubic feet, with changes geared to the price of crude oil. Had the original price formula been in existence, the price of Mexican natural gas in 1980 would have been more than $6.00 per 1,000 cubic feet.[38] Mexico several years ago ceased selling gas to the United States, based partly on continuing disagreements over price but also because Mexico found that it could use the gas at home, without flaring.[39]

The interesting aspect of this tale lies less in the details of which side was right or who charged whom with bad faith—and there were many such accusations on both sides—but in the lack of comprehension shown by each side to the sensitivities of the other.[40] Scholars in the United States could be found on either side of the issue; George Grayson showed sympathy for the U.S. position, and Richard Fagen and Henry Nau treated the incident as an example of maladroitness by the U.S. government. There may have been Mexican scholars who showed some understanding of the U.S. position, but not in print.[41] This is not unusual. When there are quarrels between the Mexican and U.S. governments, U.S. scholars will often side with the Mexicans, but it is rare, perhaps nonexistent, for Mexican scholars to agree openly with the U.S. position. This undoubtedly is a consequence of asymmetry in economic power, coupled with a history of suspicion of U.S. motives.

The negotiation showed that Mexicans who negotiate with the United States, particularly on issues concerning the petroleum industry, must keep one eye on the domestic political clamor that is inevitable. The estimate they must make is not whether there will be political objections to almost any agreement—there will be, cloaked in economic, dependence, sovereignty, security, exploitation, or other terms—but the intensity of this opposition when weighed against economic benefits.[42] Negotiators from the United States sometimes forget this, and individual members of Congress, when they interfere in the negotiating process, are hardly aware of the internal Mexican context. For its part, the Mexican government tends to forget about the separation of powers in the United States and often feels it has an agreement when it has concluded only one step of a more complex process. In the natural-gas case, the agreement with the pipeline companies never even made it through the executive branch.[43]

The Politics of Oil

Many Mexicans had grandiose ideas about the power the new oil discoveries would bring, especially in bilateral relations with the United States. Mario Ojeda, to cite a prominent Mexican analyst, thought that oil was a two-edged sword in that its presence could lead the United States to offer trade, financial, and technology concessions to convince Mexico to raise its production level, but that, at the same time, failure to increase production could result in U.S. reprisals, including even military intervention.[44] This type of analysis, a mixture of sophistication and deeply held suspicion about how the United States works, was common in Mexico. The United States undoubtedly was prepared to offer concessions for a secure source of oil, and undoubtedly still is, but that it would forcibly seize the oil fields and then operate them at the maximum technical level of output to keep oil prices down would hardly be thinkable in official U.S. circles, other than in the fantasies of a Dr. Strangelove. President Carter was thought by many to have gone too far when he described the oil situation as the "moral equivalent" of war after OPEC raised prices and declared an embargo against the United States, which is quite different from actual war.

The initial U.S. reaction combined technical expertise with ignorance of the Mexican scene. Mexico suddenly entered into the consciousness of Americans far from the border. The timing of the discoveries, just after the attempted embargo by Middle Eastern OPEC countries and the quadrupling or quintupling of crude-oil prices, encouraged this type of strategic thinking. One immediate suggestion was to forge a North American common energy market; Mexico and Canada had the oil to sell, and both presumably had vast quantities of natural gas. The United States offered a secure market. In simple economic terms, the idea might have had some validity; Canada to this day seeks a market for its natural gas in the United States. And in light of the later collapse of oil prices, Mexico might have chosen wisely if an oil-supply contract also contained assurances of a stable price.

However, this type of economic thinking, isolated from historic reality, offered nothing of substance in the first flush on Mexican oil wealth. Rather than think in terms of an assured market at a stable price, Mexico opted to limit sales to the United States. Even at the lucrative price that the U.S. pipeline companies offered to buy Mexican natural gas, the opposition to the transaction was fierce in Mexico.

The elements that go into current Mexican thinking about crude-oil and natural-gas production and sales in light of the deficiencies of the policies of 1980 include:

- Limiting production of crude oil to conserve this resource as long as possible.
- Restricting exports for the same reason.
- Cooperating with OPEC to support crude prices.
- Diversifying markets for crude oil, even if this involves some price sacrifice because of higher transportation costs to destinations other than the United States.
- Recognizing the need for crude-oil export revenue to meet Mexico's external debt burden and to carry out its development program.
- Using natural gas produced in associated wells efficiently at home.
- Facilitating conservation of these depletable natural resources by encouraging development of other energy resources, such as nuclear, and by pricing and other policies that discourage profligate use of energy resources.
- To the extent possible, adding value domestically to Mexico's petroleum and gas resources, such as through further development of the petrochemical industry.
- And, above all, not repeating the previous experience of petrolizing the Mexican economy, both directly by exploiting oil reserves and indirectly by mortgaging Mexico's future development to borrowings predicated on the existence of oil in the ground.

Table 6.7 Strategy of National Energy Program, by Stages

Objective	Consolidation Stage, 1983–1988	Diversification and Technological Stage, 1989–2000
Guarantee self-sufficiency	Increase crude and gas capacity	Increase installed capacity
	Widen electricity capacity	Improve exploitation of "dear" oil
	Increase secondary oil recuperation	Complete knowledge of country's energy potential
	Increase exploration	Reduce dependence on oil as an energy source
Assist national economic development	Maintain flexible export platform of 1.5 MMBD	Maintain sector's financial contribution
	Gradually reduce internal subsidies on energy prices	Modernize sector by forward and backward linkages
	Strengthen forward and backward linkages	
	Strengthen employment and production protection by national procurement	
Assist social development	Maintain selective subsidies for low-income groups	Gradually reduce subsidies
	Promote rural energy programs	Provide complete national energy coverage
	Correct regional inequalities	Overcome regional and environmental disequilibria
	Diminish environmental contamination	
Conserve energy by efficient use	Eliminate waste and irrational use	Promote technological change for conservation
	Set prices to stimulate conservation	Maintain oil price policy for energy conservation
	Use technical and financial means and publicity to stimulate conservation	
	Complete specific conservation programs	
Achieve a national energy balance	Introduce new thermal, geothermal, and hydroelectric projects	Consolidate coal, geothermal, and nuclear sources of energy
	Complete Laguna Verde project and start another	Extend nonconventional uses to rural areas
	Strengthen exploration and evaluation of all energy potential	Diversify nonelectrical uses
	Stimulate cogeneration and other nonconventional energy sources	

(continued)

Table 6.7 (*Continued*)

Objective	Consolidation Stage, 1983–1988	Diversification and Technological Stage, 1989–2000
Strengthen technological autonomy	Consolidate research institutions	Amplify institutional network for research
	Provide technical support to providers and users	Consolidate technological effort
	Strengthen training	
	Develop nuclear technology	
	Provide more resources to alternative energy sources, especially solar	
Achieve a more efficient and integrated energy sector	Maintain austerity in expenditures	Increase sector's productivity
	Improve financial operation of CFE[a]	Maintain austerity in expenditures
	Eliminate overloading	Achieve consistent growth
	Reach concrete productivity agreements	
	Consolidate intersectoral coordination	
Contribute to strengthening world hydrocarbons market	Maintain flexible export platform	Take advantage of opportunities to maximize export value
	Continue to fix prices in consultation with importers and other exporters	
	Maintain principle of market diversification	

[a]Comisión Federal de Electricidad.
Source: Poder Ejecutivo Federal, *Programa nacional de energéticos 1984–1988*, pp. 70–73.

These objectives are evident from Mexico's 1984 to 1988 energy program, whose main points are set forth in Table 6.7. Many details of this strategy are already out of date, but the overall philosophy that motivated it is more durable. What particularly distinguishes the 1984 to 1988 plan from the earlier policy are the emphases on pricing energy resources to encourage conservation and the explicit reference to setting prices in consultation with other exporters (and, as stated in the plan, with importers; this is included largely for cosmetic purposes and to take account of Mexico's links with oil importers in Central America and the Caribbean).[45]

Mexico's plans include the further development of nuclear energy. The troubles surrounding the first plant at Laguna Verde, in the state of Veracruz, have included long construction delays, massive cost overruns, and disagreements with the United

States under nuclear nonproliferation initiatives during the Carter administration. The Chernobyl disaster occurred more than a year before the first of Laguna Verde's two 654-megawatt boiling-water reactors was scheduled to become operational in 1987, and this stimulated intense and organized opposition to its going on line.[46] As can be seen in Table 6.7, plans made in 1984 called for a second nuclear plant, but the experience with Laguna Verde may alter this outcome or at least delay its construction.

Viewing the Oil Relationship

Energy planning in Mexico can be examined in a limited sectoral context, or, more broadly, how energy policy affects the entire economy. Similarly, Mexican energy relations with the United States can be analyzed in terms of the effect on U.S. energy decisions or on the overall bilateral relationship.

In the first flush of oil prosperity in the latter 1970s, oil *qua* oil received much attention in Mexico's official planning. Oil as the motor of overall economic growth was the theme of the main development plans put together in 1979. However, in a deeper sense, oil and its role in the political-economic development of Mexico were neglected. As one Mexican analyst has noted, the oil revenue could have been the basis for structural reforms that clearly were needed or, by contrast, been used mainly to finance the traditional growth policy. The second alternative was chosen.[47] Megaprojects were instituted, public employment was increased, import levels rose, and the economy went through a short-lived boom. The structural changes were not instituted until after the flush of the oil boom had turned into the disaster of the oil bust. It was not the oil bonanza that stimulated basic changes in the economy, but the drastic decline in oil revenues. The structural reforms Mexico undertook after 1982 were crisis-driven, not oil-driven.

The evidence of the post-1982 policy is that Mexico learned from the experience of 1976 to 1982 to use windfalls constructively. It is impossible to be certain, however, that another oil boom stimulated by a surge in prices might not lead to the abandonment of the current economic-modernization efforts and instead prompt a recrudescence of populist measures. Unemployment and underemployment in Mexico are high, real wages have declined, and political discontent is rampant. These conditions existed in 1976, albeit to a much lesser extent, and their presence was part of the explanation for the policies followed at that time. A new revenue windfall would permit actions to deal simultaneously with many current problems: spending to enhance popularity; abandonment of a nonoil export policy because the foreign exchange from oil revenues would be adequate at least temporarily; and delaying diversification in the glow of restored high overall economic growth rates. A return to a modified version of earlier policies has a low probability, but it is not zero.

The United States really had little to find fault with in Mexico's energy policy of 1976 to 1982 when viewed in the narrow framework of energy. Crude-oil production built up to substantial levels, as did exports. Mexico was essentially a price follower; it did not set the high OPEC prices, and no one could have expected the country not to take advantage of the windfall. The difficulty over natural-gas sales to the United States was essentially a sideshow to the broader picture of crude-oil production and exports.

The United States, however, was caught up in the Mexican failure to use its energy resources for modernizing its economy because the collapse of that policy led to the Mexican government's subsequent drastic measures. The decline in GDP coupled with the shortage of foreign exchange led to the sharp reduction in imports from the United States, and the fall in real wages encouraged emigration. The lack of reserves to meet debt-service payments required a rescue effort by the U.S. government. It was not Mexico's 1976 to 1982 oil policy narrowly defined that adversely affected the United States, but it was the failure by Mexico to use the oil revenue as the basis for structural reform for which the United States had to pay a price.

The United States, like Mexico, is presumably wiser today because of the earlier experience. The level of Mexican oil production, the proportion exported (whether to the United States or elsewhere), and the price charged are all important issues for the United States, but they pale in significance compared with the role of oil in Mexico's broader economic policy. Repetrolization of the Mexican economy would carry the seeds of a subsequent bust. The diversification of Mexico's economy, including particularly more efficient production and export of manufactured goods, is essential for the United States, just as for Mexico.

This is another way of phrasing the central theme of this book: what happens in Mexico has profound repercussions on the United States. A headline placed over an editorial column directed to the United States in 1979 by Carlos Fuentes read: "Mexico is . . . not an oil well."[48] It was not just the United States that thought in narrow terms at that time, but Mexico itself, and the Mexican mentality was the crucial one then, just as the Mexican outlook is the relevant one now.

Looking Ahead

This foray into the future is based on the assumption that oil will be a tool in the modernization of Mexico, but not the critical lever to the exclusion of practically all other measures, which it was before the 1982 crisis. This implies an effort at true diversification, not just of export markets for crude oil, but of production and exports generally, especially nonoil exports. Further, oil and natural gas must be priced at their scarcity value and not be used to subsidize other activities if Mexico is to avoid the repetrolization of the economy. The price assumption is made both in the interest of oil conservation in Mexico and to avoid trade disputes with the United States.

However, since oil revenue will be important to Mexico's well-being regardless of how effectively Mexico moves into other areas, diversification in oil policy will also be necessary. The establishment of the petrochemical industry was one technique for broadening the contribution of oil and gas resources. The more effective use of natural gas at home is also a form of diversification.

About 90 percent of Mexico's oil exports are in crude form. Phrased differently, Mexico's oil-export fortunes are linked to the demand for crude oil. As desirable as oil may be as a primary commodity, compared with, say, tin or sugar, it is still subject to the vagaries of commodity markets; that is, revenue from crude-oil exports is likely to be more volatile than for products with greater value added, such as manufactures. The implication of this conclusion is that Mexico would be well advised to integrate its oil and petrochemical industry, particularly the former, downstream much more than it has in the past.

Specifically, Mexico may wish to enter the retail product market outside Mexico, especially in the United States. Other countries—Venezuela and Kuwait—have done this, and Saudi Arabia is considering similar action.[49] The form that this takes—whether a sales contract, a joint venture with a group familiar with retail marketing in the United States, or ownership by Pemex itself—will depend on such considerations as financing, management needs, and concern over political sensitivity to a government-owned monopoly competing at the retail level in the United States. However, the logic of downstream integration, from crude exploration and production to refining to the retail level, is that it can reduce the volatility of export earnings. When crude prices decline, the crude becomes an input for a retail-level profit center. When crude prices are high, Mexico has a choice of profit centers.

There are many reasons why Mexico might hesitate to commit itself to this form of downstream integration. It may not believe it has enough oil to commit itself downstream, and the initial investment would be high.[50] It would require head-on competition with the major oil companies, which have exploited the logic of vertical integration from the crude-oil to the retail level for products. Pemex lacks the experience of retail competition, since it has had a domestic monopoly for about fifty years. There would be nationalistic concern that opening retail outlets in the United States would increase the economic integration between the two countries.

Mexico would have to confront one other concern if and as it considered downstream integration into the U.S. retail market. This is that the United States might impose an import fee on foreign oil. Mexico might then be caught having to provide crude to refineries for meeting its retail commitments when more desirable crude markets existed outside the United States. And it would have to compete with major oil companies drawing a proportion of their crude from domestic U.S. sources and therefore not subject to an oil-import fee. Because of internal opposition, the probability of an oil-import fee being imposed in the United States is not high, but it exists; moreover, the imposition in 1986 of a higher fee on imported than on domestic oil to help finance the U.S. superfund demonstrated that discrimination against foreign oil does take place.[51]

Mexico faces a dilemma in its arguments against an oil-import fee. Its most powerful argument, apart from the adverse repercussions on the Mexican economy (which, in turn, would affect U.S. exports to Mexico), is that by imposing an oil-import fee, the United States would compromise crude exports from its most secure source of supply—Mexico and other neighbors.[52] At the same time, Mexican policy deliberately limits its supply of crude to the United States. It would not be possible for Mexico to have it both ways if the issue of security of supply became important.

The best way for Mexico not to be affected by an oil-import fee, if one is imposed, is to reach a supply agreement with the United States, making operational the argument that Mexico is a secure source of supply, in exchange for exemption from the fee. This would involve a hard choice for Mexico, between the nationalism of energy independence and the necessity to maintain revenue, but it is a choice that would have to be faced if the United States does impose an oil-import fee.

7

THE ECONOMICS
AND POLITICS OF DEBT

Sooner or later, regulators will have to accept some form of explicit interest capitalization.

ERNESTO ZEDILLO PONCE DE LEÓN, 1986

Only if interest rates are substantially reduced and/or there are drastic international changes, will Mexico be able to service its debt in the long term.

GUILLERMO ORTÍZ AND JAIME SERRA PUCHE, 1986

Ideas which were discarded as radical or unacceptable when initially raised become, often after a very short time, generally acceptable techniques for concrete solutions [to the debt problem].

FRANCISCO DÁVILA SUÁREZ, 1986

Unbearable Burden versus Concrete Obligation

Mexico's external debt exceeded $100 billion in 1989, and the country ran a close second to Brazil as the largest debtor among developing nations. Annual interest payments on the public debt vary year by year, depending on interest rates in the United States and other capital markets, but have been $8 to $9 billion a year, about 5 to 6 percent of GDP, since 1986. Debt principal is not being repaid; reschedulings have pushed these obligations into the future. The pattern until 1987 was to borrow, thereby increasing the total outstanding debt, at the same time that current interest payments were made. No explicit capitalization of interest obligations to foreign banks has occurred, a step that commercial creditors have resisted. But in effect that was what happened until 1988 because even as current interest was paid, the total of borrowed capital increased. This implicit form of interest capitalization (that is, converting an obligation to pay interest into part of the principal) suits the regulatory and accounting practices of U.S. commercial banks. Various ways to buy back debt, thereby reducing the principal, were tried after 1987.

The immediate issue is economic—funds that leave Mexico to meet interest obligations are a drain of resources desperately needed at home. The economic cost when interest payments exceed new capital inflows is particularly onerous for a developing country such as Mexico, and meeting the external-debt obligation has been a major contributing factor to the decline in Mexico's economy since 1982. In essence, the interest burden of the external debt is being transferred back to Mexico's workers, who have suffered sharp drops in real income.

The combination of economic deterioration and social hardship, coupled with the visibility of payments to foreign banks, has made the debt situation one of Mexico's leading political issues. Mexicans see themselves suffering while creditors prosper. The sentiment for paying less interest, or paying none at all for now, is powerful.[1] Stating the problem in moral terms—who suffers most—is unlikely to stir the souls of creditors, but the social-political aspect should agitate the U.S. government.

The Mexican government, judging the burden of payment to be less costly than the economic cost of default, has continued to make payments, but has renegotiated the level of these payments on increasingly better terms. This is not, however, a calculation made once and forever; it is subject to repeated evaluations entailing a complex of factors, including the amount of payments (both in absolute terms and in relation to other economic variables in Mexico), the relationship between payments and new capital inflows, and the degree of pressure on the Mexican authorities from the internal political situation.

The calculus that Mexico must make, and then continually remake, is thus a mixture of the economic costs and benefits of meeting or suspending foreign interest payments, the domestic political cost of payments versus the short-term political benefits of suspending them, and the effect of nonpayment on Mexico's international prestige. The decision to keep paying has required some concessions from the creditors. If the decision were made to cease payments, it, too, would probably be accompanied by a negotiation; Mexico would concede that the obligation exists, but seek relief.

Creditors must make their own complex calculations. The U.S. government has a stake in Mexico's political stability, but it also is concerned with the operations of the international financial system. Private creditors in developed countries have short-term profit motives and, for the larger banks, systemic concerns as well. Official and private concerns in creditor countries are not necessarily the same, and large private creditors have a different outlook from smaller ones. Making interest payments to foreign banks means that those funds cannot be used to buy imports; thus the U.S. productive sector pays a price in reduced exports so that U.S. and non-U.S. banks can be paid.

The overall international debt situation, which includes Mexico's debt, is changing rapidly. This chapter outlines the evolution of Mexico's external debt and its effects in Mexico, and then, in the light of United States–Mexico relations, makes a recommendation.

Evolution of the Debt

The ''normal'' pattern of debt distribution taught to economics students two decades ago was that developing countries should be expected to run deficits in the current account of their balance of payments—that is, import more goods and services than they export. The current-account deficit would then be covered by capital inflows, made up of private investments, foreign loans, and credit from official sources and private lenders. The net result of such a balance-of-payments structure would be to allow developing countries to absorb resources from the rest of the world for use in their development programs. In other words, it was unexceptional for economic development to be driven partly by contracting external debt, and this was certainly the pattern for Mexico. Mexico's current account was generally negative, modestly so until the 1980s, when the deficit skyrocketed until corrective action was taken. The balance-of-payments data for the 1980s are shown in Table 4.9.

The generally accepted pattern that developed countries were exporters of capital and developing countries importers was shattered by the oil shocks of 1973 and 1974 and 1980 and 1981 and related events that went under the name of recycling petrodollars (the surpluses built up by oil-exporting countries). The shifts in trade patterns were drastic because of the large oil price increases. What is particularly germane to understanding what took place in Mexico is that the current-account surpluses of the oil exporters (Mexico was not a major oil exporter in 1973; that came a few years later) found their way into banks that acted as intermediaries and lent funds. This recycling by private institutions was encouraged by governments and even international financial institutions such as the World Bank and the International Monetary Fund because it was evident that official lending would be insufficient to cover the capital needs of developing countries. In retrospect, the encouragement to borrow laid the seeds of later trouble for those countries that heeded the siren call of available, lendable funds. The official encouragement should not bear all the blame, however; if the banks were eager lenders, countries like Mexico turned out to be willing borrowers. If sovereignty means self-determination, then Mexico bears the responsibility for its own decision to borrow. Placing blame, however, is no longer really relevant.

The traditional pattern under which developed countries were expected to be capital exporters and developing countries capital importers was finally shattered by two further developments. The first was the steady growth of U.S. current-account deficits. By 1986, the United States was not only the world's largest capital importer, but also the world's largest international debtor. It is hard to overstress the impact on Mexico and other countries of this radical and rapid shift of the United States from the world's leading creditor to its largest debtor nation, and it is a prime example of the effect that U.S. domestic policy inadvertently has on Mexico. The shift raised U.S. interest rates, which, in turn, raised Mexico's debt payments.

Another reason for the change in pattern of resource flows was the existence of the debt itself. Debt must be serviced. Interest must be paid even if principal is not amortized, and this can be done without a further debt buildup only if the country has a surplus in current account. The turnaround in the Mexican current account began in 1982, when the deficit was reduced. The shift in Mexico's current-account position between 1981 and 1983 was $18 billion, which is a gigantic number for an economy the size of Mexico's. But the cutback in merchandise imports that was required to create this shift was severe and unsustainable, and the current-account surplus declined in 1984 and 1985, then shifted back into modest deficit in 1986. A current-account surplus was restored in 1987, and a deficit reemerged in 1988.

That is the broad context in which Mexico's external debt grew, but it is equally important to look at internal explanations. Let us start with the debt buildup itself. Table 7.1 shows the growth of external debt from 1971 through 1985. Table 7.2 provides a picture of annual debt flows—that is, the inflow leading to the buildup of

Table 7.1 Mexico's External Debt, 1971–1985 (values in billions of dollars)

Year	Total	Public	Private	Public as Percent Total
1971	6.6	4.5	2.1	68.7
1972	7.7	5.1	2.6	65.8
1973	10.3	7.1	3.2	69.0
1974	14.5	10.0	4.5	68.7
1975	20.1	14.5	5.6	71.9
1976	25.9	19.6	6.3	75.7
1977	29.3	22.9	6.4	78.1
1978	33.4	26.3	7.1	78.6
1979	40.3	29.8	10.5	73.9
1980	50.7	33.8	16.9	66.6
1981	74.9	53.0	21.9	70.7
1982	84.9	58.9	26.0	69.4
1983	92.6	73.5	19.1	79.4
1984	94.2	75.7	18.5	80.4
1985	94.4	75.9	18.5	80.4

Note: External-debt figures will vary depending on how short-term debt is calculated and how much private debt is captured.

Source: Roberto Gutiérrez R., "El endeudamiento externo del sector privado de México: expansión y renegociación," p. 338.

Table 7.2 Net Flows of External Debt (values in billions of dollars)

Year	Inflows	Inflows as Percent GDP	Interest Payments	Interest as Percent Merchandise Exports
1973–76	4.8	5.1	1.2	41.1
1977	3.3	3.5	2.0	42.5
1978	3.0	2.5	2.6	42.4
1979	6.7	2.6	3.7	42.1
1980	10.5	2.5	5.5	36.2
1981	23.3	9.7	8.3	43.2
1982	10.1	3.1	11.3	51.8
1983	3.5	2.5	9.9	46.1

Source: Leopoldo Solís and Ernesto Zedillo, "The Foreign Debt of Mexico," p. 262.

Table 7.3 Profile of Mexico's Foreign Debt, 1951–1988 (billions of dollars)

	1985	1986	1987	1988
Public sector	73.5	75.3	81.4	78.5
Percent to commercial banks	78	78	77	74
Mexican banks	5.0	5.6	5.8	7.6
IMF	2.4	4.0	5.1	5.0
Private sector	18.5	16.0	13.0	10.0
Total	99.0	101.0	105.5	100.5

Note: Figures may not add due to rounding. The debt figures are not the same as those of Table 7.1 because the two sources did not use identifical definitions of debt. The differences are not signficant for purposes of this analysis.
Sources: U.S. Embassy, Mexico City, and U.S. Department of State.

debt and the outflow for interest payments. Table 7.3 profiles Mexico's foreign debt by type of creditor from 1985 through 1988. Together, the tables present a picture of the evolution of the debt buildup.

From 1971 to 1985, the debt buildup was persistent, but spurts occurred in its rate of growth (Table 7.1). The rate of buildup of external debt increased in 1973, leveled off somewhat after 1977 (following an agreement with the IMF calling for a limitation in the rate of increase of foreign debt), and then had an immense spurt in 1981. Another IMF agreement in 1982 again leveled off the rate. These agreements with the IMF were entered into both because new capital was needed and because some external disciplinary pressure was useful.

Guillermo Ortíz and Jaime Serra Puche have pointed out that the average annual rate of external debt increase between 1960 and 1972 was 6.3 percent, or less than the increase in GDP.[2] The receipt side of the current account in the balance of payments increased at the even more rapid rate of 10.4 percent a year. The implication is that Mexico's external borrowings were prudent over this period. To revert to the traditional model set forth earlier, while Mexico's current-account deficit was growing larger (at an average annual rate of 8.3 percent over this period), this reflected the absorption of resources from the rest of the world at what appeared to be a sustainable rate. Over this whole period, the debt/GDP ratio was well below 20 percent, but by 1985, it was more than 50 percent. It is now more than 60 percent.

The slowdowns and spurts in the accumulation of external debt can be seen in Table 7.2. The growth in debt buildup slowed perceptibly in 1977, then increased again markedly in 1981, only to slow down again after the IMF agreement in 1982. Table 7.2 also shows the relationship between capital inflows from new debt and payments to meet interest on old debt. The inflows exceeded the interest payments until 1981, the normal pattern if the objective is to exploit resources made available by the rest of the world. After 1982, the relationship was reversed and Mexico was providing resources to the rest of the world, a topsy-turvy situation in which the poor country, Mexico, is exporting resources, while the rich, neighboring country, the United States, is importing them.

Table 7.3 shows that bank and other commercial credit make up the majority of Mexico's external debt. The significance of the dominance of commercial-bank credit is twofold: such lending is usually shorter term than credit from official sources, such as the World Bank and the Inter-American Development Bank; and it normally carries a higher interest rate.[3] Commercial-bank credit has another particularly relevant feature—it is commercial. The behavior of commercial banks is motivated primarily by profit considerations; a Mexican appeal to commercial lenders to take into account political and social considerations by giving generous debt treatment has less resonance than when a comparable plea is made to governments or international institutions.

Why Mexico Borrowed

The motivation of the commercial-bank lenders is reasonably straightforward. They had lendable funds, primarily from the capture of petrodollars, and sovereign borrowers like Mexico, or near sovereigns like large public enterprises such as Pemex, seemed safe clients from which attractive interest-rate spreads could be obtained over the cost of the money to the banks. In other words, the lending was profitable at what seemed to be a low risk. What is less fathomable is why the banks continued to lend even after it became evident that the low-risk assumption was shaky.[4] Some possible explanations include ignorance of the size of Mexico's debt, inertia, and the conviction popular in the early 1980s that the debt problem was one of liquidity—that is, a short-term phenomenon that would pass, rather than a structural issue that would endure.

Mexico's continued large borrowings were no more justifiable than the continued bank lending. But the 1970s and early 1980s were heady years in Mexico, as the country became an oil exporter of the first rank at a time when oil prices were high. For two years, 1980 and 1981, real growth of the GDP, at 8.3 and 7.9 percent, was well above the historical norm for Mexico, and together with the accompanying increase in job creation, this was hailed in Mexico's global plan of the time as a major accomplishment, with the implication that a new growth norm had been established.[5]

The implicit assumption was that either oil prices would remain high or borrowing based on oil in the ground could be covered in due course even if prices declined temporarily. Meanwhile, oil revenues and loans could be used to create an industrial and agricultural structure by the twenty-first century that would ensure self-sustained economic growth even if oil revenue declined. As a result of such bullish thinking, Mexico's external debt increased even when oil prices were high, and then skyrocketed when oil prices declined.

Leopoldo Solís and Ernesto Zedillo undertook a detailed exercise to decompose the sources of the growth in external debt, which they attribute to the spendthrift atmosphere in Mexico at the time, typified by the popularity of those members of the cabinet who produced the grandest projects and programs.[6] Their results show that the major external causes of the growth of the foreign debt were shocks of two varieties: high oil prices, which slowed the growth in volume of exports, thereby causing oil revenue to be insufficient to meet the growing cost of imports; and the later decline in the oil price in 1981 and sharp increase in world interest rates. Solís and Zedillo cite the unprecedented increase in imports of foreign goods and capital flight as the main internal causes for the debt increase. The growth in imports resulted from the development plan and an overvalued exchange rate. This also stimulated the large capital flight by making it possible to purchase foreign exchange at a low cost in pesos, and then profit when the peso was later devalued.

There is a large literature on why countries borrow. Mark Gersovitz gives four reasons: to divorce the level of consumption from short-term income fluctuations; because the domestic marginal product of capital exceeds the world cost of capital (in layman's language, because the extra output from the activity for which the loan is used exceeds the cost of the loan); because a country wishes to adjust slowly to some shock; and to have liquidity to carry out international transactions, such as suppliers' credits for trade.[7] But these explanations are inadequate to explain the Mexican actions. There is little evidence that Mexico was meticulous in carrying out cost–benefit analyses on the use of foreign funds for specific projects, and the country's external-debt policy eventually led to shock treatment in the de la Madrid administration to stabilize the economy; the adjustment was sudden, not gradual, and as the situation deteriorated, it became increasingly difficult to obtain short-term loans at an acceptable cost.[8]

What is apparent is that purely economic explanations of why Mexico contracted external debt are incomplete. A broader political-economic explanation involving the desire to distribute economic largesse for political motives, the social goal of augmenting job creation, and the nationalistic impulse of a rush to industrialization all helped fuel the rush to debt.

Policy during the critical years of debt buildup was made in reckless disregard of the costs of faulty judgment. Mexico counted on continued high oil prices, and assumed that oil in the ground would cover all repayment contingencies. Murphy's law was not taken into account, and when oil prices declined, capital flight surged, and foreign interest rates increased, the consequences were devastating. This inexcusable recklessness constituted an abuse of leadership that adversely affected the lives of 80 million Mexicans.

As Table 7.1 shows, the debt buildup also affected Mexico's private sector. Indeed, during the critical years of buildup of foreign debt between 1980 and 1982, the private debt grew at a more rapid rate than the public, and for a reason similar to that underlying the growth of public debt—the heady atmosphere of perpetual economic growth based on petroleum.[9] At the end of 1983, the private external debt was distributed among 3,873 companies, but one-third of the total was concentrated in 9 industrial groups.[10] The most important creditors were U.S. banks.[11]

The conditions that led to the public-sector debt crisis in 1982 also brought on a crisis of the private debtors. The expectation of continued 8 percent or so growth a year turned into economic decline; this led to a sharp drop in domestic demand; new construction contracts plummeted, especially from Pemex; and the sharp devaluation of the currency increased the peso cost of debt repayment.[12] But while Mexico's private sector was no more prescient in its business forecasts than the public sector was in its economic projections, private individuals had the option to invest outside Mexico to protect the value of their capital and could turn to the government for rescue. This was handled by the Fideicomiso para la Cobertura de Riesgos Cambiarios—best known by its acronym, Ficorca—an agency that began operations at the beginning of 1983 and protects private companies against the risk of further devaluations of the peso. The operations of Ficorca are complex, and the extent of the assistance given depended on the rescheduling terms the private company could negotiate with its creditors. What the establishment of Ficorca demonstrated was that when large companies were in peril of bankruptcy because of the inability to meet foreign-exchange obligations, the government felt constrained to help. There was thus a merging of the public and the private external debts. Government rescues of large corporations are familiar in the United States as well, as in the Chrysler and Continental Illinois cases.

One other major factor in Mexico's debt buildup was capital flight, which embodies a contradiction. While the growth of public and private debt was at least partly due to the expectation of continued economic growth, capital flight takes place when there is lack of private confidence in the political or economic stability of a country. Even in 1981, when capital inflows (that is, new debt) amounted to about $23 billion, capital flight was apparently about $11 billion. Several elements characterize the reconciliation of these contradictory tendencies: companies may borrow to expand, even as individuals, both within and outside these companies, send funds abroad to protect their capital; and the very size of the capital outflows created a need to replace the foreign exchange.

Capital flight is not a precise concept. The word "flight" gives it a pejorative meaning, but much movement of capital out of a country is for legitimate investment and trade purposes, and it is not simple to separate this necessary movement from precautionary shipment of assets abroad.

Estimates of capital flight from Mexico in recent years vary with the definition used, but for the past decade as a whole capital flight was equal to one-third to one-half of the increment to foreign debt.[13] The implication is that if capital had not fled Mexico, the foreign-debt buildup would have been substantially lower, but this is an uncertain assertion because the accumulation of debt was not necessarily all used for productive purposes to compensate for capital flight. However, capital available for use in the country certainly would have been greater had there been less capital flight.

There is constant speculation among financial experts whether accumulated capital flight, which represents assets held abroad by Mexicans, can be lured back by appropriate policies. Some return of capital to Mexico did occur from 1986 through 1988, but it was motivated by the need for working capital in the face of tight credit policy as well as by high Mexican interest rates. Much of the capital sent abroad was invested in fixed assets, such as real estate, and will not return to Mexico.

One feature of capital flight from Mexico not well developed in the technical economic literature is the proximity of the United States. Deposits by Mexicans in banks on the U.S. side of the border flourished in recent years, particularly after 1982, even in those border areas with troubled economies and high unemployment, such as the lower Rio Grande Valley and Laredo. An analyst with the Federal Reserve Bank in Dallas estimated that in 1984 banks in Texas border counties held one-quarter of all Mexican deposits in the United States.[14] The proportion is remarkably high, since the U.S. border banks are relatively small. The reasons are familiarity, what the analyst in the cited article called "an old-boy network," and higher liquidity (a low ratio of loans to deposits) than banks generally offer in the United States. This assures Mexican depositors quick access to their funds without breaking the banks.[15]

The question of capital flight merits examination in the context of the Mexican debt problem because the amounts, however calculated, are extremely large and the issue arouses so much passion in both capital-fleeing and capital-receiving countries. The emotion in Mexico often centers on patriotism. The contrary view in U.S. financial circles is that a wealth holder would be a fool to needlessly risk assets by keeping them at home if objective circumstances indicated a need to send them elsewhere. There are charges from time to time that U.S. banks and other recipients of capital flight actually solicit these funds, but the solicitation would fall on deaf ears if the "frightened money" did not exist.[16]

Countries have resorted to controls to prevent capital flight, as Mexico did for a short time in late 1982, but the accepted wisdom is that these regulations can have little long-term effect in Mexico because of its proximity to and extensive economic linkages with the United States.[17] Controls on outward movement of capital would almost certainly impede the flow of capital into Mexico, since asset holders do not wish to be trapped in a cul de sac with no legal means of exit.

The World Won't Stop—It's Hard to Get Off

There is plenty of blame to share between borrowers and lenders for the problem Mexico faces in servicing its foreign debt, but blame-casting is a useful exercise only if it serves as a caution to avoid repetition of faulty policies.

When the debt crisis exploded on the international scene in the latter part of 1982, many large U.S. commercial banks were heavily exposed in Mexico; that is, loans to Mexico constituted a high proportion of their capital, and they had no graceful exit. These proportions have since been reduced, but large banks still cannot easily walk away.[18] They have thus become engaged in what has been called involuntary lending, discussed below.

The large money-center banks have an interest in the stability of the international financial system in addition to their narrow profit concern in Mexico. Smaller banks have more leeway; their exposure relative to their capital is generally less in Mexico than that of the larger banks, and they are less amenable to arguments that they must continue to lend to protect the international system. Many are taking losses and leaving Mexico.

While the foreign banks were a vital part of the process, Mexico helped get itself into trouble. The fiscal excesses of the Echeverría and López Portillo administrations are well documented.[19] Once Mexico got on the debt roller coaster, it could not easily get off. Since 1982, the government has sought to ease the disengagement by a combination of dealing with the causes of the problem (that is, the stabilization and modernization programs), easing the burden of servicing through debt rescheduling, buying old debt at a discount and replacing it with new, longer-term debt, and seeking new debt to avoid an abrupt and painful extrication.

There is a potent social issue in Mexico. The main sufferers from the stabilization efforts have been those persons and families least able to cope with hardships over and above those already present.[20] The Mexican government, friendly foreign governments such as that of the United States, and international institutions must take this hardship into account, but commercial banks, while they are evidently aware of the social-political imperatives that the Mexican authorities face, cannot be expected to allow compassion to drive their lending activities. In the final analysis, Mexico itself must deal with the human hardships, and its response to the debt problem must confront the fundamentals of development policy while aiding those who cannot wait for the long term. But Mexico needs help to do this.

The essential ingredient now is some relief for Mexico to work out escapes from past mistakes, based on a solid foundation for the future. Cooperative relations are needed, among the social groups in Mexico, between the foreign banks and the Mexican authorities, and between Mexico and creditor governments and international institutions. None can escape facing the problems each had a hand in creating.

Dealing with the Debt Issue

The current international debt problem erupted in August 1982 when Mexico's Secretary of Treasury, Jesús Silva Herzog, informed officials of the U.S. government, the IMF, the World Bank, and private commercial banks that Mexico had run out of foreign-exchange reserves and could not meet its debt-service obligations.[21] This was the first act of what has become a continuing debt drama; the United States and the international community provided bridge loans to cover the period until Mexico completed its financing negotiations with the IMF and the commercial banks.

Mexico's actions (in 1983 and 1984) following this first crisis were politically courageous, financially prudent, and socially draconian at the time. Mexico was seen as the model debtor, one willing to confront its problems by reducing its fiscal deficit, lowering real wages, and correcting the overvaluation of the peso. These key measures were incorporated in an agreement with the IMF that was to run for three years, and were the quid pro quo for the financial actions of the IMF, creditor governments, and private banks.

However, further acts have taken place in the continuing debt drama. By the end of 1985, a year in which fiscal austerity gave way to expansion, Mexico was no longer seen by the outside financial community as a model debtor. Indeed, the Mexican situation forced rethinking of what until then had been conventional wisdom about the need for economic austerity to deal with a combination of inflation and large deficits in the balance of payments. The new thinking, as it affected Mexico, was best exemplified in two specific actions: the Baker plan, named after U.S. Secretary of the Treasury James Baker, and a new agreement with the IMF.

The Baker plan was introduced in October 1985 at the annual meetings of the IMF and the World Bank in Seoul, Korea. It contained three key elements: an increase in lending to debtor countries from multilateral development institutions, such as the World Bank and the Inter-American Development Bank, over the three-year period 1986 through 1988; an increase in lending of $20 billion over the same period by commercial banks, generally in conjunction with lending by the official multilateral banks; and, as the debtor-country counterpart, a series of measures designed to foster economic growth, such as encouraging foreign investment, selling inefficient public-sector enterprises, reducing import protection, and liberalizing capital markets.

To an observer not immersed in the previous orthodoxy of stabilization programs, the proposals hardly seem radical. They are rooted in a U.S. philosophy that economic growth is best achieved when the public sector of countries plays a modest role. Indeed, they have been called the "classical approach to balance-of-payments adjustment" in that the components of correction are curtailing fiscal excesses and taking actions to promote exports and reduce imports.[22] What was "fresh" about the Baker approach was that it envisaged stabilization in an atmosphere not merely of economic austerity, but also of growth, while dealing with the cost to service past debt buildup by forcing lenders to provide new debt.[23] The Baker plan was welcomed in developing countries because its premise was that debtors could grow out of their problems rather than shrink out of them by economic decline.

Mexico's second agreement with the IMF during the de la Madrid administration was announced in November 1986.[24] In addition to features familiar to such agreements, such as monetary and credit policy designed to lower inflation and a flexible exchange-rate policy as one tool for maintaining balance-of-payments equilibrium, this standby agreement (as these IMF agreements are called) also supported the Baker proposals for stimulating growth. These proposals are worth setting forth, since they had a pathbreaking effect.

The key condition of the 1982 IMF agreement was that Mexico would drastically reduce its public-sector deficit as measured by its relationship to Mexico's GDP. This deficit, which can be referred to as a public-sector borrowing requirement (PSBR), was then in fact reduced from more than 17 percent of GDP in 1982 to 7.7 percent in 1984, after which it started to rise again. A second effort to reduce the PSBR during the final years of the de la Madrid administration almost certainly would not have been politically tenable because it would have involved even further economic contraction.

What was done instead was to recast the meaning of the public-sector deficit. Three definitions were identified: an overall deficit, an operational deficit, and a primary balance. The overall deficit is the familiar PSBR, and at the time the agreement was reached it was expected to be about 17 percent of GDP in 1986.[25] The operational deficit is calculated by subtracting the inflation component of internal public debt from the overall deficit. The economic rationale is that the increase in nominal interest payments does not represent an income transfer in real terms but instead compensates debt holders for the erosion from inflation in the real value of the principal of the debt. Translated into less technical language, if personal demand is based on real balances or wealth holdings, partial compensation of the decline in these balances from the effects of inflation will not lead to increased demand. The primary balance is the difference between public-sector receipts and outlays, excluding all interest payments, domestic and foreign. This balance is being used by the Mexican authorities to measure the results of the fiscal effort in which it is engaged. The new IMF agreement deals with both the PSBR and the operational balance, but its stipulations focus primarily on the size of the balance.

An economic basis exists for the use of different measures of the public-sector deficit, but it is evident that the IMF was also motivated by noneconomic considerations: the social hardship associated with a drastic reduction in the PSBR would almost certainly not have been acceptable in Mexico. It is here, in the actual operations of the IMF, that the shift in philosophy in the Baker proposal, from an emphasis on economic contraction to one on growth, had an impact.[26] Although many critics (including this one) argue that the Baker plan is inadequate for dealing with the debt problem, its overall implications in the continuing process of debt restructuring have not been negligible—as the Mexican case illustrates.[27]

The condition in the Baker plan that additional public and private financing should be made available to debtor countries only if they pursue market-dominated policies also found its way into the IMF agreement. Mexico made commitments to liberalize its trade regime and pursue a flexible exchange-rate policy, and its representatives said that the government would reduce the number of state enterprises.

Finally, the feature in the IMF agreement that attracted the most publicity was the insistence that private banks contribute additional lending as a necessary condition of the adjustment process. The way this was put in the IMF press release was that since Mexico was already in recession, its authorities were relying "on the financial support of all creditors that have financed Mexico's development in the past to help them implement a growth-oriented program."[28] The external financing package to Mexico's public sector, most of which was for 1986 to 1987, had the following elements: $6 billion from commercial banks; $2.3 billion from the World Bank; $4 billion from the Inter-American Development Bank; $2.5 billion from official bilateral creditors; and about $1.3 billion from the IMF.[29] Not all of this was additional lending. The package was referred to in shorthand as being of $12 billion, which was the estimate of the new funds that would enter Mexico in 1987.

Hundreds of private banks from around the world were involved in this forced lending program to Mexico, and many of them balked, especially smaller ones.[30] It took until March 1987, about five months for a program that had a life of less than a year and a half, before the private bank package was completed. We can conclude that the Baker plan premise of increased private lending to heavily indebted countries pursuing market-oriented growth programs is more easily promised than accomplished and that, based on the Mexican experience, such laborious bailing-in techniques are inadequate. This inadequacy is particularly clear for smaller banks that are not trapped by the constraints from excessive past lending and that do not share with the larger banks concerns about the viability of the international financial system. These smaller banks believe that they can get off this particular debt roller coaster, or at least that they can try, and it took considerable pressure from U.S. officials to get U.S. banks to agree to contribute new funds to the Mexico package, as it did from IMF authorities to convince banks in all creditor countries.[31] This aspect of the Baker plan clearly has no future.

New lending is only one element in dealing with the debt problem. The other is to face the service burden that Mexico must bear on old debt.

Past Debt Rescheduling

Recasting of obligations is undoubtedly as old as the oldest profession; it is a common feature of government, business, and personal finance transactions. What is different about the recent period, particularly since the Mexican rescue of 1982, is the magnitude of the debts being rescheduled and the frequency of these negotiations.

Mexico has gone to the rescheduling and refinancing well many times since August 1982. The reschedulings by both official and private creditors were at first relatively modest. Interest rates on rescheduled debt were high, and the term for repayment of principal was not extended very far into the future. But in successive negotiations, both the interest rate and the terms were eased. Mexico has, in fact, become the pioneer in the most recent rescheduling series and in extracting terms from the private creditors that became benchmarks in creditor negotiations with other countries. But although every agreement establishes some precedent for subsequent agreements, countries are still treated on a case-by-case basis, and precedent does not mean formula. To cite just one example, not every country receives most-favored-nation treatment, an interest rate and terms as favorable as the best-case treatment that preceded it. The Mexican rescheduling that accompanied the 1986 financing merits special attention because of its scope and its terms. This agreement was announced on September 30, 1986. Table 7.4 sets forth the total debt package; new loans for 1986 and 1987 represent the involuntary lending by the commercial banks incorporated into the IMF agreement.[32] The $43.7 billion of already outstanding public-sector debt with foreign commercial banks was extended to a repayment term of twenty years, with seven years of grace during which only interest is paid. In other words, repayment of principal is not to begin until the eighth year and to be fully amortized (assuming no further rescheduling) only in the year 2006. The term of the new money for 1986 and 1987, the $6 billion, is twelve years, with five years of grace. By granting such long-term repayment schedules, private commercial banks have thus agreed to act more or less as development banks.

The interest rate on both the old and the new money was set at thirteen-sixteenths

Table 7.4 Mexican Foreign Debt Package of September 1986 with Private Bank Creditors (millions of dollars)

Package Elements	Amounts
Old debt balance	43,700
Debt contracted in 1983 and 1984	8,550
New loans for 1986 and 1987[a]	6,000
Petroleum facility	720
Growth facility	500
Facility to maintain public investment	1,200
Ficorca	11,200
Interbank funds	6000
Total	77,870[b]

[a]The new lending package was not completed until March 1987.

[b]While a total is given in the source, it is misleading because some elements of the package were definite and others contingent on future events.

Source: El Mercado de Valores, October 6, 1986, p. 931.

of 1 percent above Libor (the London interbank offer rate), which comes to a spread of about 0.81 percent. (The spread refers to the difference between the cost of money to the banks in the interbank market, Libor, and the interest charged to Mexico.) This was a new low for such reschedulings—most of Mexico's earlier debt carried an interest rate of between 1.125 and 1.5 percentage points over Libor, and some had been based on the spread over the prime rate in the United States, which was higher than Libor—and quickly became a benchmark for reschedulings with other countries.[33] The Mexican authorities calculated that the savings from the lower interest rates would be $294.7 million a year, which is income forgone by the banks. This arithmetic troubles many banks and explains resistance to the settlement, especially after the development-bank terms, the twenty years and seven years of grace, and the precedent set for subsequent sovereign reschedulings.

Table 7.4 lists three contingency or special items that were part of the IMF–commercial bank package. The petroleum facility would provide up to an additional $720 million to Mexico (more accurately, up to SDR 600 million, which at the time was close to $720 million) if the petroleum price dropped below $9 a barrel. Under the investment facility, commercial banks would provide up to $1.2 billion in case of a sudden decline in the external receipts of the public sector. Under a third facility, commercial banks would provide up to $500 million in new funds if Mexican recovery did not permit a projected increase in public investment in selected projects identified as having a high domestic content of inputs and substantial secondary repercussions on the private sector. The World Bank agreed to guarantee up to 50 percent of commercial-bank disbursements under this facility.

Secretary of the Treasury Gustavo Petricioli informed the finance committee of the Mexican Chamber of Deputies on October 22, 1986, of Mexico's accomplishments in its debt negotiations and what future debt strategy would be.[34] He stressed the following points: the approximately $12 billion of new financing that was to be made available in 1986 and 1987; the generous terms and low interest rate of the rescheduling, which together with the new financing meant that net resource transfers from Mexico to other countries would decline from 5.6 percent of GDP in 1985 to 1.9 percent in 1987; the restructuring of more than $11 billion of private debt through the intermediary of Ficorca (Table 7.4); the extension for at least three years of a $6 billion interbank line of credit (Table 7.4); and the ability these features gave to allow Mexico to resume economic growth.

It would be unwise to be too exuberant about the package. While it resolved a short-term foreign-exchange problem, thereby giving the Mexican authorities breathing room to restore economic growth, it still left major problems. The most important was the continuing high rate of inflation in Mexico, and the most durable involves implementing the program to restructure the economy, particularly to make industry more competitive internationally. The total outstanding debt of more than $100 billion is still enormous, and the large interest payments deprive Mexico of resources needed for development. But the debt package did demonstrate that when the IMF, the World Bank, and the U.S. government work together, devising a growth-oriented strategy for a debtor country is possible. The challenge for the future is even more extensive international cooperation to help Mexico restore economic growth. Although the commercial banks went along in this case, it will be difficult to get them to do so again in the future.[35]

One final element of debt rescheduling should be mentioned. In addition to working out arrangements with commercial banks, Mexico renegotiated its debts with official creditors. These negotiations took place in a forum known as the Paris Club.[36] Mexico had first resorted to the Paris Club shortly after the 1982 crisis erupted; the 1986 agreement restructured those debt maturities falling due between September 22, 1986, and March 31, 1988, amounting to $1.5 billion, with a term of ten years, with five years of grace. In addition, the restructuring included 60 percent of the interest payments falling due between September 1986 and the end of 1987, or some $282 of $470 million.[37]

Mexico has chosen to meet its external-debt obligations in a renegotiated form, while other countries—including Peru, Ecuador, and Brazil—have ceased paying their contractual debt-service obligations, in whole or in part, over longer or shorter periods; in return, Mexico has been accorded favored treatment as commercial banks and creditor governments view these things. It is clear, however, that this generosity (if that is the right word) will not be enough; Mexico's entire debt situation requires further restructuring.[38]

Where Things Stand

Perhaps the best description of how creditors have handled the debt problem is "creative muddling through." The muddling through is represented by creditor insistence at first on high spreads, short repayment terms for principal, yearly renegotiations as the best way to keep pressure on debtor governments to take corrective actions to deal with their internal economies and balance of payments, and, in essence, walking away from the social-political problems this posture caused in debtor countries.[39] The hope was that debtor countries would grow out of the debt problem, that it was a passing matter of liquidity and not a pervasive structural phenomenon. Insufficient liquidity is essentially a short-term problem; structural reform is a long-term undertaking.

The creativity in the muddling manifested itself as the debt problem persisted. Spreads declined, amortization periods were lengthened, and official creditors formally capitalized interest obligations and gave debtors multiyear rescheduling agreements (known as Myras) rather than engage in year-by-year negotiations. The creativity was grudging, though. It took great pressure from the U.S. government and international agencies to bring along the private banks in the Mexican case. Banks must ask themselves why they should provide new money as old loans are sold at a deep discount.[40] When Citibank decided in May 1987 to increase its reserve against developing-country loans, this meant essentially that the bank's portfolio of these loans was being written down. The Citibank action was quickly followed by other U.S. banks. This was a decision of willingness to divest billions of dollars of existing loans to developing countries, at a discount. This decision hardly presages a willingness by banks to make new loans to the same countries whose old loans were written down.[41]

The kinds of solutions, if that is the proper word, that have been suggested for the debt problem fall into four broad categories, not necessarily mutually exclusive: to grow out of the problem; to forgive part of the debt, either directly or by sale of old loans at a discount; to push the problem forward, such as by capitalizing interest or stretching out the scheduled amortization of principal; and to pay part of the principal of the debt in local currency as opposed to foreign exchange.[42] Each of these solutions has a number of permutations, and there are many combinations among the categories.[43] There also has been a running debate about whether solutions can be generalized for all debtor countries, whether each case must be dealt with on its own merits, or whether some combination of a generalized approach differentiated in its implementation by the specific country circumstances offers the best solution.

The Baker plan assumed that debtor countries can grow out of their debt problems, and that the necessary ingredients for such growth are more short-term financing and long-term, growth-oriented restructuring of economies. The Mexican case was a significant one for testing U.S. policy because the effort under the Baker plan was greatest there. The plan played a positive role in acknowledging that Mexico could deal with its economic problems by growing instead of contracting its economy, but in other respects it must be judged a failure.

A number of scenarios can be constructed projecting Mexico's export earnings, its current-account performance, the success of its economic restructuring, and the treatment afforded to Mexican exports by the United States. The outcomes will differ depending on the world price of oil, the growth of Mexican nonoil exports, the handling of Mexico's public revenues and expenditures, and the influence of the exchange rate on trade and capital flows. Under extremely optimistic assumptions, Mexico can indeed be projected as growing out of its debt problems, but there are many skeptics (including the author).[44] Surmounting the debt problem requires a long-term view, whereas the political-social situation in Mexico requires short-term improvement in the form of renewed economic growth. The two are not incompatible, but success of the long-term program is not independent of short-term results.

Senator Bill Bradley of new Jersey has proposed a plan to forgive some principal and interest on outstanding debt. Bradley's proposal is driven primarily by the decline in U.S. exports to the large Latin American debtor countries as a result of their stabilization programs. The assumption of the plan is that the resources that are made available by debt relief will be used to buy more imports from the United States. He calls for an annual debt/trade conference by the World Bank; debtor countries agreeing at this forum to undertake economic reforms, chosen by them, would receive 3 percentage points of interest-rate relief for three years on outstanding private and official bilateral loans, plus a 3 percent write-down of principal each year for three years; and multilateral development banks, whose loans would not be written down, would commit themselves to increase their lending by $3 billion a year over the three years.[45] What happens at the end of three years would presumably depend on the international economic situation at that time.

The "hit" in the Bradley plan would be taken primarily by the commercial banks, who therefore did not welcome it. The banks and the U.S. Treasury argue that forcing the banks to bear the burden of debt forgiveness will lead to curtailed future lending to debtor countries. This is the implication of the Citibank action taking losses now on loans to debtor countries.[46] Yet there are variants of the Bradley plan under which banks are willing to write down current loans. Japanese banks in March 1987 created what is best described as an offshore factoring company to which they will sell their loans at a discount, shifting collection to the new company. In this way, the banks acquire lendable funds for other purposes rather than keep them frozen in what are largely sterile accounts.[47] By increasing their reserves against developing-country loans, U.S. banks positioned themselves to sell such loans at a discount, although they may need relief from regulators in order not to have to write down the value of loans they choose not to sell. (About one-third of all commercial-bank loans to Mexico are held by U.S. banks.)

The institution buying discounted loans need not be one created by the banks themselves. Proposals have been made for the World Bank or the IMF to play this role, permitting them to combine debt relief with their other programs.[48] The risk is that it might endanger their own credit standing in world financial markets. It is not clear just how the secondary market for the discounted sale of sovereign loans will develop.

In early 1988, Mexico, in cooperation with the U.S. Treasury and J. P. Morgan Bank, devised an innovative financing plan to take advantage of the discount at which Mexican debt was selling. Under the scheme, creditor banks were offered new Mexican bonds in exchange for the debt they already held. The new Mexican securities were attractive because the principal would be collateralized by non-marketable zero-coupon bonds issued by the U.S. Treasury.[49] Stated simply, the plan was for Mexico to buy $10 billion of twenty-year U.S. bonds, which, since they paid no interest until maturity, would cost about $2 billion. It was expected that the new bonds Mexico would issue, for which the zero-coupon bonds would be collateral, would be swapped for existing debt tendered at a discount of about 40 percent. The result would be to reduce Mexico's total outstanding debt and lower interest costs.

The actual bidding for the new bonds was disappointing. Mexico accepted bids from ninety-five foreign creditor banks covering $3.67 billion of old debt and, in turn, issued $2.56 billion of twenty-year bonds, which came to 69.77 cents of new debt for each $1 of old debt. Most large U.S. banks shunned the Mexican offer. The main bidders were large non-U.S. banks and some regional U.S. banks that found this an attractive way to exit from their old credits to Mexico.[50]

The U.S. government tacitly recognized that the Baker plan was inadequate when Secretary of the Treasury Nicholas F. Brady, in March 1989, outlined a new debt-reduction proposal. The details were left to later negotiation among creditor countries, between them and commercial banks, and with debtor countries. Brady suggested the exchange of some portion of old debt of commercial banks (the exact proportion was left vague, but it was generally understood to be about 20 percent) for new, long-term bonds whose principal and interest repayments would be partially guaranteed by the World Bank and the IMF. Adjustments would be made in regulatory procedures to permit U.S. banks to do this. Elements of the Baker plan remained: Brady's rhetorical stress was on the need for debtor countries to grow rather than stagnate out of their problems; relief would be on a case-by-case basis predicated on the pursuit by debtor countries of "sound policies"; and efforts would be made to convince banks to provide new money using a "menu" approach (employing many techniques in addition to straightforward new loans).[51] As with the Baker plan, the Brady proposals, coupled with general unease internationally about the debt issue, served to stimulate more flexible IMF policies from which Mexico benefited in 1989.

The third general type of debt solution is to push payments off into the future.

Commercial banks now do this regularly for amortization of principal. The Paris Club has done this explicitly by rescheduling interest obligations, as noted above. New loans that permit old interest to be paid do this as well in a more roundabout way. Peru has been limiting its debt service to a proportion of its export earnings (ostensibly 10 percent), which is a form of capitalization of interest (assuming that Peru someday will repay its debt). Two U.S. analysts have argued that the debt-service payments could be limited to a proportion of either GDP or earnings from exports.[52] The capitalization of interest obligations is also one of the solutions suggested by the Economic Commission for Latin America and the Caribbean (ECLAC) in a special conference held in Mexico City in January 1987.[53]

The logic of delaying payments is twofold: it permits use of the resources now for development programs that can take effect only over time; and inflation in creditor countries may effectively reduce the real burden of future payments. Inflation is also the basis of the argument that banks are well advised to sell off doubtful loans at a discount now. The motivation for the banks to establish a substantial secondary market for developing-country debt gained much credibility after the lower interest-rate spread and the long-term amortization granted in the 1986 Mexican package. Debtors prefer to pay in the future, especially in an inflationary environment; and creditors in this environment should prefer payment now, especially if the interest received is low.

The final broad type of solution is to deal with what is known in economics as the transfer problem—the need to generate foreign exchange to meet an obligation that exists in foreign currency. Beyond exchanging its old debt at a discount for new obligations, Mexico can reduce the absolute size of its foreign debt in only two ways: run a surplus in its current account, thereby permitting the outflow of resources without increasing debt, or procure an inflow of capital to acquire Mexican assets. Both techniques are being used in dealing with the debt problem.

Mexico established criteria under which debt can be exchanged for equity in Mexican companies.[54] The idea was for foreign investors to buy Mexican debt at a discount and convert these debt instruments into pesos for investment in Mexico. The Mexican regulations gave priority to investment in certain activities, especially those likely to lead to increased exports and bring advanced technology into Mexico. Preference was given to activities integrated into the economy of the country, not the kind of enclave operation that prevails for the *maquiladora*. Mexico had close to $2 billion in swaps completed or in the pipeline by early 1987, but it is unclear how much of this investment would have come anyway and whether swaps are mostly a cheap way for investors to expand activities.[55] Mexico suspended debt–equity swaps in 1987 because they increased monetary expansion, and thus aggravated inflation, as pesos were issued to buy back the debt.

Two Mexican economists, Víctor Urquidi and Saúl Trejo, proposed a twist on debt–equity swaps. Their suggestion is that part of the interest on foreign debt be paid in local currency for the account of the creditor banks, which would then use these peso funds to invest in export-oriented activities.[56] Trejo has also argued that debt must be analyzed in a broad international context and that Mexico's economic needs can be met only through an expansion of exports; if this occurred, the export interest of the United States (which is what stimulated the Bradley proposals) would also be furthered.[57] Trejo was even more explicit about the link between local-currency payments of part of the interest and investment in export-oriented industries in an article in which he quantified the consequences of the proposal for Mexico and the creditors.[58] Felix Rohatyn and Roger Altman have proposed a variant of the Urquidi–Trejo idea by suggesting that a U.S.–Mexico development-finance authority be established that would have two functions: to swap its securities for Mexican debt held by U.S. banks and to organize and finance manufacturing facilities in Mexico. The proposal calls for a guarantee from the U.S. side for the securities issued by the finance authority.[59]

The objective of all the debt-relief proposals, whether they relate specifically to Mexico or to debtor countries generally, is to stimulate economic growth. Those persons who advocate forgiving part of the debt, capitalizing some interest and extending the term for amortization, or repaying some obligations in local currency, or some combination of all of these, believe that the resources thus freed can be (would be) used for productive investment within the debtor countries. Many of the proposals seek to ensure that the resources will be so used by involving the commercial banks or the World Bank in the disposition of the resources.

Mexico has a double consideration in dealing with its external debt—minimizing the outflow of resources for debt repayment, but also continuing the inflow of new resources at a reasonable cost; it is reluctant to take an action that accomplishes the first objective at the expense of the second.

It is not hard to think up specific debt-relief schemes. If a decision is made about who takes the "hit"—the debtor country, the budgets of creditor countries, commercial banks, or all of these—programs follow logically. The problem has been the reluctance of any of these groups to accept too much of the cost of debt relief, although to date a disproportionate burden has fallen on the population of the debtor country. The creative part of the muddling-through process has occurred only when forced by a crisis that concentrated minds, and this is a disruptive way of operating.

A Recommendation

Paying the debt has been costly in more than monetary terms. The major cost has been imposed on the Mexican population. Per capita incomes declined during the *sexenio* of President de la Madrid for the first time in any administration since the 1930s; the external-debt service was not the only reason for the fall in income, but was an important factor. Resources amounting to some 5 to 6 percent of GDP must leave Mexico each year; about one-third of the foreign exchange earned from exports of goods and services goes to service the external debt. This has compelled Mexico to limit its imports and consequently its rate of economic growth. The political fallout has been substantial, and the opposition on the left based its presidential campaign in 1988 largely on the issue of declaring a debt moratorium so that the hardship on the Mexican population can be eased.

Producers in the United States have also paid a high price. Mexico's imports of goods and services are far below what they would have been with a higher rate of economic growth. If GDP growth in Mexico during the past six years had been 5 percent a year (which is slightly below the norm of the previous fifty years), cumulative imports over this period could have been $35 billion more than they were.[60] If U.S. producers captured only 60 percent of this higher figure (which is lower than the proportion they have enjoyed), U.S. exports over the six years would have been $21 billion higher. This translates into about 100,000 U.S. jobs a year.[61]

United States debt strategy has thus involved a trade-off at the margin between benefits going to financial institutions as opposed to producers of goods and services. By insisting that the debt be serviced, the choice has favored the financial institutions at the expense of the productive sector. Industrial workers in the United States have been caught up in this trade-off and were losers as well.

Relations between Mexico and the United States have suffered. While the majority of the external debt is owed to non-U.S. banks, the average Mexican sees the United States as the creditor. The blame for the hardship caused by the need to make debt payments is placed jointly on the Mexican and U.S. governments. This was evident in the speeches by Cuauhtémoc Cárdenas in his presidential campaign.

The current debt situation is thus unsatisfactory to Mexicans most in need of relief and to American producers and industrial workers. More definitive relief than step-by-step muddling through is now appropriate. So are steps to share the burden more equally among all the parties involved in the debt buildup—including the banks. The argument that debt relief will dry up new lending to Mexico would be more convincing if lending had not already dried up. A healthy, economically growing Mexico will be a better prospect for new lending than a Mexico that must live from hand to mouth.

The U.S. government, in cooperation with other creditor governments, has now twice taken the initiative to reduce Mexico's debt-service burden—the Baker and Brady proposals. Neither plan was adequate. A precise form relief should take will not be spelled out here; there are already many proposals on the table, and they can and do serve as inputs to discussions among the parties involved.[62] The relief can have the mix of elements analyzed earlier: some reduction of the total debt and annual payments; stretching out payments; and using swap techniques involving payments in pesos rather than in foreign exchange.

However, the general criteria on which debt relief should be based must be clear. These include the following points.

- The relief should be substantial enough to permit restoration of positive per capita income growth. The Baker plan contemplated that growth would take place by building the total debt further; the Brady plan included this plus some debt relief. However, substantial new lending is unlikely under current circumstances of economic stagnation in Mexico. The recommendation here is based on the belief that sufficient economic growth will be likely only if Mexico can retain more of its own resources.

- Burden sharing should be more equitably divided between the borrower (the Mexican government and its entities) and the lenders than in the past. Most banks are in a far better position to share this burden today than they were when the debt crisis first erupted in 1982.

- The debt relief should not be automatic, but require credible commitments from Mexico on its economic policy. To a great degree, Mexico has demonstrated its resolve to pursue what Brady called ''sound'' policies. Neither banks nor individual governments are well placed to extract these conditions; hence, the international financial institutions (the IMF, World Bank, and Inter-American Development Bank) should be involved.[63]

- Governments must be engaged, on both the creditor and the debtor sides, since only they are in a position to provide guarantees in the event they will be needed; or they must alter banking regulations, if this is required. And only they are in a position to place the debt situation into the broader context of the total political-economic relationship with Mexico.

The need for policy consistency by Mexico merits emphasis. Mexico has not been consistent in its stabilization policy. The internal inflation was attacked primarily by keeping wages down; apart from the hardship this caused, it was not working. Consumer prices in 1987 rose by about 160 percent. The PSBR continued to rise—it was more than 17 percent of GDP in 1987—and because of the inflation, the interest rate for government borrowing approached 200 percent. The internal debt had become far more onerous than the external debt; measured in relation to the GDP, the cost to service the external debt in 1987 was 5 percent, and that to meet interest on the internal more than three times larger, 16 percent.

The need for a more forceful approach to economic stabilization was evident, and in December 1987 the government announced what it called the Pacto de Solidaridad Económica (Economic Solidarity Pact, PSE), which has involved a combination of declines in planned levels of government spending, price and wage controls, and temporary freezing of the exchange rate.[64] The goal of this modified shock treatment was to reduce the monthly rate of inflation from about 10 to less than 2 percent.[65] The PSE was a serious program, but a substantial debt-relief package requires assurance that seriousness will endure during the Salinas administration.

The failure to work out a comprehensive debt-relief scheme for Mexico does not mean that there will be no relief. Rather, it means that the next debt package will be devised in an atmosphere of crisis, as have past arrangements. The better part of statesmanship is to act calmly in advance of what is coming in any event.

Mexico has since reached agreement on $54 billion of its commercial debt under which banks have the option of lowering the interest rate, accepting a 35 percent discount on old debt, or providing new loans. The actual decline in annual interest that Mexico will have to pay depends on the option chosen, but the total is apt to be modest, about 1 percent of GDP. The agreement will succeed if it bolsters investor confidence. In my judgment, the agreement is likely to be another chapter in the continuous debt drama, not the end of the tale.

8

THE BORDER

> If the border is not economically integrated into the rest of the country and does not see its future as working to improve the situation of all Mexicans, it will have no alternative but to turn north, with all the risks this implies.
>
> GUILLERMINA VALDÉS-VILLALVA, 1985

> Why do you have to declare yourself for the Mexicans or for the Americans?
>
> U.S. CITIZEN OF MEXICAN ORIGIN IN INTERVIEW ON BILL MOYERS' TELEVISION PROGRAM, 1986

> And thus we come to the most preoccupying problem, namely, that of underground water of the border region and its trail of consequences for future Mexico–U.S. relations and eventually for the development of very important adjoining areas.
>
> CÉSAR SEPÚLVEDA, 1982

Two Nations, One Destiny

Patterns of life are different at border regions from those at inland areas. Societies come together at borders, sometimes in mutual animosity (as at the long border between China and the Soviet Union or the shorter one between Chile and Peru), sometimes in friendly interaction (as is generally true along the extensive Canada–United States border). Even where the relationship is amicable, the mix of two sovereignties and separate cultures leads to social and political tensions.

There are scholars who specialize in border studies, but there is no comprehensive theory of borders.[1] However, even if such a theory existed, a special section would be needed for understanding the relationship where the United States and Mexico meet.

The United States–Mexico border has unique elements. The most evident (the most shocking, really) is the vast disparity in wealth. In 1984, the per capita income in the most affluent part of the U.S. border, the San Diego metropolitan area, was more than 6.5 times that of Mexico ($2,040). The disparity diminishes drastically in the poorest county on the U.S. border, but while per capita income in Starr County, Texas ($4,106), was only 30 percent that of the United States as a whole, it was still twice that of Mexico. Other Texas metropolitan areas fall in between; El Paso's per capita income was about four times that of Mexico, and Laredo's about three times.[2]

Differences in income and wealth have their consequences. Joseph Nalven has noted that the air-pollution-control office in San Diego has 100 staff positions, whereas that in Tijuana, whose population is about half that of the combined region

154

from Chula Vista to San Diego, has 5; the San Diego budget is thirty-five times that of Tijuana.[3] The differential resource availabilities are replicated for almost all services, such as water pollution, sewage treatment, and control of waste disposal.

Impulses at the border move in both directions, but there is a dominant–subordinate influence. Economic differences are manifested in assembly plants that locate in Mexico to take advantage of cheap labor. People move north, mostly to improve their economic positions. But the effects run deeper; values, aspirations, and social mores are transmitted more thoroughly from the wealthier to the poorer country.[4] Consumer habits are imported from the United States to a people who are not able to afford a U.S. market basket of consumer goods.

There is also a political effect. Democracy is entrenched in the United States, whereas it is qualified in Mexico; it is no accident that Mexico's northern border is the region most infected by the yearning for effective suffrage.

The border is a complex region. Its population grew rapidly on both sides in the 1950s and 1960s, particularly in Mexico. This growth slowed after that in Mexico. Indeed, between 1970 and 1980, border growth was less than Mexican population growth in general.[5] People living on the border have been trained in their native culture and mores, but the constant interaction adds a strong element of the foreign culture. Tijuana is as unlike Mexico City as El Paso is unlike Boston. Neither is the border mixture easily digestible. A well-known Mexican psychologist has noted, "For the Western world, one could hardly find a pair of nations that would be more intensely different in historico-sociocultural background than the United States of America and the Republic of Mexico."[6] The result "is a separate society, in a sense, with a unique culture of its own, made up of elements which overlap and come from the two mother cultures."[7]

The border is an arena of conflict and cooperation, of example and animosity, of opportunity and frustration, and of separation and blending—in each case to a degree that does not exist generally in either nation. This chapter will seek to capture these contradictions by examining each country's economic, cultural, political, and environmental impact on the other at the border—although they are not separable in practice. Because the two countries are contiguous, much U.S. demand for narcotics is met from production in Mexico or from use of that country as a transit point. Another major influence of contiguity, transnational migration patterns, will be discussed in Chapter 9. But the conclusion can be stated here: A border synthesis is inescapable.

Mutual Impacts

History contributes much to Mexican thinking about the border region. This is true for the totality of Mexico–United States relations, but the past is especially neuralgic where the two countries meet. It is hard to find a Mexican discussion of the border that does not recall the loss of Texas and other territory to the United States under the treaty of Guadalupe-Hidalgo in 1848, following the Mexican War.[8] This constant reference to Mexican weakness and U.S. imperialism is part of the educational formation of Mexican leaders. This perennial reiteration does not signify that Mexico has rejected the reality of history, but that the factors that led to the territorial loss remain an important input into current policy. For example, the region that now forms California, Arizona, New Mexico, and Texas was mostly unpopulated by Mexicans at the time of the Texas war of independence and the Mexican War, and one motivation for more recent Mexican industrial and economic programs at the border was to avoid even the possibility of history repeating itself if the area remained relatively unpopulated.[9]

While fears of a new U.S. manifest destiny are occasionally heard in Mexico, the realistic concern is not direct invasion but a loss of loyalty by border inhabitants to the very concept of a national Mexico; see, for example, the quotation from Guillermina Valdés-Villalva at the beginning of this chapter. Antonio González de León expresses uneasiness about interdependence at the border with the United States, a binational economy, or symbiosis.[10] This is another manifestation of unequal power. Mexico, the weaker country, while granting that there is a binational economy at the border—the Mexican incentives for the *maquiladora* demonstrate this acceptance—does so with misgiving and concern. The stronger country, the United States, deals with the binational economy primarily on economic grounds, but also out of a desire to avoid mass migration north. These different sensitivities, like the disparate histories, are part of the backdrop to understanding the separate viewpoints at the border.

The growth of a large Spanish-speaking population in the U.S. border region, with its own agenda on international affairs, influences the U.S. government. While the loss of sovereignty is not an issue—indeed, the inevitable growth of domestic political power by Hispanic groups constitutes an affirmation of U.S. sovereignty—the Hispanic groups in the U.S. Southwest bemoan their alienation from Washington, D.C., and even from their own state capitals. The response, however, is to organize in order to influence U.S. and state policy rather than to look to Mexico. Border concerns in the United States also deal with specific issues, such as air and water quality and hazardous-waste disposal, discussed later in the chapter.

Before going further, it is necessary to define what is meant by the border. Most allusions to the border will refer to those cities and counties on both sides that abut the other country, but this is not a rigid definition because San Diego, which is treated as a border city, is not directly on the border. The border presents itself as a series of twin cities, one in each country (Table 8.1), and these twin cities, each supporting the other to a greater or lesser degree, are the very essence of symbiosis. The totals at the bottom of Table 8.1 for border cities and counties reflect the definition of the border as used in this chapter.

Economics

Mexican actions to stimulate the border economy have always had political and social objectives. Jesús Tamayo has pointed out that the first free zone established on the Mexican side of the border in 1861 was designed to keep the locals from emigrating to Texas.[11] The border-study program of the Centro de Investigación y Docencia Económicas (Cide), one of Mexico's leading research and teaching institutions, was stimulated by unease over the region's increasing economic integration with the United States and the loss of legitimacy of the official party.[12]

Table 8.1   Population of U.S. and Mexican Border Cities, 1980 (population figures in thousands of persons)

U.S. City	Mexican City	Population 1980		Percent Growth 1950–1980	
		U.S. City	Mexican City	U.S. City	Mexican City
California	Baja California				
San Diego/Chula Vista	Tijuana	1,008	430	171	616
Calexico	Mexicali	14	342	124	429
Arizona	Sonora				
Yuma/San Luis	San Luis	43	77	374	1,780
Nogales	Nogales	16	66	155	168
Douglas	Agua Prieta	13	29	38	176
New Mexico	Chihuahua				
Columbus	Palomas	—	2	—	199
Texas					
El Paso	Ciudad Juárez	425	544	226	296
Presidio	Ojinaga	2	18	—	298
	Coahuila				
Del Rio	Ciudad Acuña	30	39	111	242
Eagle Pass	Piedras Negras	21	69	194	145
	Tamaulipas				
Laredo	Nuevo Laredo	91	202	76	250
Rio Grande City	Camargo	9	16	124	−38
Hidalgo/McAllen	Reynosa	69	195	242	471
Brownsville	Matamoros	85	189	136	312
Totals		U.S.	Mexico		
Border cities		1,819	2,199	113	171
Border counties		4,042	2,890	178	253
Border states		41,918	8,179a	113	355
Full country		226,546	69,393	50	153

Note: Totals may not add due to rounding.
— = Less than 500.
aExcludes Mexican state of Nuevo León, which abuts the border at Texas, but whose border population is negligible. However, its main city, Monterrey, while not at the border, does have many border-city attributes.
Sources: Based on tables prepared by Jerry R. Ladman, "Industry on the Southern Border of the United States," pp. 206–7, taken from U.S. Census Bureau, *U.S. Census of the Population*, 1950 and 1980; México, Secretaría de Economía, *Censo general de población*, 1950; Inegi, *Censo general de población y vivienda*, 1980.

Mexican border programs were designed to stimulate employment. Commentators have made a connection between U.S. termination in 1964 of the *bracero* program, under which Mexicans had been contracted for farm work in the United States, and the start of border programs to provide work for the returning Mexicans, but while undoubtedly a consideration, a desire to stimulate border employment irrespective of migration to the United States already existed.[13] A criticism often lodged against the border industrialization program is that it attracts immigrants to the region who then continue their journey across the border. The evidence for this sequence—of persons coming to the border to get a job in the *maquiladora*, only to end up in the United States—is not strong, although it cannot be rejected completely.[14] However, the criticism misses the point. The Mexican authorities have always had two related objectives in mind: to populate the border and to find jobs for persons there.

Border development programs have had intended and unintended consequences. They did help populate the region and provide much employment, but they also served to integrate the border more closely with the United States. The Mexican authorities thus face an intractable dilemma: continued job creation has become essential to maintain loyalty to the official party and to Mexico itself, but the more these jobs are integrated into the industrial production system of the United States, the more loyalty to Mexico City diminishes. The Mexican political authorities cannot terminate the industrial integration with the United States, since that is the basis of border development, but they must simultaneously seek ways to increase this integration with Mexico as a whole.

If one measures the increase in the number of plants, their employment, and the exports they have generated since the incentives that led to the *maquiladora* program were instituted in 1965, the *maquiladora* must be judged a success (Table 8.2). Their growth derives from a number of considerations, and while proximity to the United States plays a role, it is not the only one. On the U.S. side, most of the plants supplying inputs to the *maquiladora* are located elsewhere in the United States, particularly in the Midwest.[15] Transportation costs are therefore not the major attraction for many products assembled in *maquiladora*.

Peso devaluation has been a major stimulus to *maquiladora* growth; since 1983, this devaluation sharply reduced the dollar cost of Mexican workers paid in pesos. A Mexican analyst has calculated that U.S. salaries for comparable work were 4.7 times those of Mexican *maquiladora* workers in 1975, 5.6 times in 1980, and 14 times in 1983.[16] The exchange-rate relationship made Mexico one of the cheapest places in the world for an American corporation to hire foreign labor.

The growth of the *maquiladora* also reflects a tacit agreement between the two countries. Mexico instituted and then augmented incentives for foreign firms to locate in Mexico in their production-sharing arrangements. These benefits include the ability to import materials in bond (that is, without payment of duty) on the basis that they will later be exported after Mexican value has been added; permission to import machinery, equipment, replacement parts, and tools free of duty; general exemption from the Mexican limitation on 49 percent foreign ownership; unlimited-entry business visas for foreign plant managers; and eased regulations for land use and acquisition.[17] *Maquiladora*, because of the way they operate, generate costs rather than profits in Mexico and hence pay little or no corporate income tax there. *Maquiladora* plants were limited to the border until 1972; about 90 percent of these plants were still at the border in 1989.

The U.S. part of this unwritten agreement was to permit the continuation of the 806.30/807.00 system, under which import duties are liable on only the value added abroad.[18] Other than this, the official U.S. role has been mostly passive.[19] This passivity has been controversial among labor unions whose members make

Table 8.2 Number, Employment, and Exports of
Mexican *Maquiladora* Plants, 1965–1988

Year	Number of Plants	Total Employment[a]	Net Exports[b] ($ million)
1965	12	3,000	3
1970	120	20,327	83
1975	454	67,213	332
1980	578	119,546	772
1981	605	130,973	976
1982	585	127,049	851
1983	600	150,867	818
1984	722	202,078	1,155
1985	789	217,544	1,268
1986	844	242,234	1,285
1987	1,432	325,000	1,577
1988	1,441	390,422	2,337

[a]The border industrialization program began in 1965.
[b]Figures reflect value added in Mexico.
Sources: Export data: Banco de México, *Indicadores económicos.* Other
data: 1984–1986, *El mercado de valores*, October 27, 1986, p. 1010; 1980–
1984, Inegi, *Boletín mensual de información económica*, various issues;
1965–1979, *Comercio exterior* 33, no. 1 (January 1983): 148; *El Tiempo,*
February 7, 1988; and press release of Mexico's National Commission on
Foreign Investment on activities in 1987.

products that compete with those exported by the *maquiladora*, but it is uncertain
whether the plants actually deprive U.S. workers of jobs by encouraging runaway
industries.[20] The reverse may be true—U.S. industries may survive by providing
inputs to these plants. The survival argument was put as follows by two U.S.
analysts of *maquiladora*-type production sharing: "in many of the industries in
which import penetration has been most pronounced and trade policy most highly
charged with political pressures—sectors such as apparel, electronics, and automobiles—firms have reorganized their operations to use assembly abroad as an
integral part of their strategy for survival."[21]

While some Mexicans argue for drastic revision or abolition of the *maquiladora*
operation, the Mexican authorities have never taken the abolition option seriously.[22] Too many jobs are involved, too much foreign exchange is earned, and
too much is at stake politically to alienate the border population from the government in the Federal District. However, few Mexicans are fully satisfied with the
operations of the *maquiladora*. Their concerns fall into five categories: the lack of
integration of these plants into the Mexican economy; their vulnerability to changes
in the Mexican exchange rate and the health of the U.S. economy; their exploitative
nature, especially regarding women workers; their failure to provide meaningful
skills to Mexicans; and the tendency to exaggerate foreign-exchange earnings, since

much that is earned is spent for consumption goods and services on the U.S. side of the border.

The principal shortcoming of the *maquiladora* industry is that while located within Mexico, the only thing Mexican about it is labor. The Mexican share of the value of material inputs, the merchandise for processing and the packaging, has averaged only 1.3 percent in recent years.[23] The total value added in Mexico, based on U.S. duty assessment under 806.30/807.00, has ranged between 45 and 50 percent since 1983, composed primarily of labor costs, but also electricity, other utilities, and local transportation.[24]

Enclave activities of foreign corporations in developing countries have a long and generally turbulent history. The most frequent examples have been large mining projects, which have generated conflicts in a number of Latin American countries. Mining involves the foreign exploitation of a country's natural resources—its patrimony, as it is often phrased in Latin America—but it does resemble the *maquiladora* in limiting benefits to the developing country to employment and foreign-exchange earnings from direct exports.

In Mexico, as in other countries, the backward linkage in manufacturing—that is, developing supplier industries—was often facilitated by domestic-content provisions forcing foreign investors to use increasing proportions of local products.[25] But domestic-content provisions do not apply to *maquiladora*. Producers are happy because they are not limited in their sources, but the situation also means their support is generally limited to workers in their plants and government officials interested in the generation of foreign exchange.

In part, the enclave nature of *maquiladora* is made necessary by the underlying philosophy of U.S. tariff items 806.30/807.00. The duty exemption for U.S. components in item 806.30 refers to U.S. metal materials "exported for further processing" and in 807.00 to "articles assembled abroad in whole or in part of fabricated components, the product of the United States." However, there is nothing under either item that limits Mexican materials to less than 2 percent of total material inputs, and, in fact, other countries have generally surpassed this percentage.

Why has Mexico not done so? The reasons are varied. One is that the border nature of most of the *maquiladora* limits integration with the rest of Mexico, at least with the major manufacturing areas of Mexico City and Guadalajara, because of distance and inadequate transportation facilities. Monterrey, Mexico's second largest manufacturing center, is distant from Ciudad Juárez, Tijuana, and Mexicali, which are the three leading locations for *maquila* plants. However, since many goods move long distances in other countries, distance alone is an inadequate explanation for lack of integration. Another reason for the lack of Mexican inputs is that most *maquiladora* are owned and operated by U.S. companies, which have transferred the labor-intensive portions of operations out of the United States.[26] Foreign companies (increasingly Japanese as well as U.S.) have little incentive to seek out Mexican inputs unless there is a palpable price or quality advantage.[27]

For those who believe in the market and the salience of comparative advantage, the *maquiladora* are seen not only as a success story, but also as the wave of the future. This sharing of production exploits the abundant factor of each country, the capital and production processes of the United States and the labor of Mexico, in a least-cost combination. Foreign-exchange earnings from *maquiladora* are roughly equal to those from tourism, which is evidence of success. Yet because they are not integrated into the Mexican economy, these plants remain a fragile base on which to build an industrial structure. The major fault may be Mexico's; other countries have integrated assembly into the framework of national production. A common recommendation of Mexican analysts is to force the use of more national products in the assembly plants.[28] Other recommendations frequently made are to give credit and other incentives for Mexican investment in *maquiladora*, perhaps through joint ventures, and increased benefits for plant location away from the border, particularly at ports. One attempt to better integrate the *maquiladora* allows them, particularly if their products are not competitive with other production in Mexico, to sell up to 20 percent of output within Mexico. The main purpose of this feature is to encourage potential Mexican intermediate-goods industries. The main motive for permitting in-bond plants to locate away from the border is to integrate them into the Mexican economy.

Another source of concern over *maquiladora* is their double dependence on circumstances not within Mexican control. Since most such plants are part of the production processes of U.S. companies, their expansion depends on the state of the American economy. Equally crucial is the need for Mexican labor costs (or, more strictly, unit costs, combining wage costs and productivity) to be lower than in other areas in which assembly plants can be located, such as the Caribbean or Asia. The most important contributor to low Mexican wages in recent years has been the depreciating peso, and perpetuation of this situation merely to maintain assembly plants is hardly a viable policy.

The harshest criticism of the *maquiladora* system is that it is based on the exploitation of Mexican labor. The low wages tied to a depreciated peso are only one aspect of this exploitation charge. The more severe accusation is that the plants deliberately use women because of their docility, and that poor working conditions foster high labor turnover and leave former employees with little skills for future earnings.

In the past, women made up 80 to 90 percent of the work force of assembly operations like the *maquiladora* not just in Mexico, but in all countries. There are many reasons for female predominance: greater tractability of women than of men in the societies of most developing countries and, hence, less of a tendency to unionize; lower wages than those of males; and greater female availability, particularly in view of the large turnover in these plants. However, by 1988, due to the growing sophistication of *maquiladora* production, the male component of the work force had risen to 35 percent.[29]

The annual turnover is 30 percent.[30] Guillermina Valdés-Villalva found that in the 1982 to 1983 period, only 12.9 percent of those who left *maquila* jobs found second jobs elsewhere in the *maquila* industry, and Jorge Carrillo, in a well-documented article focusing on the labor experience in *maquiladora* in three cities—Tijuana, Ciudad Juárez, and Matamoros—found that employee rotation was a permanent feature even in plants long in existence.[31] These three cities in 1987 had 50 percent of all border *maquiladora* plants and 56 percent of employment. Length of employment varied slightly by city and the nature of the job (worker, technician, or administrator), but the general pattern was between two and one-half and three years. The principal cause of turnover until 1981 was dismissal by the employer, but there is evidence that employee initiative to leave a job has since become more frequent.[32]

The issue of exploitation of young women (Valdés-Villalva notes that the average age of female *maquila* workers in 1982 to 1983 was twenty-two) is controversial.[33] Observers have cited such conditions as boring jobs under sexist management, poor working conditions, and repetitive work with few breaks and little conversation as hardships *maquiladora* workers must bear.[34] But it is possible that these observers bring their own middle-class sense of values to the analysis of exploitation. The young women do seek the jobs, presumably after learning something about working conditions through word of mouth. Two U.S. investigators interviewed 497 female workers under controlled conditions free of management interference at two coupon-sorting plants in Ciudad Juárez, and the general conclusion of a majority of those interviewed (between 52 and 53 percent) was that the environment was pleasant, the job not filled with pressure, and the training adequate.[35]

The female predomination of *maquiladora* employment has been criticized by both Mexican and U.S. observers as being counterproductive, attracting persons who would not otherwise be in the labor force through the lure of pocket money while doing nothing for the male majority of Mexico's working population.[36] But the conclusion that young women would not enter the work force if not for the *maquiladora* has been challenged. A U.S. investigator has demonstrated that unemployment among women in Mexico is already higher than that among men and concludes, "There is no reason to assume that most women are merely working to pass time while they wait for a husband to come along. A more plausible explanation is that they work out of financial necessity."[37]

Of all the issues surrounding the *maquiladora*, none is more loaded with emotion than the recruitment of young women, many of whom are entering the labor force for the first time, to do simple, repetitive tasks. Those who criticize the structure seek to evoke memories of female-dominated sweatshops once familiar in the United States and other developed countries. The contrary argument is that working conditions are not adverse and that wages, while low by U.S. standards, are not by Mexican standards. If the wages were substantially higher, approximating those in the United States, the outcome would undoubtedly be the loss of most of the plants to other platform nations.[38]

The assembly work in *maquila* plants must be tailored to individuals with modest educations. In María Fernández-Kelly's sample, 5 percent of the workers had less than six years of schooling, 55 percent had six years, and 40 percent had between seven and eleven years.[39] The precise skills imparted, therefore, are those suitable primarily for other assembly operations. A familiar vicious circle appears: the repetitive nature of most of the chores is a factor in the high turnover, and the high turnover requires that the individual tasks be kept simple to minimize training time.

However, some work habits that are obtained may be transferable to other jobs. There is also some technology transfer from the *maquiladora*. Administrative and technical personnel are trained. The techniques for organizing processing operations are transmitted to those Mexicans in management positions. The proportion of men is increasing. Still, the argument that the *maquiladora* represent a useful stage in the industrialization of Mexico cannot be pushed too far. Their enclave, captive nature, high turnover rates, and production techniques designed for persons with modest educations have limited industrial value for Mexico as a whole. Unless the *maquiladora* are better integrated into the Mexican production process, their main value will continue to be the provision of employment and the generation of foreign exchange.

Employment in the *maquiladora* is substantial, but must be kept in perspective. The roughly 400,000 employment figure for 1987 is about 40 percent of the annual *additions* to Mexico's total labor force. The size of the labor force in Mexico is about 28 million, and *maquiladora* employment therefore constitutes only 1.5 percent of the total, significant for the border but marginal for Mexico as a whole.[40]

From time to time, Mexicans are critical of the balance-of-payments drain at the border resulting from personal purchases on the U.S. side. This is often translated to mean that the earnings from *maquiladora* exports are overstated, since the workers leave much of their wages with merchants on the U.S. side.[41] While factually accurate, the argument is superficial. Mexicans who live on the border can hardly be criticized for taking advantage of purchasing opportunities on the other side, especially when an overvalued peso provides an incentive to do so—and this is the case whether earnings come from *maquiladora* or other work. Cross-border purchases take place in both directions and are another manifestation of the fact that the border is a line of sovereignty, not necessarily one of economic or social rationality.

The *maquiladora* have been oversold and overdenounced on both sides of the border. The overselling comes from those who depict these plants as the wave of the future, as the ideal way to facilitate production sharing between the two countries. *Maquiladora* are efficient production-sharing arrangements that provide benefits to U.S. producers and to the Mexican workers and Mexico's foreign-exchange earnings, but are a fragile base on which to industrialize because their continuation (let alone their future growth) depends so heavily on relative wage and unit costs in Mexico compared with other locations.

The overdenunciation also takes place on the U.S. side of the border. Labor unions in the United States argue against *maquiladora* on the grounds of keeping jobs at home, but their case is a narrow one. The issue is not really the Mexican location for labor-intensive operations, but the choice between the United States and any foreign location. If the 806.30/807.00 facility were removed and import duties had to be paid on the total value of imports (the U.S.-produced portion plus the foreign value added), one would then have to look at each product to determine whether total manufacture would best be done in the United States or abroad. In separate studies in 1970 and 1988, the U.S. International Trade Commission concluded that U.S. labor would probably lose employment opportunities if the 806.30/807.00 system were terminated because many operations would move totally abroad.[42] If the economics of production led in this direction, maintenance of jobs in the United States would then require import restrictions. In the case of textiles and apparel, shipments from *maquiladora* plants are already restricted by U.S. import quotas. The loss of the 807.00 feature would almost certainly lead to complete manufacture of many other products outside the United States and make them targets for quota limitations similar to those now in existence for textiles and apparel.

The U.S. critics of the *maquiladora* also tend to neglect the benefits to U.S. border cities. Econometric measurement shows that the *maquiladora* have a significant impact on increasing both employment and sales in the U.S. border cities.[43] If 806.30/807.00 benefits were removed, the U.S. border cities would be penalized even if employment were increased elsewhere in the United States—and that possibility is, at best, uncertain.

The critics of the *maquiladora*, both Mexican and American, tend to downplay both the employment and the balance-of-payments importance of these operations. For while *maquiladora* employment is modest in the total Mexican employment picture, it has become crucial to the border area, and the foreign-exchange earnings are an important element in Mexico's ability to service its foreign debt. When measured on a value-added basis, *maquiladoras* in 1988 provided one-quarter of Mexico's manufactured exports. These considerations cannot be ignored by the Mexican government, nor should they be by the U.S. government.

Cultural and Living Habits

There has been a maturation in writings about the border, progressing from condescension to greater understanding. Discussions from the centers in both countries as recently as the early 1980s tended to depict the border disparagingly, as having an inferior, mongrel society, neither Mexican nor American. Americans have had a tendency to look down on Mexicans and on Mexican Americans as well. Anglos use derogatory terms to describe Mexicans and persons of Mexican origin—greaser, for example.[44] Racist language reflects cultural conditioning, and, unfortunately, such attitudes have also manifested themselves in official U.S. behavior, although this is beginning to change for the better; another "operation wetback," a paramilitary operation launched in 1954 to round up and then carry out mass deportations of suspected undocumented Mexican aliens, is not likely. Still, old habits persist; in February 1985, the United States expressed displeasure over Mexican drug-enforcement behavior by deliberately slowing down border crossings—an inferior is dealt with by punishment.[45]

Writings coming from Mexico City have long reflected a patronizing view of border residents; Mexican Americans are referred to as *pochos* (persons who speak neither Spanish nor English, but a mixture) and Americans as *gringos* (the word is derogatory when used in Mexico). The attitude was expressed clearly in 1978 by Carlos Monsiváis, an intellectual of substantial reputation in Mexico: "The border Mexican learns from his daily contact with American reality; he has come full circle, from a position of chauvinistic defiance to one of wallowing in 'the Mexican's inferiority complex.' "[46] Monsiváis saw "capitalist ideology" and American status symbols becoming real at the same time that an "indigenous recess" is maintained.[47]

Alicia Castellanos and Gilberto López y Rivas have deplored U.S. influence on the Mexican language, values, consumption, aspirations, living habits, and social mores; they argue that it devalues the "national" culture of Mexican border residents.[48] What such analyses reveal is precisely the inferiority complex to which Monsiváis referred, but it resides not with border residents, but with the critics themselves in Mexico City. The argument that national culture is being lost assumes a contest of cultures, a zero-sum game that the Americans are winning, but what is occurring is more subtle: two cultures are meeting, and the outcome is a melding of two quite different traditions. Whether the mixture is better or worse than the separate cultures is indefinable; it depends on the values brought to the assessment.

Ideology at the border is probably more capitalistic, to use Monsiváis's word, than in most of Mexico, if by that he means the dominance of private initiative, but this does not prevent Mexican border entrepreneurs from looking to Mexico City for favors. They have been so conditioned by the PRI. Perhaps the most capitalistic of cities in Mexico in terms of ideology is Monterrey, and its location near the border has much to do with this.[49]

Culture at the border is conditioned by national heritage, education, economics, cross-border kinships, and the daily interaction that comes from proximity. Habits at the border are more binational than elsewhere in the two countries. The music is both rock and Latin; the diet is both hamburgers and tacos. William Murray points out that on Halloween, children in Tijuana don costumes and go *triquitriqui*, but he fails to note that they are also conscious of the day of the dead.[50]

Border culture is distinct from national cultures, but is not uniform on both sides of the border; habits of thought are different in Laredo and Nuevo Laredo because the conditioning factors differ. Cultural patterns are also not the same in Tijuana and in Matamoros, at the other end of the border, any more than San Diego and Brownsville have identical cultures. Again, the formative features vary.

The purpose here is not to enter into a lengthy discussion of differences in Mexican and U.S. mores or to define the precise nature of the cultural mixture at various locations on both sides of the border. It is, rather, to highlight a phenomenon understood at the border but little noticed elsewhere. What occurs there directly affects millions of persons and indirectly impinges on what in the capitals is considered to be high policy. When the U.S. authorities slow down border crossings, as they do from time to time to send some sort of message to Mexico, the unscrambling device delivers something at the other end that is incomprehensible. The intention is to express dissatisfaction over some Mexican action or lack of action (say, on drug control); the result is to damage U.S. commerce and prevent cross-border cultural interaction. And the authorities in Washington repeatedly ignore the simple fact that El Paso is as reliant on Ciudad Juárez as the reverse. The Mexicans come across to work in the homes in Nogales, to shop in Laredo, and to hold down a variety of jobs in McAllen. The Americans go across to shop, manage *maquiladora* plants, and work out mutual problems relating to medical care, criminal justice, and fire services.

This constant interaction is superimposed on underlying cultural patterns and social mores. Those officials responsible for managing border cities must provide necessary services; they do not have the luxury of disdaining foreigners. Cross-border relations involve serious disputes—for example, over environmental issues—as well as cooperation, and these problems cannot be resolved by nationalistic posturing.

When one speaks to border residents, there is a common theme of cultural distance from the two capitals. The patronizing from both Washington, D.C., and Mexico City is met by hostility. The Mexican *norteños* at the border mock the *chilangos* who come from Mexico City. Yet attitudes are evolving; border studies have flourished in recent years. The Centro de Estudios Fronterizos del Norte de México (the Center for the Study of Mexico's Northern Frontier) in Tijuana became a full-fledged university, El Colegio de la Frontera Norte, in February 1986. Associations of border scholars have been formed in the United States to do research on a variety of issues, from economics to culture, from the environment to health services. The United States–Mexico Border Health Association publishes a bilingual quarterly journal (*Border Health–Salud Fronteriza*). The 1986 USITC study of the border seriously attempted to set forth options for improving the economy on the U.S. side.[51]

Those Mexicans who write about cultural alienation of border residents from their national heritage have a legitimate concern. The solution they offer of greater economic and political integration of the border into Mexico is similarly reasonable. But this will not alter the basic fact that the border culture and living habits of border residents will be different from those elsewhere in the country. The border manifests in acute form what is evident about United States–Mexico relations generally, that whether one calls it symbiosis, mutual dependency, integration, or cooperation, each side relies on the other for its well-being.

Politics

Monsiváis is undoubtedly correct that a capitalist ideology is more deep-seated at the border than in Mexico City. The *maquiladora* contribute to this, but are by no means the only reason for the economic orientation of Mexican border residents. Mexicans at the border are bombarded daily by U.S. radio and television. They visit the other side, shop in the stores, work in a variety of activities, and speak regularly with persons living in the United States. Their consumption habits are formed both by what is available in Mexico and by what they can purchase in the United States. Mexican commentators deplore the situation for stimulating a drain of foreign exchange to maintain consumption patterns suitable for Americans with higher incomes but not for Mexicans. Nevertheless, Mexican authorities have learned that they cannot decide by decree, or by the importunings of economists and social commentators, how their border nationals should spend their money. One example of this recognition was the *artículos gancho* program, under which U.S. goods were offered for sale in Mexican stores at competitive prices.

One of the problems that has perennially beset efforts at cross-border cooperation among mayors of twin cities or governors of border states is that authority is more centralized in Mexico than in the United States. Mexican authorities have fewer locally generated revenues; they are more constrained in actions they can take independently of the distant federal government.

Alejandra Salas-Porras, a Mexican analyst, has noted that the urbanization of the border has created employment for technicians, engineers, administrators, lawyers, and other professionals who constitute a group of trained persons able and prepared to make independent decisions.[52] The growth of the *maquiladora* has just added to this cadre of Mexican professionals in constant contact with U.S. counterparts, usually on technical issues.

This combination—the economic interaction, the substantive distance from Mexico City, the technical consultations among professionals, the cultural penetration—has made the northern frontier more ideologically conservative than either the political hierarchy or the bureaucracy in Mexico City. It is not known, because unregulated tests are not regularly permitted, how the northern states would vote in free elections, whether the PRI would continue to capture practically all the governorships and the overwhelming majority of mayoralties in cities. What is known is that conservative, anti-PRI sentiment is strong on the border.

Opinion surveys also consistently show that border residents have a more favorable view of the United States than persons living in Mexico City. Those who live on the border are more likely to accept the need for economic cooperation with the United States than persons polled in Mexico City.

The deficiencies of Mexico's qualified democracy have become an issue of greater moment at the border than in the interior of the country. The point should not be pushed too far because the main decisions on the political system are made in the center and not the periphery. Nevertheless, it was the periphery that attracted most attention during elections in 1986 and 1987, and this clamor has had durable reverberations in the center.

Environment

The Chilean economist Aníbal Pinto commented some years ago that the Economic Commission for Latin America, with which he was affiliated and which for many years was influential in shaping development policy in the region, neglected environmental issues.[53] This shortcoming still characterizes analyses and suggestions of those who approach development issues from an economic-political viewpoint.

But environmental survival is the most critical border issue of all. The effectiveness of the *maquiladora* in promoting Mexican industrialization and employment; the degree to which the language of Mexican and Mexican-American border residents is studded with Spanglish; even the extent to which Mexican border residents look to the United States as opposed to Mexico as the basis for their economic future—all pale by comparison.

The most significant issue in the southwestern United States and northern Mexico is the quantity and quality of the water. It serves little purpose to raise income levels in Agua Prieta (in the Mexican state of Sonora) if pollution from copper smelters on both sides of the border curtail life expectancy. The high rate of infant mortality in Nuevo Laredo—42.1 per thousand compared with 8 per thousand in infants up to one year across the border in Laredo—is caused mostly by preventable diseases resulting from inadequate water and food treatment, combined with poverty.[54]

Environmental issues are fields unto themselves that cannot be covered adequately here. Yet no discussion of the border would be complete without examining them. Beyond their intrinsic importance, they shape much of the give-and-take among authorities along the border and even the negotiations between the two federal governments. Environmental conflicts have been among the most vi- tuperative between two countries and also among the most rewarding in terms of cooperation. Let us briefly discuss three major environmental areas: water, air, and hazardous waste.

Water Quality. Apportionment of the waters of the principal rivers, the Rio Grande and the Colorado, has been accomplished under two treaties, of 1906 and 1944. Albert Utton, a U.S. water expert, has written, "By and large, we can give a good report on the apportionment of the surface flows shared by Mexico and the United States. The two countries have been able to agree amicably on the division of the major rivers, leaving only the minor rivers unapportioned."[55] According to Utton, the main unresolved problem relating to sharing the quantity of surface water is what to do in the event of an extraordinary drought or a serious accident. Utton argues that since surface water is fully appropriated, the task for the future as populations continue to increase is to institute better conservation measures by setting priorities among water uses that would allow gradual retirement of water-intensive agricultural production in favor of municipal and industrial needs, for example.[56]

The institution for carrying out the 1944 water treaty is the International Boundary and Water Commission (IBWC), described by one observer as being "as remarkable a regional water management agency as can be found anywhere."[57] Its predecessor, the International Boundary Commission (IBC), was established in 1889; the IBC was joined with the International Water Commission in 1932 to form the IBWC. The IBWC has a Mexican and an American section, each headed by a commissioner and staff. Each side pays its own expenses and accords diplomatic status and free movement in its territory to personnel of the other. The commission carries out important work, almost completely without publicity and largely divorced from the political conflicts that otherwise beset the interaction between the two nations, and has demonstrated that it is possible to have fruitful cooperation on a technical level. However, many issues are political and thus beyond the scope of the IBWC, including increasingly important groundwater and wastewater issues.

Water-pollution and sewage problems usually require solutions at the political level; the IBWC is then often given responsibility for the administration of agreements that are reached. Political procedures were outlined by an August 1983 agreement, signed in La Paz, Baja California, which deals with cooperation for the protection and improvement of the environment in the border area. Each country has appointed a national coordinator, the Environmental Protection Agency (EPA) in the United States and the Secretaría de Desarrollo Urbano y Ecología (Secretariat of Urban Development and Ecology, Sedue) in Mexico, and the overall agreement is carried out through negotiated subagreements. Thus far, they include border sanitation, air pollution, and hazardous-waste disposal and transportation, but the cooperation need not be limited to these subjects. The agreement calls for a minimum of one high-level meeting a year, but the technical nature of the issues involved requires more frequent meetings of experts. Both the Tijuana sewage and the New River agreements discussed below grew out of this framework.

Unlike surface-water allocations, water-quality issues are still controversial, and neither side has a pure record. Stephen Mumme has documented U.S. procrastination in dealing with the problem of excessive salinity in the Colorado River as it leaves the United States and enters Mexico.[58]

The water of the Colorado River supplies the needs of 15 million people in the southwestern United States and the Mexicali valley of northwestern Mexico. Following construction of the Wellton-Mohawk project in Arizona in 1961, the salinity of the Colorado River rose to unacceptable levels in Mexico, destroying an estimated 7,000 acres and forcing some 500 farmers a year to abandon their land.[59] The supposed permanent solution to this problem was not reached until 1973, when minute 242 of the IBWC was signed. The main feature of the agreement was a U.S. commitment to build a desalting plant near Yuma, Arizona, and a canal to carry off the brine. Each country committed itself to consult with the other before undertaking new water developments that might affect the other. But it is not clear that the desalting plant will fully solve the Mexican problem; the Imperial Dam, where water is stored, now has its own salt problem.

Just as the United States can be faulted for inordinate delays in dealing with the saline content of the Colorado River water provided to Mexico, so can Mexico be criticized for contaminating waters in the United States by its waste-disposal methods and inadequate sewage treatment. The greatest concerns regarding surface-water quality exist in the Rio Grande and Tia Juana River valleys. The Rio Grande is being polluted by the increasing discharge of wastewater into the river from the growing population on both sides of the border.[60] Sewage disposal and associated water-pollution problems resulting from inadequate treatment have become a major irritant in relations between the two countries.

The sewage problem attracting the most attention has been in Tijuana. Parts of the city have no sewer service, and wastewater runs downhill across the border into the Tia Juana River valley and from the river into the Pacific Ocean. The resulting high bacteria count often forces beaches on the U.S. side to close. This problem was the subject of numerous meetings over many years, both at the local level and between authorities of the two federal governments, and came to a head in 1984, when Mexico applied for a loan from the Inter-American Development Bank to expand the water supply and distribution system and double the capacity of Tijuana's sewage collection. A July 1985 agreement under which Mexico committed itself to construct, in stages, a large-scale treatment system for municipal wastewater in Tijuana should eventually alleviate the problem.[61] The monitoring of this agreement will take place through the IBWC.

One other pollution problem that received extensive publicity was that of the New River. This river rises in Mexico, near Mexicali, and flows northward into California to the Salton Sea, southeast of Palm Springs. Its contamination, from both inadequately treated sewage and industrial discharges, had long been the subject of despair on both sides of the border, but especially in the United States. The problem was publicized nationally in the United States on the television program "60 Minutes'' on December 28, 1986. Shortly before that program (and possibly because it was known that the program was being prepared), in September 1986, the two countries agreed to cooperate, through the IBWC, to improve water quality in the New River.

Among the causes of the New River pollution alleged on "60 Minutes" were discharges by *maquiladora* on the Mexican side and waste disposal in Mexico by companies operating on the U.S. side. The implications were that production in Mexico granted the freedom to pollute and that less strict waste-disposal standards led U.S. companies to carry their garbage into Mexico.

Other water-pollution problems arise elsewhere along the border. Some have been corrected—such as that of the San Pedro River, which flows north from Sonora into southeastern Arizona—while others remain to be addressed, such as at Nuevo Laredo.

The most critical unresolved water issue is the utilization rate and potential contamination of groundwater. The IBWC, with minimum legal authority in this field, has made recommendations to deal with sanitation problems, but the broad issue remains to be addressed. One U.S. legal expert has pointed to the inadequacies and differences among groundwater laws in the four U.S. border states, noting that "each of the states has a different system of groundwater law; none has adequate legislation or regulations for the protection and management of diminishing supplies within the state and along the border area."[62] Beyond this, as Utton points out, international competence over aquifers divided by the frontier is largely undefined; he calls the legal and institutional situation "chaotic."[63]

Groundwater provides about 40 percent of U.S. water for irrigation and 80 percent for all uses in U.S. rural areas. The biggest users are the border states, and there is incontrovertible evidence that groundwater is being used faster than it can be replenished. An article in the *Economist* points out that parts of west Texas above a depleted portion of the Ogallala aquifer are already dustbowls.[64] Excessive drawing from an aquifer can also lead to saturating the remaining water with harmful salts, rendering it useless. Aquifers can also be contaminated by seepage from fertilizers and pesticides, leaks from underground gasoline-storage tanks, and hazardous-waste disposal. As one expert has put it, "Groundwaters store contamination, and the process is often irreversible."[65] The data to determine the extent of groundwater contamination are generally lacking, but the problem is real and growing in such regions as the twin-city area of El Paso and Ciudad Juárez.[66] Groundwater is the chief source of water for human consumption in the area, and studies indicate that both cities are pumping at a faster rate than the aquifer, the Hueco Bolsón, is being recharged. Because of fear that the water will shortly be unfit for human consumption, El Paso filed in 1980 for permission to drill wells in the Mesilla Bolsón in New Mexico, which has thus far not been granted. Mexico is obviously an interested party in this interstate dispute in the United States.

The specialized literature, written by technicians and not by politicians given to overstatement, is filled with calamitous predictions if remedial action is not taken. Expert recommendations cite the need to develop more complete hydrological information, practice conservation, establish allocation priorities, and devise joint management of groundwaters intersected by the international boundary.

Air Quality. Air-quality problems have existed for some time all along the border, but experts cite three areas as most pressing: the San Diego–Tijuana complex; El Paso–Ciudad Juárez; and the copper-smelting triangle of Cananea and Nacozari, both in Sonora, and Douglas, Arizona. These were the three areas initially addressed by the air-quality working group of the border environmental cooperation agreement. Each has now become an issue of discussion between the two federal governments under the 1983 La Paz agreement.

One of the leading analysts of air-pollution problems along the border, Howard Applegate, has referred to past treatment of the atmosphere as a classic example of a common property resource, which "belongs to no one, so therefore belongs to everyone."[67] His recommendation is that the atmosphere be treated as a public property resource, much in the manner of national forests and grazing lands, thereby establishing the basis for entitlements, and the air shed be considered a single entity cutting across both nations.

Hazardous-Waste Disposal. Finally, management of hazardous and toxic substances presents another set of environmental issues that grow daily in complexity and importance. The regulatory framework is haphazard, varying among the border states in the United States and uncontrolled by any overarching federal standards, and hardly any regulation at all in Mexico.[68] Among the problems are the export to Mexico of substances banned in the United States (certain pesticides, for example), the shift to Mexico of operations with stringent safety standards in the United States (asbestos products are an example), and the actual dumping in Mexico of wastes generated in the United States (the earlier discussion of the pollution of the New River noted one instance of this practice).

This set of problems has been approached thus far under the bilateral environmental agreement mostly by discussion and the exchange of information. One issue of some consequence that has arisen in the La Paz framework is Mexican opposition to ocean incineration of waste as practiced by the United States.

There was a time, not much more than a decade ago, when U.S. businesses considered it shrewd to move hazardous and polluting businesses to developing countries as U.S. environmental standards became more strict. The trade-off for the developing country was between income enhancement for some and environmental degradation for all. This philosophy still prevails to some extent, as is evident from the location of copper smelters and plants working with lead and asbestos, and from the waste-disposal practices of some U.S. companies in Mexico. It is clear at the border, however, that this export of pollution, beyond the damage it does in Mexico, comes back to trouble the United States in such forms as food contaminated by domestically prohibited pesticides or sulfur oxide emissions from copper smelting in Mexico.

It is too early to assess the full impact of the La Paz agreement, but it represents a valuable step. The two countries recognized the importance of the environmental issue and made it high policy—perhaps not as high in their thinking as drug traffic, but still of great importance. The agreement provided a method to deal with political issues as well as the technical aspects of environmental issues that were within the purview of the IBWC. By combining federal coordination and working groups on local problems, some easing of the different administrative systems of the two countries—highly centralized in Mexico, less so in the United States—was made possible. But most environmental issues between the two countries remain unresolved, and the most crucial, dealing with the use and contamination of groundwater, has hardly been dealt with thus far, even *within* the two countries.

What has been recognized, however, is that the two countries are linked, that each one's garbage can make the other sick. Viewed in historical context, this is no small achievement. The bilateral environmental agreement, whatever its ultimate accomplishments, represents a shift in U.S. behavior from disdain to discussion and negotiation.

Drugs

Drug traffic is an example of proximity between countries creating problems. The United States is the world's largest market for illicit drugs, and Mexico is the most important conduit for drugs entering the United States, both those produced in Mexico and others for which Mexico is a convenient transit point. The drug problem is important in its own right, but it also contaminates the total bilateral relationship. Some background on the extent of the Mexico–United States drug trade is necessary to understand the reason for U.S. preoccupation.

The most widely used illegal drug is marijuana; an estimated 18.2 million Americans, or 10 percent of the population over age twelve, use it at least once a month.[69] An estimated 5.8 million Americans use cocaine one or more times a month, and the number of heroin addicts is estimated at 500,000. The Office of Technology Assessment (OTA) conservatively estimates the retail value of marijuana, cocaine, and heroin sold in the United States at $50 billion in 1985, with marijuana totaling $16.8 billion; cocaine, $20 billion; and heroin, $13.8 billion.

The Mexican connection varies among these three substances. Mexico does not produce the coca plant, the source for cocaine, which the Drug Enforcement Administration (DEA) considers to be the most serious problem because of its increasing use and damage to health. (Physical quantities of cocaine entering the United States are estimated to have doubled between 1981 and 1986.[70]) Rather, cocaine from South America destined for the United States comes through Mexico. The main export point is Colombia, but there is intelligence that transshipment through Mexico increased following interdiction efforts in Florida and the Caribbean.[71]

Foreign countries provided between 10,000 and 15,000 metric tons of marijuana to the United States in 1987, an estimated 80 percent of consumption. The main suppliers were Mexico and Colombia, each with about one-third; other more modest suppliers included Jamaica and Belize.[72] Mexican marijuana is produced mainly in Chihuahua, Durango, and Sinaloa, and while the Bureau of International Narcotics Matters (INM) of the U.S. Department of State has speculated that marijuana growing increased in Mexico after the 1982 economic decline, eradication also increased in 1987 and 1988 (Table 8.3).

Marijuana is produced in the United States and many other countries, and potential sources of supply are limitless for all practical purposes. Because of its rela-

Table 8.3 Mexico: Estimates of Opium Poppy and Marijuana Production and Exports, 1987 and 1988

	Opium Poppy		Marijuana	
	1987	1988	1987	1988
Hectares				
Cultivated	7,360	7,738	9,000	9,000
Eradicated	2,200	2,737	3,750	3,997
Harvested	5,160	5,001	5,250	5,003
Metric tons				
Yield	50	45–55	n.a.	n.a.
Produced (after loss factor)	1.5[a]	5	5,933	5,655
Seized in Mexico	0.07	0.08	100	278
Consumed in Mexico	n.a.	n.a.	n.a.	100
Exported to the U.S.	5[a]	5[a]	1,340	n.a.
Mexican production as percent				
total non-U.S. production	0.7–1.2	17–18	26–35	29–38

Note: It is evident from looking at successive narcotics reports on Mexico that estimates shift year after year, even for years reported earlier.
[a]Figures are for heroin base.
Source: U.S. Department of State, Bureau of International Narcotics Matters, "International Narcotics Control Strategy Report," 1988.

tively low dollar/high quantity characteristic, marijuana is usually shipped in bulk. Imports enter the United States primarily on private ships and aircraft. However, marijuana from Mexico also enters in private vehicles and on individuals.

Most heroin entering the United States is produced in Asia, but Mexico is both a producer and a major transit point.[73] The INM estimated that close to 90 percent of the heroin consumed in the United States in 1977 originated in Mexico, but that the percentage declined in the early 1980s to 30 percent due to heroin eradication efforts, only to increase again to an unknown percentage by now. One reason for the increase given by INM was the attractiveness of opium poppy cultivation in the declining economy. Heroin traffic is highly organized, and because it has a high value to low bulk ratio, heroin can be carried into the United States in small shipments by individual couriers. Table 8.3 provides data compiled by INM on opium poppy and marijuana production in Mexico.

Mexico–United States Cooperation

The budget for the U.S. State Department international anti-narcotics program totaled $118 million in U.S. fiscal year 1987; of this, $15.5 million was dedicated to Mexico, the highest for any country. As INM put it, "Mexico continues to be the highest United States narcotics control priority."[74]

The aerial-eradication program uses eighty-nine aircraft under the direction of the Mexican attorney general's office. Five fixed-wing Turbo Thrushes are provided by the United States, as are three Bell-212 and fifteen Bell-206 helicopters equipped for spraying and sometimes used for transporting troops. Table 8.3 gives U.S. estimates of crop destruction from spraying. In mid-1986, the DEA had 32 agents stationed in Mexico and 161 agents stationed in the United States along the Mexican border.[75] The U.S. agents do not have the authority to make arrests in Mexico, but they cooperate with Mexican counterparts in investigations and provide evidence gathered in the United States for prosecutions pursued in Mexico. The U.S. Customs Service, the Coast Guard, and the Federal Bureau of Investigation provide additional lines of defense within the United States.

Perhaps the most basic question of the entire program centers on the long-term value of crop-eradication programs. Their effects can be neatly quantified by hectares sprayed and tonnage of crops destroyed, but it is not self-evident that any eradication is durable. Statements by U.S. authorities relating just to Mexico are replete with admissions about the recrudescence of drug production following earlier successes of crop eradication. The main problem is that crop-control and crop-eradication programs must be pursued simultaneously in many countries. Peter Reuter has argued that U.S. drug-control efforts in foreign countries have been unsuccessful, despite individual success stories, because of limited options available to growers, absence of government control in many planting areas, and, most important, the shifting set of drug producers in the world.[76] Turkish opium, Mexican heroin, and Mexican marijuana production all declined sharply at one time or another, but new sources repeatedly came on line, as did new distribution systems. But this reasoning, even if accepted, does not necessarily lead to the conclusion that production-control programs should be abandoned; it does demonstrate, however, that demand-reduction measures are necessary to durably curtail drug traffic. This is the Mexican position—that while Mexico will pursue production-control and interdiction measures, the heart of the correction rests with the United States.

The stationing of a large number of DEA agents in Mexico is a vivid example of bilateral cooperation that holds potential for friction. The DEA agents work cooperatively with their Mexican counterparts, and when a U.S. agent is killed or abducted, it becomes an international incident.[77] The many Mexicans killed in the anti-drug campaign have gone unnoticed in the United States. Yet INM reports that 25,000 Mexican army personnel, one-quarter of the total strength, were engaged full-time in narcotic-eradication efforts in 1988; up to 50,000 army personnel were engaged in special eradication and interdiction efforts. Mexican navy and marine forces are involved in interdiction programs off both coasts. More than 65 percent of the budget of the Mexican attorney general's office went for the anti-narcotic campaign in 1987; and, despite budget stringency, the attorney general's budget was one of the few to increase in real terms.[78]

The explosive mix of U.S. agents working in Mexico, their abduction and murder, and the pervasiveness of corruption inherent in the drug trade came to a when Enrique Camarena was kidnaped, tortured, and killed in February 1985, and re-erupted when DEA agent Victor Cortez was arrested and tortured in Guadalajara by the Jalisco judicial state police, but eventually released under U.S. pressure in August 1986. The investigations in both cases, especially that of Camarena, established without doubt the complicity of police and government officials in the drug traffic in Mexico.

Both cases have been amply covered in other publications.[79] The evidence is clear that Camarena was fingered because of his work, including his role in discovering irrigated fields, tractors, and barracks with beds for 100 men, all for marijuana cultivation. The more effective the DEA agents, the more likely they are to be targets for retaliation by narcotics traffickers.

The killing of one American and the arrest of another by state police did have an impact on the Mexican anti-narcotic program that would not have occurred if only Mexicans were involved, and served to stimulate Mexican anti-drug efforts.[80] As of mid-1986, 103 drug arrests had been made, mostly in connection with the Camarena case.[81]

Despite their value in the campaign against narcotics, the presence of U.S. drug-enforcement agents is sensitive in Mexico. This presence is not publicized by the Mexican authorities, and articles in Mexican newspapers following the Camarena case expressed astonishment about the extent of the U.S. DEA presence.

Samuel del Villar, a Mexican scholar, has argued that work by DEA agents, such as Camarena, may be indispensable for the U.S. "unilateral" program, but at the same time has a corrupting effect on the Mexican legal structure. He asserts the need for symmetry, for action not just on what the United States wants Mexico to do, but also on Mexican interests in the United States.[82] The del Villar arguments— that corruption emanates from the demand in the United States and that Mexico's cooperation responds primarily to U.S. interests—are heard frequently in Mexico, although in the final analysis, they are debating points. Mexico's anti-drug campaign also serves Mexican interests.

Mexican society is not immune to the narcotics traffic no matter whether the blame lies with demand in the United States or supply in Mexico. There is evidence of increasing drug addiction by Mexicans, especially young people, and this has stimulated a serious anti-drug campaign in Mexico. The examples of political power exerted by drug dealers in other countries, particularly Colombia, have not been lost on Mexican authorities—the corrupting power of billions of dollars has no nationality.

U.S. Pressures on Mexico

The United States seeks to exert leverage over other countries' narcotics-control efforts by means of negative sanctions and positive encouragements. Negative sanctions typically tie levels of U.S. bilateral aid to the effort exerted by a recipient country and affect U.S. votes on loans in multilateral financial institutions such as the World Bank, the Inter-American Development Bank, and the International Monetary Fund. The adequacy of steps to control illicit narcotics production and trafficking is made subject to a presidential certification that, in turn, is linked to the aid. This system of punishment became a major issue of confrontation between the United States and Mexico when the U.S. Senate voted (63 to 27) on April 14, 1988, to impose sanctions on Mexico for noncooperation in halting drug traffic. The U.S.

administration opposed the decertification on the grounds that it would "cause significant damage to a broad range of U.S. interests in Mexico."[83] The decertification bill did not reach the floor of the House of Representatives.

The Senate had one clear motive, to send a warning to the Mexican government,[84] and a second more speculative one, to register an anti-drug vote for domestic political reasons in the certain knowledge that the president would veto actual sanctions. The Mexican reaction was predictably vitriolic, focusing on sovereignty.[85] What the Senate did, as the United States frequently does, was to treat Mexico as an inferior.

This type of crude leverage is sure to fail when dealing with a country as significant as Mexico. What it does, instead, is arouse national passions to defy the United States. Adrián Lajous, a Mexican known to be friendly toward the United States, commented that "we can merely rage at the arrogant, holier-than-thou pronouncement of the U.S. Senate."[86] It is possible that crude leverage using limited financial inducements can succeed in countries less significant than Mexico, but even this is doubtful because many other issues are always on the table in the bilateral relationship.[87]

Lorenzo Meyer, a respected Mexican historian and political analyst, entitled an article he wrote on United States–Mexico relations in 1985 as "A Bad Year in a Difficult Epoch."[88] He referred to efforts by the U.S. government to slow down tourist travel to Mexico by repeated public threats to issue travel advisories warning tourists that it was dangerous to visit particular areas in Mexico. The ostensible reasons for the threats were the robbery and murder of American tourists, but the general understanding in Mexico was that since there were fewer of these crimes in Mexico than in the United States itself, the motive was to pressure Mexico to take energetic action to investigate the Camarena murder. The pressure probably worked, but the attack on tourism was resented.

A Policy Prescription

Traffic in narcotics from Mexico to the United States raises immensely important issues. The argument can be made that almost any action that effectively curtails this traffic should be taken, regardless of the consequences on the bilateral relationship. But stating the proposition in this stark form reveals its defects. Effective action against narcotics production and traffic requires a cooperative relationship, a simple truth often lost in the accusatory rhetoric.

The anti-narcotics campaign is one of many issues that affect relations between the two countries. Economic interchange, political amity, the movement of people, the flow of ideas—these and many more matters define the policy approach of each country to the other. The various issues are linked, and their totality is inseparable from the anti-narcotics effort. Just one example illustrates the point. The 1987 INM report on U.S. anti-narcotics strategy in Mexico states repeatedly that much of the increase in Mexican growing can be attributed to the decline in the country's economy. Yet the pressure exerted on Mexico to be more vigorous in the Camarena murder investigation by warning against tourist travel was intended to further depress the economy, which, in turn, could heighten social instability in Mexico, thereby compromising the major U.S. policy objective—avoiding such instability.

The harsh reality that the United States has many interests in other countries renders a sanctions policy—cooperate on drug policy, or else be punished in other areas—largely ineffective. The mere threat of punishment against a country as proud of its independence as Mexico can defeat the very cooperation that is desired.

The pressure exerted is normally best done quietly, diplomatically rather than journalistically. Public accusations intended largely to arouse animosity of a domestic audience against the perfidy of officials of the other country serve no useful purpose. Some publicity is needed in the anti-narcotics campaign; the evidence is that the Camarena investigation and the release of Cortez were facilitated by the worldwide publicity that was depicting Mexico as a corrupt society. But invidious publicity must be measured and limited to special circumstances.

Staff members of the House Foreign Affairs Committee surveyed the Mexican–United States anti-narcotic effort in 1985 and made a number of recommendations.[89] In addition to the usual charges of corruption, the main recommendations were for a more active role by DEA agents in cooperation with the Mexican attorney general's office and better accounting practices for the use of aircraft provided to Mexico.[90] Many of the recommendations have since been acted on.

This staff study's first general recommendation, one applicable to the anti-narcotics campaign globally, is that the United States must better demonstrate its own commitment to the fight against narcotics.[91] The *Economist*, in an article on the war on drugs, commented that "the most cutting Mexican retort" to U.S. charges of corruption, "which has yet to be answered, is that the United States is ill placed to blame others for drug trafficking when it cannot contain its own $100 billion-a-year drug trade."[92]

The U.S. drug problem would not be eliminated if there were no corruption in Mexico. It presumably can be better contained, however, if there is genuine cooperation between the two countries. This, not mutual public scapegoating, should be the objective of policy of each country.

Joint Destiny

Mexico has a policy toward the border. The details have changed as the objective situation altered, but attention has been constant and the essential feature has been to encourage migration to the border area by providing incentives for creating jobs. The job-creating techniques have involved large expenditures on irrigation, the creation of free zones in various border states, the development of a national border program in 1961, the border industrialization program in 1965, and ad hoc actions, such as the *artículos gancho* program in the 1970s.[93] The measures adopted have been economic and, from the national Mexican viewpoint, not always ideal. The border was populated, but the people who came looked both to the United States and to Mexico. The *maquiladora* created jobs, but remain a fragile enclave to this date. And, perhaps most seriously, a large proportion of the border population developed a political outlook in variance with that of the dominant PRI.

By contrast, the United States has not had a consistent policy toward its side of the border. The Southwest Border Regional Commission was established in 1975 and then disbanded in 1981 because of inability to define its role. The federal government reacted sympathetically to the hardships caused on the border by peso devaluations, first in 1976 and then in 1982, but provided no new programs. The interests of border residents are ignored when the authorities in Washington, D.C., decide they must send some sort of message to Mexico City on the drug trade, the safety of U.S. tourists, or any other issue; the message all too often is sent by slowing down border crossings and border-city commerce. Washington's actions make it evident that the federal authorities have never grasped the binational character of the border. Authorities in the United States are uncertain whether they wish to open the border more broadly by establishing a large free zone or a productivity zone on both sides, or close it more by eliminating the special import-duty provisions of 806.30/807.00.[94]

Cross-border cooperation is extensive in such matters as providing health and fire services, but still poses great problems in other areas, especially of an environmental nature. The drug traffic prospers because the two countries share a border. But, above all, border relations cannot be divided between a U.S. side and a Mexican one without causing great damage to both. This is why U.S. actions at the border to punish Mexico, or Mexican preaching to border residents to think more like the people who live in Mexico City, are either damaging (the U.S. actions) or fatuous (the Mexican lecturing). In the interest of the millions of people who live on the border, there is no substitute for cooperation, whether in modest things, like the small joint health-research programs that exist, or in vital matters, such as working out transboundary conservation of groundwater. The La Paz agreement represents an excellent example of federal cooperation along the border. Both countries would benefit from more.

9

MIGRATION

The predominant view in the United States is that Mexican immigration is a crime-related phenomenon. . . . It overlooks the real context in which the presence of the undocumented Mexican migrant in the United States responds to an economic relation that has costs and benefits for both the country of origin and the country of destination in the migratory process.

JORGE BUSTAMANTE, 1985

[T]he strategic factor in initiating the migrant streams to fill these jobs is active recruitment on the part of employers or their agents from the developed region.

MICHAEL J. PIORE, 1979

Consequently, the net effect of an increase in labor supply due to immigration is to increase the aggregate income of the native-born population.

ECONOMIC REPORT OF THE (U.S.) PRESIDENT, 1986

Sovereignty and Morality

No more vivid example of asymmetry between nations exists than the movement of Mexicans to the United States. A variety of reasons explain this flow, but the predominant motivation is economic: to earn more money in the United States than can be earned in Mexico. This bespeaks a relative lack of opportunity in Mexico, which makes emigration at once humiliating and depressurizing. In the United States, the immigration from Mexico is desired by some groups and resented by others; the balance between the two shifts with the times, but the polar pressures always coexist.

The U.S. Immigration Reform and Control Act of 1986 (IRCA), more generally referred to by the names of its two sponsors, Senator Alan K. Simpson and Representative Peter W. Rodino, Jr., represents a manifestation of sovereignty. As phrased in the *Economic Report of the President, 1986*: "As a sovereign Nation, the United States must responsibly decide not only who may cross its borders, but also who may stay."[1] Mexico, so zealously protective of its own sovereignty, has no choice but to recognize the U.S. right to control entry of persons.

Yet there is a moral question. Entry of Mexicans into the United States, with or without proper documents, has been going on for more than a century. It has been substantial since World War II, when the United States, because of labor shortages, solicited the Mexican workers under the *bracero* program. There was, in effect, a common-law agreement between the two countries, one seeking and the other providing workers, and there is an understandable Mexican concern over one-sided change in a traditional practice involving two parties.

179

In the contest between sovereignty and morality, sovereignty inevitably won. American authorities owe their primary responsibility to U.S. nationals, not Mexicans. Morality was not neglected in the amnesty or legalization provisions of the U.S. legislation, but they could have been more generous had morality been given greater weight.

Many of the themes discussed in this book affect the people of the two countries only indirectly. The degree of democracy they enjoy is an issue uppermost in the minds of most Mexicans only from time to time. The effects of foreign trade or foreign direct investment are not apparent to most persons of the two countries. The Mexican in the barrio and the American in the inner city hardly think about issues of dependency, asymmetry, or historical grievances. But migration is different. It is a movement of people, not of goods and services. Sovereignty and morality may be abstractions, but they affect issues like deportation and amnesty or whether families can stay together or must be separated, and these issues concern people in the most direct form imaginable—where they can live, how they live, and with whom they live.

This chapter first discusses the economic basis for migration, then reviews migration from Mexico to the United States, and concludes with a discussion of the policy issues involved.

The Economic Basis of Migration

There is no single explanation of why people move from one location to another, within a country or to another country. The explanatory variables include a desire for economic betterment, political freedom, family reunion, and adventure; lifestyle habits of sending and receiving localities; and fear of physical danger from war, pestilence, and hunger. The dominant explanation, certainly for migration from Mexico to the United States, is economic, although this is clearly combined with networks established as a result of decades of earlier migration and proximity; Mexicans do not emigrate in great numbers to Europe.

The catchall phrase used to capture the economic motivation for migration is "push-pull": poor conditions in the sending country, more attractive ones in the receiving country. There is a vast literature on push–pull in general and specifically in relation to migration from Mexico to the United States.[2] Much of it seeks to determine whether the push out of Mexico or the pull into the United States predominates, but migration responds to the combination of both forces.

But economics does not explain everything. Not all Mexicans respond to the differences in earning potential between staying at home or emigrating to the United States. Many regularly leave the rural areas of their upbringing to seek opportunity and work in metropolitan job markets within Mexico rather than cross the border into the United States.[3] Some move from one location to another within Mexico, and then to a third location, either inside or outside the country. There is evidence that one move begets another by the same person—movement becomes familiar—and each of these variations responds to a self-selection; some people migrate and others do not, even when presented with identical economic stimuli.[4] Alejandro Portes has tried to capture these individual idiosyncrasies by focusing on the structural rather than economic basis for migration, but this hardly answers the question. Yet it does point out that men and women do not emigrate only because of wage differentials, and that everyone in Mexico who can earn more in the United States does not leave.[5]

Still, repeated interviews with the migrants show that their overwhelming impulse for migration is economic.[6] The stimulus may be a short-term economic downturn, a conviction by the migrant that long-term earning opportunities are greater in the United States, a sense of responsibility to family and village well-being, and a carrying out of practices that have become traditional in particular locations. The existence of networks in sending and receiving locations is an important explanatory variable. This last point is demonstrated by data that show consistency over time from the main sending areas in Mexico. The leading sending states in Mexico have been, in varying order at different times, Jalisco, Chihuahua, Michoacán, Zacatecas, and Guanajuato, although from time to time other states, such as San Luis Potosí and Coahuila, have been important senders.[7]

Sidney Weintraub and Chandler Stolp constructed a series of econometric models seeking to capture the main economic variables that explain why Mexicans emigrate.[8] Some were based on push factors, others on pull factors, and one on joint push–pull. Mexican GDP and U.S. nonagricultural wages were significant variables at the 95 percent confidence level in explaining economic migration to the United States.[9] The same study sought to project Mexican economic migration to the United States to the year 2000, and concluded that it would be unwise to anticipate an easing of emigration pressure over this period regardless of the international economic setting.[10]

The quotation from Michael Piore at the beginning of this chapter represents a significant element in understanding the Mexican reaction to the unilateral U.S. effort to curtail undocumented immigration; emigration from Mexico to the United States has a longer history and a more solid natural basis than most other instances of temporary migration. The economies of Turkey and Germany, to cite two other countries affected by extensive temporary migration, are not as integrated as those of Mexico and the United States. The very name used by the Germans, "guest workers," demonstrates that the invitation came from the receiving country, which was also the case of the U.S. *bracero* program used to recruit Mexican agricultural workers from 1942 to 1964. Even when the invitation was not explicit, as with undocumented immigration from Mexico, it was implicit. Until 1986, it was not illegal to hire an undocumented worker; the criminalization to which Jorge Bustamante refers in the opening quotation of this chapter applied only to the immigrant. There was a set of rules for Mexican emigration to the United States, and one aspect of these rules was that Mexican workers were wanted and were expected to enter the United States without papers; they would not be penalized beyond being permitted to depart voluntarily if caught, to try again another day—even the same day.[11]

The migrants have motivations—the main one is to increase their income. The sending country has motivations—the main ones are to relieve employment pressures and receive remittances to strengthen the balance of payments. The receiving countries have motivations—the main one for leaving the door half-open is to provide labor that would not otherwise be available, certainly not at the price requested by the immigrant workers. The migrant worker phenomenon thus affects all parties, and it is a systemic, not an isolated, act.

The proposition put forth by many theorists who think in these terms is that foreign workers, whether invited explicitly or tacitly through an elaborate set of rules understood by all parties, take jobs with low social status that native workers reject.[12] Status, as Piore argues, derives not from the jobs but from the labor force, a necessary qualification since the so-called low-status jobs in Germany included those on automobile assembly lines, which would have higher status in the United States.[13] But this duality, jobs for natives and other jobs for foreigners, does not stand up to close scrutiny. The difference in status of jobs held by foreigners among industrial countries demonstrates that status is created rather than inherent in the labor market, and what is created can be altered. Street cleaning is generally considered a low-status job, yet there are numerous examples of more native-worker applicants than jobs available when the pay is high.[14] A more precise statement of the position that there are jobs unwanted by native workers is that they are unwanted at the price—the wages and working conditions—offered. Status is as much an artifact of income as it is of the job.

Receiving countries have recruited foreign workers with low skills because they are generally cheaper than native workers, or at least cheaper than competing native workers would be if foreign workers were not available. This was the basis for permitting the immigration of undocumented Mexican workers. There are also hierarchical considerations for using Mexican workers, since this permits maintaining wage differentials within a work force without having to raise the entire scale. In other words, an alternative to the unwanted-jobs thesis is the desire in receiving countries to keep costs down without prejudice to most native workers. If this is the correct interpretation of what was taking place before Simpson-Rodino, it implies that some costs will increase if the legislation is successful in curtailing undocumented immigration.

The world's nontotalitarian states assume a basic right of individuals to emigrate from the country of their residence, a position built into the Helsinki agreement on European security and cooperation. U.S. legislation links the granting of most-favored-nation trade treatment to communist countries to their permitting reasonable freedom to emigrate. There is no recognized reciprocal position that countries must admit emigrants from other places; this is decided by each nation in the practice of its own sovereignty. Some countries, like the United States, are relatively generous in admitting immigrants, while others are relatively restrictive, which is increasingly the case in Western Europe, and the tendency throughout the world is toward more restriction. Countries apparently do not believe they are being inconsistent in pressing for freedom to emigrate while limiting immigration.[15]

This general philosophical position is turned on its head in the United States–Mexico situation. Mexico certainly does not seek to limit emigration, and until Simpson-Rodino, the United States did nothing effective to limit undocumented immigration from Mexico. The U.S. position has now changed, at least legislatively. Contrary to its position with respect to the Soviet Union, the United States undoubtedly would now welcome Mexican moves that made emigration of its nationals more difficult. It is the Mexicans who assert that this is not possible in a democracy.

If there were no frontiers, migration of people would be vastly greater; even now, tens of millions of people, largely without documents from the country of immigration, migrate each year. In a purely welfare sense, freedom of migration would lead to lower income disparities among countries. However, immigration restrictions are designed precisely to maintain income disparities; more exactly, they are intended to prevent an influx of low-wage labor from reducing incomes in the higher-income country.

In investigating the migration tension between Mexico and the United States, it is useful to keep these self-interested objectives in mind. The ability of its nationals to work in the United States is seen by Mexico as a social and economic benefit, at least as long as Mexico is unable to provide sufficient work at a satisfactory wage at home for all who seek it. The pressure for immigration restriction stems from a fear that unlimited immigration would alter the social and economic status of persons already in the United States.

The Facts as They Are (Un)Known

The search for objective facts about immigration from Mexico and other countries was a necessary element in fashioning the Simpson-Rodino legislation, although what emerged was a mixture of fact and compromises of different opinions.[16] Now that the legislation exists and is being carried out, the type of factual information needed has altered. Before the bill was passed, it was necessary to learn how many persons were entering the United States, with or without documentation, how long they stayed, and how they affected the U.S. labor market and economy as a whole. After the legislation was enacted, the issues changed. We know that about 1.8 million persons—of whom 1.2 million, or 70 percent, were Mexicans—sought amnesty under the legislation, but it will take more time to determine whether the threat of penalties on employers who knowingly hire undocumented aliens will curtail entries.[17] The hope of those who fashioned the legislation is that most employers will obey the law.

The factual forest is well-nigh impenetrable. Focusing only on Mexico, the kinds of questions of fact that arise are the following: What is the pool from which Mexican immigrants come? Who comes? Why do they come? How many come? What proportion includes sojourners, and what percentage will eventually become permanent immigrants? How many are here? What is the effect on the U.S. labor market? on the Mexican labor market? How is total U.S. income affected by the presence of undocumented workers? How much money do the undocumented immigrants send home? Will they continue to come if Mexican incomes rise? Will employer penalties stop them from coming? How do the two separate publics and governments feel about the immigration (emigration) of undocumented Mexican workers?

The discussion of these questions will be truncated in the interest of space and because a test is in progress under U.S. immigration legislation. This variety of questions will be dealt with under three headings:

1. What is the pool from which Mexican immigrants come?
2. What are the effects of the immigration (emigration) here (there)?
3. Is it possible to predict what measures will work to encourage Mexicans to stay at home?

The legislation will inevitably affect relations between the two countries. If the employer-penalty program succeeds in dissuading Mexicans from entering the United States, the social and employment pressures in Mexico could affect stability. Mexicans without documents who hold jobs in the United States will be reluctant to leave—to make a round trip to visit family, as they did earlier—for fear they will be asked for documents when they return. The labor markets of the two countries, like the markets for goods and services, were becoming integrated, and it remains to be seen whether U.S. restrictionism will rupture this.

The Mexican Migrant Pool

The size of the Mexican labor force—that is, those persons actively seeking work—is not a settled matter. Mexico's 1980 census estimated the labor force as 22 million in June of that year. If the labor force has risen since then by 700,000 a year, a conservative figure, this would imply a labor force at the start of 1989 of some 28 million. But by general agreement, the 1980 census was faulty and its data inconsistent with other estimates, particularly the continuing survey of occupation carried out by the Secretaría de Programación y Presupuesto (Secretariat of Programming and Budget, SPP). A year earlier, this showed the labor force at less than 20 million. But if the increase in entrants into the labor force is closer to 1 million a year, rather than 700,000, this still implies an economically active population at the start of 1989 of about 28 million.[18] Using projections made by SPP, the economically active population in the year 2000 will be between 35 and 40 million, depending on how many people voluntarily stay out of the labor market.[19] The implication of these projections is that Mexico will require consistently high overall growth rates to create sufficient jobs; even then, enough job creation to eliminate unemployment and underemployment is unlikely.

If either unemployment or inadequate income because of involuntary underemployment is the force propelling emigration, then the prospects for reducing emigration pressures for the rest of this century are dim indeed. The American economist Clark Reynolds undertook an exercise projecting the Mexican labor demand and supply and, depending on growth of GDP and the labor intensity of production (that is, whether less capital-intensive production techniques are used), concluded that the excess supply of labor in Mexico in the year 2000 could either be eliminated or reach as high as 5.6 million.[20] The Mexican economy has declined since that exercise was undertaken, and it may well be that the 5.6 million oversupply figure is low.[21] The growth in the Mexican labor pool should start tapering off around the year 2000 because of the decline in birth rates that has been apparent since the 1970s.

One additional point should be made about the potential migrant pool. The participation rate in the labor force, measured as those aged twelve years and over, has been declining modestly, but more or less consistently, for men during the past thirty years, and in 1980 was estimated to be 71.3 percent—the main reason appears to be increased years in school.[22] However, the participation rate of women has been increasing; it was 21.5 percent in 1980. The overall participation rate, therefore, has remained steady at about 45 to 46 percent, and because of the still low level of female participation in the labor force, one cannot expect a slackening of the need to create jobs in the years ahead even if more schooling continues to delay entry into the labor force. The point is that the pressure to emigrate, as measured by raw numbers of those most likely to do so, is unlikely to abate for at least the rest of this century.

How many people leave Mexico each year, or at least did so before the uncertainties created by the Simpson-Rodino legislation? Some figures are known. In recent years, between 50,000 and 75,000 legal immigrants from Mexico have been admitted each year.[23] It is clear that this figure is dwarfed by the entry of Mexicans without documentation, but it is not known by how much.

Scholars have used a variety of techniques to estimate the flow of undocumented aliens. The most easily available figure is that for apprehensions by the border patrol of the U.S. Immigration and Naturalization Service (INS). As can be seen from Table 9.1, this figure reached almost 1.8 million in U.S. fiscal year 1986, but has declined since. The high percentage of Mexicans shown in the table, around 95 percent, is a reflection of the concentration of the border patrol on the Mexican border; it is generally believed that Mexicans make up between 50 and 60 percent of

Table 9.1 Illegal Aliens Apprehended in the United States, U.S. Fiscal Years 1951–1988 (figures in thousands)

	Aliens Located	Mexicans Located	Percent Mexican
1951–1960[a]	360	344	95
1961–1970[a]	161	103	64
1971–1980[a]	832	747	90
1981	976	874	90
1982	970	887	91
1983	1,251	1,172	94
1984	1,247	1,171	94
1985	1,349	1,267	94
1986	1,767	1,671	95
1987	1,190	1,140	96
1988	1,008	950	94

[a]Annual average.
Source: Data obtained directly from the INS.

the annual flow of undocumented immigrants.[24] But the apprehension figure is unreliable: it gives a false impression that the undocumented-alien problem is over-whelmingly Mexican; it counts cases of apprehension, not of different persons apprehended, and thus overstates when the same person is apprehended more than once; it understates the undocumented-alien problem by the omission of most non-Mexicans; and it ignores many Mexicans who enter the United States without being apprehended.

In August 1978, a group of researchers from the Secretaría de Trabajo y Previsión Social (Secretariat of Labor and Social Services, STPS) stationed itself at the border locations where the INS deposited undocumented Mexicans who had been ap-prehended, and it counted fewer than 33,000, compared with the INS figure that month of 89,000.[25] There is no satisfactory explanation of the discrepancy. This same research group interviewed returning migrants during a three-week period in October and November 1977 and, with the help of data published by the INS on the length of stay of deported aliens, was able to classify the persons by the year they entered the United States. Those who returned voluntarily were also interviewed and classified by the year of entry to the United States. Ratios were determined for voluntary to involuntary departures from the United States. An estimate was also made of Mexicans who did not return, again based on data published by the INS on the length of stay of expelled aliens. The estimate of undocumented entries from 1972 and 1976 was between 630,000 and 2 million a year. Most of these persons returned to Mexico, and the net flow, equivalent to the increase in the stock of undocumented Mexican immigrants who remain in the United States, was estimated at between 50,000 and 160,000 a year.[26]

Flow and stock concepts merge and become inexact when calculating figures over long periods. Much of the literature uses a different terminology, sojourner or settler.[27] The figures for the number of Mexicans who have settled in the United States after first entering without documents is no more certain than the gross flow each year, but there are better techniques to make the estimates; in addition, an effort was made to catch this group in the 1980 U.S. census.

The U.S. Bureau of the Census estimated in the 1980 census that there were roughly 2 million undocumented aliens in the United States, of whom 55 percent were born in Mexico.[28] After revising the estimate to include persons not captured in the census count, the Census Bureau estimate of undocumented aliens in the United States in 1980 was between 2.5 and 3.5 million, of whom 1.5 to 2 million were estimated to be Mexicans. The net flow since 1980 was estimated to be between 100,000 and 300,000 a year. Putting all these figures together gives a range of between 3.2 and 5.6 million undocumented aliens in the United States at the end of 1987, of whom between 1.9 and 3.2 million were Mexicans.

Of the undocumented Mexicans estimated from the census count, only 9 percent were over age forty—Table 9.2 also shows the relative youth of native Mexicans who entered the United States from 1980 to 1986 compared with other foreign-born residents. This relatively young population can be expected to be quite prolific and increase the proportion of Mexican-origin population in the United States in the years to come, a point of some significance for the future ethnic composition of the U.S. population, as we will discuss shortly.

Table 9.2 Age of Mexican and Other Foreign-Born
Population Who Entered the United States, 1980–1986
(figures in thousands)

	Foreign-Born Population	Mexican-Born Population
Totals	4,430	965
Ages (percent of totals)		
6–14 years	17.8	21.7
15–29 years	43.5	57.5
30–44 years	24.9	15.4
45 years and older	13.9	5.4
29 years and younger	61.3	80.2

Source: Karen A. Woodrow, Jeffrey S. Passel, and Robert Warren, "Recent Immigration to the United States—Legal and Undocumented: Analysis of Data from the June 1986 Current Population Survey."

The Census Bureau estimate is not necessarily the final word on the stock of undocumented aliens in the United States, since different researchers have come to varying conclusions.[29] However, the consensus estimates for the stock of undocumented aliens in the United States in 1980 were in the range of 3 to 5 million, between 50 and 60 percent Mexican, even before the census estimate.[30] There is less agreement on the net flow since 1980 because the period coincides with a time of severe economic hardship in Mexico (and turbulence in other migrant-sending areas, especially Central America), which almost certainly affected the scope and nature of migration to the United States.

The IRCA legislation deals with this duality—flow–stock, gross flow–net flow, or sojourner–settler, however labeled—in linked fashion. The employer-penalty provisions were intended to curtail the gross flow, and the amnesty clauses to deal compassionately with the stock resulting from earlier flows. But there were derogations from both features reflecting the compromises necessary to get the bill through the Congress and then signed by the president; as will be noted later, not all of them were felicitous.

Effects of Mexican Migration

The movement of Mexicans to the United States, whether as sojourners or settlers, affects the United States, Mexico, and the relationship between the two countries. These effects are most readily analyzed by separately examining economic, social, and political outcomes, but in reality they form a seamless web. Some effects are reasonably clear. The ability of Mexicans to emigrate did ease social pressures in Mexico, and the availability of foreign workers did permit the harvesting of perishable crops at the lowest possible cost to growers and consumers. Other effects are more speculative.

Most U.S. economists, including the U.S. Council of Economic Advisers, as cited in the quotation beginning this chapter, believe that the availability of alien labor, clandestine though it was, raised the growth rate of the U.S. economy as a whole.[31] They reason straightforwardly that the presence of relatively cheap labor raised returns to other factors of production—capital, land, and other labor complementary to the undocumented labor, particularly labor with higher skills. At times of full employment, a labor shortage can be a bottleneck to overall growth, but even at times of high unemployment, labor supply may be inadequate at the price offered in particular activities—such as harvesting crops, producing some items of apparel, and working in restaurant kitchens. To the extent that the availability of alien labor keeps wages below what they otherwise would be, consumers of products made or harvested with this labor are the beneficiaries.

There are distributional effects of the use of foreign labor. Farm owners producing perishable crops benefit, while native workers migrating around the country to pick fruits and vegetables are losers. Native workers who wash dishes in restaurants do not benefit from the employment of alien workers, whereas restaurant owners do. Skilled workers higher in a firm hierarchy are likely to benefit from the presence of alien workers, whereas competing workers at the same hierarchical level are unlikely to benefit. However, when the total GNP is rising, there may be trickle-down benefits even to those workers in direct competition with the alien workers. These benefits are apt to disappear, especially for competing workers, when growth in the overall economy falters.

It is no accident, therefore, that the pressure for restriction becomes most intense at times of a stagnant or declining economy. This was true in the United States during the Great Depression, and the clamor against guest-worker programs in Europe peaked when economic growth slowed and unemployment rose after the first oil crisis in 1973 and 1974. The same restrictionist sentiment took hold in the United States during the recession of the late 1970s. Desultory economic growth in Western Europe for most of the past decade has contributed to the durability of the restrictionist sentiment there.[32]

Several efforts have been made to measure the impact on the U.S. labor market of the presence of foreign workers, both legal immigrants and undocumented aliens. This is more easily done for legal immigrants, since their fortunes can be traced over time. The impact of undocumented aliens on the U.S. labor market, particularly of competing labor, is more conjectural.

Legal immigrants who have been in the United States for upward of ten years earn higher wages than comparable native workers.[33] Several authors have entered a cautionary note, however. Recent immigrants tend to come with fewer skills and fewer years of schooling than did earlier ones, and their economic progress may not prove to be comparable. This is particularly true of Mexican immigrants, who have an average of 7.5 years of schooling compared with more than 11 years for other Hispanics and whites.[34]

A caveat is worth entering to this concern about lesser schooling and skill levels of recent immigrants. Restrictionist arguments that relatively unskilled and unschooled immigrants will become public charges have a long history, dating back to Italian and Irish immigrants in the nineteenth century, Jewish immigrants at the turn of this century, and unschooled Asian immigrants following the end of the Vietnam War. The results proved otherwise, however.

The question of economic progress over time does not arise for undocumented immigrant sojourners, since they come and go. The illegality of undocumented immigrant settlers makes their economic progress problematic; in any event, precise time-series data are not readily available as a consequence of the illegality.

Sojourners came and then came again and again because they earned more money in the United States than in Mexico. The germane labor-market question about them is not how well they do, but how they affect wages in the United States, not for labor as a whole, but for those with whom they are in competition at the lower end of the labor market. If it is accepted that under normal economic conditions the economy as a whole benefits from the presence of undocumented workers and that skilled workers also benefit in a hierarchical structure, then the most important unresolved issue is the distributional one.

How do those national workers at the bottom of the income scale, or those who are unemployed, fare from the presence of large numbers of undocumented workers? There is no easy answer to this question. Vernon Briggs believes that the persons hurt are minorities, those most vulnerable to competition from low-wage workers who do not have the ability to complain about their treatment, and argues that there should be more conscious coordination between immigration and labor policies, which translates into restrictionism.[35] George Borjas and Marta Tienda concluded that the effect of undocumented workers on native wage rates is minuscule, negative by at most a fraction of 1 percent, but that the wages of resident foreign workers are reduced by 2 to 9 percent.[36] Frank Bean, Lindsay Lowell, and Lowell Taylor similarly concluded that there is no evidence that undocumented Mexican workers depress the earnings of native-born U.S. workers, and even argue that if there is any effect, it is slightly positive for native workers. They also accept the thesis that undocumented aliens take jobs that natives do not want.[37] Thomas Muller and Thomas Espenshade find some evidence, although not overwhelming, of wage depression in California from undocumented immigrants.[38]

One reason for these inconclusive findings is that the underlying data to examine the specific consequences of undocumented immigration are problematic. In addition, a meticulous examination of labor-market impact requires a number of rigid assumptions on the homogeneity of labor, its mobility to take advantage of wage differentials, the short-term versus the long-term consequences, the price at which producers might substitute labor for capital and vice versa, and what happens in specific regions and industries as opposed to looking at labor as a whole.[39] Since undocumented aliens are unevenly distributed among the states, their impact on labor markets must vary among the regions.

Wage depression or enhancement for competing workers is a less significant outcome than job displacement. Do undocumented alien workers actually displace legally resident workers? Answering this more important question is equally speculative. It is not too much of a simplification to classify students of undocumented immigration as being either job-creation or job-displacement advocates. Job-creationists argue that undocumented foreign workers remove production bottlenecks.

A framer on a construction job opens opportunities for bricklayers, roofers, carpenters, and others; those who harvest fresh fruits and vegetables open opportunities for canners, jobbers, wholesalers, and retailers; a cutter in a garment shop is necessary if those who sew the garments, iron them, and then work in the distribution network are to have jobs. There is no single lump of labor that exists in the United States, but a complex, interrelated chain, and each link is necessary for the entire chain to fit together.

The opposite view, that of job displacement, grants the chain or network logic but argues that there is no shortage of legal workers to fill the jobs taken by undocumented aliens. This view is that the undocumented worker is hired mainly to keep wages down, and, at a time of high unemployment among unskilled workers, this translates into job displacement.

The U.S. General Accounting Office examined much literature on this theme and came up with a qualified conclusion: illegal aliens "appear" to displace native workers; its synthesis of the forty-six studies examined "suggests" widespread displacement, but displacement, like wage depression, is itself a qualified concept, dependent on the state of the U.S. economy, the region of the United States being examined, and the activity in question.[40] However—and this is the same point made for wage depression—the germane question is the distributional one. The jobs that might be displaced are those at the lower end of the wage scale. If bottlenecks are removed, the beneficiaries are likely to be persons with greater incomes than the unskilled labor used to remove the production impediments.

Perhaps the most significant long-term implication of immigration into the United States from Mexico, and increasingly from other Latin American countries, is that it is changing the ethnic mix of many states. The Latin American– and Spanish-origin population of the United States grew from 9.1 to 14.6 million between 1970 and 1980; this 60 percent growth was five times that of the total population.[41] The Mexican-origin population grew by 93 percent over that period, or eight times the growth of the total population, and five states—Arizona, California, Colorado, New Mexico, and Texas—held almost 85 percent of the Mexican-origin population in the United States in 1980. The main reasons for this rapid growth were immigration and fertility, each of which accounted for about half the increase. Some 86 percent of the undocumented Mexicans who enter the United States are under age thirty-four, which implies that procreation of this group will continue to be higher than for the U.S. population as a whole.

What has been happening, therefore, is not merely an economic phenomenon affecting the U.S. labor force, but a lasting change flowing from immigration, clandestine and open, from Mexico. The social structure of many states is changing, and the higher fertility rate of Mexican- and other Latin American–origin populations ensures continued rapid Hispanicization of these and other states. This is a pattern that occurred earlier in the United States with other ethnic groups, and they left their mark on U.S. habits, including the political direction of many municipalities and states and of the federal government. Hispanics are rapidly becoming the largest minority in the United States and those of Mexican origin the largest single group among them. This is the most durable form of integration of two countries.

The economic effects of migration for Mexico relate to the labor market there and the dollars sent back by the migrants in the United States. As is true for the United States, the consequences of the ethnic integration between the two countries will probably prove to be the most durable effect for Mexico. Mexicans are ambivalent about emigration, seeing no escape from the human movement under current population and employment pressures, but also feeling a sense of national degradation from this necessity.

This inner conflict between necessity and preference emerges in the fuzziness of the public discussion of the emigration issue. The Mexican position encompasses recognition of the U.S. sovereign right to restrict entry, but also a running commentary in the press and even the Mexican Congress about the wrongheadedness of the restriction. There is an admission that emigrants leave for personal advantage, but there are also regular attacks on the United States for maltreatment of the emigrants.[42] Mexicans often assert the need to reach understandings on migration in a bilateral framework, but then during the debate on Simpson-Rodino, the Mexican government ignored U.S. suggestions that the two countries discuss the issue.

Peter Gregory has estimated the wage impact in Mexico of the emigration, concluding that curtailment of undocumented emigration would depress wages by 3 to 4 percent in low-skill occupations.[43] This conclusion is at best an approximation, assuming price elasticities for the supply and demand for labor that are at best speculative and implicitly treating Mexico as one large labor market when in reality the country is a series of labor markets, each with different conditions.

There are no reliable data on remittances sent home by Mexican immigrants in the United States. Juan Diez-Canedo sought to calculate this based on data supplied by U.S. banks and came to a figure of $317 million in 1975.[44] Official balance-of-payments data show net transfers into Mexico of about $700 million each year in 1987 and 1988. The figure is undoubtedly higher than this, but trying to state how much higher would be sheer guesswork.

The Difficulty of Prediction

One of the most interesting findings of Mexican researchers is that it is not the very poorest who emigrate. One survey found that only 3.2 percent of the undocumented emigrants were unemployed in the month prior to leaving Mexico. Eight of ten migrants were employed in the month prior to emigrating, and the remainder was not in the labor market.[45] This corroborates what other researchers have discovered, that those who emigrate clandestinely are not the poorest Mexicans.[46] There are many explanations for this. It takes money to emigrate, thereby mostly excluding the unemployed. And as income rises, one's appetite for still more income is whetted.[47] As incomes rise, so do aspirations and horizons.

There is an analytical corollary to this finding—as Mexican wages rise, emigration may increase temporarily, implying that increased employment in Mexico is unlikely to have much deterrent effect on emigration in the short term, say, for the rest of this century. Over a longer term, if incomes in Mexico continue to rise, emigration will eventually decline.

The Mexican authorities are deeply concerned about the potential impact of the

IRCA legislation and often ask U.S. interlocutors familiar with the immigration theme whether the United States is likely to seriously enforce the employer-penalty provisions. This is immediately followed by a query about whether the U.S. authorities have calculated the damage that would be inflicted on Mexico if the clandestine traffic were effectively closed. A common Mexican attitude is that the undocumented flow of Mexicans, while messy and outside U.S. law, has served both countries well and that the consequences of curtailing the flow could bring real hardships to Mexico.[48]

The dialogue between the Mexican and the U.S. governments deals largely with political issues, such as the respective national positions toward Central America; social matters, such as the drug traffic; and, overwhelmingly, economic matters, such as trade and foreign direct investment. Migration matters, which may be more important than any of these, rarely get discussed.[49] Unless the two countries were to agree to a new *bracero* agreement under which workers would be hired, under government sanction, for temporary work in the United States, there is little to discuss about migration as such. But a new government-to-government agreement of this nature would be highly controversial in Mexico; it would be portrayed as selling Mexican workers, cheaply, to *gringo* employers and is unlikely to materialize.

There is a school of thought in both countries, however, that the Mexican workers will be increasingly needed in the United States. Clark Reynolds, in a series of essays, has projected the supply and demand for unskilled labor in both countries and concluded that there will be complementarities between them—an excess supply in Mexico and an excess demand in the United States.[50] The recommendation coming from these projections is that the labor market of the two countries should be further integrated, by specific agreement or otherwise.

These projects, like all such exercises, build in assumptions, some explicit and others implicit. Perhaps the most important of these is that U.S. productivity will grow between now and the year 2000 by 1 percent a year. If the growth is greater, the need for a given number of workers to achieve a given growth in GNP is reduced. The Reynolds exercise leaves GNP growth in the United States as the residual, or the variable to be determined; that is, a shortage of unskilled labor will lead to lower growth. Productivity could be the residual, however. Fewer available unskilled workers could lead to their more efficient use. Also, a global figure for productivity growth is misleading. According to the U.S. Bureau of Labor Statistics, productivity growth in the United States during the 1980s (1979–1985) was more than 3 percent a year for manufacturing but less than 1 percent a year overall. It is unclear in which sector of the economy Mexican workers are believed to be needed by those who foresee a shortage of low-skill labor in the United States in the 1990s.

The labor complementarity theme has become an article of faith among many Mexican analysts, who conclude that the United States is doing Mexico no favor by accepting undocumented workers, but is instead meeting U.S. needs. There undoubtedly is a mutuality of interest, else the migration would not have been as durable as it has been, and this mutuality explains why the United States has not until now vigorously carried out its immigration laws. It explains, also, why even Simpson-Rodino makes a large exception to the general rules on amnesty and undocumented workers in favor of U.S. agriculture. What is omitted from the Mexican calculus, however, is that public opinion in the United States opposes hiring foreign workers; the Mexican analysis also ignores the potential distributional impact of undocumented workers in the United States. If there is damage from their employment, whether wage depression or displacement, the impact will be on those least able to cope.

The curtailment of undocumented immigration could also lead to political instability in Mexico, which is in neither country's interest. But this is uncertain. If Gregory's calculations are even close to correct, abrupt curtailment of emigration of low-skilled workers will lead to a once-and-for-all wage reduction among this group of 3 to 4 percent, but Mexican workers have suffered real wage reduction since 1982 that totals ten times this amount. Conversely, curtailment of emigration would affect a self-selected group of adventurous young persons, who might instead turn their energies to internal agitation. The answer to this question will emerge if the employer-penalty provisions of IRCA effectively curtail undocumented immigration from Mexico, but the United States may prefer not to know the answer.

Policy: Separate and Asymmetrical

It may be useful to summarize the internal contradictions of the migration debate in each country. The reason for the long delay in enacting Simpson-Rodino was the tug between the majority, at least as measured in public-opinion polls, who wished to curtail undocumented immigration, and a number of vocal minorities, including Hispanic organizations and employer groups opposed to the employer-penalty provisions, who preferred the messy status quo under which undocumented aliens were entering the United States. These otherwise incompatible sectors of U.S. society made common cause for many years against legislation affecting undocumented immigrants. Indeed, the legislation was finally enacted only after special provisions were included catering to agricultural growers.[51]

Seasonal agriculture has always been treated as a special case for importation of foreign workers. There has been a problem with this policy: Mexicans may enter the United States to work in agriculture but then drift into other, higher-paying occupations, leaving the agricultural-worker pool in need of constant replenishment. Using data from the 1980 census, only 17 percent of undocumented Mexican workers were engaged in agriculture, compared with 35 percent in manufacturing, 11 percent in construction, and the remainder, close to 37 percent, in various service activities.[52]

Another compromise that made enactment of Simpson-Rodino possible was the amnesty program. Under the legislation, only those undocumented aliens who could demonstrate that they have lived continuously in the United States since January 1, 1982, were eligible for adjustment of status. Since the formal procedures for granting amnesty did not begin until May 1987, this meant that migrants who had become settlers over the previous five and one-half years were ineligible. The compromise was beneficial to the roughly 1.8 million persons who qualified to apply and terrifying to hundreds of thousands of persons, perhaps millions, who did not.[53]

This backdating to 1982 affects more than Mexicans. José Napoleón Duarte, former president of El Salvador, requested a delay in the forced departure of what he estimated were hundreds of thousands of Salvadorans who entered the United States after January 1, 1982, reasoning that El Salvador could not cope with this sudden influx.[54] His request was rejected.

Now that IRCA exists, however, the proper question to ask is how different policies on its implementation can affect outcomes. Are there other policies unrelated to Simpson-Rodino that can influence migration outcomes?

One such policy relates to family reunification. The evidence is clear that undocumented aliens who have become settlers are not merely young, single males.[55] Most live in households with spouses and children. Some members of these families are legally in the United States, and others are not; some qualified for amnesty, and others did not. Many persons may not have applied for amnesty for fear of family separation. A critical issue, therefore, will be the action taken by the United States to reunite families separated by the way the amnesty law was written. One of the tenets of U.S. immigration law generally is to encourage the unification of families, and there was cruel irony that an amnesty law based on humanitarian grounds did lead to some family separation.

There are two main techniques for preventing the entry of undocumented aliens. The traditional method is through the border patrol concentrated on the Mexican border; the innovation in Simpson-Rodino is the penalties against employers who knowingly hire undocumented aliens.[56] The seriousness of U.S. intent to enforce the new law can be judged over time by the budgets appropriated for the INS, particularly the border patrol, and the vigor with which employers who violate the law are penalized.[57] The expectation of persons familiar with past U.S. enforcement of immigration laws is that this one will not be vigorously enforced either, that the INS will continue to be underfunded, and that there will be reluctance to seek significant fines and other punishments of employer violators.[58] But it is by no means certain that the employer-penalty provisions of IRCA will be enforced in a lax way. Here implementation can make a big difference; the U.S. immigration door can be kept half-open, as it has been for some time, or it can be mostly shut to persons without legal papers to enter.

The ideal situation, if the United States does not wish undocumented workers and Mexico would prefer that they not have to leave, is for Mexico to provide gainful employment, at decent wages, to all who seek it. This is a long-term ideal, and Mexico's economic policy obviously affects the level of employment. Can U.S. economic policy have much effect in maximizing job creation in Mexico? At the margin, the answer is undoubtedly yes. American trade protectionism can frustrate job creation in competitive Mexican industries. As Mexican President López Portillo once stated, the United States can take either Mexican goods or Mexican people; it cannot keep out both. United States aid provided through multilateral institutions such as the World Bank and the Inter-American Development Bank can stimulate Mexican economic and social progress, and investment by U.S. firms can create jobs.[59]

More important, perhaps, than any of these conscious measures are U.S. policy decisions that affect Mexico by inadvertence. They relate to U.S. macroeconomic policy, which affects interest rates and the rate of growth in the U.S. economy, which, in turn, have profound repercussions in Mexico.[60]

It is useful to repeat, however, what was noted earlier—these admonitions, valid though they are, are prescriptions for the long-term alleviation of emigration pressures from Mexico, not for short-term curtailment. The short-term effect of modestly higher incomes in Mexico is likely to be increased emigration. As has been evident throughout the period since World War II, Mexicans emigrate, mostly as sojourners, when incomes rise and in even greater numbers as economic conditions at home worsen. Economic development that leads to curtailed emigration will be a long-term process.

Mexico's most durable problem, as well as its most valuable asset, is its population. The tragedy of emigration is that those who leave, either for short periods or for good, include many of Mexico's most adventurous young people, precisely the citizens a country wants to keep at home. The motivations of all those who leave are not the same, but large-scale emigration is a symptom of lack of opportunity in Mexico.[61]

Between now and the end of the century, Mexico will have to create 10 to 12 million jobs, almost half again as many as now exist. Mexico's annual need to create 1 million jobs is relatively higher than the 2 million need of the United States, which has three times Mexico's population. Even when economic growth was averaging 6 percent a year for a quarter of a century, Mexico was unable to create jobs at a pace to provide employment to all seekers. So even with economic recovery and sustained economic growth, the size of the problem is beyond Mexico's capacity to cure in the short to medium term.

Migration is one of the most intractable issues between Mexico and the United States. It is driven by disparate economic conditions in the two countries, a situation that cannot be altered in the short term. The migratory process has gone on for so long that it has conditioned the way individuals and families live. The economy of each country is deeply affected by whatever practice is followed, and each country will have difficulty in coping with changes in practices. It can be argued whether the U.S. economy as a whole can adjust without damage to its economic growth without a large flow of undocumented foreign workers. It is quite clear, however, that Mexico will be unable to satisfy all new entrants into the labor force over the next decade and beyond, and it is anybody's guess how the society will be affected if the emigration escape valve is effectively closed.

This difference in impact—significant but not crucial for the United States, but potentially destabilizing for Mexico—is another example of the asymmetry between the two countries.

III

SUMMING UP

10

CONCLUSIONS AND RECOMMENDATIONS

> But the exterior is seen in Mexico, for profound historical reasons, as a source of dangers, not of opportunities.
>
> GABRIEL ZAID, 1984

> I am perfectly aware how difficult it must be to deal with a country so powerful and so immediate. It is evident that one of the most difficult problems for Mexican chiefs of state is the equilibrium in this relation.
>
> MAURICIO GONZÁLEZ DE LA GARZA, 1987

> It is no exaggeration to say that the twin sisters of ignorance and arrogance define the behavior of the generality of North Americans [toward Mexico].
>
> OCTAVIO PAZ, 1986

The Motivation

I have devoted years to examining the United States–Mexico relationship in the conviction that each country is the other's most important partner. The interaction between the two countries is circumscribed by differences in history and culture and vast disparities in economic and international political power, but is also shaped by mutual necessity. This relationship has not always been a happy one, and it may never be intimate (although the word "never" covers too long a time), but it is inevitable. It can also be more productive.

What Is Happening in Mexico?

Every reader of detective stories knows that the crucial moment for Sherlock Holmes in "Silver Blaze" comes when he grasps the meaning of why the dog did not bark. The first approach to interpreting events in Mexico since 1982 is to try to understand why there was no widespread turbulence. If real wages in the United States declined by 50 percent over a six-year period and inflation soared to more than 100 percent a year, it is uncertain whether the political-economic structure of the nation would survive intact.

There is no single explanation of why the Mexican population endured what it did, surely with deep dismay, but also mostly tranquilly resigned to adversity. Most Mexicans are conservative, preferring incremental to sudden change, revolutionary rhetoric notwithstanding. Those who have suffered most from the economic policies

199

since 1982, the very poor, are too busy coping to have much time or energy for political activism. The middle class, the traditional shapers of revolutions, have weathered the stabilization experience with less hardship than their poorer brethren. The economic deterioration of individual and family situations came in discrete steps, and this left hope for improvement next year or the year after that. The underground economy also absorbed some of the shock of declining incomes.

The lack of widespread social disruption does not mean that Mexico has remained as it was before the 1980s. The evidence I have presented demonstrates the reverse—the changes taking place in Mexico are more profound than at any time since the 1930s, perhaps since the Revolution. The changes in economic policy and political patterns would have occurred in any event in the fullness of time, but their pace was accelerated by a series of simultaneous internal and external shocks. The abrupt decline in oil prices and the depletion of foreign-exchange reserves in 1982 to meet debt-service obligations made evident the exhaustion of the development-from-within model. The subsequent stabilization program led to drastic declines in per capita income; this was a new experience for modern, PRI-dominated Mexico. Inflation was out of control for some ten years, and the durable success of the so-called economic solidarity pact in force in 1988 and 1989 is uncertain.

The deficiencies of Mexican-style democracy were violently manifest in the student riots of the 1968. The political system was tested repeatedly in the 1980s as the economy declined, and it was manifest that the PRI was unprepared to face truly democratic choice. The national elections in 1988 made clear that political reform was overdue, but it is still not certain just how much popular choice will be willingly granted. The population endured severe hardship after 1982, but showed its deep discontent when offered a choice in the 1988 election.

Mexico thus faces a complex modernization dealing with its economic structure, its long-standing social inequalities, and the extent of political choice available to its population. The multifaceted, inseparable challenge pervades every aspect of Mexican society, from the crumbling social compact between the state and its people to policies for dealing with specific issues, such as education, the provision of social services, inflation, debt payment, techniques for industrialization, and relations with the external world.

There is no simple, catchall phrase to describe Mexico's political structure. Its features have counterparts elsewhere, but the totality is unique to Mexico. Other places have had durable political machines whose foundation was caring for the faithful and rendering service for the client population; this was typical of many U.S. states and cities for many years. Other countries have had sustained electoral domination by a single party at the national level; this has been the case in postwar Japan. The practice of placing leading political and governmental figures in critical jobs controlled by the government is widespread; this occurs with frequency in France, for example.

Mexico's elections have been mostly a formality. But even in the past, results adverse to the PRI were occasionally accepted at the municipal level, albeit with bad grace.[1] The near certainty of PRI victories in elections at all levels combined with other features to explain the durable one-party dominance: the concentration of power in the central government; the rewarding of loyal political and bureaucratic figures; the ability to control the leading sectors of the economy; and the sophisticated paraphernalia to co-opt significant potential dissidents. But the edifice depended on economic growth for its success and came under pressure as the economy declined.

A caveat must be entered, however. While Mexico is not a democracy with respect to effective suffrage, neither is it a dictatorship. It does have oppressive features, such as summary arrests and muzzling of dissent. The press generally echoes a government line, but opposition news and opinion media do exist. Judicial procedures vary from those in the United States, especially regarding the normal length of pretrial detention in criminal cases, but Mexico has a functioning judicial system. The legislature is not equal to the executive, nor has it had independent power, but opposition legislators conduct debates on significant issues more frequently than in the past. The power of the Chamber of Deputies is almost certain to grow now that the division between the PRI and the opposition is so narrow. Opposition political parties are rarely permitted to win, but their candidates campaign and do influence public opinion. The 1988 presidential campaign had significant candidates from the left and the right as well as from the PRI, and the outcome is a watershed on how Mexico will be governed.

In sum, Mexico has elements of democracy alongside one-party control. The presidential system has had a number of key features: they include the choice of his successor by the incumbent, presumably in consultation with key leaders of the PRI (and, in 1987, even public television presentation of their views by the leading PRI presidential precandidates); the exercise by the president during his tenure of almost absolute power; and, following his one six-year term, the president's absolution from blame for his acts while in office. Gabriel Zaid has described this arrangement as an obsolete contract that once had value as a substitute for recourse to arms by squabbling *caudillos*. He referred to this implicit contract as pre-modern and now humiliating to Mexico.[2]

An insistent clamor for more complete democracy is now being heard thunderously in Mexico. Previous presidents were subjected to public criticism after they left office; this happened to both Echeverría and López Portillo. De la Madrid was castigated publicly even while in office. Detailed articles are disseminated documenting fraud in elections.[3] The linking of democracy and morality has become widespread. "Moral renovation," one of the themes with which de la Madrid entered office, can no longer simply mean curtailment of dishonest gain by public officials; moral renovation now means the growth of democracy, the granting of effective suffrage.

There was some coincidence in the simultaneous exhaustion of both the political and the economic underpinnings of the Mexican structure (although the economic decline surely accelerated the political decline of the PRI), but pressures for change had been building for some time in both arenas. The economic policies undertaken by the de la Madrid administration, if carried to their logical conclusion, will substantially alter institutions and habits by forcing Mexico to look outward more than at any time since the Revolution. The changed structure demands developing a competitiveness that did not exist earlier, and the use of import tariffs will eliminate the role of the central government in case-by-case import licensing. Rents or unearned profits from import licenses will no longer play an enriching role for the beneficiaries.

This is a major experiment in economic development. An important question is how the economic changes will play back on Mexico's political processes. One scenario is that as the economy opens, the political structure will be forced open even more. This is the view taken here. It is also the judgment of President Carlos Salinas de Gortari. Decentralized economic decision making in which the critical factor will be the marketplace and not functionaries will gradually erode the basis for the existing bureaucratic-political machinery. Until now, the principal monetary beneficiaries of the system have been business, the middle class, and some favored labor unions.[4] Most groups will not lose their monetary benefits under the new economic policy, but they, particularly business, will have acquired more power to make their own economic decisions. The freedom to make these choices is apt to be contagious; freedom may not be able to be compartmentalized into economic and political segments.

There is a potential opposing scenario, that the shift in economic policy is so important, that the stakes for the players are so high, that political closing, at least temporarily, is the more likely outcome, despite the 1988 national elections. This pattern, prevalent in Mexico after 1982, characterized the Chilean experience under Pinochet and the development patterns in South Korea and Taiwan. But Chile, Korea, and Taiwan are not exact parallels; the political structures in those countries were more repressive than those in Mexico. Mexico, by contrast, wishes to be counted among the world's democratic societies, and a shift away from democracy to the Chilean model under Pinochet, for example, would run counter to the pattern and pressures coming from Latin America as a whole.[5] It would entail force to frustrate the popular pressure evident in the 1988 national elections for political opening.

There is a third possible scenario, that if economic reform seems to be leading to unacceptable political changes, the economic opening itself will be aborted. Many Mexicans advocate precisely this, a reversion to an economic model even more state led than the earlier development-from-within policy. This was the position of Cuauhtémoc Cárdenas in his 1988 presidential campaign. Even if adopted, this is unlikely to be a durable scenario because the Mexican market lacks the purchasing power to make it viable. It would also run counter to what is by now a worldwide trend toward less state involvement.

Mexico no longer has the luxury of avoiding decisions about the economy. Raymond Vernon wrote in 1963 that Mexico's political system had to either find the means to reduce the extent of its control over the economy in the hope that this would unleash dynamic forces generating growth, or find other ways to respond to the country's changing needs even if this sacrificed "the appearance of legitimacy."[6] Mexico was able to procrastinate in the 1960s because it was not evident to the country's political leadership that the old model had run its course. It was possible to defer restructuring in the 1970s because receipts from oil and debt masked other economic deficiencies. But the evidence that the old model was exhausted was unequivocal in the 1980s.

The thesis set forth here is that the combination of clamor for greater political participation and the growing economic opening will reinforce each other and that the end result, sooner more likely than later, will be a more open and a more democratic Mexican society than the one that now exists. Mitigation of income inequalities is apt to be delayed, but will become harder to ignore if the political system becomes more democratic. This dual pressure for a fuller political democracy and actual economic opening is the most important societal development now taking place in Mexico.

What Is Happening in the United States?

Recent U.S. economic policy has sometimes created severe problems for Mexico and sometimes been helpful. Mexico paid a heavy price for the mix of macroeconomic policy instruments used during the first phase of the Reagan administration. The high interest rates resulting from the restrictive U.S. monetary policy aggravated Mexico's debt-service obligation at the very time that oil prices plummeted. And the reduction in U.S. inflation meant that the real cost of debt servicing in dollars was higher than had been anticipated when the loans were contracted.

But the steady U.S. economic growth during the 1980s provided an outlet for Mexican exports. This was particularly true in 1986 and 1987, when Mexican exchange-rate policy coupled with other export-promotion measures led to soaring exports of manufactured goods to the United States.

These effects, the damaging and the helpful, occurred without any thought on the part of U.S. policymakers to their impact on Mexico. This point, noted earlier, is worth stressing again: the most important U.S. policy measures affecting Mexico are taken inadvertently. Those who look mainly at U.S. policy directed specifically at Mexico are missing the main show.

The United States is becoming more protectionist than at any time since the Smoot-Hawley tariff period of the 1930s, a trend frightening to Mexico. Protectionist pressures have always existed in the United States, but they were overwhelmed during the past fifty years by a trade-liberalizing philosophy. Protectionism was largely industry-specific, while trade policy generally was directed to opening markets worldwide. Mexico is partially the direct target of this new protectionism, but is mostly caught up in a general sentiment favoring what has come to be called fair trade.

The threat of U.S. protection against imports from Mexico causes a bitter reaction because current Mexican export policy conforms to repeated U.S. prodding over the years. A Mexican policymaker could hardly be blamed for concluding that the United States is willing to preach Mexican export promotion as a general proposition only to restrict imports when the lecture is heeded.

The U.S. protectionist threat has contributed to changes in Mexican trade policy. The 1985 agreement with the United States on subsidies and countervailing duties came in response to a raft of fair-trade petitions directed against imports from Mexico. The trade understanding (or framework arrangement for fostering consultation) between the two countries signed in November 1987 permits Mexico and the United States to consult on each other's trade practices within thirty days of a request and called for immediate discussions on textile, agricultural, steel, and electronics products, all of which are subject to actual or threatened U.S. import restrictions.[7] (These consultations led to a new textile agreement and a modest increase in Mexico's steel quota in the United States.) The Mexican authorities were willing to sign this agreement and face domestic criticism from the left about excessive bilateral trade relations with the United States because they were concerned that the greater risk was U.S. protectionism.[8]

The United States also has begun a more restrictive immigration policy. Again, the stimulation for this is primarily internal, but will affect developments in Mexico if the flow of undocumented workers is sharply curtailed.

The contrast between recent tendencies in the United States and those in Mexico is worth drawing with some precision. Mexico is increasingly looking outward on trade matters as the United States moves to protect its home market. Restriction of undocumented immigrants in the United States comes at the very time that Mexican population policy is working to reduce population growth rates. Mexico has been willing to inflict hardships on its domestic population to meet interest payments on its external debt at a time when practically every U.S. politician flees from the very thought of burdening the U.S. population with higher taxes. The overall impression is that Mexico is showing greater economic courage than the United States.

What Is Happening to the Relationship?

The trauma of the 1980s forced Mexico to look closely at its options. One result of this examination was to stress economic cooperation with the United States. This is evident in the trade opening, the increasing welcome to foreign investment, the seeking out of the U.S. market for nonoil exports, and the signing of two bilateral trade agreements. But the United States is distrusted by many Mexicans, especially intellectuals, so that much internal rhetoric still stresses nationalism and distancing from the United States, even as Mexico's economic policy brings the two nations closer.[9]

The U.S. response has been a mixture of acceptance of the new Mexican initiatives and harshness over what are seen as Mexico's shortcomings. Acceptance is best exemplified in the two trade agreements; harshness, in the drug issue. It is doubtful, however, that the United States will again neglect relations with Mexico to the degree it did as recently as a decade ago; U.S. self-interest in Mexico's well-being is now evident. Turmoil in Mexico cannot be contained at the border, and U.S. policy must do what it can to prevent this outcome. Mexico is also a significant supplier of oil and the third-largest market for U.S. exports even at a time when its economy is not prospering; the market potential is vast once Mexico prospers again. Mexico's inability to meet its debt service in 1982 concentrated financial minds in the United States about the importance of its southern neighbor, and U.S. presidential candidates in 1988 found it necessary to set forth a specific policy toward Mexico dealing with such issues as trade and investment, debt, migration, oil, and hemispheric security.

The industrial integration of the two economies is also impressing itself on the minds of policymakers in the two countries. This is apt to be the most important defense against U.S. restrictions on imports from Mexico. Protectionism would affect U.S. producers and workers who provide intermediate and capital goods to Mexico and purchase needed intermediate goods from Mexican suppliers. These cross-border alliances between mutually dependent producers are growing more powerful daily.[10]

Mexico is now becoming both an ally and a competitor of the United States in the industrial arena. The alliances are taking place in particular industries; the competition in both markets. Mexico is developing an economic relationship with the United States similar to those we have with more industrialized countries. Because it is a poorer country, the economic competition/cooperation is less extensive than that with Canada, the other U.S. land neighbor, but is moving in a similar direction.

The industrialists with cross-border alliances are conscious of what is occurring in the bilateral relationship. But the general populations in the two countries are not. The population in Mexico is still fed a diet of nationalism and distrust of U.S. motives. The United States, as stated by Gabriel Zaid in the quotation beginning this chapter, is regarded more as a danger, an exploitative country, than as a neighbor whose presence offers opportunities for Mexican economic growth. Zaid could also have been writing about the United States, whose public does not see Mexico as providing an economic opportunity, but as a country whose main exports are problems we would rather not have.

The deeper reality is not the dangers, but the potential for mutual benefits from the growing trans-border economic and industrial cooperation. That is the purpose of this book, to stress this promise so that it is understood by the publics in the two countries.

The nature of the political structure in Mexico is an internal issue, but it inevitably affects relations with the United States. The talk of a special relationship with Mexico arises from time to time, but "special" always had a different degree of warmth when applied to Mexico compared with other countries where the word is used, such as Great Britain. This is so for historical reasons and because the affection for a democracy is deeper than for a country that is still authoritarian. A difference exists between a relationship born out of necessity and one conceived in respect. The conviction that Mexico's institutions foster corruption also reduces U.S. confidence in the relationship, for although the United States is not without corruption, Mexico's is perceived to be more extensive. These descriptions—authoritarian and corrupt—are changing, although just how far the change will go is uncertain.

The qualifications to its democracy have implications for Mexican foreign policy much broader than relations with the United States. Delal Baer has noted that much of Mexico's past foreign policy was based on general principles rather than international reality.[11] Moral arguments, such as those favoring international economic justice, have less resonance with audiences in democratic countries when they are seen as coming from a country that itself is authoritarian; and these Mexican pronouncements are regarded in the United States as intended for a Mexican audience, not for serious foreign consideration. An analogy can be made with Mexico's trade posture. As long as Mexico was outside the GATT, its statements on trade issues were received as those of a free rider. This has now changed. So too will Mexico's moral influence on other global issues as its political system becomes more open.

The vast economic and power disparities between Mexico and the United States are not amenable to changes in the short term. The two countries have dissimilar historical and cultural formations. Beyond this, the relationship is often inflamed by hostile behavior by both sides. Their disrespectful discourse is a vivid example of this. The episodic official U.S. attention to Mexico is evidence of condescension, even though Mexico is no longer a country run by *caudillos*, but by sophisticated politicians and technocrats.

Mexico, for its part, does not abet a cooperative relationship by continuing to believe that it can obtain economic concessions even as it constantly lambasts the United States at home and in foreign-policy forums. Officials in the United States read what is disseminated by the Mexican authorities for the domestic audience, and this influences their responses to what Mexico requests when it speaks internationally.

Despite their differences, despite the frequent incivility, the two countries have a joint destiny determined by geography. This is not disputable intellectually, and it is now being recognized increasingly in action as well.

Main Recommendations

The broad conclusion from the analysis in this book is that for better or worse, in good times and especially in bad, the behavior of either Mexico or the United States deeply affects the other. The marriage metaphor may be too legalistic, but there is certainly an inseparable meaningful relationship. The key recommendation that flows from this analysis, stated simply, is that the two countries should make the most of this situation. The first step in improved relations is to accept the intimate nature of the relationship, since only then can other cooperative actions follow, as many have during the recent years of Mexican adversity.

The policy chapters of this book deal with specific functional issues in the relationship. Not all the recommendations in the separate chapters will be repeated here; the main ones will be summarized. Some suggestions are directed to Mexico, others to the United States. However, optimizing the relationship requires taking a broader view than function-by-function activities. It is necessary that the authorities of each country recognize the problems, limitations, idiosyncrasies, culture, and historic formation of the other. Mexico will not be taken seriously if it repeatedly abuses the United States in international and domestic forums; the real and the verbal aspects of the relationship are not easily separable. The United States will not be seen as a friend if it continues to approach relations with Mexico in a condescending way; this, unfortunately, has been typified in recent years by name calling in the effort to control drug traffic and by patronizing lecturing by U.S. officials.

Neither country is a unified whole when it comes to attitudes toward the other. This is evident, but worth stating nevertheless. The United States should not attribute to all of Mexico what is an essentially anti-American press. Mexicans should not conclude that anti-Mexican views of particular U.S. senators or representatives reflect the view of the whole Congress, let alone of the United States.

The specific functional recommendations build on developments in each country. The most important of these relate to the role reversals in trade policy, the opening in Mexico and the closing in the United States. Throughout this book, the viewpoint is that Mexico's economic opening is the correct path toward renewed and sustainable economic growth because the internal market is inadequate for Mexico to meet its economic growth aspirations. Even during the phase of easy import substitution, in the decades when the growth of GDP was consistently high, almost half of Mexico's population benefited only marginally. Assuming that Mexico continues the trade policy direction it has chosen, the principal recommendation must be directed to the U.S. government, which must support this Mexican policy in word and deed. This means U.S. industries will have to adjust as Mexican industry becomes more competitive; many U.S. workers will be hurt, and they deserve support, but through financial adjustment and retraining rather than by frustrating the Mexican effort through U.S. import restraints. The totality of U.S. industry and workers will benefit if Mexico prospers. The requirement for U.S. policy is to compensate those individuals who are hurt from the much larger benefits that accrue to U.S. society as a whole.

One additional point should be made about U.S. protection. It is generally specific to industries in which wages make up a significant portion of total unit costs. American industry cannot compete with Mexican production on the basis of which country pays the lower wages. Mexican wages will invariably be lower at this stage of the countries' respective histories. The more productive attitude is for each country to establish a policy framework that encourages industrial complementarity. This has been called managed industrial integration here. It requires modest or even zero levels of protection in each country for the import of inputs from the other. Official agreements under which the governments decide the sectors in which private entrepreneurs should operate are neither needed nor desirable; this is precisely the type of microeconomic decision the market is able to handle. The best example is the development of the *maquiladora* in which private parties took advantage of policy frameworks established separately by the two countries.

The combination of relatively open markets and industrial production sharing should lead to a quantum leap in bilateral trade. The two countries would become even more economically integrated than they are now. Would this also make Mexico more vulnerable to decisions made in the United States? Perhaps, but since about 80 percent of Mexico's exports of manufactures already go to the United States, it is hard to conceive of even greater concentration. Production sharing involves mutual vulnerabilities. It also generates cross-border alliances that are probably the best protection against excessive protectionism. While Mexico–United States trade should increase in absolute terms under this combination of relatively open markets and more extensive production sharing, increased competitiveness of Mexican industry should augment its ability to diversify markets.

Why managed integration? Why not let nature (events) take its (their) course? The management recommended here is an assurance of a policy framework and not direct government involvement in the details of industrial complementation. Each government will inevitably involve itself in policy aspects of its industrial development, from health and safety requirements to minimum wages. Managed integration is a way to assure investors that the two governments support a policy of fostering complementarity.

Neither side is now confident that the other will not take actions prejudicial to its well-being. These potential actions deal mostly with domestic matters in each country, primarily macroeconomic policy. Regular meetings of U.S. and Canadian foreign ministers and Treasury and central bank officials take place precisely to avoid surprises. The Organization for Economic Cooperation and Development in Paris and various other groupings of developed countries (the group of five, of seven, of ten, and other sizes), plus the regular economic summits of the leading industrial democracies, also serve this consultative purpose. It is a measure of the inferior position that Mexico has played in U.S. thinking that, until 1989, nothing comparable existed, except for dealing with specific issues or sectors, such as trade generally or oil. Consultation is not coordination. There is no way to fully shield Mexico from the inadvertent consequences of U.S. policy. At the margin, however, some U.S. policies might be modified, or Mexico might be able to take some ameliorative action if forewarned. The consultation would be in both directions, since Mexico also takes actions that affect U.S. nationals.

There is no functional area in which it is more vital for each side to be aware of the official thinking of the other than on Mexico's foreign debt. The debt issue is potentially explosive in Mexico. The decline in Mexican incomes in recent years has been attributed by the opposition on the left, and even by the *corriente democrática* faction of the PRI from which Cuauhtémoc Cárdenas comes, to Mexico's decision to keep paying interest on its foreign debt. These interest payments in recent years have been about 5 to 6 percent of GDP and therefore represent a significant outflow of resources. The peso counterpart of these payments limits the government's budgetary options. The Mexican authorities have refused to declare a unilateral moratorium on meeting external-debt service, but maintaining this position requires that the burden of the payments becomes less onerous. Obtaining some relief from the debt burden is a political imperative if President Carlos Salinas de Gortari is to have a successful *sexenio*.

The official U.S. approach to the debt is that Mexico can grow out of its stagnation with only modest easing in its interest payments. The judgment expressed here is that this does not go far enough. If Salinas is not able to show significant results on debt relief, the entire policy of restructuring the economy will be endangered. Further debt shocks are conceivable, indeed likely, such as higher world interest rates that would increase Mexico's resource outflow or drastic curtailment of bank lending. The two countries tried to avoid the crisis atmosphere that prevailed during the previous two debt restructurings, in 1982 and 1986, by promoting negotiations in 1989 to reduce the interest cost of Mexico's external debt. Only time will tell if the effort succeeded.

A final precise recommendation deals with petroleum relations between the two countries. This, too, is sensitive, although for a different reason from debt. Oil represents Mexico's national heritage, and selling oil and associated resources to the

United States, even at a large profit, is not universally welcome in that country; this was evident from the reaction to the plan to sell natural gas to the United States in 1977 and 1978. It has also been evident that reliance on oil exports is a mixed blessing.[12] This reliance not only petrolized the economy, but also led to income volatility as oil prices changed. One way to minimize this volatility is for Mexico to integrate its oil industry downstream, abroad as well as at home, including to the retail level in the United States, as has been done by Venezuela. Downstream integration into the United States would permit taking the profit on crude sales when these prices are high and on product sales when the crude is treated as an input cost. This would emulate the behavior of the oil majors.

While the immediate danger is not great, it is possible that the United States will one day impose an oil-import fee. Mexico has argued that it should be exempt from any such levy in the interest of U.S. security of supply. The logic of the Mexican position would be more convincing if there were a long-term-supply agreement. As politically sensitive as this issue is in Mexico, there is merit for both countries in examining this possibility.

Concluding Comments

Great tension marks the United States–Mexico relationship—differences separate the two countries while their mutual dependence brings them together. The two pulls are always present. The unifying impulse dominates when Mexico reaches out for help because there is no place to turn except to the United States. The instinct to separate is most powerful when Mexico feels strong and confident, an attitude that has dominated for most of the period since World War II. Mexico has looked outward when in trouble and inward when prospering.

Mexico is now looking outward in a more profound way than at any time since the Revolution. The shift in approach is not a one-shot affair, like a bridge financing or a debt rescheduling, but a continuing reordering of the economy. Whatever the durability of the present phase of modernization, there can be no looking back. But the United States is not responding in kind. Trade protectionism is threatened. Mexican officials are publicly charged with dishonesty. Both the Congress and the executive make threats to punish Mexico if it does not cooperate in whatever field happens to be the current fancy, whether it is the momentary politics of drugs, the treatment of particular foreign investors, or the refusal to hew to the U.S. posture in Central America. The important and enduring aspects of the relationship are being sacrificed to the relatively trivial or temporal. The impression that is left is that the U.S. government has not grasped what is taking place in either the Mexican economy or political structure.

Mexico will not jettison its heritage and will continue to look south to Latin America and to Spain for cultural nourishment even as it moves ever closer to the United States in its economic programs and the ethnic intermingling of the two countries. The United States will not alter its heritage either, and will continue to look to Europe for spiritual sustenance even as its political and economic interests flourish with Mexico. What is required, however, is a recognition that each country can sustain multiple interests. Each can look in other directions even as it looks to the other. They can cooperate, even with pressures for mutual distancing. Each can accept the importance of the other even as it has relationships with third countries. But the United States and Mexico can and must recognize that their relationship will inevitably be the most important for each of them because they are where they are.

NOTES

Introduction

1. While English as the official language is not the law in Texas, a nonbinding referendum in favor of this position was passed overwhelmingly in the Republican state primary on March 8, 1988. According to *Newsweek*, seventeen states then had statutes proclaiming English as the official language (February 20, 1989, p. 22).
2. Other countries in Latin America without credible external threats do have large military or paramilitary forces. The reasons for the relatively modest Mexican military force are also economic, to conserve resources and limit the political role of the military.
3. Robert A. Pastor and Jorge G. Castañeda argue that different interests must inevitably result in misperceptions (*Limits to Friendship: The United States and Mexico*). I question the validity of this thesis.
4. This percentage is derived by using either minimum wages, which apply for many workers, or industrial wages.
5. Stephen D. Krasner, *Structural Conflict: The Third World Against Global Liberalism*, p. 5.
6. Jorge G. Castañeda, "Don't Corner Mexico!" p. 89.
7. Stanley Hoffmann, *Gulliver's Troubles, or the Setting of American Foreign Policy*, p. 147.
8. The difficulty of altering income distribution patterns is discussed in Pedro Aspe and Paul E. Sigmund, eds., *The Political Economy of Income Distribution in Mexico*.

Chapter 1

1. Anti-Americanism among Mexicans can often be extreme. Marlise Simons quotes the Mexican historian Gaston García Cantú: "I refuse to speak the language of the empire. It's easier not to be contaminated that way" ("The People Next Door," p. 2). He may refuse to speak English, but many senior Mexican officials, including President Carlos Salinas de Gortari and his predecessor, Miguel de la Madrid, were educated in the United States, traders do much of their business in English, and migrant workers will do better if they learn English.
2. "Shadows of the Past," *Economist*, September 5, 1987, p. 22.
3. The figure is based on U.S. customs data.
4. The relationship of 25,000 jobs per $1 billion of exports is often used by the U.S. Department of Commerce.
5. U.S. Embassy Mexico telegram 2214, January 29, 1986, to Department of State, based on Mexican data.
6. Data are from the Bank of Mexico.

7. U.S. Embassy Mexico telegram 9896, May 30, 1985, to Department of State, based on data compiled by the Mexican Directorate General for Foreign Investment. The percentages of other countries were: West Germany, 8.6; Japan, 6.3; Switzerland, 5.0; and Great Britain, 3.0. The U.S. proportion has remained about the same since then.

8. Karl W. Deutsch, "Transaction Flows as Indicators of Political Cohesion."

9. Data are from the Immigration and Naturalization Service, Washington, D.C. In fiscal year 1987, of the 293 million persons who entered the United States via Mexico, 116 million were aliens.

10. Banco de México, *Indicadores económicos*.

11. That the same symbols of consumerism are used in Mexico as elsewhere is evident from the title of an article by one of Mexico's distinguished social commentators, Carlos Monsiváis: "Civilización y Coca-Cola."

12. *New York Times*, November 17, 1986, p. 6 (Southwest edition). Subsequent references to this poll are from the same source.

13. Mario Ojeda, "The Future of Relations Between Mexico and the United States."

14. Banco de México, *Indicadores económicos*.

15. Based on data from an industrial park operator in Ciudad Juárez, and confirmed by minimum-wage data for the area as of January 1989 as reported in *El Mercado de Valores*, January 1, 1989, p. 27.

16. Olga Pellicer de Brody, "Mexico in the 1970s and Its Relations with the United States."

17. The November 1986 strike at the Delco Electronics plant in Kokomo, Indiana, which makes electronic control units to govern engine operations for General Motors cars, was caused by a plan to shift production from the United States to Mexico. This strike idled 7,500 workers at the Delco plant and nearly 50,000 workers at various GM plants around the United States (*New York Times*, November 22, 1986, p. 7 [Southwest edition]). The plant stayed in Kokomo, at least for the time being.

18. Production sharing ís discussed in Joseph Grunwald and Kenneth Flamm, *The Global Factory: Foreign Assembly in International Trade*. Chapter 4 (pp. 137–179) deals specifically with assembly in Mexico. So does U.S. International Trade Commission (USITC), *The Use and Economic Impact of TSUS Items 806.30 and 807.00*.

19. Rolando Cordera and Carlos Tello, "Prospects and Options for Mexican Society." It is worth noting that this essay was written in 1981, before Tello had an opportunity to test some of his ideas when he served as director general of the Bank of Mexico at the end of 1982.

20. Cordera and Tello were reacting to a proposal by Clark W. Reynolds, "Mexican–U.S. Interdependence: Economic and Social Perspectives." What I have proposed would undoubtedly also be labeled neoliberal. Cordera and Tello make a parody of this approach by insisting that it would arrest labor organization, limit education to specialities needed for industry, gut social welfare programs to trim the size of the public sector, and end up by consolidating dominance by an industrial elite, presumably in alliance with confederates in the United States.

21. Carlos Rico F., "'Interdependencia' y trilateralismo: orígenes de una estrategia," p. 88.

22. Carlos Rico F., "Prospects for Economic Cooperation."

23. See Chapter 8 for an explanation of this statement.

24. Bela Balassa, ed., *European Economic Integration*, p. 117.

25. In what they called "managed interdependence," a phrase that did not register with me until after I had hit on the expression "managed integration," Guy F. Erb and Cathryn Thorup advocated precisely this kind of bilateral framework agreement ("U.S.–Mexican Relations: The Issues Ahead").

26. The IBM agreement is discussed in Chapter 5.

27. Ojeda, "Future of Relations Between Mexico and the United States," is based on this thesis.

28. I. William Zartman and Maureen R. Berman, *The Practical Negotiator*, p. 204.

29. Richard Newfarmer, ed., *Profits, Progress and Poverty: Case Studies of International Industries in Latin America*, deals with MNC bargaining in the following industries: cigarettes, electrical, iron and steel, automobiles and tires, pharmaceuticals, tractors, and food processing. Some sources of what are called monopolistic MNC advantages that are emphasized in the final analytical chapter by Gary Gereffi and Richard S. Newfarmer are from technology that the MNCs bring, economies of scale, and product differentiation ("International Oligopoly and Uneven Development: Some Lessons from Industrial Case Studies").

30. Jesús Puente Leyva, "The Natural Gas Controversy."

31. Thomas Colosi, "A Model for Negotiation and Mediation," p. 17.

32. These negotiating alliances are discussed in Richard E. Feinberg, "Bureaucratic Organization and United States Policy Toward Mexico," and Richard R. Fagen, "The Politics of the United States–Mexico Relationship."

33. Raymond Vernon, *Sovereignty at Bay: The Multinational Spread of U.S. Enterprises.*

34. Van R. Whiting, Jr., "Transnational Enterprise in the Food Processing Industry," pp. 343, 383.

35. Patrick H. Heffernan, "Conflict over Marine Resources."

36. The $1 billion figure is high because the interest on debt to official institutions does not normally float up and down, as does the interest rate on debt to private commercial creditors. The latter debt makes up some 85 percent of the outstandings.

37. David Goldsbrough and Iqbal Zaidi make the evident point that the magnitude of these transmissions depends on the structures of the developing countries ("Transmission of Economic Influences from Industrial to Developing Countries").

38. Feinberg, "Bureaucratic Organization and United States Policy Toward Mexico," p. 39.

39. Ibid.

40. I base this statement on discussions with U.S. government officials.

41. The Bilateral Commission on the Future of United States-Mexican Relations recommended in a report the reincarnation of a high-level coordinator for U.S. government policy toward Mexico (*The Challenge of Interdependence: Mexico and the United States*, p. 164).

42. United Nations Association of the U.S.A., "Relationships in the North American Economic Area."

43. Rafael Fernández de Castro, "Mexican Government Influence on the Outcome of U.S. Legislation"; tables on Canadian and Mexican lobbying presented by George Grayson at a symposium on Mexico at the Foreign Service Institute of the U.S. State Department, December 8–9, 1986.

Chapter 2

1. Plutarco Elías Calles established the Partido Revolucionario in 1929. Lázaro Cárdenas changed the name in 1938 to the Partido de la Revolución Mexicana. The Partido Revolucionario Institucional, the PRI, was born in 1946.

2. Mancur Olson, *The Rise and Decline of Nations: Economic Growth, Stagflation, and Social Rigidities.*

3. Pablo González Casanova's *Democracy in Mexico* was extremely influential in the formation of intellectual thinking in Mexico when originally published in Spanish in 1965. Many U.S. works on Mexico focus on inequality, either using a Marxist, class-struggle framework, such as James D. Cockcroft, *Mexico: Class Formation, Capital Accumulation, and the State*, or pointing out the failure of the Mexican economic model to benefit the majority, such as Susan Eckstein, *The Poverty of Revolution: The State and the Urban Poor in Mexico*, and Judith Adler Hellman, *Mexico in Crisis.*

4. Sidney Weintraub, *Free Trade between Mexico and the United States?*, pp. 84–91. The small-scale industrialists, mostly conservative in political philosophy, were aided by intellectuals of the left, who opposed entry into the GATT out of fear that entry would tie Mexico's economy even more closely to the United States.

5. There are many studies of Mexican business organizations, including John J. Bailey, *Governing Mexico: The Statecraft of Crisis Management*; M. Basañez, *La lucha por la hegemonia en México, 1968–1980*; and R. J. Shafer, *Mexican Business Organizations.*

6. Discussion of Canacintra as a captive group can be found in Dale Story, *Industry, the State, and Public Policy in Mexico*, p. 86.

7. There are many examples of this criticism. For example, see the press release of the speech by Claudio X. González, CCE president, of September 5, 1986, analyzing the 1986 *Informe* of President de la Madrid.

8. Francisco Alba, "Logros y limitaciones en la absorción de la fuerza de trabajo en México," p. 559.

9. Peter Gregory, *The Myth of Market Failure: Employment and the Labor Market in Mexico*, p. 20.

10. Ibid., p. 23.

11. Centro de Estudios Económicos del Sector Privado, *La economía subterranea en México*, p. 104.

12. Leopoldo Solís, *Economic Policy Reform in Mexico: A Case Study for Developing Countries*, p. 100.

13. Instituto Nacional de Estadística, Geografía e Informática (Inegi), *Sistema de cuentas nacionales de México, 1981–1983*, p. 1. The Comisión Económica para América Latina y el Caribe (Cepal) gives salaries as a proportion of GDP in 1984 as 27 percent (*Estudio Económico de América Latina y El Caribe 1984: México*, p. 5). The exact percentages are different if one looks at disposable national income. The decline in the share of salaries in this calculation was from 41 to 32.5 percent, and the increase in the share to capital from 53.7 to 62.3 percent. However, the picture remains the same. The shares for the United States come from *Economic Indicators* (prepared monthly by the Council of Economic Advisers for the Joint Economic Committee of the Congress), January 1989.

14. The percentage of industrial workers organized is from U.S. Department of Labor, "Profile of Labor Conditions."

15. *New York Times*, March 27, 1986, p. 4 (Southwest edition).

16. A fascinating study of the winter vegetable trade between Mexico and the United States is David R. Mares, "Agricultural Trade: Domestic Interests and Transnational Relations."

17. Edward J. Williams, "The Evolution of the Mexican Military and Its Implications for Civil–Military Relations."

18. David Ronfeldt, "The Modern Mexican Military: Implications for Mexico's Stability and Security," p. 6.

19. The *New York Times* points out that about 2,000 favored intellectuals do get stipends from the government (September 27, 1987, sec. 4, p. 2). This is not corruption, but it is a form of bribery.

20. This theme is taken up in an article in the *New York Times*, October 21, 1986, p. 1. This was one of a series of analytical articles the newspaper ran at that time on Mexico.

21. This is the sense of the papers presented by U.S. scholars of Mexico at a conference at the State Department on December 12, 1985. See Roderic A. Camp, ed., *Mexico's Political Stability: The Next Five Years*.

22. However, in addition to the bloody suppression of the 1968 student demonstrations, there is evidence of other violence and of police brutality. Carmen Cano Gordón and María Teresa Cisneros Gudiño deal with incidents of violence stemming from land-tenure disputes (*La dinámica de la violencia en México*). Amnesty International documents cases of detention, torture, and murder, especially of peasants opposed to the PRI-affiliated CNC (*Mexico: Human Rights in Rural Areas. Exchange of Documents with the Mexican Government on Human Rights Violations in Oaxaca and Chiapas*). The publication also contains a detailed denial, case by case, by the Mexican government. Many journalists have been murdered and many more detained by authorities over the years, seemingly on political grounds; see *Proceso*, July 21, 1985, pp. 26–29, and August 4, 1986, pp. 24–27, and *Newsweek*, November 17, 1986, p. 62. When rubble was cleared following the earthquake that devastated parts of Mexico City on September 19, 1985, bodies were found of persons who had apparently been tortured while in police custody (*Wall Street Journal*, October 15, 1985, pp. 1, 22). There is an organization called the National Front Against Repression, made up of persons who claim to have relatives being held as political prisoners, Mexican *desaparecidos*, or disappeared ones (*Austin American-Statesman*, August 24, 1986, p. D5). There was violence directed against PAN candidates in elections in the border state of Coahuila in October 1987.

23. William P. Glade, "Mexico: Party-Led Development."

24. Rogelio Sada, the chief executive of Vitro, a large glass company in Monterrey, was forced to resign in 1985, reportedly because he supported the PAN candidate for mayor of Monterrey. This allegation was widely circulated and generally believed to be accurate (see the column by David Asman, *Wall Street Journal*, July 24, 1986, p. 22).

25. The English translation is *For a Democracy Without Adjectives*. The book was a collection of magazine articles written over a number of years. The title of the book caught the eye in 1986 in a way that it might not have half a dozen years earlier.

26. I have made this argument in "Economic Sources of Political Instability in Mexico."

27. Cepal, "Daños causados por el movimiento telúrico en México y sus repercusiones sobre la economía del país."

28. An AP story on the earthquakes around the time of the second anniversary reported on the homeless (*Austin American-Statesman*, September 19, 1987, p. B10).

29. *Wall Street Journal*, October 15, 1985, p. 1.

30. For example, a column by Jorge A. Bustamante, a prominent Mexican sociologist, in *Excélsior*, Mexico City's leading newspaper, praised the American people and institutions for their generosity, but the main thrust was hostile: he said that U.S. television portrayed Mexico as incapable of dealing with the catastrophe, and that the U.S. ambassador had the audacity to contradict official figures on the number of deaths (October 7, 1985, p. 6A). A column on the front page of *Excélsior* by Gastón García Cantú, a Mexican historian known for his intense hatred of the United States, contained the following language: "More than 200 years of affronts, invasions, and a war of conquest are [intended to be] obliterated thanks to a temblor of grade 8.1." This history cannot be erased by "a million dollars carried by a smiling Nancy [Reagan] and additional shipments of used clothing and potable water." Mexico should not accept this "fraternal" aid because the United States "has been, is, and will be an adversary of Mexico" (October 7, 1985, p. 1).

31. The activities of the embassy were recounted in an article by Robert L. L. Cohoes in *State*, the in-house magazine of the State Department, November 1985.

32. See *Excélsior*, October 11, 1985.

33. In this discussion, I have drawn heavily on the four papers by M. Delal Baer, "The Mexican Midterm Elections."

34. The Federal Electoral Commission puts another face on the 1986 electoral reform, that it contributes to the "integral democratization of society" by giving the opposition a greater voice (*The New Mexican Electoral Legislation*, p. vii).

35. John J. Bailey argues that one motivation for a multiparty system is to reduce the influence of the United States acting through a single, large opposition party, such as the PAN (*Governing Mexico: The Statecraft of Crisis Management*). My own judgment is that this sounds more like rationalization than primary intention.

36. The PRI appears to have wanted to guard against losing its absolute legislative majority.

37. Partial renovation of the Senate at each election was the system contemplated in the 1917 constitution, but later altered.

38. Both Bailey (*Governing Mexico*) and Baer ("Mexican Midterm Elections") contain fuller discussions of the opposition parties.

39. The PAN's history and current positions are discussed in Dale Story, "The PAN, the Private Sector, and the Future of the Mexican Opposition."

40. Cary Hector omits the PPS from his definition of the left, presumably because it is generally considered to be a captive of the PRI. Hector stresses that the left as constituted in 1985 to 1986 did not pose a strong electoral alternative ("La izquierda mexicana hoy: una mirada aproximación y en perspectiva").

41. Baer, "Mexican Midterm Elections," report 4, p. 17. My own judgment is that politically conscious Mexicans were well aware of the gap between myth and reality when it came to the PRI's grasp of power well before the 1985 elections.

42. M. Delal Baer, "The 1986 Mexican Elections: The Case of Chihuahua," p. 2.

43. *Proceso*, October 13, 1986, p. 10.

44. Juan Molinar Horcasitas, "Regreso a Chihuahua."

45. *Proceso*, July 7, 1986, p. 6.

46. That this was an important reversal was evident from the speculation in the Mexican press that Bartlett had improved his chances of being chosen as the PRI candidate for president because of his effective intervention. He eventually was not chosen. The plan to not hold mass was a serious and potentially explosive development. The Mexican constitution forbids clerics to participate in politics as clerics, and this, in a sense, was precisely what the bishops were proposing. They could argue that the constitution also forbids electoral fraud, but that would be a debating point. The intention to not hold mass was reminiscent of the Cristero rebellion when, for three years starting in early 1926, the Roman Catholic church in Mexico withheld sacraments to protest anticlerical provisions of the constitution. It is understandable that the Vatican did not want a repetition of the Cristero rebellion.

47. See Roderic A. Camp, *Intellectuals and the State in Twentieth-Century Mexico*, p. 100.

48. *Proceso*, August 18, 1986, p. 71.

49. The election results given in this and the next paragraph come from *Proceso*, July 19, 1988, pp. 23–25. Challenges to the vote count may alter the figures.

50. *New York Times*, July 11, 1988, p. 6 (Southwest edition).
51. *Proceso*, discusses this (July 25, 1988, pp. 26–31). It is of some interest that the majority of the members of the petroleum workers' union, the STPRM, voted for Cárdenas. This may provide some explanation of why the Salinas government moved in January 1989 to reduce the union's power and arrest its leader, Joaquín Hernández Galicia, known as La Quina. The union also had the reputation of being corrupt, and Salinas's action was therefore popular.
52. Some defections have occurred.
53. *Proceso* notes that many PRI legislative candidates proposed by the CTM, the labor confederation affiliated with the party, were defeated (July 18, 1988, pp. 30–33). These included Joaquín Gamboa Pascoe, the CTM leader in the Federal District, who was defeated in his quest for a Senate seat. The gist of the *Proceso* article is that the long-time leader of the CTM, Fidel Velázquez, is now obsolete.
54. See Chapter 7 for a discussion of the debt theme.
55. E. V. K. Fitzgerald discusses precisely these issues ("Mexico, A New Direction in Economic Policy.") So do countless works by Mexican authors.

Chapter 3

1. An interesting account of how President Johnson tried to inject warmth into the relationship with his Mexican counterpart, President Gustavo Díaz Ordaz, is in E. V. Niemeyer, Jr., "Personal Diplomacy: Lyndon B. Johnson and Mexico, 1963–1968."
2. In my own experience as a U.S. government official, I often picked up the telephone in Washington to chat with a counterpart in Ottawa about an issue between the two countries. This was typical of what other officials did as well. I never did this with a Mexican counterpart, nor, to my knowledge, did my colleagues. Such direct conversations now take place to some extent between officials from the two Treasury departments or the Federal Reserve and the Bank of Mexico. Debt has made for communication.
3. Examples of both types of actions are legion. John Gavin was thoroughly disliked by Mexican officials and intellectuals when he was ambassador to Mexico from 1981 to 1986 precisely because he publicly lectured Mexico on its internal and external policies. A two-page advertisement was inserted in the *New York Times* containing a letter to President Reagan signed by thirty-five members of Congress warning of the Communist threat in Mexico, including that coming from Mexican officials (October 1, 1982, pp. A16–17). When President Carter visited Mexico in 1979, the well-publicized toast he received from President López Portillo referred to "sudden deceit" by the United States in connection with negotiations for the sale of Mexican natural gas. The Mexican ambassador to the United Nations, Mario Moya Paléncia, referred to a "week of infamy" in October 1986 because of discriminatory fees imposed on oil imported into the United States to help finance the environmental superfund and passage of U.S. immigration legislation that contained an employer-penalty provision (*Proceso*, October 27, 1986, p. 10).
4. The interchange between academics of the two countries is much more informal than that between officials, but even this is influenced by the relative national powers and economic inequalities. This can be seen in attacks in the Mexican press against U.S. academics whose views do not conform with Mexican positions. An example of such attacks can be seen in *Proceso*, October 27, 1986, pp. 10–15, in an article about the series on Mexico carried in the *New York Times* from October 19 to 25, 1986, which contained comments on Mexico from various U.S. academic specialists.
5. The terminology of positive and negative sanctions can be found in David A. Baldwin, *Economic Statecraft*. I have used the phrase "positive sanctions," even though I find it an oxymoron.
6. The Mexican left considers sales to the strategic petroleum reserve as beneficial to the United States and harmful to Mexico by depleting a scarce resource.
7. Donald L. Wyman, "Dependence and Conflict: U.S. Relations with Mexico," p. 133.
8. The argument on determinants of foreign investment will not withstand careful scrutiny in that much U.S. and other foreign investment went to Mexico despite its restrictive laws. The main determinant has been the state of the Mexican economy and its political situation rather than its laws. This is evident from the data given in Chapter 5.
9. Brian Latell, *Mexico at the Crossroads: The Many Crises of the Political System*. Jorge Castañeda,

in *Proceso*, discussed both the CIA evaluation of Mexican stability and the essay by Latell (September 1, 1986, pp. 30–34).

10. Ibid., p. 13.

11. I wonder how U.S. officials would react if a Mexican government official asserted that there was an increase in U.S. corruption because many business persons, rather than politicians, were placed in senior positions. The evidence could also be superficially convincing.

12. Roberta Lajous de Solana and Jesús Velasco Márquez, "Visión de México en la prensa de Estados Unidos: 1984."

13. The program was aired on February 23, 1986.

14. Juan M. González, Yolanda Muñoz Pérez, Georgina Núñez, and Priscila Sosa, "El impacto de las audencias Helms en la relación bilateral."

15. The *New York Times* series ran from October 19 to 25, 1986.

16. Sally Shelton Colby in an op-ed piece in the *Washington Post*, May 28, 1986. Jorge Castañeda had an op-ed column in the *New York Times* on May 21, 1986. The *Wall Street Journal* ran an editorial, "Putting Down Mexico," on May 30, 1986. Mexico bashing was well exemplified by "Mexico: Broken Promises," *Newsweek*, March 17, 1986 (international edition). The content of this cover story is fairly summarized in the following sentence: "Mexico looks like a country in danger of being overwhelmed by its own inefficiency, pollution, poverty and corruption, a country rotting from within" (p. 6).

17. The *Wall Street Journal* ran three articles documenting this corruption on November 19, 20, and 25, 1986. The *Journal* frequently runs exposé articles on wrongdoing, domestic and foreign, so that the argument that Mexico was singled out for opprobrium will not stand up to scrutiny.

18. On August 31, 1986, an Aeroméxico DC-9 was destroyed in the skies near Los Angeles International Airport, with a loss of eighty-two lives, when a single-engine Piper crashed into its tail section. The fault was apparently that of the pilot of the small airplane and perhaps of the U.S. air-traffic controllers. There was much speculation in Mexico at the time that if the situation had been reversed, if a U.S. commercial airliner had crashed with much loss of life because of mishandling over a Mexican airport, the official and press commentary in the United States would have been devastating to the effect that this Mexican inefficiency is only what one would expect.

19. Daniel Cosío Villegas, *American Extremes*, p. 39.

20. Mario Ojeda, "México ante los Estados Unidos en la coyuntura actual," p. 52. While I have translated the word *funestas* as "unfortunate," it has the sense of "mournful"—that is, something stronger than unfortunate but not quite tragic.

21. Octavio Paz, *The Other Mexico: Critique of the Pyramid*, pp. 11, 35–36.

22. Octavio Paz, *Sor Juana Inés de la Cruz o las trampas de la fe*, p. 67.

23. Octavio Paz, "Reflections: Mexico and the United States," p. 142.

24. Ibid., p. 150.

25. Francisco Javier Alejo, "Complementation and Conflict: A Mexican View," p. 262. Scholarly literature in Mexico is replete with criticisms of the lack of U.S. generosity in its trade preferences for Mexico. See, for example, Isabel Molina, "La renovación del sistema generalizado de preferencias arancelarias y sus implicaciones para México," and Gustavo Vega Cánovas, "Comercio y política en Estados Unidos: librecambismo versus proteccionismo desde la segunda guerra mundial."

26. Mario Ojeda, *Alcances y límites de la política exterior de México*, pp. 197–198.

27. U.S. Department of State, "Report to Congress on Voting Practices in the United Nations," p. II-5. In 1986, Mexico agreed with the United States in 17 percent of plenary votes in the General Assembly.

28. Jorge G. Castañeda, "Don't Corner Mexico!"

29. Enrique Krauze, "*Vecinos distantes* de Alan Riding," p. 36.

30. Lorenzo Meyer, "Historical Roots of the Authoritarian State in Mexico," pp. 11–13.

31. The definitions come from Webster's *New World Dictionary of the American Language*.

32. My family has experienced this. One example was when a car in which my wife was a passenger was stopped twice on the short trip from Cuernavaca to Mexico City, each time for a police request for payment of a fine for a nonexistent traffic infraction.

33. See Chapters 4 and 5 for a discussion of Mexico's trade and industrial policies.
34. George W. Grayson asserts that "of all the constraints (on taking advantage of the oil boom in the 1970s) the most important is the inefficiency of Pemex" ("Mexico's Opportunity: The Oil Boom," p. 75). Grayson cites the political influence in awarding contracts, the bloated bureaucracy, and the power and venality of the oil union in Pemex.
35. The most complete discussion of STPRM can be found in Angelina Alonso and Roberto López, *El sindicato de trabajadores petroleros y sus relaciones con Pemex y el estado, 1970–1985*. Brief discussions in English of the union can be found in George W. Grayson, *The Politics of Mexican Oil*, pp. 81–102, and Alan Riding, *Distant Neighbors: A Portrait of the Mexicans*, pp. 171–179.
36. Octavio Paz has noted that "political reform is inseparable from intellectual and moral reform" ("Remache: burocracia y democracia en México," p. 63).
37. Daniel Levy and Gabriel Székely, *Mexico: Paradoxes of Stability and Change*, p. 110.
38. Sissela Bok, *Lying: Moral Choice in Public and Private Life*, pp. 114–115.
39. The attempt to alter the operations and intellectual protection of the U.S. pharmaceutical industry operating in Mexico, discussed in Chapter 5, is an example of U.S. resistance to a Mexican industrial-policy measure. The U.S. response to Mexican export subsidies by means of countervailing duties is another example of nonacceptance of a practice that Mexico justified on the grounds of being a developing country.
40. Supporters of the PAN have welcomed criticism of the PRI coming from the U.S. press—which Mexicans, used to their own cozy press–government relationship, assume is stimulated by the U.S. government.
41. *Proceso* cites Jorge Alcocer, a PSUM deputy, as stating that the cover story in the international edition of *Newsweek* of March 17, 1986, was part of a well-orchestrated campaign organized by the U.S. State Department directed against the president of Mexico (March 24, 1986, p. 7).
42. I base these assertions on a number of factors, including many conversations with Mexicans in which these suspicions were expressed. Many articles cited earlier in this chapter urging the United States to allow Mexico freedom to maneuver in its foreign policy, especially in Central America, grow out of this same suspicion that Mexico is being punished for its positions.
43. Edward J. Williams, "The Evolution of the Mexican Military and Its Implications for Civil–Military Relations."
44. René Herrera and Mario Ojeda, *La política de México hacia Centroamérica (1979–1982)*, p. 100.
45. Octavio Paz, *The Labyrinth of Solitude: Life and Thought in Mexico*, p. 24.

Chapter 4

1. Robert S. Spich argues that free trade was the ideology and then seeks to make the case that this is inconsistent with real conditions in the world ("Free Trade as Ideology, Fair Trade as Goal: Problems of an Ideological Approach to U.S. Trade Policy"). Spich may be correct that official rhetoric harped on free markets, but it was clear to all engaged in policy-making that completely free trade was not policy.
2. Raymond Vernon, "International Trade Policy in the 1980s: Prospects and Problems."
3. During the AFL-CIO meeting in Miami Beach in October 1987, Jackie Presser, president of the International Brotherhood of Teamsters, appeared on television repeating over and over, "fair trade, not free trade."
4. Helen Hughes has argued that the combination of dependency ideology and structural economic views of the time left a legacy of economic distortion and political chaos (*Policy Lessons of the Development Experience*).
5. Jorge G. Castañeda notes that the current buzzword for political and economic policy in Mexico is "modernization" ("Mexico's Coming Challenges"). This encompasses the kind of structural change inherent in trade liberalization.
6. There is another role reversal in this tension. Mexican intellectuals tend to view the United States as pragmatic, a word that when used by them has overtones of unprincipled. They see Mexico as more ideologically dedicated to legal principles. In the case of a special relationship, the ideology was mostly on the U.S. side and the quest for pragmatism in its favor on the Mexican side.

7. The word "discrimination" was used loosely in the U.S. government citation in the opening quotation. Discrimination refers to differential treatment of foreign nations, not to measures to protect the domestic market.

8. An excellent study of Mexican development policy in the postwar period until the 1970s is Roger D. Hansen, *The Politics of Mexican Development*.

9. U.S. Department of Commerce, International Trade Administration, *United States Trade: Performance in 1985 and Outlook*, p. 137.

10. Trade figures would not be the same if Mexican data were used. It would not be proper to compare the two sets of data, not only because the timing of recording data would throw off the numbers, but also because the methodologies and definitions differ. For example, for tariff items 806.30 and 807.00 (discussed below), U.S. data show as imports the gross value of these products, including that portion originally exported from the United States. Mexican data do not show these items in the merchandise trade account, but elsewhere in the current account.

11. An analysis of changes in U.S. imports from Mexico shows that the ten products whose shares of total manufactured imports increased most between 1981 and 1985 were nonair piston engines (from 2.1 to 10.6 percent); radio broadcast receivers (0.3 to 5.3); trucks (0 to 2.6); insulated wire and cable (5.1 to 7.3); hydrocarbons, that is, oil products (0 to 1.8); passenger vehicles (0 to 1.3); office machines (2.2 to 3.4); television receivers (0 to 1.0); various other motor-vehicle parts (4.3 to 5.3); and cement (0.1 to 1.0). The percentages were calculated from four-digit U.S. SITC data. The leading U.S. agricultural imports from Mexico were live cattle and fresh vegetables, especially tomatoes; and the leading U.S. agricultural exports to Mexico were oilseeds and corn.

12. Internal tables from the Office of the U.S. Trade Representative (USTR). The method for calculating the utilization rate in 1988 exaggerates the increase over previous years.

13. The utilization percentages for the other four countries shipping most products to the United States under GSP were, in 1985: Taiwan, 90; South Korea, 82; Brazil, 91; and Hong Kong, 72.

14. Imports into the United States under GSP in 1987 from the five leading providers were, in billions of dollars: Taiwan, 3.4; South Korea, 2.8; Mexico, 2.2; Hong Kong, 1.9; and Singapore, 1.8.

15. USITC, *The Impact of Increased United States–Mexico Trade on Southwest Border Development*, p. 57. It would be incorrect to assume that all of this benefit went to Mexican exporters, since there was undoubtedly a sharing between importers and exporters of the unpaid duty.

16. Gustavo del Castillo V., *U.S.–Mexican Trade Relations: From the Generalized System of Preferences to a Formal Bilateral Agreement*, p. 18. He provides no documentation to support this assertion.

17. Isabel Molina, "La renovación del sistema generalizado de preferencias arancelarias y sus implicaciones para México."

18. Organization of American States, *The United States Generalized System of Preferences: Caribbean Basin Initiative*, p. 66; U.S. Trade Representative, press release on GSP review, January 2, 1987.

19. The beer exclusion was based on representations by a U.S. producer unable to gain entry for its beer in Mexico. This has not really impeded U.S. imports of Mexican beer, which were $175 million in 1988.

20. The dollar-value limit increases each year with the increase in U.S. GNP. In 1984, the last year under the original legislation, it was $63.8 million. The limit was $76.1 million in 1987.

21. In preparing the paragraphs that follow on 806.30/807.00, I drew extensively on the USITC, *Impact of Increased United States–Mexico Trade on Southwest Border Development*.

22. This issue was the subject of an article in the *New York Times*, December 29, 1986, p. 1.

23. USITC, *The Use and Economic Impact of TSUS Items 806.30 and 807.00*.

24. This is contained in the most recent bilateral agreement, signed in January 1988 to run until the end of 1991.

25. USITC, *Impact of Increased United States–Mexico Trade on Southwest Border Development*, p. 91. According to this source, U.S. textile and apparel imports from Mexico in 1985 came to $413 million, of which $275 million were covered by the MFA. United States imports from Mexico under the MFA rose by 69 percent in value between 1976 and 1985 and 40 percent in quantity, to 224 million square-yard equivalents. Both these growth rates were substantially lower than for U.S. MFA-controlled imports as a whole.

26. Ibid., pp. 94, 100. I have been told by Mexican textile producers that they welcome the MFA for this very reason.
27. Ibid., p. 101.
28. Office of the United States Trade Representative, press release, December 30, 1987.
29. An analysis was made of the twenty four-digit SITC commodities whose market share from Mexico increased most in the United States from 1983 to 1984; it showed SITC item 6783, iron and steel tubes and pipes, in seventeenth place. United States imports of this item from Mexico rose from $55 to $92 million, an increase of 68 percent and increasing its share of U.S. imports from 0.33 to 0.52 percent.
30. I first became aware of this phrase from the writings of a Canadian trade expert, Rodney de C. Grey. See, for example, "A Note on U.S. Trade Practices."
31. In preparing this paragraph, I have drawn on Stephen L. Lande and Craig VanGrasstek, *The Trade and Tariff Act of 1984: Trade Policy in the Reagan Administration.*
32. This paragraph draws on USITC, *Impact of Increased United States–Mexico Trade on Southwest Border Development*, pp. 106–107.
33. In addition to the discussion in the foregoing citation, further details on this case can be found in Sidney Weintraub, *Free Trade between Mexico and the United States?*, pp. 48–53, and Maury Bredahl, Jimmye Hillman, Robert Rothenberg, and Nicolas Gutierrez, *Technical Change, Protectionism, and Market Structure: The Case of International Trade in Fresh Winter Vegetables*, pp. 20–48. David R. Mares discusses the interlocking Mexican and U.S. interests in the production of winter vegetables in Mexico, largely in the state of Sinaloa, and its marketing in the United States ("Agricultural Trade: Domestic Interests and Transnational Relations").
34. Sidney Weintraub, "Mexican Subsidies and U.S. Law: Potential Collision Course."
35. Allan E. Gotlieb, "The Canada–United States Relationship," pp. 30–31.
36. The superfund tax was antiforeign. It was 8.2 cents a barrel for domestic petroleum and 11.7 cents a barrel for imported petroleum. A GATT panel acting on a complaint from Mexico, Canada, and the European Community found the U.S. action inconsistent with Article II:2 of the GATT, and the United States agreed to rescind the disparate treatment (GATT *Focus*, July–August 1987, p. 1).
37. One example is USTR, *Annual Report on National Trade Estimates, 1985*: "Even before Mexico's economic crisis, the U.S. government repeatedly emphasized the importance of liberalizing Mexico's trade regime" (p. 151).
38. The basis for these calculations is given in Figure 4.1.
39. The protocol of accession was published in *Comercio Exterior* 36, no. 10 (October 1986): 876–877.
40. In joining the GATT, Mexico declared that it would unilaterally establish a maximum tariff of 50 percent *ad valorem* and then lower most tariffs that were between 20 and 50 percent over a period of thirty months. The tariff escalation was scheduled to be as follows at the end of the thirty-month period: zero to 10 percent for raw materials and articles of popular consumption not produced in Mexico or produced in insufficient quantity; 20 to 30 percent for other articles, depending on their degree of processing; and 50 percent for articles intended to be excluded from importation. In fact, tariffs were reduced even more at the end of 1987, to a ceiling of 20 percent for most items. The bound rates (that is, those for which there is a contractual obligation in the GATT) would start at the 50 percent level, and lower bindings will be on a product-by-product basis in the context of multilateral tariff negotiations. In early 1989, Mexico raised many duties from zero to 10 percent as part of a program to unify rates, which are now largely between 10 and 20 percent.
41. Discussion of the differences between different forms of trade regimes can be found in Anne O. Krueger, *Foreign Trade Regimes and Economic Development: Liberalization Attempts and Consequences*, and Anne O. Krueger and Constantine Michalopoulos, "Developing-Country Trade Policies and the International Economic System."
42. Saúl Trejo Reyes and Gustavo Vega Cánovas stress the point that GATT membership will require Mexico to completely reformulate its industrial and commercial policies ("El ingreso al GATT y sus implicaciones para el futuro de México").
43. Tomás Peñaloza Webb, "La adhesión de México al GATT."
44. Ricardo Peña Alfaro, "Ventajas y desventajas del ingreso de México al GATT," p. 35.
45. Weintraub, *Free Trade between Mexico and the United States?*, pp. 84–91.

46. The subsidies and countervailing duties agreement with the United States, which is pure bilateralism, was concluded in April 1985. Daniel C. Levy and Gabriel Székely point out that Mexico's foreign office (Secretaría de Relaciones Exteriores) had opposed this agreement (''Mexico, Challenges and Responses''). SRE has the reputation of being opposed to bilateralism with the United States.

47. Gustavo Vega Cánovas argues that the bilateral approach is prejudicial to Mexico (''El entendimiento sobre subsidios e impuestos compensatorios entre México y los Estados Unidos: implicaciones económicas y políticas,'' p. 152).

48. See discussion in Chapter 1.

49. For a discussion of the Cambridge recommendations, see Robert E. Looney, *Economic Policymaking in Mexico: Factors Underlying the 1982 Crisis*, pp. 173–178.

50. Instituto Mexicano de Comercio Exterior (IMCE), *La protección efectiva en México, 1979–1983*. The study examines nominal protection (the percentage difference in internal and external prices of products), effective protection (the percentage difference in value added at internal and external prices, which requires examining the pricing of inputs to final products), and effective subsidies. IMCE has since been abolished as a separate organization.

51. Ibid., p. 22 n. 3.

52. A domestic resource cost (DRC) ratio seeks to measure the economic cost, using shadow prices, of the domestic factors needed to produce a unit of value added at international prices. Ratios below 0.9 indicate a product as internationally competitive, between 0.9 and 1.1 as of uncertain competitiveness, and more than 1.1 as uncompetitive. World Bank analysis for 1980 showed roughly half of Mexico's industrial sector as being noncompetitive or of uncertain competitiveness.

53. A second loan, for $250 million, was approved in January 1987, and a third was under negotiation in early 1989.

54. Agreements were concluded between the two countries under the umbrella of the framework accord on trade in steel, textiles, and beer, wine, and distilled spirits.

Chapter 5

1. United Nations, *The Economic Development of Latin America and Its Principal Problems*.

2. Banco de México, *Indicadores económicos*.

3. A thorough study of Mexico's industrial policy since World War II is Saúl Trejo Reyes, *El futuro de la política industrial en México*.

4. Similar legislation has been introduced in recent years in the U.S. Congress for the automobile industry, but never enacted.

5. Nacional Financiera and Organización de las Naciones Unidas para el Desarrollo Industrial (UNIDO), *México: los bienes de capital en la situación económica presente*.

6. Poder Ejecutivo Federal, *Programa nacional de fomento industrial y comercio exterior 1984–1988* (Pronafice), pp. 20, 143, 147. See also René Villarreal Arrambide, ''The New Industrialization Strategy in Mexico for the Eighties,'' p. 58.

7. Rafael Izquierdo expressed the consensus judgment well: ''Protectionism, in spite of its shortcomings, has unquestionably been beneficial, even indispensable'' (''Protectionism in Mexico,'' p. 289).

8. Gerardo Dávila Jiménez, ''La política de precios y subsidios,'' p. 236. The World Bank calculated a slightly higher proportion (13.7 percent) in 1981.

9. Ruth Rama and Robert Bruce Wallace, using a technique of measuring actual value added by sector and comparing this with what value added would have been in each sector using world prices, found significant transfers from agriculture and mining in favor of industry (''La política proteccionista mexicana: un análisis para 1960–1970''). Their conclusion from the years they measured, 1960 to 1970, was that the primary sector of the Mexican economy (agriculture and mining) was forced to pay a disproportionately high cost of the industrialization policy. Clark W. Reynolds has pointed out that much of the foreign-exchange cost of the early stages of industrial development came from agricultural exports (*The Mexican Economy: Twentieth Century Structure and Growth*). This be-

came increasingly difficult and then impossible to continue in the 1980s as the accumulated travails of the sector led to increasing agricultural imports.

10. The figures in this paragraph are from the World Bank, *Mexico: Future Directions of Industrial Strategy*, pp. 11–19.

11. Poder Ejecutivo Federal, *Plan global de desarrollo 1980–1982*, vol. I, p. 154.

12. Steven E. Sanderson, *The Transformation of Mexican Agriculture: International Structure and the Politics of Rural Change*, pp. 241–249.

13. The percentages are based on data from the Banco de México. Shipments neither to nor from in-bond plants, the *maquiladora*, are included in foreign-trade statistics. They are captured in the balance of payments under frontier transactions.

14. Pronafice, p. 88.

15. The plan went through many modifications as different groups were consulted. The team in the Ministry of Commerce and Industrial Development (Secofi) that put the plan together was later disbanded.

16. Douglas C. Bennett and Kenneth E. Sharpe reproduce a diplomatic note of February 1, 1978, from the U.S. government to Mexico (*Transnational Corporations versus the State: The Political Economy of the Mexican Auto Industry*, pp. 277–278). On the U.S. industry position, see "Statement of the Motor Vehicle Manufacturers Association of the United States" to the U.S. International Trade Commission. The statement concludes that "Mexican automotive performance requirements have not been harmful to U.S. industry or foreign investment abroad."

17. USITC, *Foreign Industrial Targeting and Its Effects on U.S. Industries*, p. ix.

18. This discussion does not include the *maquiladora*, which are dealt with in Chapter 8. The *maquiladora* have a distinct legislative and regulatory framework.

19. The legislative and administrative apparatus is contained in "Foreign Investment Climate in Mexico," a report of the U.S. embassy in Mexico City, June 1985. This report is normally updated annually.

20. Kurt Unger, "El comercio exterior de manufacturas modernas en México: el papel de las empresas extranjeras," p. 443.

21. *Economist*, February 8, 1985, p. 62.

22. A few can be cited here. In Spanish: Fernando Fajnzylber and Trinidad Martínez Tarrago, *Las empresas transnacionales*; Bernardo Sepúlveda Amor and Antonio Chumacero, *La inversión extranjera en México*; Bernardo Sepúlveda Amor, Olga Pellicer de Brody, and Lorenzo Meyer, *Las empresas transnacionales en México*; Miguel S. Wionczek, *El nacionalismo mexicano y la inversión extranjera*. In English: John M. Connor, "A Quantitative Analysis of the Market Power of United States Multinational Corporations in Brazil and Mexico"; John M. Connor and Willard F. Mueller, *Market Power and Profitability of Multinational Corporations in Brazil and Mexico*; Richard S. Newfarmer and Willard F. Mueller, *Multinational Corporations in Brazil and Mexico: Structural Sources of Economic and Noneconomic Power*; Richard S. Weinert, "The State and Foreign Capital." Three U.S. industry studies in the dependency-school tradition are Bennett and Sharpe, *Transnational Corporations versus the State*; Gary Gereffi, *The Pharmaceutical Industry and Dependency in the Third World*; and Sanderson, *Transformation of Mexican Agriculture*.

23. Quoted in "Mexican Pharmaceutical Industry Being Forced to Swallow a Bitter Pill," *Business Mexico*, August 1986, p. 50.

24. Unger, "El comercio exterior de manufacturas modernas en México." Issues of monopolistic competition and industrial technology are dealt with at greater length in Kurt Unger, *Competencia monopólica y tecnología en la industria mexicana*.

25. Tomás Peñaloza, "El comercio de manufacturas entre México y los Estados Unidos." Dale Story also provides the trade balance of foreign enterprises in Mexico and compares it with Mexico's overall trade balance (*Industry, the State, and Public Policy in Mexico*, p. 65).

26. USITC, *Background Study of the Economies and International Trade Patterns of the Countries of North America, Central America, and the Caribbean*, p. 163.

27. Robert O. Keohane, *After Hegemony: Cooperation and Discord in the World Political Economy*, p. 55.

28. The incident that stands out is known as the Bucareli agreements (from the name of the street in which representatives met in 1923), which in essence was a trade of U.S. diplomatic recognition of

the government of President Alvaro Obregón in return for protection of the property rights of the oil companies.

29. Inegi gives the fiscal "sacrifice" for the automotive industry during the 1970s at between 35 and 45 percent of all fiscal subsidies (*La industria automotriz en México*, p. 17).

30. Bennett and Sharpe, *Transnational Corporations versus the State*; Mark Bennett, *Public Policy and Industrial Development: The Case of the Mexican Auto Parts Industry*; Rhys Owen Jenkins, *Dependent Industrialization in Latin America: The Automotive Industry in Argentina, Chile and Mexico*; James P. Womack, "Prospects for the U.S.–Mexican Relationship in the Motor Vehicle Sector."

31. *El Mercado de Valores*, April 8, 1985, p. 330. There was a 50 percent increase in the physical volume of production in 1985 and a sharp decline of some 20 percent in 1986.

32. Womack, "Prospects for the U.S.–Mexican Relationship in the Motor Vehicle Sector," p. 113.

33. Bennett and Sharpe show the dominant position of Transmisiones y Equipos Mecánicos (Tremac), affiliated with Clark Equipment, which had more than 40 percent of all parts exports in 1975 (*Transnational Corporations versus the State*, p. 177).

34. Bennett, *Public Policy and Industrial Development*, pp. 31–39.

35. These were among the conclusions of a conference of international automotive experts held in Cuernavaca in July 1986 and reported in an article by Adolfo Gilly in *Proceso*, August 11, 1986, pp. 33–35.

36. Neil D. Schuster, "The U.S. Motor Vehicle Industry: Emerging Trends and Impacts on Mexico."

37. This investment material comes from "The Mexican Automobile Industry: Gearing Up to Export," *Business Mexico*, February 1985, pp. 50–75, and *El Mercado de Valores*, April 15, 1988, pp. 32–34.

38. Renault, which also operated earlier, withdrew from the Mexican market in 1986 after persistent losses. AMC (now Chrysler) jeeps are still produced, as are engines for export.

39. Alan Altshuler, Daniel Roos et al., *The Future of the Automobile*, pp. 12, 34.

40. Ibid., p. 189.

41. The implications for the U.S. industrial base of the movement of engine production to Mexico are examined in Harley Shaiken and Stephen Herzenberg, *Automation and Global Production: Automobile Engine Production in Mexico, the United States, and Canada*.

42. This is evident from the extensive advertising abroad that Mexico has undertaken in its effort to encourage foreign investment. One example of this is a full-page advertisement, "Myths and Facts About Foreign Investment in Mexico," placed in the *New York Times*, by the Dirección General de Difusión y Estudios Sobre Inversión Extranjera (August 29, 1986, p. 35 [Southwest edition]).

43. The data in this paragraph are from Wallace y Asociados, "Profile of Mini and Micro Computer Systems Market, Mexico," as reported in "Mexico's Dynamic Computer Industry," *Business Mexico*, November 1985, p. 74.

44. Ibid., pp. 62–66, 74. Data for 1988 are from the U.S. Department of Commerce.

45. The advertisement cited in note 42 publicizes this flexibility by calling attention to the 100 percent foreign ownership of IBM's investment as well as those of Ford for its plant in Hermosillo, Nissan in Aguascalientes, Xerox, and others.

46. What follows comes from the press and interviews with persons involved in the negotiations. Valuable information is also found in Julia Christine Vindasius, "Mexico and IBM: A New Look at State-TNC Negotiation and Bargaining Power" (M.A. thesis, Massachusetts Institute of Technology, 1986).

47. The U.S. Department of Commerce reported that in 1988, computer exports exceeded imports by more than $100 million ($276 million exports, $158 million imports). Computer imports were limited by being subject to import licensing while most other products were freed from this requirement.

48. "Mexican Pharmaceutical Industry Being Forced to Swallow a Bitter Pill," p. 68; U.S. Department of Commerce.

49. United Nations, Center on Transnational Corporations, *Transnational Corporations in the Pharmaceutical Industry of Developing Countries*, p. 111.

50. One exception is the steroid hormone industry. See Gary Gereffi, "Drug Firms and Dependency in Mexico: The Case of the Steroid Hormone Industry."

51. "Mexican Pharmaceutical Industry Being Forced to Swallow a Bitter Pill" makes much of the lack of innovation in Mexico. Joan Brodovsky argues that technological advance in Mexico's pharmaceutical industry is impeded by price controls and a legal-regulatory framework that discourages foreign licensing ("The Mexican Pharmochemical and Pharmaceutical Industries," pp. 197–198).
52. This is discussed in Chapter 4.
53. According to the U.S. Census Bureau, the U.S. surplus in 1986 was $39 million. The trade data include medicinal chemicals and botanicals, pharmaceutical preparations, and biologicals.
54. The preamble to the decree made a point of noting that 75 majority-owned foreign companies controlled 72 percent of the Mexican market, and 242 companies with majority Mexican ownership, only 28 percent (*Diario Oficial*, February 23, 1984, pp. 11–20).

Chapter 6

1. David Ronfeldt, Richard Nehring, and Arturo Gandara, *Mexico's Petroleum and U.S. Policy: Implications for the 1980s*, p. vii.
2. A thorough history of the expropriation can be found in Lorenzo Meyer, *Mexico and the United States in the Oil Controversy, 1917–1942*.
3. Miguel S. Wionczek, "Some Reflections on Mexican Energy Policy in Historical Perspective," p. 146.
4. Michele Snoeck, *El comercio exterior de hidrocarburos y derivados en México, 1970–1985*, p. 36.
5. The DOE study cited in this and subsequent paragraphs is by William D. Dietzman, Charles J. Jirik, William E. Lyle, Jr., Naim R. Rafidi, and Thomas A. Ross, *The Petroleum Resources of Mexico*.
6. Petróleos Mexicanos (Pemex), *Anuario estadístico 1987*, p. 3. Pemex notes the decline in new exploration in 1988 because of budgetary restrictions (*Memoria de labores 1988*, p. 2).
7. The U.S. EIA explains the differences between its estimate and that generally shown in the published literature as stemming from four causes: (1) the inclusion of condensate reserves with crude oil in the published literature; (2) an estimate of proved reserves of the Chicontepec paleocanal area of 10.9 billion barrels in the literature versus 2.5 billion barrels in the EIA estimate; (3) a difference in what is considered proved in some structures in the Bay of Campeche; and (4) the absence of precise data for the Huimanguillo fields in southern Mexico, which prompted the EIA to omit a quantification of reserves.
8. The material in this paragraph comes from Dietzman et al., *Petroleum Resources of Mexico*.
9. Pemex, *Memoria de labores 1986*, p. 57. Pemex refers to the region in its annual report as the southeast zone, the maritime zone, and Chicontepec.
10. Snoeck, *El comercio exterior de hidrocarburos y derivados en México*, p. 44.
11. Ibid., p. 56.
12. Oil prices rose during the second half of 1986. Pemex points out that the average price in July was only $8.61 a barrel compared with an average price in December of $13.67 a barrel (*Memoria de labores 1986*, p. 13).
13. Jaime Mario Willars A., *El petróleo en México: efectos macroeconómicos, elementos de política y perspectivas*, p. 65.
14. Cited in Snoeck, *El comercio exterior de hidrocarburos y derivados en México*, p. 84. This point is also made in Ronfeldt, Nehring, and Gandara, *Mexico's Petroleum and U.S. Policy*, p. xii.
15. The 20 percent limit was exceeded for the beneficiary countries under the San José agreement (discussed below) and for Israel.
16. Dietzman et al. concluded that Mexico could produce oil until the year 2085 at a constant rate of 2.5 million barrels a day, until 2053 at 3.5 MMB/d, and until 2036 at 4.5 MMB/d, based on an estimate of 115 billion barrels of recoverable oil (*Petroleum Resources of Mexico*). These estimates of the durability of oil supplies at different levels of extraction take on added meaning because there have been no significant new oil finds since the projections were made.
17. Jaime Corredor states explicitly that the "strong growth of foreign indebtedness . . . is considered to be more advantageous than increasing volumes of hydrocarbon exports" ("The Economic Significance of Mexican Petroleum from the Perspective of Mexican–United States Relations," p. 161).

18. Gabriel Székely points out that investment opportunities not even dreamed of a few months before López Portillo became president were pursued (*La economía política del petróleo en México, 1976–1982*, p. 145).

19. Poder Ejecutivo Federal, *Plan global de desarrollo 1980–1982*; Secretaría de Patrimonio y Fomento Industrial, *Plan nacional de desarrollo industrial, 1979–1982*.

20. It was this subsidization of energy prices that led to clamor by U.S. competitors for countervailing duties when products incorporating this energy, such as cement and petrochemicals, especially fertilizer, were shipped to the United States. These so-called upstream or natural-resource subsidies were a major legislative issue between 1983 and 1985, but have since become less pressing as Mexico has reduced or eliminated energy subsidies.

21. Willars, *El petróleo en México*, pp. 54–57.

22. Ibid., p. 33.

23. Poder Ejecutivo Federal, *Programa nacional de energéticos 1984–1988*, p. 102.

24. Ibid., p. 45.

25. Snoeck, *El comercio exterior de hidrocarburos y derivados en México*, pp. 47–48; George W. Grayson, *The Politics of Mexican Oil*, pp. 144–148. Mexico, to use a pejorative economic term, was essentially a "free rider" of the OPEC activities. One of the arguments made by the Colegio Nacional de Economistas when it opposed Mexico's entry into the GATT in 1979 was that Mexico could obtain the benefits of most-favored-nation treatment without joining GATT, just as it enjoyed higher oil prices without joining OPEC (Sidney Weintraub, *Free Trade between Mexico and the United States?*, p. 85).

26. Pemex, *Information Bulletin*, January 1987, p. 1. Mexico joined with other non-OPEC producers in April 1988 in offering to cut production if OPEC producers did the same.

27. Most of Mexico's crude-oil exports are referred to as either Maya or Isthmus. Isthmus is a lighter crude (32 degrees API), generally more in demand by purchasers. Maya is heavier (23 degrees API), with a high content of sulfur and metals, and is less in demand because of the greater technical difficulties in handling at the refineries. The mix of crude exports in 1988 was 35.7 percent Isthmus and 58.8 percent Maya, and 5.5 percent Olmeca (39.5 degrees API and a low sulfur content). The average price in 1986 was $12.24 per barrel, derived from a price of $13.85 for Isthmus, $11.08 for Maya, and $14.22 for Olmeca.

28. Calculated from data in Pemex, *Anuario estadístico 1987*, p. 68.

29. I have drawn for background in this section on USITC, *Study of the Petrochemical Industries in the Countries of the Northern Portion of the Western Hemisphere*. This study points out that olefins are produced in olefin plants and as by-products in oil refineries (vol. 1, p. 15). Feedstocks derived from natural gas are called natural gas liquids and include ethane and propane. Feedstocks derived from crude petroleum include naptha and gas oil. Aromatics are produced in refineries and as by-products in olefin plants that use heavy liquid feedstocks (vol. 1, p. 18).

30. Pemex, *Memoria de labores 1988*, pp. 128–140.

31. *El Mercado de Valores*, April 13, 1987, p. 387.

32. Pemex, *Memoria de labores 1988*, pp. 153, 155.

33. Figures are from Pemex, *Memoria de labores* for 1982 and 1988. Other data in this section, unless otherwise specified, come from *Memoria de labores* or Pemex, *Anuario estadístico* for 1985 and 1987.

34. Adrián Lajous-Vargas, "Natural Gas in Mexico," p. 61.

35. George W. Grayson, *The United States and Mexico: Patterns of Influence*, p. 75. This source, as well as George W. Grayson, "Mexico and the United States: The Natural Gas Controversy," were drawn on for background of the natural-gas controversy. Other sources used were Richard R. Fagen and Henry R. Nau, "Mexican Gas: The Northern Connection"; Jesús Puente Leyva, "The Natural Gas Controversy"; and Snoeck, *El comercio exterior de hidrocarburos y derivados en México*, pp. 96–100.

36. Puente Leyva refers to the half-truths of Heberto Castillo, one of the most vocal proponents of such a scheme, for ignoring the enormous costs and environmental dangers of liquefying and transporting natural gas ("Natural Gas Controversy," p. 159).

37. Not only was Senator Stevenson opposed by legislators from gas-producing states, but I know from

private conversations that he was warned by U.S. State Department officials that he was venturing into a hornet's nest of Mexican nationalism that he did not understand. He did not heed the advice.

38. Grayson, *Politics of Mexican Oil*, p. 202.

39. The director general of Pemex notified Border Gas, the importer for the U.S. pipeline systems, by letter on October 19, 1984, that Pemex was temporarily suspending gas exports, as permitted under the contract.

40. Ronfeldt, Nehring, and Gandara state that the incident demonstrated that each side lacked correct information about how the other side's government worked (*Mexico's Petroleum and U.S. Policy*, p. 61n).

41. At least I have not found any.

42. The substantial Mexican sales of oil to the U.S. strategic petroleum reserve have been criticized for precisely these reasons.

43. Lajous-Vargas, who is an official of Pemex, included an interesting note in "Natural Gas in Mexico": "The history of these negotiations has been documented mostly by U.S. authors, and the treatment given to the interaction between domestic and export markets has been inadequate and frequently in error" (p. 63).

44. Mario Ojeda, "El poder negociador de petróleo: el caso de México," pp. 63–64.

45. Mexico and Venezuela agreed, under an agreement signed in San José, Costa Rica, in August 1980 to provide oil on favorable credit terms to countries in Central America, plus Panama, and the Caribbean. For a discussion of the agreement, see Victoria Sordo-Arrioja, "The Mexico–Venezuela Oil Agreement of San José: A Step Toward Latin American Cooperation."

46. Rogelio Ruíz summarizes the experiences with Laguna Verde ("Experiences of the First Mexican Nuclear Plant at Laguna Verde"). An article in the *New York Times* describes the organized opposition to putting Laguna Verde on line (May 2, 1987, p. 4 [Southwest edition]). In October 1987, some forty prominent Mexican intellectuals and technicians charged that unnecessary risks were being run in entering into this dangerous venture and asked that the Laguna Verde project be halted (*Proceso*, October 19, 1987, pp. 22–24).

47. Székely, *La economía política del petróleo en México*, pp. 63–64.

48. *Washington Post*, February 11, 1979, p. L-1.

49. Articles on downstream diversification (refining and retail sales) by oil-producing countries can be found in the *New York Times*, February 25, 1988, p. D1; the *Economist*, March 26, 1988, pp. 59–60; and the *Wall Street Journal*, April 20, 1988, p. 1.

50. The *Economist* cites the danger that downstream competition among many oil-producing countries could lead to overcapacity and price squeezes (December 10, 1988, pp. 73–74).

51. The tax imposed was 11.7 cents per barrel on imported petroleum products compared with 8.2 cents on domestic production. The action was successfully challenged by several countries under Article III of the GATT, which prohibits applying higher excise taxes on imported than on domestic products.

52. For the arguments being used by Mexico against an oil-import fee, see *Pemex Information Bulletin*, March 1987, pp. 1–3. These are, in brief, that it would hurt the U.S. economy, stimulate protectionism, discriminate against heavier Mexican oil, and rupture U.S. security by endangering the reliability of crude from nearby sources.

Chapter 7

1. There was a substantial conflict within the PRI, epitomized in the person of Cuauhtémoc Cárdenas Solorzano, about the anti-democratic nature of the party. Cárdenas, the son of Lázaro Cárdenas and a former governor of the state of Michoacán, was part of the *corriente democrática*, a *cardenista* or *echeverrista* wing of the party. Cárdenas then became a candidate for president in 1988 under the banner of a group of small parties. As the *Economist* pointed out, the decision of the government to continue to meet its debt obligations was one element of the leftist opposition within the PRI (March 21, 1988, pp. 37–38). Cárdenas proposed a moratorium on interest payments until they were substantially reduced.

2. Guillermo Ortíz and Jaime Serra Puche, "La carga de la deuda externa de México," p. 173.

3. The term of commercial-bank credit is elusive as long as the principal of the debt is regularly

rescheduled. While commercial-bank loans normally carry a higher interest rate than those from the multilateral financial institutions, including the IMF, the latter are not on concessional terms for Mexico.

4. This has been called "disaster myopia" by Jack M. Guttentag and Richard J. Herring, *Disaster Myopia in International Banking*.

5. Poder Ejecutivo Federal, *Plan global de desarrollo 1980–1982*, makes explicit reference to surpassing historical norms (p. 48).

6. Leopoldo Solís and Ernesto Zedillo, "The Foreign Debt of Mexico," p. 273.

7. Mark Gersovitz, "Banks' International Lending Decisions: What We Know and Implications for Future Research," p. 62.

8. Solís and Zedillo, "Foreign Debt of Mexico," p. 275.

9. Roberto Gutiérrez R., "El endeudamiento externo del sector privado de México: expansión y renegociación," p. 338.

10. Gutiérrez lists these nine in order of the size of the debt at the end of 1983 as Alfa, Visa, Mexicana de Cobre, Vitro, Tubos de Acero de México, Cydsa, Celanese Mexicana, Cervecería Moctezuma, and Asesores de Finanzas (ibid., p. 339). Alfa alone had more than 10 percent of the total private-sector external debt.

11. Ibid. These were, in rank order of outstanding credit at the end of 1983, Citibank, Bank of America, Chase Manhattan, Manufacturers Hanover Trust, Morgan Guaranty Trust, and Continental Illinois. These six U.S. banks accounted for 26 percent of the credit outstanding to the Mexican private sector at that time.

12. Ibid., p. 340.

13. It is impossible to be precise about capital flight because of its clandestine nature. The most meticulous calculations of capital flight from Mexico make it clear that the amounts were substantial, indeed greater than for any other developing country over the past decade. Morgan Guaranty Trust Company estimated capital flight from Mexico at $36 billion between 1976 and 1982 plus $17 billion between 1983 and 1985, for a total of $53 billion for the ten years 1976 to 1985 (*World Financial Markets*, March 16, 1986). John T. Cuddington, using two definitions, came to figures between $32.7 billion and $36.3 billion from 1974 to 1982 (*Capital Flight: Estimates, Issues, and Explanations*). Two economists from the World Bank and the IMF estimated capital flight from Mexico between 1974 and 1982 at between $29.4 and $32.7 billion (Mohsin S. Khan and Nadeem Ul Haque, "Capital Flight from Developing Countries"). David Felix and Juana Sanchez found capital flight from Mexico from 1971 to 1985 to be $56 billion ("Capital Flight Aspect of the Latin American Debt Crisis").

14. *New York Times*, November 29, 1986, pp. 17, 19 (Southwest edition).

15. This statement is based on personal conversations with U.S. bankers on the border and with Mexican depositors. The U.S. border city is seen as an extension of Mexico, where business can be done in Spanish, and much safer than in Mexico itself, where dollar accounts are subject to seizure and forced conversion into pesos from which the wealth holders are fleeing in the first instance.

16. The quoted phrase comes from an article in the *Wall Street Journal* discussing havens for capital from developing countries (May 27, 1986, p. 2).

17. Without endorsing capital controls, Cuddington (*Capital Flight*, pp. 33–34) and Khan and Ul Haque ("Capital Flight from Developing Countries," p. 5) state that such controls can have short-term dampening effects on capital outflows, even though the controls attack symptoms and not causes.

18. According to the *Economist*, survey section on international banking, the exposure of large U.S. banks in the four major Latin American debtor countries—Mexico, Brazil, Argentina, and Venezuela—was the following as of September 30, 1986: Citicorp, 80 percent; BankAmerica, 95 percent; Manufacturers Hanover, 126 percent; Chase Manhattan, 101 percent; J. P. Morgan, 69 percent; and Chemical, 93 percent (March 21, 1987, p. 18). The percentages are outstanding debt to the four countries divided by the primary capital of the banks.

19. An excellent discussion of the elements that led to the Mexican debt crisis can be found in Ernesto Zedillo Ponce de León, "The Mexican External Debt: The Last Decade."

20. Robert R. Kaufman makes the point that, on balance, capitalists (owners of enterprises) are in a relatively good position to come out ahead in stabilization programs ("Democratic and Authoritarian Responses to the Debt Issue: Argentina, Brazil, Mexico," p. 194).

21. The story of this mission and the subsequent financial "rescue" is set forth in Joseph Kraft, *The Mexican Rescue*.

22. Morgan Guaranty Trust Company, *World Financial Markets*, February 1986, p. 1.

23. The word "fresh" comes from the citation in note 22.

24. *IMF Survey*, December 1, 1986, pp. 378–379.

25. It turned out to be 16.8 percent of GDP.

26. A rigorous examination of the effect on Mexico of the previous IMF program is Angel Calderon Madrid, "Un análisis de los programas de condicionalidad del Fondo Monetario Internacional a la luz de la experiencia de la economía mexicana durante 1983 y algunas consideraciones sobre la política de estabilización y industrialización en un contexto de escasez de divisas," 1985. The author argues for more flexibility to deal with unexpected developments, which in fact turned out to be IMF policy after this study was completed. The study was the winner of a prize for economic research in 1986 awarded by the Banco Nacional de México.

27. One of the harsher criticisms of the plan can be found in Peter Hakim, "The Baker Plan: Unfulfilled Promises." This article contains the sentence: "Yet, in the year since the plan was put forth, it is difficult to point to a single contribution that it has made toward alleviating debt or restoring growth" (p. 55). What such criticisms miss is that a philosophical shift from economic contraction to growth as the preferred path for dealing with countries in economic disequilibrium has a dynamic that can have useful effects over time.

28. *IMF Survey*, December 1, 1986, p. 378.

29. Ibid., p. 379.

30. The objection of Citicorp of the United States to the interest rate involved, thirteen-sixteenths of a percentage point above Libor (the London interbank offer rate), was well publicized (*Wall Street Journal*, February 4, 1987, p. 6). The reluctance of the Swiss Bank Corporation to participate was reported in the *Wall Street Journal*, August 13, 1986, p. 23.

31. I asked several executives of large U.S. banks how much pressure was put on them by U.S. government officials to make these new loans at the agreed interest rate, and the answers are typified by one of the responses: "Maximum feasible pressure."

32. The official Mexican statement on this agreement is in *El Mercado de Valores*, October 6, 1986, pp. 929–931. This source was used for much of the material that follows on the rescheduling.

33. For example, a Chilean rescheduling completed in February 1987 had a spread of 1 point over Libor compared with the 1.375 percent it was paying earlier.

34. *El Mercado de Valores*, November 3, 1986, pp. 1017–1027. This source was used in preparing this paragraph.

35. An article in the *Wall Street Journal* discusses this issue as a contest between the economic interest of commercial banks in avoiding such generous financing to troubled debtor countries and political interest of creditor governments in keeping the international financial structure functioning (March 3, 1987, pp. 1, 22). The United States also has an obvious interest in Mexico's political stability, which requires economic growth.

36. Discussions of the Paris Club can be found in Alexis Rieffel, *The Role of the Paris Club in Managing Debt Problems*, and K. Burke Dillon and Gumersindo Oliveros, *Recent Experience with Multilateral Official Debt Rescheduling*.

37. *El Mercado de Valores*, November 3, 1986, p. 1023.

38. Shortly after his inauguration, President Salinas stressed this point repeatedly in speeches and interviews. See, for example, the *Wall Street Journal*, December 5, 1988, p. A10.

39. Pedro-Pablo Kuczynski discusses actions taken to deal with Latin American debt (*Latin American Debt*).

40. According to the *Economist*, survey section on international banking, sales of Mexican debt in the secondary market took place at between 65 and 69 cents on the dollar in February 1986 and between 56 and 58 cents on the dollar in February 1987 (March 21, 1987, p. 23). The price in early 1989 was less than 50 cents on the dollar.

41. Discussions of the Citibank action and its emulation by other banks can be found in an article written by Martin Feldstein in the *Economist*, June 27, 1987, pp. 21–25, and in the *Wall Street Journal*, May 28, 1987, p. 6.

42. Peru has paid some debt in products, which is a form of countertrade.

43. *Between Bailout and Breakdown: A Modular Approach to Latin America's Debt Crisis.* William Guttman gives an inventory of ways to ease debt problems.

44. In essence, the position of U.S. economist William R. Cline is that Mexico can grow out of its problems (*Financial Times*, May 14, 1986, p. 17).

45. Peter Whitlock, "The Baker v. Bradley Debate," p. 3. Patricia Wertman summarizes the elements of the Bradley Plan and suggestions by other members of Congress ("The International Debt Problem: Congressional Proposals").

46. *Wall Street Journal*, July 2, 1987, p. 1.

47. Karin Lissakers discusses the decision by the Japanese banks in an op-ed article in the *New York Times*, March 24, 1987, p. 27 (Southwest edition).

48. Many of these proposals are outlined in the *Wall Street Journal*, March 12, 1987, p. 60.

49. The financing plan is described in the *IMF Survey*, January 11, 1988, pp. 7–8.

50. A Wall Street analysis of the scheme can be found in Kenneth L. Telljohann and Richard H. Buckholz, "The Mexican Bond Exchange Offer." There was extensive press description and commentary on the proposal because of its novel nature. Newspaper accounts of the results of the plan include those in the *Wall Street Journal*, March 4, 1988, p. 3, and the *New York Times*, March 5, 1988, p. 15 (Southwest edition).

51. The quotation marks reflect Brady's words from the press release of his statement.

52. Norman A. Bailey and Richard Cohen, *The Mexican Time Bomb*, pp. 49–51.

53. ECLAC, "Latin American and Caribbean Development: Obstacles, Requirements, and Options," pp. 102–110. The ECLAC secretariat said that other approaches were also possible, including forgiving the principal, reducing interest payments to below market prices, paying interest in the debtor's currency, and coupling any of these with increased disbursements to debtor countries by multilateral institutions.

54. Mexico's National Commission for Foreign Investment issued a manual in 1986 for carrying out debt-equity swaps, "Manual operativo para la capitalización de pasivos y sustitución de deuda pública por inversión."

55. The Chilean experience is summarized in the *Economist*, March 7, 1987, pp. 87–88, 90; the estimate for Mexico comes from a story in the *Wall Street Journal* that cites the Treasury Secretary (March 27, 1987, p. 12). What swaps do is give a preferential exchange rate to investors. They are hardly a panacea for resolving Mexico's debt problem.

56. *Novedades*, June 1, 1986, p. A4.

57. Saúl Trejo Reyes, "El contexto económico internacional de la deuda: implicaciones para México."

58. Saúl Trejo Reyes, "Deuda externa. Una alternativa de solución."

59. *Wall Street Journal*, November 26, 1986, p. 20.

60. The calculation is based on 5 percent annual growth compounded over six years; and a ratio between imports and GDP growth of 1 : 1.

61. I have used the ratio of 25,000 jobs for each $1 billion of U.S. exports.

62. The most ambitious of recent proposals is that by James D. Robinson III, chairman and chief executive officer of American Express Company, "A Comprehensive Agenda for LDC Debt and World Trade Growth." Another proposal is from Shafiqul Islam, "Breaking the International Debt Deadlock."

63. Whatever debt relief is granted to Mexico will become a precedent for comparable relief for other countries. The international financial institutions are well situated for dealing generally with this issue.

64. The Brazilian and Argentine shock treatments, after initial successes, eventually failed. The Israeli shock treatment has had more durable success and was used as a model for Mexico's PSE. Reviews of these and other cases of shock treatment are in José Luis Alberro and David Ibarra, eds., "Programas heterodoxos de estabilización."

65. Increases in the minimum wage were pegged to the projected inflation in the coming month of a basic market basket of goods. The risk of freezing the exchange rate was based on the premise that the peso was undervalued and that holding the rate steady as an anti-inflation measure would not unduly prejudice the incentive to export. However, during the first three months of 1988, the accumulated inflation was 31.5 percent and the controlled devaluation was only 2.7 percent. The exchange rate was completely frozen for most of 1988, despite an inflation of 52 percent. There

were complaints by exporters that they were being hurt and that the use of the exchange rate to combat inflation was excessively risky. It will take a year or more to evaluate the results of the shock treatment. The PSE, under a new name, was extended to March 31, 1990.

Chapter 8

1. Thomas Weaver presents the beginnings of a theoretical framework for looking at borders in "The Social Effects of the Ecology and Development of the United States–Mexico Border," but the essay focuses on the United States–Mexico border.
2. A discussion of this issue can be found in James T. Peach, "Income Distribution in the U.S.–Mexico Borderlands."
3. Joseph Nalven, "Social and Cultural Aspects of Transborder Environmental Cooperation," p. 115. The budget comparisons are for 1981, but the ratio remains similar. The differences are even greater than implied by the simple comparisons because the office in San Diego has only one purpose, while that in Tijuana is a multipurpose office.
4. Alicia Castellanos Guerrero and Gilberto López y Rivas depict this influence pejoratively, leading to the devaluation of national Mexican values ("La influencia norteamericana en la cultura de la frontera norte de México"). The fact that cultural influence runs more powerfully from the strong to the weak is thus seen as another illustration of dependency, from which Mexico must escape.
5. Víctor L. Urquidi and Mario M. Carrillo, "Desarrollo económico e interacción en la frontera norte de México," p. 1063.
6. Rogelio Díaz-Guerrero, "Mexicans and Americans: Two Worlds, One Border . . . and One Observer," p. 285.
7. Weaver, "Social Effects of the Ecology and Development of the United States–Mexico Border," p. 246.
8. A good example of this is Romeo R. Flores Caballero, *Evolución de la frontera norte*.
9. The populations when Mexico lost the territory are discussed in Niles Hansen, *The Role of Mexican Labor in the Economy of the Southwest United States*. In Texas, Anglos outnumbered Mexicans at the time of independence. The one area in which there apparently was a relatively large number of Hispanics, 60,000 in 1850, was what is now New Mexico. There were 7,500 Mexicans in what is now California and fewer than 2,000 in what is now Arizona.
10. Antonio González de León, "Factores de tensión internacional en la frontera," p. 24. Niles Hansen emphasizes the symbiotic relationship at the border in *The Border Economy: Regional Development in the Southwest*, p. 102. My own view, repeated throughout this book, is that the United States and Mexico do have a joint destiny, a conclusion whose force is greatest at the border.
11. Jesús Tamayo, "Borderlands, Border Policies, and National Policies."
12. Frida Espinoza and Jesús Tamayo, "El estado de la investigación nacional acerca de la frontera norte de México."
13. Frank Meissner makes the connection with the *bracero* program, "Mexican Border and Free Zone Areas: Implications for Development," p. 257), while Francisco Alba emphasizes Mexico's desire to stimulate border employment irrespective of the termination of the *bracero* program ("Mexico's Northern Border: A Framework of Reference," p. 26).
14. The evidence is examined in Mitchell A. Seligson and Edward J. Williams, *Maquiladoras and Migration: A Study of Workers in the Mexican–United States Border Industrialization Program*.
15. USITC, *The Impact of Increased United States–Mexico Trade on Southwest Border Development*, pp. 89–90.
16. Sergio Rivas F., "La industria maquiladora en México," pp. 1076–1077.
17. USITC, *Impact of Increased United States–Mexico Trade on Southwest Border Development*, summarizes the Mexican legal provisions regarding *maquila* plants (pp. 21–23). The basic policy document regulating the *maquiladora* is the "Decreto para el fomento y operación de la industria maquiladora de exportación," *Diario Oficial*, August 15, 1983.
18. See Chapter 4 for a description of tariff items 806.30/807.00.
19. United States agencies did publicize the advantages to U.S. business of the Mexican *maquiladora*. *Business America*, the publication of the U.S. Department of Commerce, carried at least two articles

by Roger Turner, who was on the Mexican desk, on the *maquiladora*: "Mexico's In-Bond Industry Continues Its Dynamic Growth" and "Mexico Turns to Its In-Bond Industry as a Means of Generating Exchange." Each article, in 1983 and 1984, carried a blurb that the Department of Commerce would provide further information on Mexico's in-bond industry, on request. Successful pressure to cancel Commerce Department financing of a conference on the in-bond industry in Mexico was touched on in a letter to the editor by Owen Bieber, president of the United Auto Workers, *Wall Street Journal*, January 15, 1987, p. 19.

20. This controversy is set forth in the letter by Owen Bieber cited in note 19; a letter by William H. Bywater, president of the International Union of Electronic Workers of the AFL-CIO, *New York Times*, January 26, 1987, p. 20 (Southwest edition); and an article in the *New York Times*, December 29, 1986, p. 1.

21. Joseph Grunwald and Kenneth Flamm, *The Global Factory: Foreign Assembly in International Trade*, p. 8.

22. María Patricia Fernández-Kelly makes strong anti-*maquiladora* arguments in *For We Are Sold: I and My People*.

23. Rivas, "La industria maquiladora en México," p. 1079. The period for which detailed data were available to Rivas to make this calculation ran through 1983. Subsequent analysis puts the share of Mexican inputs at about 2 percent overall, but higher in nonborder area *maquiladoras* such as in Guadalajara and Monterrey.

24. USITC, *Impact of Increased United States–Mexico Trade on Southwest Border Development*, p. 84.

25. The concept of backward linkages is from Albert O. Hirschman, *The Strategy of Economic Development*.

26. An article by Edward J. Wygard in a special advertising section of the *Wall Street Journal* refers to the *maquiladora* plants as "captives" (June 23, 1986, p. 13). The purpose of the section was to disseminate Mexico's welcome to foreign investment.

27. The growth of Japanese-owned *maquiladora* is discussed in the *New York Times*, May 26, 1987, p. 25 (Southwest edition). The growth in third-country *maquiladora* (Japanese, Korean, Taiwanese) is also discussed in U.S. Embassy Mexico City airgram 12356, "*Maquiladora* Developments— 1986," June 30, 1987.

28. This recommendation is in Rivas, "La industria maquiladora en México," and in José Luis Fernández and Jesús Tamayo, "Industry on the Northern Border of Mexico." Rivas suggests a local-content timetable similar to that which Mexico used for other industries, such as automobiles. Fernández and Tamayo suggest that greater Mexican content is best achieved through transformation of natural resources.

29. Data are from Instituto Nacional de Estadística, Geografía, e Informática (Inegi).

30. Guillermina Valdés-Villalva, "New Policies and Strategies of Multinational Corporations During the Mexican National Crisis 1982–1983," p. 162.

31. Jorge Carrillo, "Conflictos laborales en la industria maquiladora de exportación," p. 50.

32. Ibid., p. 51.

33. Fernández-Kelly found from data collected in 1978 and 1979 in Ciudad Juárez that the age varied by type of industry. In her sample, 84 percent were twenty-seven or younger for industry as a whole; 97 percent were twenty-seven or younger in electronics plants; but only 63 percent were twenty-seven or younger in apparel factories (*For We Are Sold*, p. 50).

34. Carrillo, "Conflictos laborales en la industria maquiladora de exportación"; María Patricia Fernández-Kelly, "Las maquiladoras y las mujeres."

35. G. William Lucker and Adolfo J. Alvarez, "Exploitation or Exaggeration: A Worker's-Eye View of 'Maquiladora' Work." The survey was taken in the fall of 1983. The authors acknowledge that a sample of workers from just two plants may not reflect the generality of *maquiladora* plants.

36. See, for example, Wolfgang König, "Efectos de la actividad maquiladora fronteriza en la sociedad mexicana," p. 103.

37. Susan B. Tiano, "Export Processing, Women's Work, and the Employment Problem in Developing Countries: The Case of the *Maquiladora* Program in Northern Mexico," p. 12. Fernández-Kelly also states that women join the work force because their wages are vital for the subsistence of their families (*For We Are Sold*, p. 54).

38. I have visited many *maquiladora* plants as well as many other small manufacturing operations in

Mexico. I have seen plants in which working conditions could have been improved, but, by the same token, I found the conditions in many *maquiladora* plants better than those in other Mexican factories. The work is repetitive, but the young women are mostly untrained for other jobs. Other than the evidence that *maquiladora* workers who leave one job seldom find other *maquiladora* work, I am not aware of studies that have followed the lives of these workers after leaving the original job.

39. Fernández-Kelly, *For We Are Sold*, p. 52.

40. The 400,000 employment figure does not take into account the spinoff employment effects in other Mexican activities. I have calculated these based on the structure of the Mexican economy at about 100,000. Gerald Godshaw et al. arrived at a similar figure for 1992 ("The Implications for the U.S. Economy of Tariff Schedule Item 807 and Mexico's Maquila Program"). The employment multiplier is low precisely because the *maquiladora* are not more integrated into Mexico's economy.

41. Rivas makes this argument ("La industria maquiladora en México," p. 1084).

42. U.S. Tariff Commission, *Economic Factors Affecting the Use of Item 807.00 and 806.30 of the Tariff Schedules of the U.S.*, and USITC, *The Use and Economic Impact of TSUS Items 806.30 and 807.00*. USITC is the successor agency of the Tariff Commission.

43. Richard J. Holden examined these effects on Brownsville, McAllen, Laredo, and El Paso ("Maquiladoras on the Texas/Mexico Border: An Econometric Evaluation of Employment and Retail Sales Effects on Four Texas SMSAs"). While the exact measures of elasticity of the *maquiladora* on employment and sales in the U.S. sister city may be questioned, the importance of the production on the Mexican side to the health of the urban area on the U.S. side is clear. The equations used were based on various aspects of *maquiladora* employment and wages and their effect on employment and sales in the sister city. The elasticities ranged from 0.2 to 0.4 for employment and 0.7 to 2.3 for sales; the equations explained between 86 and 96 percent of the variation in employment in the four Texas urban areas and 72 to 93 percent of a sales proxy value.

44. Americo Paredes, "The Problem of Identity in a Changing Culture: Popular Expressions of Culture Conflict Along the Lower Rio Grande Border." Paredes cites H. L. Mencken that the American language has a large stock of derogatory names directed chiefly at aliens (*The American Language*).

45. This was done in the aftermath of the murder in February 1985 of Enrique Camarena, an agent of the U.S. Drug Enforcement Administration (DEA).

46. Carlos Monsiváis, "The Culture of the Frontier: The Mexican Side," p. 65.

47. Ibid. What we are getting, of course, are some of Monsiváis's own biases.

48. Castellanos and López y Rivas, "La influencia norteamericana en la cultura de la frontera norte de México," p. 81.

49. Mario Cerutti, "Frontera, burguesía regional y desarrollo capitalista. El caso de Monterrey. Referencias sobre el período 1860–1910."

50. William A. Murray, "A Reporter at Large: Twins," p. 72.

51. USITC, *Impact of Increased United States–Mexico Trade on Southwest Border Development*.

52. Alejandra Salas-Porras, "*Maquiladoras* and the Sociopolitical Structure in the Northern States of Mexico: Chihuahua, Sonora, and Baja California."

53. Cited in C. Richard Bath, "U.S.–Mexico Experience in Managing Transboundary Air Resources: Problems, Prospects, and Recommendations for the Future," p. 430.

54. Alfonso Ortíz, "Comparative Study of Infant Mortality in the Texas–Mexico Border Area of Laredo/Nuevo Laredo," p. 3.

55. Albert E. Utton, "An Assessment of the Management of U.S.–Mexican Water Resources: Anticipating the Year 2000," pp. 368–369.

56. Ibid., pp. 369–370.

57. Stephen P. Mumme, "Engineering Diplomacy: The Evolving Role of the International Boundary and Water Commission in U.S.–Mexico Water Management," p. 73.

58. Stephen P. Mumme, "U.S.–Mexican Groundwater Problems: Bilateral Prospects and Implications."

59. Scott Whiteford, "Agriculture, Irrigation, and Salinity in the Mexicali Valley," p. 22.

60. Utton, "Assessment of the Management of U.S.–Mexican Water Resources," p. 373. A thorough discussion of water issues of the Rio Grande can be found in David J. Eaton and John M. Andersen, eds., *The State of the Rio Grande–Rio Bravo: A Study of Water Resources Issues Along the Texas–Mexico Border*.

61. John Conway argues that the optimum solution to the year 2000 and beyond would have been a joint

wastewater treatment plant on the U.S. side and a long ocean overfill ("Sewage and Public Health: The San Diego–Tijuana Region"). Political cooperation has not yet gone this far at the border, and instead a Mexican solution was adopted.

62. Robert Emmet Clark, "Overview of Groundwater Law and Institutions in United States Border States," p. 282. Discussions of groundwater laws in California, New Mexico, and Texas are in César Sepúlveda and Albert E. Utton, eds., *The U.S.–Mexico Border Region: Anticipating Resource Needs and Issues to the Year 2000*, pp. 289–336.

63. Utton, "Assessment of the Management of U.S.–Mexican Water Resources," p. 378.

64. *Economist*, October 4, 1986, pp. 35–38.

65. Ludwik A. Teclaff, "Principles for Transboundary Groundwater Pollution Control," p. 338.

66. This issue is discussed in Utton, "Assessment of the Management of U.S.–Mexican Water Resources," and in C. Richard Bath, "Environmental Issues in the United States–Mexico Borderlands." Both sources were used in preparing this paragraph.

67. Howard G. Applegate, "Transnational Air Pollution," p. 128.

68. The following discussion of management and hazardous and toxic substances draws on Bath, "Environmental Issues in the United States–Mexico Borderlands."

69. U.S. Congress, Office of Technology Assessment (OTA), *The Border War on Drugs*, p. 9. The data are for 1985. This source was used for other data given in this paragraph. The OTA study deals primarily with interdiction, or efforts to intercept or deter shipments of illegal drugs from foreign countries to the United States. The study draws on such data sources as the DEA and the National Narcotics Intelligence Consumers Committee.

70. U.S. Department of Justice, Drug Enforcement Administration (DEA), *Special Report: Worldwide Drug Assessment: Threat to the United States*, p. 2.

71. U.S. Congress, OTA, *Border War on Drugs*, p. 24.

72. *New York Times*, March 2, 1988, p. 1.

73. Ibid.

74. U.S. Department of State, Bureau of International Narcotics Matters (INM), "International Narcotics Control Strategy Report," 1987, p. 19.

75. U.S. Congress, House of Representatives, Committee on Foreign Affairs, *United States–Mexican Cooperation in Narcotics Control Efforts*, p. 16.

76. Peter Reuter, "Eternal Hope: America's International Narcotic Efforts." This source was used for other material in this paragraph.

77. This point is brought out in an article in the *Wall Street Journal*, November 25, 1986, p. 1. This was the third article in a series on drugs and corruption in Mexico, the first two of which appeared on November 19 and 20, 1986.

78. Data in this paragraph are from U.S. Department of State, INM, "International Narcotics Control Strategy Report," 1988, and from the Mexican embassy in Washington, D.C.

79. One or both of these cases are covered in the *Wall Street Journal* series cited in note 77; U.S. Congress, House of Representatives, Committee on Foreign Affairs, *United States–Mexican Cooperation in Narcotics Control Efforts*; and James Mills, *The Underground Empire: Where Crime and Governments Embrace*.

80. James Van Wert points out that before the arrest of Rafael Caro Quintero and Ernesto Rafael Fonseca Carrillo in connection with the Camarena murder, no important drug trafficker had been arrested in Mexico for seven years ("El control de los narcóticos en México. Una década de institucionalización y un asunto diplomático," pp. 98–99).

81. U.S. Congress, House of Representatives, Committee on Foreign Affairs, *United States–Mexican Cooperation in Narcotics Control Efforts*, p. 23. However, as of August 30, 1987, nobody had been tried in either case *New York Times*, August 30, 1987, p. 6 [Southwest edition]).

82. Samuel I. del Villar, "La narcotización de la cultura en Estados Unidos y su impacto en México," pp. 77, 87.

83. *New York Times*, April 15, 1988, p. 9 (Southwest edition). The struggle between the administration and the Congress over Mexican certification arose again in 1989.

84. The way Senator Pete Wilson of California put it was that Senate passage would "send a message to the government of Mexico" (*Austin American Statesman*, April 15, 1988, p. A5).

85. The *New York Times* story reporting the Senate vote was on p. 9. The response by Mexico's

presidential candidate Carlos Salinas de Gortari earned a banner headline on p. 1 of Mexico City's leading daily, *Excelsior*, on April 20.

86. Column in the *Wall Street Journal*, May 6, 1988, p. 15.
87. Rensselaer W. Lee III takes this position in "The Latin American Drug Connection," p. 243.
88. Lorenzo Meyer, "1985: un mal año en una época difícil."
89. U.S. Congress, House of Representatives, Committee on Foreign Affairs, *U.S. Narcotics Control Programs Overseas: An Assessment*.
90. Ibid. The language on corruption is as follows: "It is clear that corruption is the single biggest obstacle to effective anti-narcotics efforts in Mexico" (p. 34). The recommendations on Mexico are on pp. 39–40.
91. Ibid., p. 2.
92. *Economist*, June 7, 1986, pp. 23–24. As can be seen, this estimate of the size of the retail drug trade is double the estimate in the OTA report.
93. Jerry R. Ladman details some of the Mexican border-policy measures ("Industry on the Southern Border of the United States," pp. 210–211).
94. These suggestions are discussed in USITC, *Impact of Increased United States–Mexico Trade on Southwest Border Development*. The free-trade-zone idea was first proposed by Abelardo L. Valdés; his suggestion was to have a zone running perhaps 100 miles into each country for the length of the border in which manufacturing would take place in-bond for later privileged entry into each country. This would be a sort of super *maquiladora* combined with a super 806.30/807.00. The USITC discussion is on pp. 68–80. The productivity zone idea is similar in that a strip would be designated on both sides of the border, perhaps 15 miles wide, in which the main incentive for investment on the U.S. side would be the privilege of hiring Mexican workers in some fixed proportion with U.S. workers. It is discussed on pp. 123–126 of the USITC publication. Both proposals raise serious problems, as the USITC points out.

Chapter 9

1. *Economic Report of the President, 1986*, p. 234.
2. For an indication of the richness of the literature on this subject, see R. Burciaga Valdez, Kevin F. McCarthy, and Connie M. Moreno, *An Annotated Bibliography of Sources on Mexican Immigration*
3. According to Nacional Financiera, the urban population in Mexico increased from 12 percent in 1900 to 60 percent in 1980 (*La economía mexicana en cifras*, 1981). This rural–urban shift conforms to a general pattern in most of the world.
4. Juan Diez-Canedo Ruiz seeks to explain internal migration largely by the push factor of subsistence living in rural areas and external migration by the combination of push from rural areas plus the pull of higher wages in the United States than in the urban areas of Mexico (*La migración indocumentada de México a los Estados Unidos: Un nuevo enfoque*, pp. 111–132). This can hardly be the full explanation because many people stay in Mexico even though they can earn more in the United States.
5. Alejandro Portes, "Toward a Structural Analysis of Illegal (Undocumented) Immigration."
6. One example of this is from Wayne A. Cornelius, "Mexican Migration to the United States: Causes, Consequences, and U.S. Responses," p. 39.
7. Diez-Canedo, *La migración indocumentada de México a los Estados Unidos*, p. 67.
8. Sidney Weintraub and Chandler Stolp, "The Implications of Growing Economic Interdependence."
9. The examination was flawed by the lack of consistent data over time and the use of the sum of legal immigrants and apprehended illegal aliens as a proxy for economic migration. For these reasons, the results of the examination should be viewed as suggestive rather than conclusive. The value of the modeling is that it systematically examined data for an extended period, 1955 to 1983, and supported empirically what has been suggested from both theory and interviews.
10. Weintraub and Stolp, "Implications of Growing Economic Interdependence," p. 157.
11. Jorge A. Bustamante deals with the migration process involving employers, workers, the two governments, the *coyotes* or facilitators on the Mexican side, and the recruiters in "Mexican Migration to the United States: De Facto Rules."

12. This is a central thesis of Michael J. Piore, *Birds of Passage: Migrant Labor and Industrial Societies.*

13. Ibid., p. 27.

14. Vernon M. Briggs, Jr., has used this example in many of his writings. See, for example, *Immigration Policy and the American Labor Force.*

15. This is the major theme of Alan Dowty, *Closed Borders: The Contemporary Assault on Freedom of Movement.*

16. See Sidney Weintraub and Stanley R. Ross, *"Temporary" Alien Workers in the United States: Designing Policy from Fact and Opinion.*

17. The amnesty figure exceeds 3 million if those who applied under the special agricultural worker (SAW) program are included. Data are from the Immigration and Naturalization Service.

18. These issues are discussed in Francisco Alba, "Logros y limitaciones en la absorción de la fuerza de trabajo en México," and Peter Gregory, *The Myth of Market Failure: Employment and the Labor Market in Mexico,* especially pp. 14–100.

19. "Logros y limitaciones de la absorción de la fuerza de trabajo en México," p. 577.

20. Clark W. Reynolds, "The U.S.–Mexican Labor Market of the Future."

21. Reynolds was trying to show the need in the United States for the Mexican labor, a point taken up later.

22. Gregory, *Myth of Market Failure,* p. 20. Other data in this paragraph come from this source.

23. U.S. Department of Justice, Immigration and Naturalization Service (INS), *1987 Statistical Yearbook of the Immigration and Naturalization Service,* p. 7. In U.S. fiscal year 1987, 72,351 Mexicans were admitted as immigrants, which was 12 percent of all immigrants admitted, more than for any other single country. During fiscal years 1980 to 1986, a total of 458,300 Mexicans were admitted as immigrants, 11.5 percent of the total.

24. Of the almost 1.2 million aliens located by the border patrol in U.S. fiscal year 1988, 94 percent were Mexicans. Of the Mexicans, 99.7 percent were located in two INS regions, the southern and western, which together take in California, Texas, and Arizona. Mexicans have made up 70 percent of undocumented aliens who applied for amnesty under the regular provisions of IRCA, and 82 percent under the SAW program. The high percentage of Mexicans under the regular program is explainable by the exclusion of many Central Americans by the January 1, 1982, cutoff date.

25. Manuel García y Griego, *El volumen de la migración de mexicanos no documentados a los Estados Unidos (nuevas hipóteses).*

26. Ibid.

27. This terminology is used by Cornelius, "Mexican Migration to the United States," pp. 24–28.

28. Jeffrey S. Passel, "Undocumented Immigrants," p. 190. Data in this paragraph come from this source as well as from Jeffrey S. Passel, "Estimating the Number of Undocumented Aliens."

29. The Census Bureau did not actually count undocumented aliens. It tried to count everybody, and the figure for undocumented aliens was then estimated from the numbers over and above persons legally in the United States. The existence of INS alien registration data facilitated the making of this estimate.

30. Frank D. Bean, Allan G. King, and Jeffrey S. Passel analyze many of the estimates in "Estimates of the Size of the Illegal Migrant Population of Mexican Origin in the United States: An Assessment, Review, and Proposal." The estimating technique involved examining separate data sets that should have given the same total populations, and the number of undocumented persons was then estimated from the discrepancies. These data sets included Social Security and income tax material, reported deaths compared with those that should have been reported under normal death rates, and current population survey material compared with data from the INS. These statistical techniques had already dispelled scare numbers of the stock given earlier by the INS or from using arbitrary getaway ratios—that is, how many persons got away from the border patrol for each one caught.

31. I base this statement on an extensive review of the literature.

32. Edwin Harwood points out that polls taken in the United States during the past ten years show consistent opposition, in the 80 percent range and above, to permitting continued undocumented immigration ("American Public Opinion and U.S. Immigration Policy," pp. 205, 208). This was so even though those polled were evenly divided over whether undocumented workers displaced workers legally in the United States or took jobs the latter did not want.

33. George J. Borjas and Marta Tienda, "The Economic Consequences of Immigration," p. 648; Barry R. Chiswick, "The Economic Progress of Immigrants: Some Apparently Universal Patterns."
34. Barry R. Chiswick, "Mexican Immigrants: The Economic Dimension," p. 97. The data are from the 1980 census.
35. Briggs, *Immigration Policy and the American Labor Force.*
36. Borjas and Tienda, "Economic Consequences of Immigration," p. 64.
37. Frank D. Bean, B. Lindsay Lowell, and Lowell J. Taylor, "Undocumented Mexican Immigrants and the Earnings of Other Workers in the United States."
38. Thomas Muller, Thomas J. Espenshade et al., *The Fourth Wave: California's Newest Immigrants,* p. 112.
39. Michael J. Greenwood and John M. McDowell seek to deal rigorously with many of these questions in "The Factor Market Consequences of U.S. Immigration."
40. U.S. Congress, General Accounting Office, *Limited Research Suggests Illegal Aliens May Displace Native Workers,* pp. 17–18.
41. Harley L. Browning and Ruth M. Cullen, "The Complex Demographic Formation of the U.S. Mexican Origin Population," pp. 37–38. Other figures in this paragraph also come from this source; the data come from U.S. census figures.
42. *U.S.–Mexico Report* contains monthly translations of articles from the Mexican press. A sample of the commentary on migration from vol. 6, nos. 4 and 5 (April and May 1987), contains such themes as the racist nature of Simpson-Rodino, the shooting of a Mexican youth from Ciudad Juárez by the U.S. border patrol, the extortion of undocumented Mexicans by U.S. police, the failure to pay the minimum wage to undocumented workers, the setting up of concentration camps to hold undocumented immigrants, and concern that the return of the Mexican migrants will aggravate unemployment in Mexico.
43. Gregory, *Myth of Market Failure,* p. 206.
44. Diez-Canedo, *La migración indocumentada de México a los Estados Unidos,* p. 40.
45. Centro Nacional de Información y Estadísticas del Trabajo (Ceniet), "Los trabajadores mexicanos en los Estados Unidos." This is the final version of a paper provided to me; the paper itself was never published.
46. David S. North and Marion Houstoun, *The Characteristics and Role of Illegal Aliens in the U.S. Labor Market: An Exploratory Study.*
47. There is a theoretical exception that goes under the label of target incomes or backward-bending supply curves. It argues that when certain persons attain a target income, they are no longer interested in further work, at least for the time being. The labor-supply curve, which normally slopes upward and to the right as wages increase, might shift to the left once a target wage is exceeded. There may be such persons, but not likely many of them among Mexicans who have low incomes.
48. Jorge G. Castañeda, "Why Mexico Fears Our Immigration Law," op-ed column, *New York Times,* May 8, 1987, p. 27 (Southwest edition).
49. Congress, in the Simpson-Rodino legislation, created the Commission for the Study of International Migration and Cooperative Economic Development to examine areas of economic cooperation that would mitigate emigration pressures. This commission, whose mandate was until mid-1990, did receive cooperation from Mexican authorities to study development issues related to migration.
50. Reynolds, "U.S.–Mexican Labor Market of the Future"; Clark W. Reynolds, Raúl Ramos, and Robert McCleery, "The Impact of Foreign Trade and Export Strategies on Distribution of Income for Low-Income Households in Mexico."
51. There are a number of special provisions: immigration agents can no longer enter open fields to seek out undocumented workers without search warrants; aliens who have worked in seasonal agriculture for at least ninety days between May 1, 1985, and May 1, 1986, can be granted temporary residence and ultimately permanent resident status; if after October 1, 1989, U.S. authorities find there is a shortage of farm labor, the replenishment of foreign workers will be permitted, and the workers can be granted temporary and ultimately permanent resident status.
52. Frank D. Bean, Harley L. Browning, and W. Parker Frisbie, "What the 1980 United States Census Tells Us About the Characteristics of Illegal and Legal Mexican Immigrants." The 17 percent for agriculture includes mining, but the bulk pertains to agriculture.

53. The *Wall Street Journal* reported on undocumented aliens not eligible for amnesty and unable to change jobs without showing documents that they are legally in the United States. These persons, according to one description given in the article, "feel like slaves" (September 2, 1987, p. 42).
54. José Napoleon Duarte, letter to the editor, *New York Times*, May 12, 1987.
55. Sidney Weintraub, "Illegal Immigrants in Texas: Impact on Social Services and Related Considerations"; Bean, Browning, and Frisbie, "What the 1980 United States Census Tells Us About the Characteristics of Illegal and Legal Mexican Immigrants."
56. Wilfred J. Ethier seeks to rigorously calculate the costs of immigration enforcement and concludes that the costs will be lowest when there is a mixture of both techniques, those at the border and the domestic measures ("Illegal Immigration: The Host-Country Problem").
57. The media reported much confusion by employers when the employer-penalty provisions became effective in June 1987. There were also reports of widespread use of fraudulent documents to demonstrate legal presence in the United States.
58. Manuel García y Griego and Francisco Giner de los Ríos take the view that the United States is unlikely to be too restrictive because of adverse internal economic and social effects ("¿Es vulnerable la economía mexicana a la aplicación de políticas migratorias estadunidenses?" p. 272).
59. The limited impact these measures can have is discussed in Sidney Weintraub, "Treating the Causes: Illegal Immigration and U.S. Foreign Economic Policy."
60. The main policy recommendation in Michael Teitelbaum, *Latin Migration North: The Problem for U.S. Foreign Policy*, is that the United States should pay more attention to the effects of its domestic economic policy on Latin American economies and migration (pp. 66–67).
61. Kevin F. McCarthy and R. Burciaga Valdez classify immigrants as short-term, cyclical, and permanent and note that each group has different objectives and characteristics (*Current and Future Effects of Mexican Migration in California*).

Chapter 10

1. When municipal elections went against the PRI, the people in the cities that voted against the party expected that the central government would mete out punishment—for example, by withholding funds. Jeffrey W. Rubin discusses the aftermath of a leftist victory in 1980 in the city of Juchitán, Oaxaca ("Elections, Repression, and Limited Reform: Update on Southern Mexico").
2. Gabriel Zaid, "La propiedad privada de las funciones públicas."
3. The most notable example of this is Juan Molinar Horcasitas, "Regreso a Chihuahua." This article carefully documents the fraud in the 1986 elections in that state. The evidence presented shows more registrations than the populations of various municipalities and the frivolous manner in which complaints by the opposition (such as opening of polling places before the scheduled time and incorrect counting of votes) were dealt with by the formal electoral college or investigating body.
4. Daniel Cosío Villegas makes this point, as have others (*El sistema político mexicano: las posibilidades de cambio*, p. 34).
5. Octavio Paz argues that the true friends of Mexico, the countries with which Mexico shares a history, culture, and community of interests, are the Latin American democracies and Spain ("Contrarronda: México, Estados Unidos, América Central, etcetera," p. 16). The further closing of the political system in Mexico at this time, when the trend is in precisely the opposite direction elsewhere in Latin America, would make Mexico a pariah, just as Chile was under Pinochet and Paraguay under Stroessner.
6. Raymond Vernon, *The Dilemma of Mexico's Development: The Roles of the Private and Public Sectors*, pp. 189–190.
7. The United States requested immediate consultation on two areas of Mexican policy: technology transfer and protection of intellectual property, and investment matters.
8. Carlos Salinas de Gortari, in his television address on August 28, 1987, as a PRI precandidate, said that modern politics requires that Mexico "achieve more benefits from negotiation than from confrontation" (Foreign Broadcast Information Service, as reported in *U.S.–Mexico Report* 6, no. 10 [October 1987]: 33). The statement did not deal with the bilateral trade framework agreement with the United States, but is consistent with that action.

9. Indeed, in his television talk as a precandidate for the presidency of Mexico, Salinas referred to a "popular, nationalistic modernization" and a "defense of sovereignty."
10. The point is made in Cathryn L. Thorup, ed., *The United States and Mexico: Face to Face with New Technology*, pp. 15–16. It is also made more generally about worldwide corporate alliances in an opinion column by Daniel A. Sharp in the *Wall Street Journal*, June 1, 1987, p. 18.
11. M. Delal Baer, "Mexico: Ambivalent Ally," p. 106.
12. Oil issues are discussed in Pamela Falk, ed., *Petroleum and Mexico's Future*.

BIBLIOGRAPHY

Books and Monographs

English

Alba, Francisco. *The Population of Mexico: Trends, Issues, and Policies.* New Brunswick, N.J.: Transaction Books, 1982.

Altshuler, Alan, Daniel Roos et al. *The Future of the Automobile: The Report of MIT's International Automobile Program.* Cambridge, Mass.: MIT Press, 1984.

Amnesty International. *Mexico: Human Rights in Rural Areas. Exchange of Documents with the Mexican Government on Human Rights Violations in Oaxaca and Chiapas.* London: Amnesty International Publications, 1986.

Aspe, Pedro, and Paul E. Sigmund, eds. *The Political Economy of Income Distribution in Mexico.* New York: Holmes & Meier, 1984.

Bailey, John J. *Governing Mexico: The Statecraft of Crisis Management.* New York: St. Martin's Press, 1988.

Bailey, Norman A., and Richard Cohen. *The Mexican Time Bomb.* New York: Priority Press Publications for the Twentieth Century Fund, 1987.

Balassa, Bela, ed. *European Economic Integration.* Amsterdam and Oxford: North-Holland, 1975.

Baldwin, David A. *Economic Statecraft.* Princeton, N.J.: Princeton University Press, 1985.

Bennett, Douglas C., and Kenneth E. Sharpe. *Transnational Corporations versus the State: The Political Economy of the Mexican Auto Industry.* Princeton, N.J.: Princeton University Press, 1985.

Bennett, Mark. *Public Policy and Industrial Development: The Case of the Mexican Auto Parts Industry.* Boulder, Colo.: Westview Press, 1986.

Bilateral Commission on the Future of United States-Mexican Relations. *The Challenge of Interdependence: Mexico and the United States.* Lanham, Md.: University Press of America, 1989.

Bok, Sissela. *Lying: Moral Choice in Public and Private Life.* New York: Pantheon Books, 1978.

Bredahl, Maury, Jimmye Hillman, Robert Rothenberg, and Nicolas Gutierrez. *Technical Change, Protectionism, and Market Structure: The Case of International Trade in Fresh Winter Vegetables.* Technical Bulletin, no. 249. Tucson: College of Agriculture, University of Arizona, 1983.

Briggs, Vernon M., Jr. *Immigration Policy and the American Labor Force.* Baltimore: Johns Hopkins University Press, 1985.

Camp, Roderic A. *Mexico's Leaders: Their Education and Recruitment.* Tucson: University of Arizona Press, 1980.

————. *Intellectuals and the State in Twentieth-Century Mexico.* Austin: University of Texas Press, 1985.

————, ed. *Mexico's Political Stability: The Next Five Years.* Boulder, Colo.: Westview Press, 1986.

Cockroft, James D. *Mexico: Class Formation, Capital Accumulation, and the State*. New York: Monthly Review Press, 1983.

Connor, John M. "A Quantitative Analysis of the Market Power of United States Multinational Corporations in Brazil and Mexico." Ph.D. diss., University of Wisconsin, 1976.

Connor, John M., and Willard F. Mueller. *Market Power and Profitability of Multinational Corporations in Brazil and Mexico*. Report prepared for the Senate Committee on Foreign Relations, 95th Cong., 1st sess. Washington, D.C.: Government Printing Office, 1977.

Cornelius, Wayne A. "Mexican Migration to the United States: Causes, Consequences, and U.S. Responses." Cambridge, Mass.: Migration and Development Study Group, Center for International Studies, Massachusetts Institute of Technology, 1978.

Cosío Villegas, Daniel. *American Extremes*. Austin: University of Texas Press, 1964.

Cuddington, John T. *Capital Flight: Estimates, Issues, and Explanations*. Study in International Finance, no. 58. Princeton, N.J.: Department of Economics, Princeton University, December 1986.

del Castillo V., Gustavo. *U.S.–Mexican Trade Relations: From the Generalized System of Preferences to a Formal Bilateral Trade Agreement*. Research Report Series, no. 14. San Diego: Center for U.S.–Mexican Studies, University of California, 1985. Published in Spanish as "Relaciones comerciales: México–Estados Unidos: Del sistema generalizado de preferencias a un acuerdo bilateral de comercio." *Comercio Exterior* 36, no. 3 (March 1986): 230–240.

Dillon, K. Burke, and Gumersindo Oliveros. *Recent Experience with Multilateral Official Debt Rescheduling*. Washington, D.C.: International Monetary Fund, 1987.

Dominguez, Jorge I., ed. *Mexico's Political Economy: Challenges at Home and Abroad*. Beverly Hills, Calif.: Sage, 1982.

Dowty, Alan. *Closed Borders: The Contemporary Assault on Freedom of Movement*. New Haven, Conn.: Yale University Press, 1987.

Eaton, David J., and John M. Andersen, eds. *The State of the Rio Grande–Rio Bravo: A Study of Water Resources Issues Along the Texas–Mexico Border*. Tucson: University of Arizona Press, 1987.

Eckstein, Susan. *The Poverty of Revolution: The State and the Urban Poor in Mexico*. Princeton, N.J.: Princeton University Press, 1977.

Erb, Richard D., and Stanley R. Ross, eds. *U.S. Policies Toward Mexico: Perceptions and Perspectives*. Washington, D.C.: American Enterprise Institute, 1979.

Fagen, Richard R., and Olga Pellicer, eds. *The Future of Central America: Policy Choices for the U.S. and Mexico*. Stanford, Calif.: Stanford University Press, 1983.

Falk, Pamela, ed. *Petroleum and Mexico's Future*. Boulder, Colo.: Westview Press, 1987.

Federal Electoral Commission (of Mexico). *The New Mexican Electoral Legislation*. México, D.F.: Talleres Gráficos de la Nación, 1987.

Fernández de Castro, Rafael. "Mexican Government Influence on the Outcome of U.S. Legislation." Master's professional report, Lyndon B. Johnson School of Public Affairs, University of Texas at Austin, 1986.

Fernández-Kelly, María Patricia. *For We Are Sold. I and My People*. Albany: State University of New York Press, 1983.

Gentleman, Judith, ed. *Mexican Politics in Transition*. Boulder, Colo.: Westview Press, 1987.

Gereffi, Gary. *The Pharmaceutical Industry and Dependency in the Third World*. Princeton, N.J.: Princeton University Press, 1983.

Gibson, Lay James, and Alfonso Corona Rentería, eds. *The United States and Mexico: Borderland Development and the National Economies*. Boulder, Colo.: Westview Press, 1985.

Godshaw, Gerald et al. "The Implications for the U.S. Economy of Tariff Schedule Item 807 and Mexico's Maquila Program." Bala Cynwyd, Pa.: WEFA Group and CIEMEX-WEFA for the U.S. Department of Labor, May 1988. Mimeograph.

González Casanova, Pablo. *Democracy in Mexico*. New York: Oxford University Press, 1970.

Grayson, George W. *The Politics of Mexican Oil*. Pittsburgh: University of Pittsburgh Press, 1980.

———. *The United States and Mexico: Patterns of Influence*. New York: Praeger, 1984.

Gregory, Peter. *The Myth of Market Failure: Employment and the Labor Market in Mexico*. Baltimore: Johns Hopkins University Press for the World Bank, 1986.

Grunwald, Joseph, and Kenneth Flamm. *The Global Factory: Foreign Assembly in International Trade.* Washington, D.C.: Brookings Institution, 1985.

Guttentag, Jack M., and Richard J. Herring. *Disaster Myopia in International Banking.* Essay in International Finance, no. 164. Princeton, N.J.: Department of Economics, Princeton University, 1986.

Guttman, William. *Between Bailout and Breakdown: A Modular Approach to Latin America's Debt Crisis.* Washington, D.C.: Center for Strategic and International Studies, 1989.

Hansen, Niles. *The Role of Mexican Labor in the Economy of the Southwest United States.* Austin: Mexico–U.S. Border Research Program, University of Texas, 1979.

————. *The Border Economy: Regional Development in the Southwest.* Austin: University of Texas Press, 1981.

Hansen, Roger D. *The Politics of Mexican Development.* Baltimore: Johns Hopkins University Press, 1971.

Hellman, Judith Adler. *Mexico in Crisis.* New York: Holmes & Meier, 1978.

Herzog, Lawrence A., ed. *Planning the International Border Metropolis: Trans-Boundary Policy Options for the San Diego–Tijuana Region.* San Diego: Center for U.S.–Mexican Studies, University of California, 1986.

Hirschman, Albert O. *The Strategy of Economic Development.* New Haven, Conn.: Yale University Press, 1958.

Hoffmann, Stanley. *Gulliver's Troubles, or the Setting of American Foreign Policy.* New York: McGraw-Hill for the Council on Foreign Relations, 1968.

Holden, Richard J. "Maquiladoras on the Texas/Mexico Border: An Econometric Evaluation of Employment and Retail Sales Effects on Four Texas SMSAs." Master's professional report, Lyndon B. Johnson School of Public Affairs, University of Texas at Austin, 1984.

Hughes, Helen. *Policy Lessons of the Development Experience.* New York: Group of Thirty, 1985.

Jenkins, Rhys Owen. *Dependent Industrialization in Latin America: The Automotive Industry in Argentina, Chile, and Mexico.* New York: Praeger, 1977.

Kalifa-Assad, Salvador. "Income Distribution in Mexico: A Reconsideration of the Distribution Problem." Ph.D. diss., Cornell University, 1977.

Keohane, Robert O. *After Hegemony: Cooperation and Discord in the World Political Economy.* Princeton, N.J.: Princeton University Press, 1984.

Kraft, Joseph. *The Mexican Rescue.* New York: Group of Thirty, 1984.

Krasner, Stephen D. *Structural Conflict: The Third World Against Global Liberalism.* Berkeley: University of California Press, 1985.

Krueger, Anne O. *Foreign Trade Regimes and Economic Development: Liberalization Attempts and Consequences.* Cambridge, Mass.: Ballinger for the National Bureau of Economic Research, 1978.

Kuczynski, Pedro-Pablo. *Latin American Debt.* Baltimore: Johns Hopkins University Press, 1988.

Lande, Stephen L., and Craig VanGrasstek. *The Trade and Tariff Act of 1984: Trade Policy in the Reagan Administration.* Lexington, Mass.: Lexington Books, 1986.

Latell, Brian. *Mexico at the Crossroads: The Many Crises of the Political System.* Stanford, Calif.: Hoover Institution, 1986.

Levy, Daniel, and Gabriel Székely. *Mexico: Paradoxes of Stability and Change,* 2nd ed. Boulder, Colo.: Westview Press, 1987.

Looney, Robert E. *Economic Policymaking in Mexico: Factors Underlying the 1982 Crisis.* Durham, N.C.: Duke University Press, 1985.

Mares, David R. *Penetrating the International Market: Theoretical Consideration and a Mexican Case Study.* New York: Columbia University Press, 1987.

Marsden, Keith. *Trade and Employment Policies for Industrial Development.* Washington, D.C.: World Bank, 1982.

McCarthy, Kevin F., and R. Burciaga Valdez. *Current and Future Effects of Mexican Immigration in California.* Santa Monica, Calif.: Rand, 1985.

Meyer, Lorenzo. *Mexico and the United States in the Oil Controversy: 1917–1942.* Austin: University of Texas Press, 1977.

Mills, James. *The Underground Empire: Where Crime and Governments Embrace*. Garden City, N.Y.: Doubleday, 1986.

Muller, Thomas, Thomas J. Espenshade et al. *The Fourth Wave: California's Newest Immigrants*. Washington, D.C.: Urban Institute Press, 1985.

Musgrave, Peggy B., ed. *Mexico and the United States: Studies in Economic Interaction*. Boulder, Colo.: Westview Press, 1985.

Newell, G. Roberto, and Luis Rubio F. *Mexico's Dilemma: The Political Origins of Economic Crisis*. Boulder, Colo.: Westview Press, 1984.

Newfarmer, Richard S., ed. *Profits, Progress and Poverty: Case Studies of International Industries in Latin America*. Notre Dame, Ind.: University of Notre Dame Press, 1985.

Newfarmer, Richard, and Willard F. Mueller. *Multinational Corporations in Brazil and Mexico: Structural Sources of Economic and Noneconomic Power*. Report prepared for the Senate Committee on Foreign Relations, 94th Cong., 1st sess. Washington, D.C.: Government Printing Office, 1975.

North, David S., and Marion Houstoun. *The Characteristics and Role of Illegal Aliens in the U.S. Labor Market: An Exploratory Study*. Report prepared for the Employment and Training Administration, U.S. Department of Labor. Washington, D.C.: Linton, 1976.

Olson, Mancur. *The Rise and Decline of Nations: Economic Growth, Stagflation, and Social Rigidities*. New Haven, Conn.: Yale University Press, 1983.

Pastor, Robert A., and Jorge G. Castañeda. *Limits to Friendship: The United States and Mexico*. New York: Knopf, 1988.

Paz, Octavio. *The Labyrinth of Solitude: Life and Thought in Mexico*. New York: Grove Press, 1961. See also Spanish original, *El laberinto de la soledad*.

———. *The Other Mexico: Critique of the Pyramid*. New York: Grove Press, 1972.

Piore, Michael J. *Birds of Passage: Migrant Labor and Industrial Societies*. New York: Cambridge University Press, 1979.

Purcell, Susan Kaufman, ed. *Mexico–United States Relations*. New York: Praeger for the Academy of Political Science, 1981.

Reyna, José Luis, and Richard S. Weinert, eds. *Authoritarianism in Mexico*. Philadelphia: Institute for the Study of Human Issues, 1977.

Reynolds, Clark W. *The Mexican Economy: Twentieth Century Structure and Growth*. New Haven, Conn.: Yale University Press, 1970.

Reynolds, Clark W., and Carlos Tello, eds. *U.S.–Mexico Relations: Economic and Social Aspects*. Stanford, Calif.: Stanford University Press, 1983.

Riding, Alan. *Distant Neighbors: A Portrait of the Mexicans*. New York: Knopf, 1985.

Rieffel, Alexis. *The Role of the Paris Club in Managing Debt Problems*. Essay in International Finance, no. 161. Princeton, N.J.: Department of Economics, Princeton University, 1985.

Ronfeldt, David, Richard Nehring, and Arturo Gandara. *Mexico's Petroleum and U.S. Policy: Implications for the 1980s*. Santa Monica, Calif.: Rand for the U.S. Department of Energy Press, 1980.

———. "The Modern Mexican Military: Implications for Mexico's Stability and Security." Santa Monica, Calif.: Rand, 1985.

Ross, Stanley R., ed. *Views Across the Border: The United States and Mexico*. Albuquerque: University of New Mexico Press, 1978.

———. *Ecology and Development of the Border Region*. México, D.F.: Asociación Nacional de Universidades e Institutos de Enseñanza Superior, 1983.

Sanders, Sol. *Mexico: Chaos on Our Doorstep*. Lanham, Md.: Madison Books, 1986.

Sanderson, Steven E. *The Transformation of Mexican Agriculture: International Structure and the Politics of Rural Change*. Princeton, N.J.: Princeton University Press, 1986.

Seligson, Mitchell A., and Edward J. Williams. *Maquiladoras and Migration: A Study of Workers in the Mexican-United States Border Industrialization Program*. Tucson: University of Arizona Press, 1980.

Sepúlveda, César, and Albert E. Utton, eds. *The U.S.–Mexico Border Region: Anticipating Resource Needs and Issues to the Year 2000*. El Paso: Texas Western Press of the University of Texas at El Paso, 1984.

Shafer, R. J. *Mexican Business Organizations*. Syracuse, N.Y.: Syracuse University Press, 1973.

Shaiken, Harley, and Stephen Herzenberg. *Automation and Global Production: Automobile Engine*

Production in Mexico, the United States, and Canada. San Diego: Center for U.S.–Mexican Studies, University of California, 1987.

Smith, Gordon W., and John T. Cuddington, eds. *International Debt and the Developing Countries.* Washington, D.C.: World Bank, 1985.

Smith, Peter H. *Labyrinths of Power: Political Recruitment in Twentieth-Century Mexico.* Princeton, N.J.: Princeton University Press, 1979.

Solís, Leopoldo. *Economic Policy Reform in Mexico: A Case Study for Developing Countries.* New York: Pergamon Press, 1981.

Story, Dale. *Industry, the State, and Public Policy in Mexico.* Austin: University of Texas Press, 1986.

Teitelbaum, Michael. *Latin Migration North: The Problem for U.S. Foreign Policy.* New York: Council on Foreign Relations, 1985.

Thorup, Cathryn L., ed. *The United States and Mexico: Face to Face with New Technology.* New Brunswick, N.J.: Transaction Books for the Overseas Development Council, 1987.

United Nations Association of the United States of America. "Relationships in the North American Economic Area." Economic Policy Council, New York, February 1981.

Valdez, R. Burciaga, Kevin F. McCarthy, and Connie M. Moreno. *An Annotated Bibliography of Sources on Mexican Immigration.* Santa Monica, Calif.: Rand, 1987.

Vernon, Raymond. *The Dilemma of Mexico's Development: The Roles of the Private and Public Sectors.* Cambridge, Mass.: Harvard University Press, 1963.

————. *Sovereignty at Bay: The Multinational Spread of U.S. Enterprises.* New York: Basic Books, 1971.

————. *Storm Over the Multinationals: The Real Issues.* Cambridge, Mass.: Harvard University Press, 1977.

————, ed. *Public Policy and Private Enterprise in Mexico.* Cambridge, Mass.: Harvard University Press, 1964.

Villarreal Arrambide, René Patricio. "External Disequilibrium and Growth Without Development: The Import Substitution Model—The Mexican Experience (1929–1975)." Ph.D. diss., Yale University, 1976.

Vindasius, Julia Christine. "Mexico and IBM: A New Look at State-TNC Negotiation and Bargaining Power." Master's thesis, Massachusetts Institute of Technology, 1986.

Weil, Thomas E. et al. *Area Handbook for Mexico.* Washington, D.C.: Government Printing Office, 1975.

Weintraub, Sidney. *Free Trade between Mexico and the United States?* Washington, D.C.: Brookings Institution, 1984.

————, ed. *Industrial Strategy and Planning in Mexico and the United States.* Boulder, Colo.: Westview Press, 1986.

Weintraub, Sidney, and Gilbert Cárdenas. *The Use of Public Services by Undocumented Aliens in Texas.* Austin: Lyndon B. Johnson School of Public Affairs, University of Texas, 1984.

Weintraub, Sidney, and Stanley R. Ross. *"Temporary" Alien Workers in the United States: Designing Policy from Fact and Opinion.* Boulder, Colo.: Westview, Press, 1982.

Wionczek, Miguel S., and Ragaei El Mallakh, eds. *Mexico's Energy Resources: Toward a Policy of Diversification.* Boulder, Colo.: Westview Press, 1985.

Wionczek, Miguel S., and Luciano Tomassini. *Politics and Economics of External Debt Crisis: The Latin American Experience.* Boulder, Colo.: Westview Press, 1985.

Zartman, I. William, and Maureen R. Berman. *The Practical Negotiator.* New Haven, Conn.: Yale University Press, 1982.

Spanish

Alonso, Angelina, and Roberto López. *El sindicato de trabajadores petroleros y sus relaciones con Pemex y el estado, 1970–1985.* México, D.F.: El Colegio de México, 1986.

Basáñez, M. *La lucha por la hegemonía en México, 1968–1980.* México, D.F.: Siglo Veintiuno, 1981.

Calderon Madrid, Angel. "Un análisis de los programas de condicionalidad del Fondo Monetario Internacional a la luz de la experiencia de la economía mexicana durante 1983 y algunas consideraciones sobre la política de estabilización e industrialización en un contexto de escasez de divisas." Mimeograph version, 1985, combining two articles: "Programa de condicionalidad del

Fondo Monetario Internacional: El case de México durante 1983,'' *Revista A* [publication of Ciencias Sociales y Humanidades of the Universidad Autónoma Metropolitana] 5, no. 13 (September–December 1984), and ''Algunas consideraciones de la política de estabilisación y industrialisación en un contexto de escase de dursas,'' Documento de trabajo, no. 2. Programa Universitario Justo Sierra de la Coordinación de Humanidades de la Universidad Nacional Autónoma de México, 1984.

Cano Gordón, Carmen, and María Teresa Cisneros Gudiño. *La dinámica de la violencia en México.* México, D.F.: Escuela Nacional de Estudios Profesionales Acatlan, Universidad Nacional Autónoma de México, 1980.

Centro de Estudios Económicos del Sector Privado (CEESP). *La economía subterranea en México.* México, D.F.: CEESP, 1986.

Cosío Villegas, Daniel. *El sistema político mexicano: las posibilidades de cambio.* México, D.F.: Editorial Joaquín Mortiz, 1972.

———. *El estilo personal de gobernar.* México, D.F.: Editorial Joaquín Mortiz, 1974.

———. *La sucesión presidencial.* México, D.F.: Editorial Joaquín Mortiz, 1975.

———. *La sucesión: desenlaces y perspectivas.* México, D.F.: Editorial Joaquín Mortiz, 1975.

Diez-Canedo Ruiz, Juan. *La migración indocumentada de México a los Estados Unidos: un nuevo enfoque.* México, D.F.: Fondo de Cultura Económica, 1984.

Fajnzylber, Fernando, and Trinidad Martínez Tarrago. *Las empresas transnacionales.* México, D.F.: Fondo de Cultura Económica, 1976.

Flores Caballero, Romeo R. *Evolución de la frontera norte.* Monterrey: Facultad de Economía, Centro de Investigaciones Económicas, 1982.

García Rocha, Adalberto. *La desigualdad económica.* México, D.F.: El Colegio de México, 1986.

García y Griego, Manuel. *El volumen de la migración de mexicanos no documentados a los Estados Unidos (nuevas hipóteses).* Estudios no. 4. México, D.F.: Centro Nacional de Información y Estadísticas del Trabajo (CENIET), 1980.

González de la Garza, Mauricio. *Carta a Miguel de la Madrid: con copia a los mexicanos.* México, D.F.: Editorial Posada, 1987.

González Salazar, Roque, ed. *La frontera del norte: integración y desarrollo.* México, D.F.: El Colegio de México, 1981.

Herrera, René, and Mario Ojeda. *La política de México hacia Centroamérica (1979–1982).* México, D.F.: El Colegio de México, 1983.

Instituto Mexicano de Comercio Exterior y Academía de Arbitraje y Comercio Internacional. *El comercio exterior de Mexico,* 3 vols. México, D.F.: Siglo Veintiuno Editores, 1982.

Krauze, Enrique. *Por una democracia sin adjetivos.* México, D.F.: Joaquín Mortiz/Planeta, 1986.

Lomnitz, Larissa A. de. *Cómo sobreviven los marginados.* México, D.F.: Siglo Veintiuno Editores, 1975.

Minello, Nelson. *Siderúrgica Lázaro Cárdenas-Las Truchas: Historia de una empresa.* México, D.F.: El Colegio de México, 1982.

Ojeda, Mario. *Alcances y límites de la política exterior de México.* México, D.F.: El Colegio de México, 1976.

Paz, Octavio. *El laberinto de la soledad.* México, D.F.: Fondo de Cultura Económica, 1959. See also English version, *The Labyrinth of Solitude.*

———. *Sor Juana Inés de la Cruz o las trampas de la fe.* Barcelona and México, D.F.: Seix Barral/Biblioteca Breve, 1982.

Sepúlveda Amor, Bernardo, and Antonio Chumacero. *La inversión extranjera en México.* México, D.F.: Fondo de Cultura Económica, 1973.

Sepúlveda Amor, Bernardo, Olga Pellicer de Brody, and Lorenzo Meyer. *Las empresas transnacionales en México.* México, D.F.: El Colegio de México, 1974.

Snoeck, Michele. *La industria petroquímica básica en México, 1970–1982.* México, D.F.: El Colegio de México, 1986.

———. *El comercio exterior de hidrocarburos y derivados en México, 1970–1985.* México, D.F.: El Colegio de México, 1987.

Solís, Leopoldo. *La realidad económica mexicana: retrovisión y perspectivas,* 14th ed. México, D.F.: Siglo Veintiuno Editores, 1985.

Székely, Gabriel. *La economía política del petróleo en México, 1976–1982*. México, D.F.: El Colegio de México, 1983.

Tello, Carlos. *La política económica en México 1970–1976*. México, D.F.: Siglo Veintiuno Editores, 1979.

_____. *La nacionalización de la banca en México*. México, D.F.: Siglo Veintiuno Editores, 1984.

Trejo Reyes, Saúl. *El futuro de la política industrial en México*. México, D.F.: El Colegio de México, 1987.

Unger, Kurt. *Competencia monopólica y tecnología en la industria mexicana*. México, D.F.: El Colegio de México, 1985.

Willars A., Jaime Mario. *El petróleo en México: efectos macroeconómicos, elementos de política y perspectivas*. México, D.F.: El Colegio de México, 1984.

Wionczek, Miguel S. *El nacionalismo mexicano y la inversión extranjera*. México, D.F.: Siglo Veintiuno Editores, 1967.

Articles and Chapters

English

Alba, Francisco. "Mexico's Northern Border: A Framework of Reference." In César Sepúlveda and Albert E. Utton, eds., *The U.S.–Mexico Border Region: Anticipating Resource Needs and Issues to the Year 2000*. El Paso: Texas Western Press of the University of Texas at El Paso, 1984, pp. 22–35.

Alejo, Francisco Javier. "Complementation and Conflict: A Mexican View." In Sidney Weintraub, ed., *Industrial Strategy and Planning in Mexico and the United States*. Boulder, Colo.: Westview Press, 1986, pp. 245–263.

Applegate, Howard G. "Transnational Air Pollution." In Stanley R. Ross, ed., *Ecology and Development of the Border Region*. México, D.F.: Asociación Nacional de Universidades e Institutos de Enseñanza Superior, 1983, pp. 127–137.

Baer, M. Delal. "The Mexican Midterm Elections." 4 reports. Center for Strategic and International Studies, Georgetown University, Washington, D.C., June–November 1985.

_____. "The 1986 Mexican Elections: The Case of Chihuahua." Center for Strategic and International Studies, Georgetown University, Washington, D.C., September 1986.

_____. "Mexico: Ambivalent Ally." *Washington Quarterly* 10, no. 3 (Summer 1987): 103–113.

Bailey, John J. "The Impact of Major Groups on Policy-Making Trends in Government–Business Relations in Mexico." In Roderic A. Camp, ed., *Mexico's Political Stability: The Next Five Years*. Boulder, Colo.: Westview Press, 1986, pp. 119–142.

_____. "What Explains the Decline of the PRI and Will It Continue?" In Roderic A. Camp, ed., *Mexico's Political Stability: The Next Five Years*. Boulder, Colo.: Westview Press, 1986, pp. 159–183.

Balassa, Bela. "Structural Policies in the European Common Market." In Bela Balassa, ed., *European Economic Integration*. Amsterdam and Oxford: North-Holland, 1975, pp. 225–274.

Bath, C. Richard. "U.S.–Mexico Experience in Managing Transboundary Air Resources: Problems, Prospects, and Recommendations for the Future." In César Sepúlveda and Albert E. Utton, eds., *The U.S.–Mexico Border Region: Anticipating Resource Needs and Issues to the Year 2000*. El Paso: Texas Western Press of the University of Texas at El Paso, 1984, pp. 419–439.

_____. "Environmental Issues in the United States–Mexico Borderlands." *Journal of Borderland Studies* 1, no. 1 (Spring 1986): 49–72.

Bean, Frank D., Harley L. Browning, and W. Parker Frisbie. "What the 1980 United States Census Tells Us About the Characteristics of Illegal and Legal Mexican Immigrants." Texas Population Research Center, University of Texas at Austin, 1984.

Bean, Frank D., Allan G. King, and Jeffrey S. Passel. "Estimates of the Size of the Illegal Migrant Population of Mexican Origin in the United States: An Assessment, Review and Proposal." In Harley L. Browning and Rodolfo O. de la Garza, eds., *Mexican Immigrants and Mexican Americans: An Evolving Relation*. Austin: Center for Mexican American Studies, University of Texas, 1986, pp. 13–36.

Bean, Frank D., B. Lindsay Lowell, and Lowell J. Taylor. "Undocumented Mexican Immigrants and the Earnings of Other Workers in the United States.'' Paper presented at the annual meeting of the Population Association of America, San Francisco, April 1986.

Bergsman, Joel. ''Income Distribution and Poverty in Mexico.'' World Bank staff working paper, no. 395, June 1980.

Borjas, George J., and Marta Tienda. ''The Economic Consequences of Immigration.'' *Science*, February 6, 1987, pp. 645–651.

Brodovsky, Joan. ''The Mexican Pharmochemical and Pharmaceutical Industries.'' In Cathryn L. Thorup, ed., *The United States and Mexico: Face to Face with New Technology*. New Brunswick, N.J.: Transaction Books for the Overseas Development Council, 1987, pp. 187–213.

Brown, Hal. ''Air Pollution Problems in the Tijuana–San Diego Air Basin.'' In Lawrence A. Herzog, ed., *Planning the International Border Metropolis: Trans-Boundary Options for the San Diego–Tijuana Region*. San Diego: Center for U.S.–Mexican Studies, University of California, 1986, pp. 39–44.

Browning, Harley L., and Ruth M. Cullen. ''The Complex Demographic Formation of the U.S. Mexican Origin Population, 1970–1980.'' In Harley L. Browning and Rodolfo O. de la Garza, eds., *Mexican Immigrants and Mexican Americans: An Evolving Relation*. Austin: Center for Mexican American Studies, University of Texas, 1986, pp. 37–54.

Bustamante, Jorge A. ''Commodity Migrants: Structural Analysis of Mexican Immigration to the United States.'' In Stanley R. Ross, ed., *Views Across the Border: The United States and Mexico*. Albuquerque: University of New Mexico Press, 1978, pp. 183–203.

———. ''Mexican Migration to the United States: De Facto Rules.'' In Peggy B. Musgrave, ed., *Mexico and the United States: Studies in Economic Interaction*. Boulder, Colo.: Westview Press, 1985, pp. 185–205.

Camp, Roderic A. ''An Overview.'' In Roderic A. Camp, ed., *Mexico's Political Stability: The Next Five Years*. Boulder, Colo.: Westview Press, 1986, pp. 1–18.

———. ''Potential Strengths of the Political Opposition and What It Means to the PRI.'' In Roderic A. Camp, ed., *Mexico's Political Stability: The Next Five Years*. Boulder, Colo.: Westview Press, 1986, pp. 185–210.

Castañeda, Jorge G. ''Don't Corner Mexico!'' *Foreign Policy*, no. 60 (Fall 1985): 75–90.

———. ''Mexico at the Brink.'' *Foreign Affairs* 64, no. 2 (Winter 1985/86): 287–303.

———. ''Mexico's Coming Challenges.'' *Foreign Policy*, no. 64 (Fall 1986): 120–139.

Chiswick, Barry R. ''The Economic Progress of Immigrants: Some Apparently Universal Patterns.'' In William Fellner, ed., *Contemporary Economic Problems 1979*. Washington, D.C.: American Enterprise Institute, 1979, pp. 357–399.

———. ''Mexican Immigrants: The Economic Dimension.'' *Annals of the American Academy of Political and Social Science* 487 (September 1986): 92–101.

Clark, Robert Emmet. ''Overview of Groundwater Law and Institutions in United States Border States.'' In César Sepúlveda and Albert E. Utton, eds., *The U.S.–Mexico Border Region: Anticipating Resource Needs and Issues to the Year 2000*. El Paso: Texas Western Press of the University of Texas at El Paso, 1984, pp. 279–287.

Cohoes, Robert L. L. ''Earthquake: U.S. Embassy Staffers Swing into Action to Assist Mexico.'' *State* [in-house magazine of the State Department], no. 283 (November 1985): 2–8.

Colosi, Thomas. ''A Model for Negotiation and Mediation.'' In Diane B. Bendahmane and John W. McDonald, Jr., eds., *International Negotiation: Art and Science*. Washington, D.C.: Foreign Service Institute, U.S. Department of State, 1984, pp. 15–33.

Conway, John. ''Sewage and Public Health: The San Diego–Tijuana Region.'' In Lawrence A. Herzog, ed., *Planning the International Border Metropolis: Trans-Boundary Policy Options for the San Diego–Tijuana Region*. San Diego: Center for U.S.–Mexican Studies, University of California, 1986, pp. 27–31.

Cordera, Rolando, and Carlos Tello. ''Prospects and Options for Mexican Society.'' In Clark W. Reynolds and Carlos Tello, eds., *U.S.–Mexico Relations: Economic and Social Aspects*. Stanford, Calif.: Stanford University Press, 1983, pp. 47–81.

Corredor, Jaime. ''The Economic Significance of Mexican Petroleum from the Perspective of Mexico–United States Relations.'' In Clark W. Reynolds and Carlos Tello, eds., *U.S.–Mexico Relations: Economic and Social Aspects*. Stanford, Calif.: Stanford University Press, 1983, pp. 138–165.

De la Madrid H., Miguel. "Mexico: The New Challenges." *Foreign Affairs* 63, no. 1 (Fall 1984): 62–76.

Deutsch, Karl W. "Transaction Flows as Indicators of Political Cohesion." In Philip E. Jacob and James V. Toscano, eds., *The Interpretation of Political Communities*. Philadelphia and New York: Lippincott, 1964, pp. 75–97.

Díaz-Guerrero, Rogelio. "Mexicans and Americans: Two Worlds, One Border . . . and One Observer." In Stanley R. Ross, ed., *Views Across the Border: The United States and Mexico*. Albuquerque: University of New Mexico Press, 1978, pp. 283–307.

dos Santos, Theatonio. "The Structure of Dependence." *American Economic Review* 60, no. 2 (May 1970): 231–236.

Erb, Guy F., and Cathryn Thorup. "U.S.–Mexican Relations: The Issues Ahead." Development Paper, no. 35. Washington, D.C.: Overseas Development Council, 1984.

Ethier, Wilfred J. "Illegal Immigration: The Host-Country Problem." *American Economic Review* 76, no. 1 (March 1986): 56–71.

Fagen, Richard R. "The Realities of U.S.–Mexican Relations." *Foreign Affairs* 55, no. 4 (July 1977): 685–700.

————. "The Politics of the United States–Mexico Relationship." In Clark W. Reynolds and Carlos Tello, eds., *U.S.–Mexico Relations: Economic and Social Aspects*. Stanford, Calif.: Stanford University Press, 1983, pp. 331–347.

Fagen, Richard R., and Henry R. Nau. "Mexican Gas: The Northern Connection." Working paper, no. 15. The Wilson Center, Washington, D.C., 1978.

Feinberg, Richard E. "Bureaucratic Organization and United States Policy Toward Mexico." In Susan Kaufman Purcell, ed., *Mexico–United States Relations*. New York: Praeger, 1981, pp. 32–42.

Felix, David. "Income Distribution Trends in Mexico and the Kuznets Curves." In Sylvia Hewlett and Richard S. Weinert, eds., *Brazil and Mexico: Patterns in Late Development*. Philadelphia: Institute for the Study of Human Issues, 1982, pp. 265–316.

Felix, David, and Juana Sanchez. "Capital Flight Aspect of the Latin American Debt Crisis." Working paper, no. 106. Department of Economics, Washington University, St. Louis, February 1987.

Fernández, José Luis, and Jesús Tamayo. "Industry on the Northern Border of Mexico." In Sidney Weintraub, ed., *Industrial Strategy and Planning in Mexico and the United States*. Boulder, Colo.: Westview Press, 1986, pp. 197–202.

Fitzgerald, E. V. K. "Mexico, A New Direction in Economic Policy." *Bank of London & South America Review* 12, no. 10 (October 1978): 528–538.

Gereffi, Gary. "Drug Firms and Dependency in Mexico: The Case of the Steroid Hormone Industry." *International Organization* 32, no. 1 (Winter 1978): 237–286.

Gereffi, Gary, and Richard S. Newfarmer. "International Oligopoly and Uneven Development: Some Lessons from Industrial Case Studies." In Richard S. Newfarmer, ed., *Profits, Progress and Poverty: Case Studies of International Industries in Latin America*. Notre Dame, Ind.: University of Notre Dame Press, 1985, pp. 385–436.

Gersovitz, Mark. "Banks' International Lending Decisions: What We Know and Implications for Future Research." In Gordon W. Smith and John T. Cuddington, eds., *International Debt and the Developing Countries*. Washington, D.C.: World Bank, 1985, pp. 61–78.

Gil Díaz, Francisco. "Mexico's Path from Stability to Inflation." In Arnold C. Harberger, ed., *World Economic Growth: Case Studies of Developed and Developing Nations*. San Francisco: Institute for Contemporary Studies, 1984, pp. 333–376.

Glade, William P. "Mexico: Party-Led Development." In Robert Wesson, ed., *Politics, Policies, and Economic Development in Latin America*. Stanford, Calif.: Hoover Institution Press, 1984, pp. 94–123.

————. "How Will Economic Recovery Be Managed?" In Roderic A. Camp, ed., *Mexico's Political Stability: The Next Five Years*. Boulder, Colo.: Westview Press, 1986, pp. 47–72.

Goldsbrough, David, and Iqbal Zaidi. "Transmission of Economic Influences from Industrial to Developing Countries." In Research Department of the International Monetary Fund, *Staff Studies for the World Economic Outlook*. Washington, D.C.: IMF, 1986, pp. 150–195.

González Casanova, Pablo. "The Economic Development of Mexico." *Scientific American*, September 1980, pp. 192–204.

Gordon, David. "Mexico: A Survey." *Economist*, April 22, 1978, pp. 1–34.

Gotleib, Allan E. "The Canada–United States Relationship." In David H. Flaherty and William M. McKercher, eds., *Southern Exposure: Canadian Perspectives on the United States*. Toronto: McGraw-Hill Ryerson, 1986, pp. 23–33.

Grayson, George W. "Mexico's Opportunity: The Oil Boom." *Foreign Policy*, no. 29 (Winter 1977): 65–89.

———. "Mexico and the United States: The Natural Gas Controversy." *Inter-American Economic Affairs* 32, no. 3 (Winter 1978): 3–27.

———. *Técnicos* vs. *Políticos*: The Aftermath of the Mexican Earthquakes. *Caribbean Review* 15, no. 4 (Spring 1987): 20–21, 36–37.

Greenwood, Michael J., and John M. McDowell. "The Factor Market Consequences of U.S. Immigration." *Journal of Economic Literature* 24, no. 4 (December 1986): 1738–1772.

Grey, Rodney de C. "A Note on U.S. Trade Practices." In William R. Cline, ed., *Trade Policy in the 1980s*. Washington, D.C.: Institute for International Economics, 1983, pp. 243–257.

Hakim, Peter. "The Baker Plan: Unfulfilled Promises." *Challenge* 29, no. 4 (September–October 1986): 55–59.

Harwood, Edwin. "American Public Opinion and U.S. Immigration Policy." *Annals of the American Academy of Political and Social Science* 487 (September 1986): 201–212.

Heffernan, Patrick H. "Conflict over Marine Resources." In Susan Kaufman Purcell, ed., *Mexico–United States Relations*. New York: Praeger, 1981, pp. 168–180.

Islam, Shafiqul. "Breaking the International Debt Deadlock." Critical Issues series, Council on Foreign Relations, New York, 1988.

Izquierdo, Rafael. "Protectionism in Mexico." In Raymond Vernon, ed., *Public Policy and Private Enterprise in Mexico*. Cambridge, Mass.: Harvard University Press, 1964, pp. 241–289.

Kaufman, Robert R. "Democratic and Authoritarian Responses to the Debt Issue: Argentina, Brazil, Mexico." In Miles Kahler, ed., *The Politics of International Debt*. Ithaca, N.Y.: Cornell University Press, 1986, pp. 187–217.

Khan, Mohsin S., and Nadeem Ul Haque. "Capital Flight from Developing Countries." *Finance and Development* 24, no. 1 (March 1987): 2–5.

Krueger, Anne O., and Constantine Michalopoulos. "Developing-Country Trade Policies and the International Economic System." In Ernest H. Preeg, ed., *Hard Bargaining Ahead: U.S. Trade Policy and Developing Countries*. New Brunswick, N.J.: Transaction Books for the Overseas Development Council, 1985, pp. 39–57.

Ladman, Jerry R. "Industry on the Southern Border of the United States." In Sidney Weintraub, ed., *Industrial Strategy and Planning in Mexico and the United States*. Boulder, Colo.: Westview Press, 1986, pp. 203–227.

Lajous-Vargas, Adrián. "Natural Gas in Mexico." In Miguel S. Wionczek and Ragaei El Mallakh, eds., *Mexico's Energy Resources: Toward a Policy of Diversification*. Boulder, Colo.: Westview Press, 1985, pp. 55–63.

Lee, Rensselaer W., III. "The Latin American Drug Connection." *Foreign Policy*, no. 61 (Winter 1985/86): 142–159.

Levy, Daniel. "The Implications of Central American Conflicts for Mexican Politics." In Roderic A. Camp, ed., *Mexico's Political Stability: The Next Five Years*. Boulder, Colo.: Westview Press, 1986, pp. 235–264.

———. "The Political Consequences of Changing Socialization Patterns." In Roderic A. Camp, ed., *Mexico's Political Stability: The Next Five Years*. Boulder, Colo.: Westview Press, 1986, pp. 19–46.

Levy, Daniel, and Gabriel Székely. "Mexico: Challenges and Responses," *Current History* 85, no. 507 (January 1986): 16–20.

Lucker, G. William, and Adolfo J. Alvarez. "Exploitation or Exaggeration: A Worker's-Eye View of 'Maquiladora' Work." *Southwest Journal of Business and Economics* 1, no. 4 (Summer 1984): 11–18.

Mares, David R. "Agricultural Trade: Domestic Interests and Transnational Relations." In Jorge I. Dominguez, ed., *Mexico's Political Economy: Challenges at Home and Abroad*. Beverly Hills, Calif.: Sage, 1982, pp. 79–132.

María y Campos, Mauricio de. "Mexico's New Industrial Development Strategy." In Cathryn L. Thorup, ed., *The United States and Mexico: Face to Face with New Technology*. New Brunswick, N.J.: Transaction Books for the Overseas Development Council, 1987, pp. 67–81.

Meissner, Frank. "Mexican Border and Free Zone Areas: Implications for Development." In Michael R. Czinkota, ed., *U.S.–Latin American Trade Relations: Issues and Concerns*. New York: Praeger, 1983, pp. 253–278.

"The Mexican Automobile Industry: Gearing Up to Export." *Business Mexico* 2, no. 2 (February 1985): 50–75.

"Mexican Pharmaceutical Industry Being Forced to Swallow a Bitter Pill." *Business Mexico* 3, no. 4 (August 1986): 66–70.

"Mexico's Dynamic Computer Industry." *Business Mexico* 3, no. 1 (November 1985): 60–76.

Meyer, Lorenzo. "Historical Roots of the Authoritarian State in Mexico." In José Luis Reyna and Richard S. Weinert, eds., *Authoritarianism in Mexico*. Philadelphia: Institute for the Study of Human Issues, 1977, pp. 3–22.

Monsiváis, Carlos. "The Culture of the Frontier: The Mexican Side." In Stanley R. Ross, ed., *Views Across the Border: The United States and Mexico*. Albuquerque: University of New Mexico Press, 1978, pp. 50–67.

Mumme, Stephen P. "U.S.–Mexican Groundwater Problems: Bilateral Prospects and Implications." *Journal of Interamerican Studies and World Affairs* 22, no. 1 (February 1980): 31–55.

―――. "Engineering Diplomacy: The Evolving Role of the International Boundary and Water Commission in U.S.–Mexico Water Management," *Journal of Borderland Studies* 1, no. 1 (Spring 1986): 73–108.

Mumme, Stephen P., C. Richard Bath, and Valerie J. Assetto. "Political Development and Environmental Policy in Mexico." *Latin American Research Review* 23, no. 1 (1988): 7–34.

Murray, William A. "A Reporter at Large: Twins." *New Yorker*, December 29, 1986, pp. 63–75.

Nalven, Joseph. "Social and Cultural Aspects of Transborder Environmental Cooperation." *Mexican Studies/Estudios Mexicanos* 2, no. 1 (Winter 1986): 107–127.

Newfarmer, Richard S. "International Industrial Organization and Development: A Survey." In Richard S. Newfarmer, ed., *Profits, Progress and Poverty*. Notre Dame, Ind.: University of Notre Dame Press, 1985, pp. 13–61.

Niemeyer, E. V., Jr. "Personal Diplomacy: Lyndon B. Johnson and Mexico, 1963–1968." *Southwestern Historical Quarterly* 90, no. 2 (October 1986): 159–186.

Ojeda, Mario. "The Future of Relations Between Mexico and the United States." In Clark W. Reynolds and Carlos Tello, eds., *U.S.–Mexico Relations: Economic and Social Aspects*. Stanford, Calif.: Stanford University Press, 1983, pp. 315–330.

―――. "Mexican Policy Toward Central America in the Context of U.S.–Mexico Relations." In Richard R. Fagen and Olga Pellicer, eds., *The Future of Central America: Policy Choices for the U.S. and Mexico*. Stanford, Calif.: Stanford University Press, 1983, pp. 135–160.

Ortíz, Alfonso. "Comparative Study of Infant Mortality in the Texas–Mexico Border Area of Laredo/Nuevo Laredo." Working paper, no. 29. Lyndon B. Johnson School of Public Affairs, University of Texas at Austin, 1984.

Paredes, Americo. "The Problem of Identity in a Changing Culture: Popular Expressions of Culture Conflict Along the Lower Rio Grande Border." In Stanley R. Ross, ed., *Views Across the Border: The United States and Mexico*. Albuquerque: University of New Mexico Press, 1978, pp. 68–94.

Passel, Jeffrey S. "Estimating the Number of Undocumented Aliens." *Monthly Labor Review* 109, no. 9 (September 1986): 33.

―――. "Undocumented Immigrants." *Annals of the American Academy of Political and Social Science* 487 (September 1986): 181–200.

Paz, Octavio. "Reflections: Mexico and the United States." *New Yorker*, September 17, 1979, pp. 136–153.

Peach, James T. "Income Distribution in the U.S.–Mexico Borderlands." In Lay James Gibson and Alfonso Corona Rentería, eds., *The United States and Mexico: Borderland Development and the National Economies*. Boulder, Colo.: Westview Press, 1985, pp. 57–80.

Pellicer de Brody, Olga, "Mexico in the 1970s and Its Relations with the United States." In J. Cotler and R. Fagen, eds., *Latin America and the United States: The Changing Political Realities.* Stanford, Calif.: Stanford University Press, 1974, pp. 314–333.

———. "A Mexican Perspective." In Susan Kaufman Purcell, ed., *Mexico–United States Relations.* New York: Praeger, 1981, pp. 4–12.

———. "U.S. Trade Policy Toward Mexico: Are There Reasons to Expect Special Treatment?" Working paper, no. 9. Program in U.S.–Mexican Studies, University of California, San Diego, 1981.

Portes, Alejandro. "Toward a Structural Analysis of Illegal (Undocumented) Immigration." *International Migration Review* 12, no. 4 (Winter 1978): 469–484.

Puente Leyva, Jesús. "The Natural Gas Controversy." In Susan Kaufman Purcell, ed., *Mexico–United States Relations.* New York: Praeger, 1981, pp. 158–167.

Purcell, Susan Kaufman. "Mexico–U.S. Relations: Big Initiatives Can Cause Big Problems." *Foreign Affairs* 60, no. 2 (Winter 1981/82): 379–392.

Reuter, Peter. "Eternal Hope: America's International Narcotic Efforts." Rand Paper Series. Rand Corporation, Santa Monica, Calif., February 1985.

Reynolds, Clark W. "The Structure of the Economic Relationship." In Susan Kaufman Purcell, ed., *Mexico-United States Relations.* New York: Praeger, 1981, pp. 125–135.

———. "The U.S.–Mexican Labor Market of the Future." Paper presented at a conference on United States–Mexico relations at The Woodlands, Houston, Texas, November 7–10, 1982.

———. "Mexican–U.S. Interdependence: Economic and Social Perspectives." In Clark W. Reynolds and Carlos Tello, eds., *U.S.–Mexico Relations: Economic and Social Aspects.* Stanford, Calif.: Stanford University Press, 1983, pp. 21–45.

Reynolds, Clark W., Raúl Ramos, and Robert McCleery. "The Impact of Foreign Trade and Export Strategies on Distribution of Income for Low-Income Households in Mexico." In Pedro Aspe and Paul E. Sigmund, eds., *The Political Economy of Income Distribution in Mexico.* New York: Holmes & Meier, 1984, pp. 203–246.

Rico F., Carlos. "Prospects for Economic Cooperation." In Susan Kaufman Purcell, ed., *Mexico–United States Relations.* New York: Praeger, 1981, pp. 189–194.

Robinson, James D., III. "A Comprehensive Agenda for LDC Debt and World Trade Growth." *AMEX Bank Review*, special paper, no. 13 (March 1988).

Rubin, Jeffrey W. "Elections, Repression, and Limited Reform: Update on Southern Mexico," *LASA Forum* [Latin American Studies Association] 18, no. 2 (Summer 1987): 1–5.

Ruíz, Rogelio. "Experiences of the First Mexican Nuclear Plant at Laguna Verde." In Miguel S. Wionczek and Ragaei El Mallakh, eds., *Mexico's Energy Resources: Toward a Policy of Diversification.* Boulder, Colo.: Westview Press, 1985, pp. 87–108.

Salas-Porras, Alejandra. "*Maquiladoras* and the Sociopolitical Structure in the Northern States of Mexico: Chihuahua, Sonora, and Baja California." Paper presented at the annual conference of the Association of Borderland Scholars, Reno, Nevada, April 23–26, 1986.

Schuster, Neil D. "The U.S. Motor Vehicle Industry: Emerging Trends and Impacts on Mexico." In Sidney Weintraub, ed., *Industrial Strategy and Planning in Mexico and the United States.* Boulder, Colo.: Westview Press, 1986, pp. 181–194.

"Shadows of the Past" [survey of Mexico], *Economist*, September 5, 1987, survey pp. 1–22.

Simons, Marlise. "The People Next Door." *Wilson Quarterly* 3, no. 3 (Summer 1979): 117–129.

Smith, Peter H. "Leadership and Change: Intellectuals and Technocrats in Mexico." In Roderic A. Camp, ed., *Mexico's Political Stability: The Next Five Years.* Boulder, Colo.: Westview Press, 1986, pp. 101–117.

Solís, Leopoldo, and Ernesto Zedillo. "The Foreign Debt of Mexico." In Gordon W. Smith and John T. Cuddington, eds., *International Debt and the Developing Countries.* Washington, D.C.: World Bank, 1985, pp. 258–288.

Sordo-Arrioja, Victoria. "The Mexico–Venezuela Oil Agreement of San José: A Step Toward Latin American Cooperation." In Miguel S. Wionczek and Ragaei El Mallakh, eds., *Mexico's Energy Resources: Toward a Policy of Diversification.* Boulder, Colo.: Westview Press, 1985, pp. 109–121.

Spich, Robert S. "Free Trade as Ideology, Fair Trade as Goal: Problems of an Ideological Approach to U.S. Trade Policy." *International Trade Journal* 1, no. 2 (Winter 1986): 129–154.

"Statement of the Motor Vehicle Manufacturers Association of the United States on the Impact of Foreign-Trade Related Performance Requirements on U.S. Industry and Foreign Investment Abroad." Prepared for the U.S. International Trade Commission, August 19, 1982.

Story, Dale. "The PAN, the Private Sector, and the Future of the Mexican Opposition." In Judith Gentleman, ed., *Mexican Politics in Transition*. Boulder, Colo.: Westview Press, 1987, pp. 261–279.

Tamayo, Jesús. "Borderlands, Border Policies, and National Policies." Paper presented at the fourth symposium of Mexican and U.S. universities, Santa Fe, New Mexico, April 16–18, 1986.

Teclaff, Ludwik A. "Principles for Transboundary Groundwater Pollution Control." In César Sepúlveda and Albert E. Utton, eds., *The U.S.–Mexico Border Region: Anticipating Resource Needs and Issues to the Year 2000*. El Paso: Texas Western Press of the University of Texas at El Paso, 1984, pp. 337–351.

Telljohann, Kenneth L., and Richard H. Buckholz. "The Mexican Bond Exchange Offer: An Analytical Framework." Salomon Brothers, January 1988.

Tiano, Susan B. "Export Processing, Women's Work, and the Employment Problem in Developing Countries: The Case of the Maquiladora Program in Northern Mexico." Center for Inter-American and Border Studies, University of Texas at El Paso, 1985.

Turner, Roger. "Mexico Turns to Its In-Bond Industry as a Means of Generating Exchange." *Business America* 6, no. 24 (November 28, 1983): 27–33.

———. "Mexico's In-Bond Industry Continues Its Dynamic Growth." *Business America* 7, no. 24 (November 26, 1984): 26–30.

Urquidi, Víctor L. "A Mexican Perspective." In Richard D. Erb and Stanley R. Ross, eds., *U.S. Policies Toward Mexico: Perceptions and Perspectives*. Washington, D.C.: American Enterprise Institute, 1979, pp. 23–30.

Utton, Albert E. "Shared Water Resources in the United States–Mexico Border Region: Past Successes and Future Problems." In Stanley R. Ross, ed., *Ecology and Development of the Border Region*. México, D.F.: Asociación Nacional de Universidades e Institutos de Enseñanza Superior, 1983, pp. 167–181.

———. "An Assessment of the Management of U.S.–Mexican Water Resources: Anticipating the Year 2000." In César Sepúlveda and Albert E. Utton, eds., *The U.S.–Mexico Border Region: Anticipating Resource Needs and Issues to the Year 2000*. El Paso: Texas Western Press of the University of Texas at El Paso, 1984, pp. 365–389.

Valdés-Villalva, Guillermina. "New Policies and Strategies of Multinational Corporations During the Mexican National Crisis 1982–1983." In Lay James Gibson and Alfonso Corona Rentería, eds., *The United States and Mexico: Borderland Development and the National Economies*. Boulder, Colo.: Westview Press, 1985, pp. 159–174.

Vernon, Raymond. "International Trade Policy in the 1980s: Prospects and Problems." *International Studies Quarterly* 26, no. 4 (December 1982): 483–510.

Villarreal Arrambide, René, "The New Industrialization Strategy in Mexico for the Eighties." In Sidney Weintraub, ed., *Industrial Strategy and Planning in Mexico and the United States*. Boulder, Colo.: Westview Press, 1986, pp. 47–59.

Villarreal Arrambide, René, and Rocío de Villarreal, "Mexico's Development Strategy." In Susan Kaufman Purcell, ed., *Mexico–United States Relations*. New York: Praeger, 1981, pp. 97–103.

Wallace y Asociados, A.C. "Profile of Mini and Micro Computer Systems Market, Mexico." Prepared for the International Market Research Program, U.S. Department of Commerce, 1985.

Weaver, Thomas. "The Social Effects of the Ecology and Development of the United States–Mexico Border." In Stanley R. Ross, ed., *Ecology and Development of the Border Region*. México, D.F.: Asociación Nacional de Universidades e Institutos de Enseñanza Superior, 1983, pp. 232–270.

Weinert, Richard S. "The State and Foreign Capital." In José Luis Reyna and Richard S. Weinert, eds., *Authoritarianism in Mexico*. Philadelphia: Institute for the Study of Human Issues, 1977, pp. 109–128.

Weintraub, Sidney. "Mexican Subsidies and U.S. Law: Potential Collision Course." *Mexican Forum* 1, no. 2 (April 1981): 7–9.

_____. "Economic Sources of Political Instability in Mexico." *Mexican Forum*, special number (December 1982): 16–19.

_____. "Treating the Causes: Illegal Immigration and U.S. Foreign Economic Policy." In Demetrios G. Papademetriou and Mark J. Miller, eds., *The Unavoidable Issue: U.S. Immigration Policy in the 1980s*. Philadelphia: Institute for the Study of Human Issues, 1983, pp. 185–214.

_____. "Illegal Immigrants in Texas: Impact on Social Services and Related Considerations." *International Migration Review* 18, no. 3 (Fall 1984): 733–747.

_____. "Trade and Structural Change." In Peggy B. Musgrave, ed., *Mexico and the United States: Studies in Economic Interaction*. Boulder, Colo.: Westview Press, 1985, pp. 79–107.

Weintraub, Sidney, and Chandler Stolp. "The Implications of Growing Economic Interdependence." In Organization for Economic Cooperation and Development, ed., *The Future of Migration*. Paris: OECD, 1987, pp. 137–167.

Wertman, Patricia. "The International Debt Problem: Congressional Proposals." Congressional Research Service, Library of Congress, November 28, 1988.

Whiteford, Scott. "Agriculture, Irrigation, and Salinity in the Mexicali Valley." *Mexican Forum*, special issue (1986): 21–25.

Whiting, Van R., Jr. "Transnational Enterprise in the Food Processing Industry." In Richard S. Newfarmer, ed., *Profits, Progress and Poverty: Case Studies of International Industries in Latin America*. Notre Dame, Ind.: University of Notre Dame Press, 1985, pp. 343–383.

Whitlock, Peter. "The Baker v. Bradley Debate." *Development Forum* 15, no. 2 (March 1987): 3, 5.

Williams, Edward J. "The Evolution of the Mexican Military and Its Implications for Civil–Military Relations." In Roderic A. Camp, ed., *Mexico's Political Stability: The Next Five Years*. Boulder, Colo.: Westview Press, 1986, pp. 143–158.

_____. "The Implications of the Border for Mexican Policy and Mexican–United States Relations." In Roderic A. Camp, ed., *Mexico's Political Stability: The Next Five Years*. Boulder, Colo.: Westview Press, 1986, pp. 211–233.

Wionczek, Miguel S. "Some Reflections on Mexican Energy Policy in Historical Perspective." In Miguel S. Wionczek and Ragaei El Mallakh, eds., *Mexico's Energy Resources: Toward a Policy of Diversification*. Boulder, Colo.: Westview Press, 1985, pp. 145–163.

Womack, James P. "Prospects for the U.S.–Mexican Relationship in the Motor Vehicle Sector." In Cathryn L. Thorup, ed., *The United States and Mexico: Face to Face with New Technology*. New Brunswick, N.J.: Transaction Books for the Overseas Development Council, 1987, pp. 101–125.

Woodrow, Karen A., Jeffrey S. Passel, and Robert Warren. "Recent Immigration to the United States— Legal and Undocumented: Analysis of Data from the June 1986 Current Population Survey." Paper presented at the annual meetings of the Population Association of America, Chicago, April 29–May 2, 1987.

Wyman, Donald L. "Dependence and Conflict: U.S. Relations with Mexico." In Robert L. Paarlberg, ed., *Diplomatic Dispute: U.S. Conflict with Iran, Japan, and Mexico*. Harvard Studies in International Affairs, no. 39. 1979.

Zedillo Ponce de León, Ernesto. "The Mexican External Debt: The Last Decade." In Miguel S. Wionczek and Luciano Tomassini, eds., *Politics and Economics of External Debt Crisis: The Latin American Experience*. Boulder, Colo.: Westview Press, 1988, pp. 294–324.

Spanish

Alba, Francisco. "Logros y limitaciones en la absorción de la fuerza de trabajo en México." *Demografía y Economía* 18, no. 4 (1984): 557–580.

Alberro, José Luis, and David Ibarra, eds. "Programas heterodoxos de estabilización." *Estudios Económicos*, special number (October 1987): 3–11.

Carrillo, Jorge. "Conflictos laborales en la industria maquiladora de exportación," *Comercio Exterior* 36, no. 1 (January 1986): 46–57.

Castellanos Guerrero, Alicia, and Gilberto López y Rivas. "La influencia norteamericana en la cultura de la frontera norte de México." In Roque González Salazar, ed., *La frontera del norte: integración y desarrollo*. México, D.F.: El Colegio de México, 1981, pp. 68–84.

Cerutti, Mario. "Frontera, burguesía regional y desarrollo capitalista. El caso de Monterrey. Referencias sobre el período 1860–1910." In Roque González Salazar, ed., *La frontera del norte: integración y desarrollo*. México, D.F.: El Colegio de México, 1981, pp. 196–234.

Cruz Miramontes, Rodolfo. "Los tratados de límites con los Estados Unidos y los problemas más relevantes derivados de su aplicación." In Roque González Salazar, ed., *La frontera del norte: integración y desarrollo*. México, D.F.: El Colegio de México, 1981, pp. 278–312.

Dávila Jiménez, Gerardo. "La política de precios y subsidios." In Hector E. González M., ed., *El sistema económico mexicano: un análisis sobre su situación*. México, D.F.: Premia Editora, 1982, pp. 228–249.

Dávila Suárez, Francisco. "La crisis de la deuda externa y el desarrollo." *Comercio Exterior* 36, no. 12 (December 1986): 1109–1113.

del Villar, Samuel I. "La narcotización de la cultura en Estados Unidos y su impacto en México." In Gabriel Székely, ed., *México–Estados Unidos, 1985*. México, D.F.: El Colegio de México, 1986, pp. 63–88.

Espinoza, Frida, and Jesús Tamayo. "El estado de la investigación nacional acerca de la frontera norte de México." Centro de Investigación y Docencia Económicas (CIDE), México, D.F., August 1985.

Fernández-Kelly, María Patricia. "Las maquiladores y las mujeres." *Los Universitarios*, nos. 139–142 (1979).

García y Griego, Manuel, and Francisco Giner de los Ríos. "¿Es vulnerable la economía mexicana a la aplicación de políticas migratorias estadunidenses?" In Manuel García y Griego and Gustavo Vega, eds., *México–Estados Unidos, 1984*. México, D.F.: El Colegio de México, 1985, pp. 221–272.

González de León, Antonio. "Factores de tensión internacional en la frontera." In Roque González Salazar, ed., *La frontera del norte: integración y desarrollo*. México, D.F.: El Colegio de México, 1981, pp. 7–25.

González M., Juan, Yolanda Muñoz Pérez, Georgina Núñez, and Priscila Sosa. "El impacto de las audiencias Helms en la relación bilateral." In *Relaciones México–Estados Unidos: entre el conflicto y la cooperación*, Carta de Política Exterior Mexicana, Centro de Investigación y Docencia Económicas (CIDE) 6, no. 2 (April–June 1986): 5–19.

Gutiérrez R., Roberto. "El endeudamiento externo del sector privado de México: expansión y renegociación." *Comercio Exterior* 36, no. 4 (April 1986): 337–343.

Hector, Cary. "La izquierda mexicana hoy: una mirada aproximación y en perspectiva." *Mexican Studies/Estudios Mexicanos* 2, no. 1 (Winter 1986): 1–33.

König, Wolfgang. "Efectos de la actividad maquiladora fronteriza en la sociedad mexicana." In Roque González Salazar, ed., *La frontera del norte: integración y desarrollo*. México, D.F.: El Colegio de México, 1981, pp. 95–105.

Krauze, Enrique. "*Vecinos distantes* de Alan Riding." *Vuelta*, no. 104 (July 1985): 35–39.

Lajous de Solana, Roberta, and Jesús Velasco Márquez. "Visión de México en la prensa de Estados Unidos: 1984." In Manuel García y Griego and Gustavo Vega, eds., *México–Estados Unidos, 1984*. México, D.F.: El Colegio de México, 1985, pp. 31–41.

María y Campos, Mauricio de. "La industria farmacéutica en México," *Comercio Exterior* 27, no. 8 (August 1977): 889–912.

Meyer, Lorenzo. "México–Estados Unidos: lo especial de una relación." In Manuel García y Griego and Gustavo Vega, eds., *México–Estados Unidos, 1984*. México, D.F.: El Colegio de México, 1985, pp. 15–30.

———. "1985: un mal año en una época difícil." In Gabriel Székely, ed., *México–Estados Unidos, 1985*. México, D.F.: El Colegio de México, 1986, pp. 13–25.

Molina, Isabel. "La renovación del sistema generalizado de preferencias arancelarias y sus implicaciónes para México." In Manuel García y Griego and Gustavo Vega, ed., *México–Estados Unidos, 1984*. México, D.F.: El Colegio de México, 1985, pp. 155–171.

Molinar Horcasitas, Juan. "Regreso a Chihuahua." *Nexos* 10, no. 11 (March 1987): 21–32.

Monsiváis, Carlos. "Civilización y Coca-Cola." *Nexos* 9, no. 104 (August 1986): 19–29.

Ojeda, Mario. "México ante los Estados Unidos en la coyuntura actual." In Rosario Green et al., *Continuidad y cambio en la política exterior de México: 1977*. México, D.F.: El Colegio de México, 1977, pp. 37–60.

———. "El poder negociador del petróleo: el caso de México." *Foro Internacional* 21, no. 1 (July–September 1980): 44–64.

Ortíz, Guillermo, and Jaime Serra Puche. "La carga de la deuda externa de México." *Estudios Económicos* 1, no. 1 (January–June 1986): 171–191.

Paz, Octavio. "Remache: burocracia y democracia en México." *Vuelta*, no. 127 (June 1987): 62–63.
––––––. "Contraronda: México, Estados Unidos, América Central, etcetera." *Vuelta*, no. 131 (October 1987): 14–21.
Peña Alfaro, Ricardo. "Ventajas y desventajas del ingreso de México al GATT." *Comercio Exterior* 36, no. 1 (January 1986): 33–45.
Peñaloza Webb, Tomás. "El comercio de manufacturas entre México y los Estados Unidos." *Foro Internacional* 19, no. 2 (October–December 1978): 363–376.
––––––. "La adhesión de México al GATT." *Comercio Exterior* 35, no. 12 (December 1985): 1160–1168.
Rico, Carlos. "'Interdependencia' y trilateralismo: origines de una estrategia." *Cuadernos Semestrales* 2, no. 3 (May 1978): 17–88.
––––––. "Las relaciones mexicano–norte americano y los significados de la 'interdependencia.'" *Foro Internacional* 19, no. 2 (October–December 1978): 256–291.
Rivas F., Sergio. "La industria maquiladora en México." *Comercio Exterior* 35, no. 11 (November 1985): 1071–1084.
Sepúlveda, César. "Los recursos hidraúlicos en la zona fronteriza México–Estados Unidos. Perspectiva de la problemática hacia el año 2000—algunas recomendaciones." In César Sepúlveda and Albert E. Utton, eds., *The U.S.–Mexico Border Region: Anticipating Resource Needs and Issues to the Year 2000.* El Paso: Texas Western Press of the University of Texas at El Paso, 1984, pp. 353–364.
Trejo Reyes, Saúl. "La política industrial en el período de la postguerra." In Hector E. González M., ed., *El sistema económico mexicano: un análisis sobre su situación actual.* México, D.F.: Premia Editora, 1982, pp. 176–193.
––––––. "El contexto económico internacional de la deuda: implicaciones par México." *Comercio Exterior* 36, no. 4 (April 1986): 323–326.
––––––. "Deuda externa. Una alternativa de solución." *Estudios Económicos* 1, no. 2 (July–December 1986): 139–157.
Trejo Reyes, Saúl, and Gustavo Vega Cánovas. "El ingreso al GATT y sus implicaciones para el futuro de México." *Comercio Exterior* 37, no. 7 (July 1987): 519–526.
Unger, Kurt. "El comercio exterior de manufacturas modernas en México: el papel de las empresas extranjeras." *Comercio Exterior* 35, no. 5 (May 1985): 431–443.
Urquidi, Víctor L., and Mario M. Carrillo. "Desarrollo económico e interacción en la frontera norte de México." *Comercio Exterior* 35, no. 11 (November 1985): 1060–1070.
Van Wert, James. "El control de los narcóticos en México. Una década de institucionalización y un asunto diplomático." In Gabriel Székely, ed., *México–Estados Unidos, 1985.* México, D.F.: El Colegio de México, 1986, pp. 89–104.
Vega Cánovas, Gustavo. "Comercio y política en Estados Unidos: librecambismo versus proteccionismo desde la segunda guerra mundial." In Manuel García y Griego and Gustavo Vega, eds., *México–Estados Unidos, 1984.* México, D.F.: El Colegio de México, 1985, pp. 111–154.
––––––. "El entendimiento sobre subsidios e impuestos compensatorios entre México y Estados Unidos: implicaciones económicas y políticas." In Gabriel Székely, ed., *México–Estados Unidos, 1985.* México, D.F.: El Colegio de México, 1986, pp. 117–152.
Zaid, Gabriel. "Pagar la deuda." *Vuelta*, no. 89 (April 1984): 5–9.
––––––. "México: el modelo tibetano." *Vuelta*, no. 117 (August 1986): 10–12.
––––––. "La propiedad privada de las funciones públicas." *Vuelta*, no. 120 (November 1986): 25–32.

Official Publications

United States Government

Dietzman, William D., Charles J. Jirik, William E. Lyle, Jr., Naim R. Rafidi, and Thomas A. Ross. *The Petroleum Resources of Mexico.* Washington, D.C.: Department of Energy, 1983.
Economic Indicators, January 1989. Washington, D.C.: Council of Economic Advisers for Joint Economic Committee, 1989.
Economic Report of the President, 1986. Washington, D.C.: Government Printing Office, 1986.
"North American Trade Agreements." A study mandated in Section 1104 of Trade Agreements Act of 1979, July 26, 1981, transmitted by letter of August 4, 1981, from the president to the Congress.

U.S. Bureau of the Census. *Highlights of U.S. Export and Import Trade*. Report FT 990. Washington, D.C.: 1970–1986.

U.S. Congress. General Accounting Office. *Limited Research Suggests Illegal Aliens May Displace Native Workers*. Washington, D.C., April 1986.

_____. *Drug Control: International Narcotics Control Activities of the United States*. Washington, D.C., 1987.

U.S. Congress. House. Committee on Foreign Affairs. *U.S. Narcotics Control Programs Overseas: An Assessment*. Report of a staff study mission to Southeast Asia, South America, Central America, and the Caribbean. H. Doc. 43-780. 99th Cong., 1st sess. Washington, D.C.: Government Printing Office, 1985.

_____. *United States–Mexican Cooperation in Narcotics Control Efforts*. Hearing, July 17, 1986. H. Doc. 64-3820. 99th Cong., 2nd sess. Washington, D.C.: Government Printing Office, 1986.

U.S. Congress. Office of Technology Assessment. *The Border War on Drugs*. Washington, D.C., 1987.

U.S. Department of Commerce. *1986 U.S. Foreign Trade Highlights*. Washington, D.C., 1987.

_____. International Trade Administration. *United States Trade: Performance in 1985 and Outlook*. Washington, D.C.: Government Printing Office, 1986.

U.S. Department of Energy. *International Energy Annual 1987*. Washington, D.C.: Government Printing Office, 1988.

U.S. Department of Justice. Drug Enforcement Administration. *Special Report: Worldwide Drug Assessment: Threat to the United States*. Washington, D.C., 1986.

_____. Immigration and Naturalization Service. *Statistical Yearbook of the Immigration and Naturalization Service*. Washington, D.C.: Government Printing Office, various years.

U.S. Department of Labor. Bureau of International Labor Affairs. "Profile of Labor Conditions." December 1982.

U.S. Department of State. "Report to Congress on Voting Practices in the United Nations." Washington, D.C., 1986, 1987.

_____. Bureau of International Narcotics Matters (INM). "International Narcotics Control Strategy Report." Reports submitted to the House Committee on Foreign Affairs and the Senate Committee on Foreign Relations. March 1, 1987, 1988, and 1989.

U.S. Embassy, Mexico City. "Foreign Investment Climate in Mexico." June 1985 and subsequent years. Mimeograph.

U.S. Information Agency. "The Climate of Opinion in Mexico City in Mid-1983." Results of a survey of 500 adults in Mexico City, September 1983.

_____. "Domestic and International Economic Problems Top Concerns of Urban Mexicans." Results of a survey of 2,657 adults in 30 cities with more than 50,000 population, February 28, 1985.

U.S. International Trade Commission (USITC). *Study of the Petrochemical Industries in the Countries of the Northern Portion of the Western Hemisphere*. Publication no. 1123. Washington, D.C.: USITC, 1981.

_____. *Background Study of the Economies and International Trade Patterns of the Countries of North America, Central America, and the Caribbean*. Publication no. 1176. Washington, D.C.: USITC, 1981.

_____. *Foreign Industrial Targeting and Its Effects on U.S. Industries, Phase III: Brazil, Canada, the Republic of Korea, Mexico, and Taiwan*. Publication no. 1632. Washington, D.C.: USITC, 1985, pp. 173–226.

_____. *The Impact of Increased United States–Mexico Trade on Southwest Border Development*. Publication no. 1915. Washington, D.C.: USITC, 1986.

_____. *Imports under Items 806.30 and 807.00 of the Tariff Schedules of the United States, 1982–1985*. Publication no. 1920. Washington, D.C.: USITC, 1986.

_____. *The Use and Economic Impact of TSUS Items 806.30 and 807.00*. Publication no. 2053. Washington, D.C.: USITC, 1988.

_____. *Imports under Items 806.30 and 807.00 of the Tariff Schedules of the United States, 1984–1987*. Publication no. 2144. Washington, D.C.: USITC, 1988.

U.S. Select Commission on Immigration and Refugee Policy. *U.S. Immigration Policy and the National Interest*. Final report, staff report, plus Appendixes A through I. Washington, D.C., 1981.

U.S. Tariff Commission. *Economic Factors Affecting the Use of Item 807.00 and 806.30 of the Tariff Schedules of the U.S.* Washington, D.C., 1970.

U.S. Trade Representative. *Annual Report on National Trade Estimates, 1985*. Mandated by Section 303 of the Trade and Tariff Act of 1984. Washington, D.C., undated.

Mexican Government

Banco de México. *Informe anual*. México, D.F., various years.

———. *La distribución del ingreso en México*. México, D.F.: Fondo de Cultura Económica, 1974.

Centro Nacional de Información y Estadísticas del Trabajo (Ceniet). "Informe final: Los trabajadores mexicanos en los Estados Unidos." Internal discussion document. Secretaría del Trabajo y Previsión Social, México, D.F., February 1982.

Comisión Nacional de Inversiones Extranjeras (Comisión). *Manual operativo para la capitalización de pasivos y sustitución de deuda pública por inversión*. México, D.F.: Comisión, 1986.

Instituto Mexicano de Comercio Exterior (IMCE). *La protección efectiva en México, 1979–1983*. 2 vols. (summary and complete study). México, D.F.: IMCE, 1984.

Instituto Nacional de Estadística, Geografía e Informática (Inegi). *La industria automotriz en México*. México, D.F.: Secretaría de Programación y Presupuesto (SPP), 1983.

———. *Estadísticas históricas de México*. México, D.F., 1985.

———. *Anuario estadístico de los Estados Unidos Mexicanos*. México, D.F.: SPP, various years.

———. *Sistema de cuentas nacionales de México*. México, D.F.: SPP, various years.

Nacional Financiera, S.A. (Nafinsa). *La economía mexicana en cifras*. México, D.F.: Nafinsa, 1981.

Nafinsa and Organización de las Naciones Unidas para el Desarrollo Industrial (UNIDO). *México: estrategia para desarrollar la industria de bienes de capital*. México, D.F.: Nafinsa, 1977.

———. *México: los bienes de capital en la situación económica presente*. México, D.F.: Nafinsa, 1985.

Petróleos Mexicanos (Pemex). *Anuario estadístico*. México, D.F., various years.

———. *Memoria de labores*. México, D.F., various years.

Poder Ejecutivo Federal. *Plan global de desarrollo 1980–1982*. 2 vols. México, D.F.: SPP, 1980.

———. *Plan nacional de desarrollo 1983–1988*. México, D.F.: SPP, 1983.

———. *Programa nacional de financiamiento del desarrollo 1984–1988*. México, D.F.: Secretaría de Hacienda y Crédito Público, 1984.

———. *Programa nacional de fomento industrial y comercio exterior 1984–1988*. México, D.F.: Secretaría de Comercio y Fomento Industrial, 1984.

———. *Programa nacional de energéticos 1984–1988*. México, D.F.: Secretaría de Energía, Minas e Industria Paraestatal, 1985.

Presidencia de la República. *Criterios generales de política económica para la iniciativa de ley de ingreso y el proyecto de presupuesto de egresos de la federación, correspondientes a 1987*. México, D.F.: Presidencia, November 1986.

———. *V informe de gobierno 1987*. México, D.F., 1987.

Procuraduría General de la República. "The Mexican Effort: The Permanent Campaign Against Drug Traffic and Drug Addiction, 1985–1986 Statistics." Mexico, D.F., September 1986. Mimeograph.

Secretaría de Energía, Minas e Industria Paraestatal. *Balance nacional: energía 1982–1984*. México, D.F., 1986.

———. *Balance nacional: energía 1985*. México, D.F., 1986.

Secretaría de Patrimonio y Fomento Industrial. *Plan nacional de desarrollo industrial, 1979–1982*. México, D.F., 1979.

Secretaría de Programación y Presupuesto (SPP). *La industria petrolera en México*. México, D.F., 1979.

———. *Sistema de cuentas nacionales, oferta y utilización de bienes y servicios, 1981*. México, D.F., 1982.

International Organizations*

Inter-American Development Bank (IDB). *Economic and Social Progress in Latin America*. Washington, D.C.: IDB, various years.

*Staff papers representing the views of individuals in official national or international organizations are listed by author's name.

Nowicki, A. et al. *Mexico: Manufacturing Sector: Situation, Prospects and Policies*. Washington, D.C.: World Bank, March 1979.

Organization for Economic Cooperation and Development (OECD). *The Future of Migration*. Paris: OECD, 1987.

Organization of American States (OAS). *The United States Generalized System of Preferences: Caribbean Basin Initiative*. Washington, D.C.: OAS, 1985.

United Nations. *The Economic Development of Latin America and Its Principal Problems*. Lake Success, N.Y.: U.N. Department of Economic Affairs, 1950.

United Nations. Center on Transnational Corporations. *Transnational Corporations in the Pharmaceutical Industry of Developing Countries*. New York: United Nations, 1984.

United Nations. Comisión Económica para América Latina y el Caribe (Cepal). *Estudio Económico de América Latina y El Caribe 1984: México*. United Nations Economic and Social Council (ECOSOC) LC/L.330/Add. 12, August 1985.

_____. "Daños causados por el movimiento telúrico en México y sus repercusiones sobre la economía del pais." México: ECOSOC, LC/G.1367, October 15, 1985. Mimeograph.

United Nations. Economic Commission for Latin America and the Caribbean (ECLAC). "Latin American and Caribbean Development: Obstacles, Requirements, and Options." Paper prepared for a special conference, Mexico City, January 19–23, 1987, LC/G.1440 (Conf. 79/3).

World Bank. *Mexico: Future Directions of Industrial Strategy*. Washington, D.C., 1983.

_____. *World Development Report*. Washington, D.C., various years.

Periodicals

United States and Non-Mexican Publications

Austin American-Statesman (Austin, Texas, daily newspaper)
Bulletin (published monthly by the U.S. Department of State)
Business America (published biweekly by the U.S. Department of Commerce)
Economist
Euromoney
Financial Times
IMF Survey (published twenty-three times a year)
Mexican Studies/Estudios Mexicanos (published biannually)
Newsweek
New Yorker
New York Times (Southwest edition)
Survey of Current Business (published monthly by the U.S. Department of Commerce)
U.S.–Mexico Report (monthly translations from the Mexican press)
Wall Street Journal
Washington Post
World Financial Markets (published monthly by the Morgan Guaranty Trust Company)

Mexican Publications

Business Mexico (published quarterly by the American Chamber of Commerce of Mexico, A.C.)
Comercio Exterior (published monthly by the Banco Nacional de Comercio Exterior [Bancomext])
Demografía y Economía (published quarterly by El Colegio de México [Colmex])
Diario Oficial (the official record of laws and regulations)
Estudios Económicos (published semiannually by Colmex)
Excélsior (Mexico City daily newspaper)
Foro Internacional (published quarterly by Colmex)
Indicadores económicos (issued monthly by the Banco de México)
Information Bulletin (published monthly by Pemex)
El Mercado de Valores (published weekly and subsequently twice monthly by the Nacional Financiera [Nafinsa])

Mexico Update (published twice monthly by the economics department of the American Chamber of Commerce of Mexico, A.C.)

Nexos (monthly magazine)

Novedades (Mexico City daily newspaper)

Proceso (weekly magazine of news and opinion)

Review of the Economic Situation of Mexico (published monthly in Spanish and English by the Banco Nacional de México [Banamex])

El Trimestre Económico (published quarterly)

Vuelta (monthly magazine)

ABBREVIATIONS

ACP	African-Caribbean-Pacific countries associated with the EEC
AFL-CIO	American Federation of Labor-Congress of Industrial Organizations
ALADI	Asociación Latinoamericana de Integración (Latin American Integration Association)
ANIERM	Asociación Nacional de Importadores y Exportadores de la República Mexicana (National Association of Importers and Exporters of the Republic of Mexico)
API	American Petroleum Institute
Banamex	Banco Nacional de México (National Bank of Mexico)
Bancomext	Banco Nacional de Comercio Exterior (National Bank of Foreign Trade)
CAD/CAM	Computer-aided design/computer-aided manufacturing
Canacintra	Cámara Nacional de la Industria de Transformación (National Chamber of Manufacturing Industries)
CBS	Columbia Broadcasting System
CCE	Consejo Coordinador Empresarial (Businessmen's Coordinating Council)
CEESP	Centro de Estudios Económicos del Sector Privado (Private Sector Center for Economic Studies)
Cemai	Consejo Empresarial Mexicano para Asuntos Internacionales (Mexican Enterpreneurial Council for International Affairs)
Ceniet	Centro Nacional de Información y Estadísticas del Trabajo (National Center of Labor Information and Statistics)
Cepal	Comisión Económica para América Latina y el Caribe (see ECLAC)
CFE	Comisión Federal de Electricidad (Federal Electricity Commission)
CIA	U.S. Central Intelligence Agency
CIDE	Centro de Investigación y Docencia Económicas (Center for Economic Research and Teaching)
CIF	Cost, insurance, freight
CMHN	Consejo Mexicano de Hombres de Negocios (Mexican Council of Businessmen)
CNC	Confederación Nacional Campesina (National Peasants' Confederation)
CNOP	Confederación Nacional de Organizaciones Populares (National Confederation of Popular Organizations)

259

Colmex El Colegio de México (The College of Mexico)

Conasupo Companía Nacional de Subsistencias Populares (National Staple Products Company)

Concamin Confederación de Cámaras Industriales (Confederation of Industrial Chambers)

Concanaco Confederación de Cámaras Nacionales de Comercio (Confederation of National Chambers of Commerce)

Coparmex Confederación Patronal de la República Mexicana (Mexican Employers' Confederation)

CTM Confederación de Trabajadores Mexicanos (Confederation of Mexican Workers)

CVD Countervailing duty

DEA U.S. Drug Enforcement Administration

DOE U.S. Department of Energy

DRC Domestic resource cost ratio

ECLAC Economic Commission for Latin America and the Caribbean (formerly ECLA)

ECOSOC United Nations Economic and Social Council

EEC European Economic Community

EFTA European Free Trade Association

EIA Energy Information Administration of the U.S. Department of Energy

EPA U.S. Environmental Protection Agency

FAS Free alongside

FDI Foreign direct investment

FDN Frente Democrático Nacional (National Democratic Front [group that supported Cuauhtémoc Cárdenas for president in 1988])

Ficorca Fideicomiso para la Cobertura de Riesgos Cambiarios (Trust Fund for the Covering of Foreign-Exchange Risks)

GAO U.S. General Accounting Office

GATT General Agreement on Tariffs and Trade

GDP Gross domestic product

GNP Gross national product

GSP Generalized system of preferences (in this book, refers to the U.S. system)

IBC International Boundary Commission

IBRD International Bank for Reconstruction and Development (World Bank)

IBWC International Boundary and Water Commission

IDB Inter-American Development Bank

IMCE Instituto Mexicano de Comercio Exterior (Mexican Institute of Foreign Trade)

IMF International Monetary Fund

Inegi Instituto Nacional de Estadística, Geografía, e Informática (National Institute of Statistics, Geography, and Information)

INM Bureau of International Narcotics Matters, U.S. Department of State

INS U.S. Immigration and Naturalization Service

IRCA U.S. Immigration Reform and Control Act of 1986

ISI Import-substituting industrialization

LAC Latin American and Caribbean countries

Libor London inter-bank offer rate

Mcf thousand cubic feet

MFA Multifiber arrangement

MFN Most-favored-nation treatment

MMB/d Millions of barrels a day

MNC Multinational corporation

Myra Multiyear debt restructuring agreement

Nafinsa Nacional Financiera, S.A. (National Financing Institution), Mexico's development bank

NIC Newly industrializing country

OPEC Organization of Petroleum Exporting Countries

OTA Office of Technology Assessment

PAN Partido Acción Nacional (National Action Party)

PARM Partido Auténtico de la Revolución Mexicana (Authentic Party of the Mexican Revolution)

PC Personal computer

PDM Partido Demócrata Mexicano (Mexican Democratic Party)

Pemex Petróleos Mexicanos (Mexican Petroleum Company)

PMS Partido Socialista Mexicano (Mexican Socialist Party)

PMT Partido Mexicano de los Trabajadores (Mexican Workers' Party)

PNR Partido Nacional Revolucionario (National Revolutionary Party [a predecessor of the PRI])

PPS Partido Popular Socialista (Popular Socialist Party)

PRI Partido Revolucionario Institucional (Institutional Revolutionary Party)

PRM Partido de la Revolución Mexicana (Party of the Mexican Revolution [predecessor of the PRI])

Pronafice Programa nacional de fomento industrial y comercio exterior 1984–1988 (National program of industrial development and foreign trade, 1984–1988)

PRT Partido Revolucionario de los Trabajadores (Workers' Revolutionary Party)

PSBR Public sector borrowing requirement

PSE Pacto de Solidaridad Económica (Economic Solidarity Pact)

PST Partido Socialista de Trabajadores (Socialist Workers' Party)

PSUM Partido Socialista Unificado Mexicano (Unified Socialist Party of Mexico)

Secofi Secretaría de Comercio y Fomento Industrial (Secretariat of Commerce and Industrial Promotion)

Sedue Secretaría de Desarrollo Urbano y Ecología (Secretariat of Urban Development and Ecology)

Semip Secretaría de Energía, Minas, e Industria Paraestatal (Secretariat of Energy, Mines, and Parastatal Industry)

SHCP Secretaría de Hacienda y Crédito Público (Secretariat of the Treasury and Public Credit)

Sicartsa Siderúrgica Lázaro Cárdenas–Las Truchas (Lázaro Cárdenas–Las Truchas steel mill)

SIN Spanish International Network (Univisión)

SITC Standard international trade classification

SPP Secretaría de Programación y Presupuesto (Secretariat of Programming and Budgeting)

SRE Secretaría de Relaciones Exteriores (Secretariat of Foreign Relations)

STPRM Sindicato de Trabajadores Petroleros de la República Mexicana (Union of Petroleum Workers of the Republic of Mexico)

STPS Secretaría de Trabajo y Previsión Social (Secretariat of Labor and Social Service)

TNC Transnational corporation

TSUS Tariff schedules of the United States

USITC U.S. International Trade Commission

USTR U.S. Trade Representative

VA/M Value added to imports in Mexico

INDEX

263